REFERENCE

DISCARDED

The NEW ENCYCLOPEDIA *of* SOUTHERN CULTURE

VOLUME 16 : SPORTS AND RECREATION

Volumes to appear in

The New Encyclopedia of Southern Culture

are:

The NEW

ENCYCLOPEDIA *of* SOUTHERN CULTURE

CHARLES REAGAN WILSON General Editor

JAMES G. THOMAS JR. Managing Editor

ANN J. ABADIE Associate Editor

VOLUME 16

Sports & Recreation

HARVEY H. JACKSON III   Volume Editor

Sponsored by

THE CENTER FOR THE STUDY OF SOUTHERN CULTURE

at the University of Mississippi

THE UNIVERSITY OF NORTH CAROLINA PRESS

Chapel Hill

This book was published with the
assistance of the Anniversary Endowment Fund
of the University of North Carolina Press.

Designed by Richard Hendel
Set in Minion types by Tseng Information Systems, Inc.
Manufactured in the United States of America
The paper in this book meets the guidelines for permanence and
durability of the Committee on Production Guidelines for Book
Longevity of the Council on Library Resources.
The University of North Carolina Press has been a member
of the Green Press Initiative since 2003.
Library of Congress Cataloging-in-Publication Data
Sports and recreation / Harvey H. Jackson III, volume editor.
p. 24 cm. — (The new encyclopedia of Southern culture ; v. 16)
"Sponsored by The Center for the Study of Southern Culture at the
University of Mississippi."
Includes bibliographical references and index.
ISBN 978-0-8078-3441-1 (cloth : alk. paper) —
ISBN 978-0-8078-7173-7 (pbk. : alk. paper)
1. Sports—Southern States—Encyclopedias. 2. Recreation—
Southern States—Encyclopedias. 3. Leisure—Social aspects—
Southern States—Encyclopedias. 4. Popular culture—Southern
States—Encyclopedias. 5. Southern States—Social life and
customs—Encyclopedias. I. Jackson, Harvey H. II. University of
Mississippi. Center for the Study of Southern Culture. III. Series.
F209 .N47 2006 vol. 16
[GV584.S68]
975.003 s—dc22
2010655074
The *Encyclopedia of Southern Culture*, sponsored by the Center for
the Study of Southern Culture at the University of Mississippi, was
published by the University of North Carolina Press in 1989.
cloth   15 14 13 12 11   5 4 3 2 1
paper   15 14 13 12 11   5 4 3 2 1

Tell about the South. What's it like there.

What do they do there. Why do they live there.

Why do they live at all.

WILLIAM FAULKNER

Absalom, Absalom!

CONTENTS

In 1989 years of planning and hard work came to fruition when the University of North Carolina Press joined the Center for the Study of Southern Culture at the University of Mississippi to publish the *Encyclopedia of Southern Culture*. While all those involved in writing, reviewing, editing, and producing the volume believed it would be received as a vital contribution to our understanding of the American South, no one could have anticipated fully the widespread acclaim it would receive from reviewers and other commentators. But the *Encyclopedia* was indeed celebrated, not only by scholars but also by popular audiences with a deep, abiding interest in the region. At a time when some people talked of the "vanishing South," the book helped remind a national audience that the region was alive and well, and it has continued to shape national perceptions of the South through the work of its many users—journalists, scholars, teachers, students, and general readers.

As the introduction to the *Encyclopedia* noted, its conceptualization and organization reflected a cultural approach to the South. It highlighted such issues as the core zones and margins of southern culture, the boundaries where "the South" overlapped with other cultures, the role of history in contemporary culture, and the centrality of regional consciousness, symbolism, and mythology. By 1989 scholars had moved beyond the idea of cultures as real, tangible entities, viewing them instead as abstractions. The *Encyclopedia*'s editors and contributors thus included a full range of social indicators, trait groupings, literary concepts, and historical evidence typically used in regional studies, carefully working to address the distinctive and characteristic traits that made the American South a particular place. The introduction to the *Encyclopedia* concluded that the fundamental uniqueness of southern culture was reflected in the volume's composite portrait of the South. We asked contributors to consider aspects that were unique to the region but also those that suggested its internal diversity. The volume was not a reference book of southern history, which explained something of the design of entries. There were fewer essays on colonial and antebellum history than on the postbellum and modern periods, befitting our conception of the volume as one trying not only to chart the cultural landscape of the South but also to illuminate the contemporary era.

When C. Vann Woodward reviewed the *Encyclopedia* in the *New York Review of Books*, he concluded his review by noting "the continued liveliness of interest in the South and its seeming inexhaustibility as a field of study." Research on the South, he wrote, furnishes "proof of the value of the *Encyclopedia* as a scholarly undertaking as well as suggesting future needs for revision or supplement to keep up with ongoing scholarship." The two decades since the publication of the *Encyclopedia of Southern Culture* have certainly suggested that Woodward was correct. The American South has undergone significant changes that make for a different context for the study of the region. The South has undergone social, economic, political, intellectual, and literary transformations, creating the need for a new edition of the *Encyclopedia* that will remain relevant to a changing region. Globalization has become a major issue, seen in the South through the appearance of Japanese automobile factories, Hispanic workers who have immigrated from Latin America or Cuba, and a new prominence for Asian and Middle Eastern religions that were hardly present in the 1980s South. The African American return migration to the South, which started in the 1970s, dramatically increased in the 1990s, as countless books simultaneously appeared asserting powerfully the claims of African Americans as formative influences on southern culture. Politically, southerners from both parties have played crucial leadership roles in national politics, and the Republican Party has dominated a near-solid South in national elections. Meanwhile, new forms of music, like hip-hop, have emerged with distinct southern expressions, and the term "dirty South" has taken on new musical meanings not thought of in 1989. New genres of writing by creative southerners, such as gay and lesbian literature and "white trash" writing, extend the southern literary tradition.

Meanwhile, as Woodward foresaw, scholars have continued their engagement with the history and culture of the South since the publication of the *Encyclopedia*, raising new scholarly issues and opening new areas of study. Historians have moved beyond their earlier preoccupation with social history to write new cultural history as well. They have used the categories of race, social class, and gender to illuminate the diversity of the South, rather than a unified "mind of the South." Previously underexplored areas within the field of southern historical studies, such as the colonial era, are now seen as formative periods of the region's character, with the South's positioning within a larger Atlantic world a productive new area of study. Cultural memory has become a major topic in the exploration of how the social construction of "the South" benefited some social groups and exploited others. Scholars in many disciplines have made the southern identity a major topic, and they have used a variety of methodologies to suggest what that identity has meant to different social groups. Literary critics have adapted cultural theories to the South and have raised the issue of postsouthern literature to a major category of concern as well as exploring the links between the literature of the American South and that of the Caribbean. Anthropologists have used different theoretical formulations from literary critics, providing models for their fieldwork in southern communities. In the past 30 years anthropologists have set increasing numbers of their ethnographic studies in the South, with many of them now exploring topics specifically linked to southern cultural issues. Scholars now place the Native American story, from prehistory to the contemporary era, as a central part of southern history. Comparative and interdisciplinary approaches to the South have encouraged scholars to look at such issues as the borders and boundaries of the South, specific places and spaces with distinct identities within the American South, and the global and transnational Souths, linking the American South with many formerly colonial societies around the world.

The first edition of the *Encyclopedia of Southern Culture* anticipated many of these approaches and indeed stimulated the growth of Southern Studies as a distinct interdisciplinary field. The Center for the Study of Southern Culture has worked for more than three decades to encourage research and teaching about the American South. Its academic programs have produced graduates who have gone on to write interdisciplinary studies of the South, while others have staffed the cultural institutions of the region and in turn encouraged those institutions to document and present the South's culture to broad public audiences. The center's conferences and publications have continued its long tradition of promoting understanding of the history, literature, and music of the South, with new initiatives focused on southern foodways, the future of the South, and the global Souths, expressing the center's mission to bring the best current scholarship to broad public audiences. Its documentary studies projects build oral and visual archives, and the New Directions in Southern Studies book series, published by the University of North Carolina Press, offers an important venue for innovative scholarship.

Since the *Encyclopedia of Southern Culture* appeared, the field of Southern Studies has dramatically developed, with an extensive network now of academic and research institutions whose projects focus specifically on the interdisciplinary study of the South. The Center for the Study of the American South at the University of North Carolina at Chapel Hill, led by Director Harry Watson and Associate Director and *Encyclopedia* coeditor William Ferris, publishes the lively journal *Southern Cultures* and is now at the organizational center of many other Southern Studies projects. The Institute for Southern Studies at the University of South Carolina, the Southern Intellectual History Circle, the Society for the Study of Southern Literature, the Southern Studies Forum of the European American Studies Association, Emory University's SouthernSpaces.org, and the South Atlantic Humanities Center (at the Virginia Foundation for the Humanities, the University of Virginia, and Virginia Polytechnic Institute and State University) express the recent expansion of interest in regional study.

Observers of the American South have had much to absorb, given the rapid pace of recent change. The institutional framework for studying the South is broader and deeper than ever, yet the relationship between the older verities of regional study and new realities remains unclear. Given the extent of changes in the American South and in Southern Studies since the publication of the *Encyclopedia of Southern Culture*, the need for a new edition of that work is clear. Therefore, the Center for the Study of Southern Culture has once again joined the University of North Carolina Press to produce *The New Encyclopedia of Southern Culture*. As readers of the original edition will quickly see, *The New Encyclopedia* follows many of the scholarly principles and editorial conventions established in the original, but with one key difference; rather than being published in a single hardback volume, *The New Encyclopedia* is presented in a series of shorter individual volumes that build on the 24 original subject categories used in the *Encyclopedia* and adapt them to new scholarly developments. Some earlier *Encyclopedia* categories have been reconceptualized in light of new academic interests. For example, the subject section originally titled "Women's Life" is reconceived as a new volume, *Gender*, and the original "Black Life" section is more broadly interpreted as a volume on race. These changes reflect new analytical concerns that place the study of women and blacks in broader cultural systems, reflecting the emergence of, among other topics, the study of male culture and of whiteness. Both volumes draw as well from the rich recent scholarship on women's life and black life. In addition, topics with some thematic coherence are combined in a volume, such as *Law and Politics* and *Agriculture and Industry*. One new topic, *Foodways*, is the basis of a separate volume, reflecting its new prominence in the interdisciplinary study of southern culture.

Numerous individual topical volumes together make up *The New Encyclopedia of Southern Culture* and extend the reach of the reference work to wider audiences. This approach should enhance the use of the *Encyclopedia* in academic courses and is intended to be convenient for readers with more focused interests within the larger context of southern culture. Readers will have handy access to one-volume, authoritative, and comprehensive scholarly treatments of the major areas of southern culture.

We have been fortunate that, in nearly all cases, subject consultants who offered crucial direction in shaping the topical sections for the original edition have agreed to join us in this new endeavor as volume editors. When new volume editors have been added, we have again looked for respected figures who can provide not only their own expertise but also strong networks of scholars to help develop relevant lists of topics and to serve as contributors in their areas. The reputations of all our volume editors as leading scholars in their areas encouraged the contributions of other scholars and added to *The New Encyclopedia*'s authority as a reference work.

The New Encyclopedia of Southern Culture builds on the strengths of articles in the original edition in several ways. For many existing articles, original authors agreed to update their contributions with new interpretations and theoretical perspectives, current statistics, new bibliographies, or simple factual developments that needed to be included. If the original contributor was unable to update an article, the editorial staff added new material or sent it to another scholar for assessment. In some cases, the general editor and volume editors selected a new contributor if an article seemed particularly dated and new work indicated the need for a fresh perspective. And importantly, where new developments have warranted treatment of topics not addressed in the original edition, volume editors have commissioned entirely new essays and articles that are published here for the first time.

The American South embodies a powerful historical and mythical presence, both a complex environmental and geographic landscape and a place of the imagination. Changes in the region's contemporary socioeconomic realities and new developments in scholarship have been incorporated in the conceptualization and approach of *The New Encyclopedia of Southern Culture*. Anthropologist Clifford Geertz has spoken of culture as context, and this encyclopedia looks at the American South as a complex place that has served as the context for cultural expression. This volume provides information and perspective on the diversity of cultures in a geographic and imaginative place with a long history and distinctive character.

The *Encyclopedia of Southern Culture* was produced through major grants from the Program for Research Tools and Reference Works of the National Endowment for the Humanities, the Ford Foundation, the Atlantic-Richfield Foundation, and the Mary Doyle Trust. We are grateful as well to the College of Liberal Arts at the University of Mississippi for support and to the individual donors to the Center for the Study of Southern Culture who have directly or indirectly supported work on *The New Encyclopedia of Southern Culture*. We thank the volume editors for their ideas in reimagining their subjects and the contributors of articles for their work in extending the usefulness of the book in new ways. We acknowledge the support and contributions of the faculty and staff at the Center for the Study of Southern Culture. Finally, we want especially to honor the work of William Ferris and Mary Hart on the *Encyclopedia of Southern Culture*. Bill, the founding director of the Center for the Study of Southern Culture, was coeditor, and his good work recruiting authors, editing text, selecting images, and publicizing the volume among a wide network of people was, of course, invaluable. Despite the many changes in the new encyclopedia, Bill's influence remains. Mary "Sue" Hart was also an invaluable member of the original encyclopedia team, bringing the careful and precise eye of the librarian, and an iconoclastic spirit, to our work.

This volume shows the decisions that the people of the American South have made about how to spend their leisure time. Consideration of sports and recreation connects with larger issues of southern cultural development. It tells much, for example, about everyday life. Beginning in an agrarian society, southerners became hunters and they fished the waters of the region. Recreation in those days was often tied to subsistence; as generations passed, though, southerners continued to embrace those activities as sports that kept them close to the environment and nurtured particular cultural values. Women drew from domestic work recreational activities that nurtured their spirits; quilting bees, for example, became not only functional and aesthetically pleasing activities but entertaining ones as well. People refreshed themselves with play and pastimes in semipublic places as well, passing the time at the country store, barbershop, and beauty parlor and sitting on the iconic porch, conversing with neighbors, friends, and passersby. In the 20th century, sports and recreation became spectacle as modern mass culture and consumerism entered the region and made lovers of sports into spectators. Professional sports franchises were slow to come into the South, but college football and basketball developed fan bases. More recently, teams like the Atlanta Braves and the Dallas Cowboys become regional icons. The football success of the New Orleans Saints in the years after Hurricane Katrina made the team a rallying point, raising pride and spirits throughout the hard-hit Gulf Coast. Giant sports stadia and arenas in cities mark the landscape of people who invest considerable meaning in loyalty to their local teams.

The South's sporting and recreational life was long structured around institutions and activities that reflected a patriarchal and racially conscious society. Women and African Americans established separate spheres. Women's domestic recreations and their participation in women's bowling, basketball, and other leagues showed their embrace of an individual competitive urge and yet also community-based recreational interaction. Negro baseball leagues, Historically Black College and University marching bands and football games, and juke joints were only a few of the institutions that African Americans used as venues for distinctive talk, storytelling, and other cultural expressions. Further, some recreational choices reflect social class preferences, as in the working-class embrace of stock car racing and the middle class of tennis and golf. Other recreational activities bring southerners together across all sorts of social borders.

Sports and Recreation demonstrates the breadth of recreational activities in the South. Readers can consider the transition from recreations popular in rural areas and according to agricultural calendars to recreations that are more commercial and often more self-conscious. Readers can vicariously stroll through amusement parks and participate in the Annual Interstate Mullet Toss. They can catch the history and flavor of the Kentucky Derby, the sounds of Austin's South by Southwest, and the pleasures of the region's beaches. Rituals are well represented, from all-day singings, to family reunions, to *quinceañeras*, to square dancing. Included are places as diverse as the Appalachian Trail, Colonial Williamsburg, Dogpatch USA, Hilton Head, and the Redneck Riviera. The reader unaware of the South's local ways will discover surprises, such as fireballing in Alabama and the adventuresome fisherman's noodling (the latter of which graces the volume's cover). Dogs seem to run through the volume, whether fox hunting, quail hunting, in field trials, or simply as beloved family pets. Articles cover the sports gamut from the wildly popular football, basketball, and baseball, to sports with ancient regional roots (blood sports, hunting, fishing), to such newly popular activities as rafting and canoeing, rock climbing, and running.

Other volumes of *The New Encyclopedia of Southern Culture* explore how southerners have worked over time, but this volume's contribution is exploring the social life of people rooted in places that afforded extended opportunities for outdoor activities and for a variety of leisure time events that helped them carve out distinctive identities around play.

The NEW ENCYCLOPEDIA *of* SOUTHERN CULTURE

VOLUME 16 : SPORTS AND RECREATION

LEISURE, SPORTS, AND
ALL SORTS OF RECREATION

C. Vann Woodward begins his *American Counterpoint* with a lengthy treatment of southern leisure. He points out that, like so many other myths about the South, this one tends to be "Janus-faced," to present contrary aspects that change depending on the observer's point of view. For some, southern leisure has been a gracious thing, involving careful attention to nonpecuniary values and activities in a world mad with materialistic frenzy. Others, looking at the reverse side, see the unattractive countenance, the Lazy South, the "Sahara of the Bozart," with all its blemishes—"idleness, indolence, slothfulness, languor, lethargy, and dissipation."

Leisure/Laziness Myth. These two contrary aspects notwithstanding, the leisure/laziness myth has consistently involved two distinct cultural subjects—work and nonwork—and has represented the typical southerner as less interested in the former than most Americans and more interested in the latter. The myth's Janus-faced quality becomes clear only when values have been assigned to work and to leisure. Some northern observers and proponents of the "new Industrial South" have focused on the South's distaste for work, viewing it as a destructive anachronism that needed to be reformed, and dismissed the various claims about the virtues of free time. But apologists for the South have tended to emphasize the value of leisure as a time for human culture, spiritual reflection, contemplation, friends, family, nature—those things that make life worth the effort—and at the same time to criticize the American preoccupation with busy work, mindless growth, and the resultant spiritual and cultural exhaustion.

This myth, then, has generated two kinds of statements, those about facts and those about values. As such, it may be analyzed on two levels. On the one hand, one may attempt to determine the extent to which the myth is true—the extent to which southern attitudes and behavior correspond to the stereotype. The social scientist, for example, may test southern mass attitudes and behavior and speculate about their causes. On the other hand, the myth may be accepted on its own terms, as an expression of values and as a part of the larger cultural dialogue or "counterpoint" that has existed between the South and the rest of the country. In this regard historians and literary critics may investigate the opinions of articulate and influential writers concerning work and leisure in order to show how at its highest reaches culture emerges in dialogue about questions of values, about what should or might be, rather than about what already exists.

The cultural debate surrounding the leisure/laziness myth goes back a long way. During the mid-18th century, southerners such as John Hammond portrayed their region as a land of tropical abundance where tranquillity and leisure were the rule. Such idyllic descriptions, echoed by men such as Robert Beverley and William Byrd, were mainly designed to counter a bad European press and attract settlers. But still these early allurement accounts sounded one major mythic value that by the Civil War was completely developed — that work should be a means to an end, that it should be a way to earn a livelihood and to free oneself from time to time for more important things.

During the antebellum period, southern spokesmen expanded, developed, and defended the leisure myth. According to people such as Virginia's Governor Henry Wise, leisure was indispensable for the natural aristocrat, providing the opportunity for learning and public service, freeing him from the servile arts and drudgery for the liberal arts and the creation of new culture, a culture that would benefit all classes. The second part of the myth included an indictment of northern money grubbing, business, and harsh treatment of workers. The North had made money its god, work an end in itself, and had forgotten about human nonpecuniary needs and the importance of leisure.

But even as the myth developed, critics from both the North and South recognized that the ideal did not match the reality, that the lack of work was more a problem than an opportunity. They pointed out that free time in the South was more the occasion for drunkenness, idleness, and dissipation than for learning, culture, and service. It was work and the discipline of work that held a people together, not the freedom of leisure. It was in the marketplace, not the saloon, that culture grew.

This sort of dialogue, involving a blend of voices, some enthusiastic, others ironic or even cynical, smoldered after the Civil War, especially in the works of southern writers such as Sidney Lanier. It was later rekindled and flared briefly in the 20th century as a response to rapid industrial changes.

Agrarians and the New South. As did many of their contemporaries and the majority of historians who have written about the period, the 12 Agrarians of *I'll Take My Stand* believed that American industry and business had taken a new direction in the 1920s—had shifted attention from production to consumption. According to the Agrarians, "It [was] an inevitable consequence of industrial process that production [outran] the rate of natural consumption." This overrun had resulted in chronic overproduction and unemployment. But instead of dealing with these consequences of success in a humane fashion, American business had "romanticized" industry and work and developed a "new gospel of consumption." Promoting "the incessant extension of industrialism," the multiplication of luxuries, and the cultivation of fantastic and even lethal desires for them, this new gospel "never proposed a specific goal; it initiated the infinite series"—a squirrel-cage existence where growth was for growth's sake, work purposeless and never ending, and consumption artificial and manipulated.

The Agrarians proposed a traditionally southern alternative to this mindless "progress." Instead of work that was brutal, harried, and meaningless, they offered "a form of labor that [was] pursued with intelligence and leisure"—was more natural and task oriented, connected to the soil and to a stable social order. Instead of free time that was lost to consumption, satiety, and aimlessness, they suggested a leisure in the "culture of the soil" where art and religion flourished, where "a free and disinterested approach to existence" was possible; the amenities of life such as manners, conversation, sympathy, family life, and romantic love were carried on; and the enjoyment of life could be spontaneous. To the Agrarians, leisure should be an integral part of life. It should be a part of work, with a social and economic place. Unlike industrial free time, it should not alienate people more than it brings them together.

Walter Hines Page agreed that leisureliness was a hallmark of regional identity. But unlike the Agrarians, he welcomed industry to the New South because, in addition to its material blessings, it would offer "the inestimable boon of leisure." For Page, leisure was an industrial product as important as consumer goods because it could be used to redeem parts of southern culture even as the traditional forms of work were being lost.

But spokesmen for the New South have generally dismissed these dreams. People such as Henry W. Grady and Richard Edmunds welcomed industry with none of Page's hopes for leisure and saw the South's casual approach to work as a curable weakness. Grady saw the South falling "in love with its work"; Edmunds observed that his compatriots had learned that "time is money." New southern businessmen have been as busy as their northern friends promoting goods and services designed for the "leisure market." City fathers court industry, boasting that the work ethic is stronger in their region than elsewhere. Following the na-

Watching the bathers at Gulfport, Miss., postcard, early 20th century (Ann Rayburn Paper Americana Collection, Archives and Special Collections, University of Mississippi Library, Oxford)

tional trend, southerners as a group have lost interest in increased leisure and have remained content with 40 hours' work a week for over 40 years—this after a 20-year period of rapid reduction of the hours of labor.

Even southern historians, while not so much welcoming the Puritan work ethic, have joined in the general condemnation of leisure. W. J. Cash saw the old southern assumptions about leisure—"that the first end of life is living itself"—woefully out of date, a way of degeneration and "incompatible with success." David Bertelson saw leisure as the traditional myth, but laziness as the traditional reality. According to Bertelson, laziness worked against a sense of community because it fragmented southerners and encouraged a preoccupation with self instead of the community.

The discussion has largely ended. Even though a few echoes are heard from time to time, southern life and leisure are no longer seriously proposed as alternatives to industrialism nor is increasing free time offered as a way for the South to accommodate modernism and retain its identity. The lively exchanges about what was more meaningless, work in the industrial squirrel cage or free time in a disintegrating culture, are mostly forgotten. But yet the perception in its simplest form—that southerners prefer leisure more and work less—remains.

In magazine articles, in newspaper Sunday supplements, and even in advertisements, the region's lazy-leisurely reputation continues to be spread, even internationally. Occasionally a journalist will editorialize and condemn or praise the lazy, leisurely South. But usually, these portrayals are not serious business. Rather they tend to be amusing reports about a charming, regional peculiarity. Public attitudes tend to conform to these popular reports. John Shelton Reed and others have demonstrated that college students North and South still hold on to this regional stereotype. Apparently, the old dialogue produced a vivid enough image in the public awareness to survive its passing.

But another possibility remains—that the myth is true, and the dialogue, too, about both a reality and an ideal. Those who engaged in the dialogue often thought of themselves as reporters as well as leaders and spokesmen. Even the Agrarians, calling their region back to tradition, made claims about historical truth and existing culture. The extent to which myth matches reality has been approached empirically with some interesting results.

Distinctive Southern Behavior. Statistical evidence for the first three decades of the 20th century indicates that southerners did prefer leisure more and work for wages less than other Americans. For example, in 1920 a typical northern worker making the same hourly wage as his southern brother worked longer hours. If he got a raise he would work even longer hours while the typical southerner would take more time off at higher income levels. But this regional difference disappeared by the 1940s and the South, like the rest of the nation, became content with the 40-hour week.

When investigators study attitudes about work directly, instead of opinions about stereotypes, they have so far failed to find regional variations. There is simply not enough evidence to support or contradict the belief that southerners value work more or less than other Americans. Nor is there much in the way of systematic evidence about southern attitudes toward leisure.

But indications can be found that southerners are distinctive when it comes to leisure behavior. The evidence comes from a variety of sources, and it is remarkably consistent. By and large, southerners simply do less in their leisure time than other Americans—or at least less of most things that social scientists and market researchers are interested in.

The U.S. Department of Labor's surveys of consumer expenditures show that southerners spend a smaller percentage of their income on "recreational goods and services" than other Americans—from the lowest to the highest income classification. Research undertaken by private marketing firms also shows that southerners engage in less "commercially relevant behavior" in their leisure than others. In general, these studies have found that the South is not as good a market as its population would suggest and that it is a particularly bad market for recreational products that are used in sports like jogging, golf, camping, bowling, and racquetball. However, southerners hold their own if the recreational products can be used in hunting and fishing.

Other studies show lower levels of magazine and newspaper circulation, though when they read, southerners are more likely to read *Field & Stream*, *Sports Afield*, *Outdoor Life*, *Shooting Times*, *Gun World*, and *American Cooner* than *Ski*, *Skiing*, *Dune Buggies*, *Cycle World*, *Water Skiier*, *Skin Diver*, *Yachting*, or *Salt Water Sports*. In the South one also finds fewer miles driven per year (a stand-in for billboard advertising), less television watching and radio listening, and low levels of memberships in sports and hobby groups. Southerners are well represented in the National Wildlife Federation and the National Rifle Association, but not many join groups like the Izaak Walton League, the Amateur Trapshooting Association, the National Field Archery Association, the American Badminton Association, and the National Horseshoe Pitchers Association. Southerners are also few in the American Philatelic Society, the American Numismatic Society, the National Model Railroad Association, and the International Brotherhood of Magicians. Southerners participate less than other Americans in what the National Endowment for the Humanities (NEH) called the fine or beaux arts (with the exceptions found by the 1973 Louis Harris Poll of singing in a choir, listening to religious music, and listening to country and western music).

These regional differences are not enormous. Region makes less difference than education does, for instance. But regional differences are about the same size as differences between black and white—about the same size, that is, of some other "cultural" or "ethnic" differences in the United States.

One may reasonably ask at this point what do southerners do when they are not consuming, watching television, reading the newspaper or magazines, or participating in clubs? A Harris Poll in 1978 found a number of these things that were included in the same NEH study. According to this poll, southerners spend more time fixing things around the house, helping others, having a good time with friends and relatives, resting after work, getting away from problems, taking naps, and "just doing nothing." More recent studies suggest these inclinations still remain.

One good way to summarize these findings is to point out that the South has a pattern of leisure that is more "time intensive" and less "goods intensive." Southerners are likely to choose activities that take more time but less money than other early 21st-century Americans. From all indications the modern South is still holding on to vestiges of a preindustrial folk culture in its leisure. Considering that he wrote more than 80 years ago about a South he feared was vanishing, John Crowe Ransom's observations in *I'll Take My Stand* that the arts of the South are the "social arts of dress, conversation, manners, the table, the hunt, politics, oratory, the pulpit, the arts of living and not the arts of escape . . . ; community arts in which every class of society could participate after its kind," are remarkably accurate today.

Since the myth, if not the proven reality, has been around so long, there is certainly no shortage of explanations for the lazy-leisurely South. H. L. Mencken's view, echoed more recently by the Kentucky-born gonzo journalist Hunter Thompson, was that white southerners are genetically disposed to idleness and vicious habits. The South Carolina poet Josephine Pinckney, on the other hand, argued that these are innate black traits, somehow spread to whites by contagion. Southerners' favorite explanation—or excuse—has probably been the weather. In its old version, favored by Robert Beverley and William Byrd, this argument has it that it is too easy to get by where food grows almost by itself and nobody needs many clothes. A version more applicable to the urban, industrial South says that it is just too hot to do much of anything. Another popular theory points to the effects of slavery, producing laziness in slaves and slaveholders alike, and also leading nonslaveholders to believe that exertion was for slaves and beneath their dignity. Still another recalls the earlier, fanciful notion that the South's supposed Cavalier heritage produced individuals fleeing Puritan constraints while pursuing a hedonistic, "long-haired" lifestyle in the southern climes.

C. Vann Woodward, on the other hand, saw a distinctive skepticism emerging in the South after the Civil War about the American dream of endless progress, industrial work, and human perfectibility in general. Resulting from the regional experience of defeat, failure, sin, poverty, and guilt, this skepticism has produced a people less caught up in the fervid rush of modern life and more content with the leisurely enjoyment of the simple present. Finally, the old myth and debate about the defects and virtues of work and leisure may have percolated down through the South, so that the culture comes to resemble what its mythmakers imagined. George B. Tindall has shown how southern myths have a definite way of influencing regional realities. For the lazy-leisurely South, it may be a case of nature imitating art.

Whatever their origins, southern attitudes toward work and leisure are part of the regional culture. Like other cultural traits, these are not things that individuals work out for themselves. They are learned from those around us while we are growing up and from each other after we are grown. A large part of any culture is made up of shared views of what is appropriate; success in any culture depends on learning what those views are and, ordinarily, on coming to share them. One is not born knowing what to do with leisure time, nor do indi-

Cartoon from the Mobile Press-Register

viduals make it up as they go along. People learn how to pass the time appropriately. Those who share the same culture—a regional culture, for instance—have learned more or less similar lessons.

W. J. Cash, while he was writing about how the old southern assumption "that the first end of life is living itself" had become out of date by the 1930s, was also writing about another aspect of southern culture, one rooted in the frontier experience, which he credited with making Dixie what it was. Looking at the origins of the white southerner's attitude toward leisure and what to do when he had it, Cash wrote that it was not a "hoary and sophisticated class tradition that dictated the proper sport for gentlemen. It was not even that the southerner knew how English squires behaved or that they hungered to identify themselves with them by imitation. It was simply and primarily for the same reasons that, in the southerner's youth and often into late manhood, he ran spontaneous and unpremeditated footraces, wrestled, drank Gargantuan quantities of raw whiskey, let off wild yells, and hunted the possum—because the thing was already in his mores when he emerged from the backwoods; because on the frontier it was the obvious thing to do; because he was a hot, stout fellow, full of blood and reared to outdoor activity; because of a primitive and naïve zest for the pursuit at hand."

It is, of course, out of fashion to fall back on Cash today. He wrote not about the South but about a relatively small portion of it, mostly the North Carolina Piedmont. He wrote almost exclusively about men—about white men, mostly. And yet, it seems that in assessing the relationship between southerners and leisure and sports, W. J. Cash was onto something. And that something was competition. Cash focused on the individual, and indeed team sports came late to Dixie. Although men and boys (and occasionally women and girls) might go out a-hunting, they went as a collection of persons, and continue to do so today. Other sports—horseracing, dog running, even fishing—pitted an individual against an adversary in a singular trial of skill or endurance. Participation came in many forms. To wager on a race brought the spectator into the contest (it also, as so often with southern sports, brought elements of honor into play). So it followed that individual southerners took sporting events seriously and defeat personally.

Southerners seemed inclined to seek out competition and turn everything they could into a contest—Confederate soldiers were said to hold lice and tick races to wile away the hours while waiting to march and fight. But of competition as a team there is little to judge by apart from the war itself—and just how well southerners were organized, or could be organized into a fighting unit, remains a matter of debate.

Cajun children fishing, Schriever, La., 1940 (Marion Post Wolcott, photographer, Library of Congress [LC-UCF-54259-D], Washington, D.C.)

Much has been made of Civil War southerners taking up what was becoming the "national pastime," and evidence suggests isolated cases of Confederate soldiers giving the sport a try. However, the most famous baseball-related incident on the southern side of the war was not a contest between competing "nines" but the story of Confederate skirmishers attacking a group of Yankees at play, breaking up the game, stealing the ball, and shooting the right fielder—which Roy Blount Jr. notes was the least competitive position on the field. This, of course, has been reduced to imagery and imagination, which is both natural and appropriate where southern sports are concerned.

It was with the New South, the often Yankee-inspired effort to bring southerners into the national mainstream, that Dixie's individual sportsmen were organized into teams. Though not enough study has been done on this, a relationship between the movement from farm to factory and the change in sporting attitudes does exist. How much to make of similarity, however, is another thing all together, for though individuality was sacrificed for the team, it was sacrificed only so far. Baseball, for example, became a near obsession as mill-town squads battled it out with each other (note, please, the use of military terms to describe the contests). As a team, the players became a single individual and, as such, an extension of the spectators—"their" team, as it were. Yet at the same time individual players continued to stand out and be recognized for personal accomplishments—as they continue to do in "team" sports like NASCAR today. And at the core of it all was the competition, the struggle, and the need to win. It was, studies have suggested, a tribal thing, where teams replaced warriors (or became warriors) in a contest between competing clans, where victory brought honor and glory and defeat did not.

Football was slow to replace baseball because football was associated with an institution that had little relevance to the majority of southerners—college. But as the sport filtered down from higher education to schools closer to home, communities began to invest the same emotion in high school rivalries as alumni and students invested in their college elevens. It was, and still remains, the competition, the test, the need to win and affirm superiority.

The emphasis southerners place on sports, and more specifically on winning, has come under criticism from many quarters. When lists of schools in trouble with the NCAA for recruiting violations are compiled, southern schools rise to the top, and when critics note how cheating to win finds few critics in the Bible Belt, their charges of hypocrisy are cavalierly ignored. Studies also suggest that community rivalries born and bred on the gridiron have prevented towns and counties from cooperating in economic development and cultural affairs. Thus, frontier individualism is transferred to the community level, and local boosters willingly accept the limitations imposed as necessary by-product of the competition.

In the latter half of the 20th century, as cities replaced towns, urban areas first competed to attract professional teams and then promoted rivalries that in some cases matched those found among colleges. Cities competed for major sporting events that, when successful, were touted as more evidence of the victor's "arrival." Atlanta's quest for the Olympics is a classic example of how far a city will go to prove itself worthy while at the same time revealing, not coincidentally, the problems being southern created for image makers once the victory was won. (Some southerners still get night sweats dreaming of belles in hoop skirts dancing among chrome-plated pickup trucks.)

Much has been written, though perhaps not enough, about how football became, for Dixie at least, another way to fight the Civil War to a different outcome. The University of Alabama's fabled victories in the Rose Bowl, despite Yankee sportswriters who said they did not deserve to be there, were seen in many quarters as revenge for Appomattox. All-Star contests such as the Senior Bowl and the Blue-Gray Game were (and still are) pitched as a contest with the hated Yankee, and integration has not seemed to make southerners less partisan, sectionally speaking. Indeed, black players generally display the same regional loyalty as their white teammates, though without the same attachment to Confederate symbols and symbolism.

On the other hand, sports are often credited with breaking down racial barriers and easing the South into integration, as attested to by bumper stickers on white-driven Georgia pickup trucks proudly proclaiming "Herschel Walker is my cousin." Bear Bryant's decision to recruit black athletes after his unintegrated Alabama team spent the afternoon chasing Southern Cal's Sam "Bam" Cunningham is the stuff of legend, but there can be no denying the impact sports has had on desegregation in the South. Football has hardly been alone in this. Basketball, for many, has become the game of choice, and out of that cauldron of competition have come regional heroes Michael Jordan and Charles Barkley.

While less attention has been paid to the rise of women's sports in Dixie, the emergence of female athletics as both spectator and participatory contests has had an impact on the diversity of sports in the South and on the "image" of the southern belle. Of course, there have always been contests within the "women's sphere," and anyone who doubts the intensity of this competition need only drop by the "domestic arts" tent at a southern county or state fair and look at contestants with their jams and jellies, cakes and pies, quilts and comforters, to know just how serious this competition is. However, these are "sports" that corresponded to the role southern women were expected to play in the order of things. To engage in anything similar to that in which men were engaged was not "ladylike" and thus discouraged. The result is well known. Pick up a high school or college yearbook from before Title IX of the Education Amendments of 1972 became law, and you will see just how little women's sports, especially team sports, were funded and encouraged. There you will see in picture and print just how limited the sports in which athletic women could participate were. (Ask anyone who was in school then, and they will recall one of the "girls" on one of the few women's teams the schools allowed, sigh, and say, "If she only had the opportunity, she could have been an All Star.") How much talent went to waste is incalculable.

As children, though, young girls played on equal footing with boys. But once they reached puberty girls were discouraged, and in many cases prohibited, from playing sports that might compromise their femininity. Despite this, southern women pushed the boundaries of the "sphere" that defined and limited what they should and could do as athletes. Usually competing as individuals rather than a member of a team, they rode horses, skied on water (mostly) and snow (occasionally), swam, hunted, fished, and engaged in a host of other athletic and recreational activities. Thus accustomed to individual competition and achievement, when given the chance they embraced team sports with the same enthusiasm as men, and since that time women's teams have grown in number, participation, and popularity.

Interestingly, perhaps ironically, women's entry into the work force and gaining access to higher education increased options for participation in sports—especially team sports. Once women became part of an organized unit, be it a mill or a college, they sought and found recreational outlets in sports. Women's teams, especially basketball, became a frequent feature at textile mills, fostering worker loyalty to the organization as well as offering women an opportunity to have a good time away from the looms. During World War II, aviation manufacturers also promoted women's teams that barnstormed around the region and competed with others. Meanwhile, as more women attended colleges, the demand for recreational opportunities increased, and having had a limited exposure to team sports at the high school level, it was only natural that women sought more opportunities as coeds.

Today the mill town teams are a thing of the past; however, southern high schools and colleges regularly field a host of women's teams, with basketball, volleyball, soccer, and softball drawing large and enthusiastic crowds. Women participate in track events, and lately field hockey and even lacrosse are gaining in popularity. Although few high schools sponsor gymnastics teams, the network of private gyms and instructors who train female gymnasts has grown with the attention television has paid to the sport. These gymnasts go on to compete in college and in some cases on national teams in international competition. Private gyms also train cheerleaders, for acrobatic and coordinated cheerleading has been recognized as a sport as competitive as any other. Sports television has recognized the popularity of these contests and regularly broadcasts women's events. Though the day is still far away when a national championship in softball will get the same attention as a bowl victory or a men's team making basketball's final four, no one can deny that southern women play with the same skill and intensity as southern men and that they value victory just as much.

Yet even though some observers feel that this love of the game, the contest, the competition, suggests that southerners are drifting into the national mainstream—claiming that LSU or Tennessee or Florida fans (be it football, baseball, or something else) are no more passionate than counterparts at Ohio State, Nebraska, or UCLA (well, maybe not UCLA)—the tribal culture so often associated with southern partisans continues to stand out when placed alongside fans from north of Mason and Dixon or west of Texas (as most recently revealed in Warren St. John's *Rammer Jammer Yellow Hammer: A Journey into the Heart of Fan Mania*).

Indeed, if there is a place where the often-alluded-to "Dixification of America" can be seen in both reality and aspiration, it is in efforts on behalf of sportsmen throughout the nation to be a little more like the South—something mass marketers and television sports networks anticipate with glee because, as the entries and essays that follow reveal, there is more to "southern recreation and leisure" than football and fishing—not to take anything away from those noble pastimes. The list shows that the things southerners do for fun are as many and varied as southerners themselves. The ways southerners entertain themselves also reflect changes in southern society that some applaud while others condemn—gambling and recreational drinking, for example. Entries also reveal the growing affluence of some segments of southern society, for though regional elites have always enjoyed places and events only they could afford—a week at Seaside or Hilton Head perhaps—in recent years a rising southern middle class has taken to heart places like Disney World and Dogpatch USA. Meanwhile, the income and level of education of NASCAR fans continues to amaze folks from somewhere other than here.

The "redneck" South, characterized by what comedian Jeff Foxworthy calls its "glorious lack of sophistication," remains and continues to contribute to the recreational culture of Dixie. But while noodling for catfish, tossing mullet, and

The Flora-Bama Lounge and Package, located about six feet from the Florida-Alabama state line (on the Florida side), has been a popular southern beach-bar hangout since 1964. It is commonly referred to as "The Last Great American Roadhouse." (Image courtesy of Harvey H. Jackson III)

participating in a variety of blood sports are considered characteristic activities of certain elements within the region, southerners also contribute in both participants and places to sports like golf, tennis, and even gardening. As the following essays show, southerners have turned what were once personal, even private, pleasures into cultural events. Back-porch jam sessions have become music festivals. Church dinners on the grounds and family reunions where folks gathered to sample wonders whipped up by local cooks have evolved into gastrotourism, where autotourists wander Dixie's highways and byways in search of yet another culinary delight. And whenever possible, which is usually, they make a contest of it—as doubters who claim their barbecue is better will quickly learn.

As a collection, these essays and entries reveal how southern recreational activities are broadening as Dixie's population diversifies—woe be to the high school soccer team without at least one Latino player. At the same time, southerners continue to enjoy traditional activities in traditional settings that are nationally known but appreciated for their regional flavor—Dollywood, the Daytona and Talladega speedways, the Flora-Bama Lounge and Package, Silver Dollar City, and South of the Border.

Meanwhile southern sports enthusiasts, armchair and otherwise, find their heroes among coaches and players who have brought glory not only to their respective schools and teams but to the region itself: Bear Bryant, Eddie Robinson, Dale Earnhardt, Bobby Jones, Junior Johnson, Pete Maravich, Kenny Stabler, Herschel Walker, and all the Mannings, to name only a few.

In the final analysis, what southerners do, where they go, and what they expect to accomplish in their spare time, their "leisure," reveal the cultural values, the class and racial similarities and differences, and the historical perspectives of those participating in whatever is going on, wherever it is being done. They may be reenacting a battle long ago lost, they may be gathered around as nimble hands and nimble minds play pool checkers, they may be attending a Mardi Gras ball or jammed along the parade route shouting for beads. Where they are and what they are doing tell us a lot about who they are and what makes them so.

That is what this volume is all about.

JOHN SHELTON REED
University of North Carolina at Chapel Hill

BENJAMIN K. HUNNICUTT
University of Iowa

HARVEY H. JACKSON III
Jacksonville State University

David Bertelson, *The Lazy South* (1967); H. C. Brearley, *American Scholar* (Winter 1949); W. J. Cash, *The Mind of the South* (1941); Norval Glenn and Charles Weaver, *Texas Business Review* (November–December 1982); Pamela Grundy, *Learning to Win: Sports, Education, and Social Change in Twentieth Century North Carolina* (2001); Pamela Grundy and Susan Shackelford, *Shattering the Glass: The Dazzling History of Women's Basketball from the Turn of the Century to the Present* (2005); Fred C. Hobson, *Alabama Heritage* (Summer 1986); Robert W. Ikard, *Just for Fun: The Story of AAU Women's Basketball* (2005); Lewis Killian, *White Southerners* (1970); Forrest McDonald and Grady McWhiney, *American Historical Review* (December 1980); Peter Marsden et al., *Social Forces* (June 1982); H. L. Mencken, *Prejudices, Second Series* (1920); Patrick B. Miller, ed., *The Sporting World of the Modern South* (2002); Ted Ownby, *Subduing Satan: Religion and Manhood in the Rural South, 1865–1920* (1990); Josephine Pinckney, in *Culture in the South*, ed. W. T. Couch (1934); Nicholas W. Proctor, *Bathed in Blood: Hunting and Mastery in the Old South* (2002); John Shelton Reed, *The Enduring South: Regional Persistence in Mass Society* (1974), *North Carolina Historical Review* (April 1983), *One South: An Ethnic Approach to Regional Culture* (1982), *Southerners: The Social Psychology of Sectionalism* (1983); Warren St. John, *Rammer Jammer Yellow Hammer: A Road Trip into the*

Heart of Fan Mania (2004); Richard D. Starnes, ed., *Southern Journeys: Tourism, History, and Culture in the Modern South* (2003); Joe Gray Taylor, *Eating, Drinking, and Visiting in the South: An Informal History* (1982); George B. Tindall, *The Ethnic Southerners* (1976); Twelve Southerners, *I'll Take My Stand: The South and the Agrarian Tradition* (1930); Rupert B. Vance, *Human Geography of the South: A Study in Regional Resources and Human Adequacy* (1935); C. Vann Woodward, *American Counterpoint: Slavery and Racism in the North-South Dialogue* (1964), *The Burden of Southern History* (1960); Jim Wright, *Fixin' to Git: One Fan's Love Affair with NASCAR's Winston Cup* (2002).

All-Day Singings

All-day singing has long been one of the most cherished social institutions of the rural South. The term has been applied to a wide range of musical affairs and even has its counterpart in the all-night singings of modern gospel quartet music, but it is most closely associated with the shape-note singing convention.

Singing conventions are events that feature the performance of shape-note music, of both the four-shape and seven-shape varieties. The four-shape conventions have always been the most conservative in that they adhere to the use of one songbook, usually the venerable *Sacred Harp*, first published by Benjamin F. White in 1844, and they tend to resist newer songs and innovative styles of performing them (they instead preserve the Fasola style of singing). In short, the four-shape people try to remain faithful to the music and, in some respects, the way of life of their ancestors. The seven-shape conventions, which are by far the most numerous of these events, were originally marked by their acceptance of the do-re-mi system of singing, and they have generally been receptive to innovations in songs and singing style. The singers at such conventions sing not from one book but from a wide variety of paperback shape-note hymnals generally published twice a year by such companies as Vaughan, Winsett, and Stamps-Baxter. The song repertoire therefore includes both the older, familiar religious material and the newest songs "hot off the press." Although everyone in attendance is encouraged to sing, performances are also made by soloists, duets and trios, and often by visiting professional quartets. People clearly attend these conventions not merely to sing but also to be entertained.

Whatever the style of singing, the singing conventions meet regularly throughout the rural and small-town South, often on a monthly basis in the case of the seven-shape singers, but much more infrequently in the case of the Fasola people. (Sacred Harp singings actually occur all over the United States, particularly after being displayed in the popular movie *Cold Mountain*.) Singers gather at a church or at the county courthouse, renew old acquaintances, sing for several hours under the guidance of experienced song leaders, and then sit down at long tables for a sumptuous feast of fried chicken, ham, potato salad, assorted pastries, and other delectables brought by the guests and participants. The practice of combining food and religious music long ago gave rise to the term "all-day singing with dinner on the grounds," which describes one of the most common events in the rural South.

BILL C. MALONE
Madison, Wisconsin

Alan Lomax, commentary on *All Day Singing from "The Sacred Harp,"* Prestige Records 25007.

Amusement and Theme Parks

In the first decades of the 20th century, more than 1,000 amusement parks dotted the American landscape. Generally built on the outskirts of towns and cities, many of these parks operated like small self-contained villages with their own electrical and plumbing systems. They boasted gardens, pavilions, lakes, and electric rides, often surrounded by a barrier separating the park's lush grounds from the outside world. Historian Lauren Rabinovitz describes these early 20th-century amusement parks as "an Erector-set world of mechanical thrill rides, shows of human and animal oddities, saloons and swimming pools, beer gardens and ballrooms, restaurants and roller skating rinks . . . characterized by its dynamism—its brash colors, constant noise, and continual movement of people and machinery." While the parks featured and advertised a host of rides, shows, and attractions, they were often built on the site of a popular picnic grove or spring, which locals had traditionally used as a leisure spot. Hoping to capitalize on the already-popular grounds, enterprising individuals bought the site, setting up a menagerie of mechanical attractions to draw more patrons.

Local streetcar companies owned many early amusement parks. Referred to as "trolley parks," these enclosed parks were situated at the end of a trolley line. Although many trolley parks offered free or reduced admission, trolley companies benefited financially in other ways. For example, the park's location at the end of a trolley line assured that cars traveled at near full capacity during their entire route. Also, because many of these parks were outside cities, companies could charge an added 5¢ or 10¢ fare for a ride to the park. For these reasons, the trolley park coached people to see and use the trolley for weekend leisure activities in addition to daily transit during the workweek. Whether owned by an individual, a small cohort of entrepreneurs, or a trolley company, most early amusement parks offered similar attractions. Parks generally had a Ferris wheel and a giant of some sort, along with the popular shoot-the-chutes and the scenic railway rides. As amusement parks like those on Coney Island became more popular and financially lucrative, smaller versions opened outside towns and cities in the North and South. Equipped with novel rides and attractions, these parks drew enthusiastic patrons from the local area. But not everyone was welcomed through the front gate. Owners of private parks, particularly those in the South, routinely enforced Jim Crow laws to offer only white patrons admission and, when applicable, their African American servants.

The Pontchartrain Beach Amusement Park, opened in 1928 and closed in 1983, once hosted concerts by famous entertainers, including Elvis Presley, and housed dozens of popular rides and attractions such as the Monster, the Zephyr, and the Ragin' Cajun roller coasters, a haunted house, the Ghost Train, bumper cars, a Ferris wheel, and a large petting zoo. (Charles Reagan Wilson Collection, Center for the Study of Southern Culture, University of Mississippi)

In 1905 the white-only Fontaine Ferry Park opened in Louisville's West End. Boasting more than 50 rides and attractions, including Hilarity Hall (a funhouse), Gypsy Village (a dance spot), and four popular roller coasters, Fontaine Ferry became the most successful park in the area. African American Louisvillians, however, were not permitted entry to Fontaine until 1964, 10 years after the city's parks were desegregated. Fontaine Ferry was sold in 1969, a year after Louisville's race riots in the West End. While white patrons likely remember the carousel, scooters, and lindy planes, many black Louisvillians cite the park as a reminder of the city's segregation.

Stringent Jim Crow laws, however, did not prevent some African American southerners from enjoying early mechanical amusements. In Nashville, for example, two trolley parks served the local population. Glendale Park opened in 1897 to whites, eventually offering patrons a casino, carousel, shooting galleries, and a small zoo. Approximately six miles away, Preston Taylor, a black entrepreneur, opened Greenwood Park in 1905. Greenwood offered black Nashvillians their own swimming pool, ball diamond, and amusement rides. Similarly, in Norfolk, Va., many white sailors attended the famous Ocean View Park, while black servicemen visited nearby Seaview Beach and Sunset Lake. By and large, however, white parks eclipsed black amusement parks, in size, number, and quality.

Although popular, white-only trolley parks such as Atlanta's Ponce de Leon Park and Charlotte's Lakewood Park called themselves the "Coney Islands" of the South, southern states boasted fewer amusement parks than New England, mid-Atlantic, and even some midwestern states at the beginning of the 20th century. While more than 60 parks operated in Pennsylvania, across the border in Virginia there were fewer than a dozen; Mississippians had just Meridian's Highland Park and possibly a few scattered amusements in Gulfport. A more rural population, rigid segregation laws, and most southerners' lack of disposable income dissuaded many entrepreneurs from establishing amusement parks in southern states.

Parks serving small communities around the South began to shut down as early as the 1920s and 1930s, and the popularity of amusement parks declined significantly after World War II, with just a few remaining open into the 1960s and 1970s. However, a number of independently owned theme parks opened as these early parks closed. Theme parks came to dominate the outdoor amusement business. With settings based on comic strips, holidays, or an imagined past, these parks set up to attract visitors from around the South and the nation. Disneyland in Anaheim, Calif., has served as a model for the contemporary theme park from its opening in 1954. In 1971 the Burbank-based Walt Disney Company opened the Magic Kingdom, its first southern park, outside Orlando, Fla. The company currently operates several Florida parks—including Epcot, MGM Studios, Animal Kingdom, Blizzard Beach, and Typhoon Lagoon—in the inclusive Walt Disney World Resort. After the success of the Disney World parks, the company launched a line of Caribbean cruises affiliated with the Florida resort. Disney also went on to develop the town of Celebration, Fla.—a community designed for Disney employees that links directly to the Walt Disney World Resort.

Since Disney World came to the South, southerners have fashioned their own unique heritage and traditions to theme park entertainment. Southern theme parks offer the region's history, music, food, religion, art, and humor to attract both southern and nonsouthern families. Although some people might argue that the picture of southern culture offered in the theme park setting is often an idealized and stereotypical view of life in the South, millions of visitors flock to the parks every summer, attracted not by their authenticity but by the simple, family entertainment they offer.

The prototype of southern-oriented theme parks was Opryland USA, in

Nashville, which opened in the summer of 1972 and closed in 1997 (only to be replaced by a shopping mall). Opryland capitalized on Nashville's reputation as the center of the country music industry and on the rise in popularity of the music in the 1970s. Opryland offered a variety of music, including rock and roll from the 1950s and contemporary tunes, music of the American West (from such musicals as *Annie Get Your Gun*), Dixieland jazz, and folk music. Much of the music is country and western, but it was not the rough sound found in the honky-tonks around Nashville. Many of the music shows at the park, like those at other modern theme parks, were staged in elaborate, air-conditioned theaters and resembled Broadway productions in costuming, music, and choreography. In addition to live musical entertainment, Opryland offered rides, food, shops, games, art, and crafts—all with a southern flavor and often a country or musical theme. The food at the park, for example, in keeping with the southern image, included fried chicken, iced tea, and ham and biscuits in establishments such as the Country Kitchen. Vendors on the sidewalks sold ice cream bars in the shapes of musical instruments. Numerous shops allowed tourists to buy a wide assortment of music memorabilia, replicas of frontier clothing and implements, craft items such as handmade dulcimers and carved wooden figures, and various products bearing the Confederate flag. Consistent with Opryland's theme were rides called the Tennessee Waltz, Grizzly River Rampage, the Old Mill Scream, and the Wabash Cannon Ball. Opryland even incorporated a carnival midway into its offerings, complete with contest booths and prizes commonly found at county fairs. Opryland's early success inspired other parks across the South, such as the also-defunct Libertyland in Memphis, Tenn.

Since Opryland's relative success, country music culture has provided the theme for other southern parks such as Dollywood, country music star Dolly Parton's 400-acre park outside Pigeon Forge, Tenn. The park's inspiration is Parton's childhood, which she spent in the Smoky Mountain foothills where the park is located, and her career in music and films. Parton was involved in the planning of the park, which includes a replica of the house in which she was born and an outdoor concert stage that is a copy of the porch where she and her family used to sing together. Like Opryland, Dollywood tries to keep the theme consistent throughout the park. A restaurant called Aunt Granny's All-You-Care-to-Eat Buffet (originally called Aunt Granny's Dixie Fixin's) serves biscuits and gravy. Smoky Mountain heritage is featured in exhibits of quilting and dulcimer making.

Other country music celebrities followed suit and became the focus of southern theme parks, such as Conway Twitty, who lived and worked inside an entertainment complex once called Twitty City. Twitty City, located just outside Nashville, contained the memorabilia of Twitty and several other country music stars and included a concession-entertainment pavilion and an audio-visual show that told Twitty's life story. Open year round, Twitty City drew hundreds of visitors during the Christmas season, when the park was decorated with 250,000 lights and added 40 special exhibits, including a life-size nativity scene. Following Twitty's death in 1993, Twitty City changed hands and is now a Christian music venue called Trinity Music City, USA, complete with a replica of the Via Dolorosa—the street in Jerusalem upon which Jesus walked on his way to the Crucifixion—and the Gold, Frankincense, and Myrrh Bible Book Store. Other country music stars who created parks in their names include Loretta Lynn (Loretta Lynn's Ranch in Hurricane Mills, Tenn.) and George Jones (George Jones Country Music Park outside Colmesneil, Tex.).

A similar regional theme was portrayed at Arkansas's Dogpatch USA, a park based on the characters from Al Capp's *Li'l Abner* comic strip. The events at Dogpatch featured the hillbilly characters, and the attractions (such as canoe rides) supposedly reflected their lifestyle. The park also highlighted the Ozark Mountain culture, offering such exhibits as an authentic gristmill, one of the largest wooden waterwheels in the world, and shops specializing in the area's many arts and crafts. The region's natural beauty, including waterfalls and spring-fed lakes, was also spotlighted there. By 1991, though, the park was struggling, in part because of its close proximity to the newer and grander Silver Dollar City near Branson, Mo., as well as a result of the outdated comic-strip theme of *Li'l Abner*, which had been out of print for more than 10 years. By 1993, Dogpatch USA's doors had been shuttered for good.

A late 20th-century development in the southern outdoor amusement business was the religious theme park. The biggest of these was Heritage USA, a resort in Fort Mill, S.C., opened in 1977 by Pentecostal television evangelists Jim and Tammy Faye Bakker and closed in 1989 because of extensive damage during Hurricane Hugo. The park, which had been called a "spiritual Disneyland," was part of a complex covering 2,300 acres and encompassing time-sharing vacation homes, rental apartments, condominiums, campsites, the five-story Heritage Grand Hotel, a halfway house for ex-convicts, and a home for unwed mothers. Heritage USA offered the world's largest wave pool and a 52-foot water slide, evangelist Billy Graham's childhood home, a Passion play staged in Heritage's own 3,000-seat amphitheater, tours of the Christian broadcasting studio on the grounds, amusement rides such as Jonah in the Belly of the Whale, and shopping at Main Street USA—designed in turn-of-the-century style with cobblestone streets and quaint storefronts. In 1985 Heritage USA attracted almost 5 million visitors, making it third only to Disneyland and Disney World in attendance. The park cultivated an image as the preserver of old-time values and old-time southern religion, sometimes calling itself the modern equivalent of camp meetings or Christian campgrounds. Although Heritage USA was by far the largest, other southern theme parks, such as the Living Waters in Johnson City, Tex., also offered biblical messages.

Other theme parks in the South use state histories as the basis for their entertainment, such as Six Flags over Texas in Arlington and Six Flags over Georgia in Atlanta. Busch Gardens (the Dark Continent) in Tampa, Fla., displays the exotic environment of Africa, and Busch Gardens (the Old Country) in Williamsburg, Va., highlights the history and culture of Europe. Both Busch Gardens parks feature elaborate animal and plant exhibits and are now owned by Blackstone.

Six Flags, Dollywood, Busch Gardens, and Disney World, unlike many of their predecessors and contemporaries, continue to be ranked among the best and most profitable theme parks in the world. Of the popular corporate amusement parks operating in the South today, though, all are headquartered outside the region. Although Texan Angus Wynne started Six Flags with the opening Six Flags over Texas in Arlington in 1961, the park was purchased by the Pennsylvania and New York Central Transportation Company (Penn Central) five years later and headquartered outside the American South. Penn Central, however, opened the second Six Flags park, Six Flags over Georgia, outside Atlanta just a year later. Through Penn Central, Six Flags expanded to include parks in the Border South states of Texas, Missouri, and Oklahoma before the company changed hands in the 1980s. By 1993, Time Warner owned the Six Flags Company, which included parks outside Louisville and Baltimore. The last southern Six Flags to open was Six Flags New Orleans, which opened in 2000. The park, however, closed just five years later as a result of Hurricane Katrina.

Although a number of amusement parks have been scattered around the American South in the past 120 years, their intended purpose and audience have changed substantially. Early parks attracted people from the nearby town, restricting patrons to one race or the other. Later, small theme parks sought to attract families from surrounding counties and states by being located near natural attractions or along popular vacation routes. Larger corporate-owned parks focused their attention wider, seeking not only to attract people from nearby metropolitan areas but to turn the park into, in some instances, an all-inclusive resort and nationally known tourist destination. All these parks, however, have one goal in common: they generate revenue by entertaining an audience with increasing disposable income and a taste for extravagant leisure activities.

University of Mississippi

Emory University

Jackson Clarion-Ledger (31 August 1986); *Southern Living* (June 1981); Lauren Rabino-vitz, *For the Love of Pleasure: Women, Movies, and Culture in Turn-of-the-Century Chicago* (1998); Jeff Ulmer, *Amusement Parks of America: A Comprehensive Guide* (1980).

Baseball

Throughout baseball history, only four former Confederate cities have enjoyed major league baseball status. Richmond was in the American Association for part of a single season in 1884, and the current Houston organization began play in 1962. The move that really counted in southern terms was the move of the Milwaukee Braves to Atlanta in 1966. When the expansion Washington Senators became the Texas Rangers in 1972, the picture was completed.

Exclusion from the big leagues for so long did not mean the South had been divorced from baseball. Far from it. The region had produced many major leaguers, including some of the greatest and most colorful, such as Ty Cobb. The South contributed some of the most influential broadcasters the game has had, including Jay "Dizzy" Dean and Pee Wee Reese, who worked television's game of the week in the 1950s and early 1960s, and radio's Mel Allen and Red Barber. Major southern cities such as Memphis, Nashville, Birmingham, Louisville, and Little Rock have long supported minor league teams and industrial leagues, and southern college teams have dominated competition. The South manufactured the great majority of the game's bats, including the Louisville Slugger, and since 1886 it has been the site of spring training camps.

What then explains the absence of major league membership for so long? The overpowering heat and humidity of the South was one consideration, especially in an age preceding night games, air-conditioning, and summer-weight uniforms. Connie Mack and Clark Griffith, two of the most influential major league owners in the first half of the 20th century, insisted that the weather in St. Louis, Cincinnati, and Washington sapped the strength of players on their teams even before midseason. Mack stated that those teams "must be 25 percent better than any other in order to win a pennant." Players spoke of soaking their feet, baseball spikes and all, in pails of ice water, then sloshing into the steamy fields in those cities. They bemoaned the nights of fitful sleep in roasting hotel rooms, and recalled soaking their bed sheets in tub water, then wrapping themselves in them for relief. Thoughts of playing in locations farther south were not broadly entertained.

Another basic problem was travel. The population centers of the South, which might have supported major league play, were too far removed from the long established northern teams. Perhaps even more important, they were separated by great distances from each other. Not until 1958 and the age of convenient and extensive airline travel did the majors open up the West Coast, which was far from populous. In this respect, the South was not far behind.

Until the 1960s southern culture was exported to the nation's baseball fans in the personalities of its regional sons who made major league rosters. Often what this meant was little more than an image of Snuffy Smith in the dugout. A short biographical sketch of Mississippian Guy "Joe" Bush appeared in a 1932 issue of the baseball bible, the *Sporting News*, for example. Its opening sentence was "No lazy bones in the body of this Cub pitcher, his Southern birth notwithstanding." An earlier generation had grown up with the illiteracy of "Shoeless" Joe Jackson, a South Carolinian who had been so frightened of the big cities of the North that he fled from his first train ride en route to the major leagues. He had needed an adult babysitter to ensure his later arrival in Philadelphia. Fans would shout from the grandstands, asking him to spell cat. It was good storytelling and reinforced a powerful stereotype America had of it southern citizens.

Jackson's contemporary, Ty Cobb, epitomized the violent southerner. All big league teams had their sons of the South. They made good copy for baseball writers, many of whom were noted for their cynicism and expertise with one-line putdowns. To be sure, all players from the South were not reported in comic or glaring fashion, but more than enough were. Especially demeaning was when a player's statements were spelled in dialect. Georgian Luke Appling, a Hall of Fame shortstop who played in the majors for two decades, sometimes referred to in print as a cracker, was repeatedly quoted as saying such words as "jes" (for just), "shucks," "gonna," "'spect," "cain't," "reckon," "uster" (for used to), and "nuthin." "Leg" somehow even became "laig" in Appling's mouth, as reported by the *New York Times*. Fellow Georgian Cecil Travis, another long-time American Leaguer, was once referred to as a "Geawgian."

Yet, a pair of broadcasters from the Deep South—Mel Allen and Red Barber—brought their homespun qualities to New York, the biggest baseball market in the world, and became the most respected of their profession. Both men, extremely fair and balanced in their reportage, represented baseball at its ideal, sportsmanlike best. In doing so, their colloquialisms gained undenied respect. Barber's talk about tearing up the pea patch swept Brooklyn. His "catbird seat" was shared by millions of Dodger fans. Nevertheless, the players remained the focus.

Baseball in the South involved nearly every hamlet on its map, though decades went by before the sport was played on a par with other regions. The game's early history in Dixie featured men from north of the Mason-Dixon Line taking leadership. Indeed, quite a few of these early baseball "teachers" carried the label of "carpetbagger." Returning Confederate veterans had preceded them, many of whom had learned the game from Union soldiers. They created a taste for the sport among the white citizenry. Ex-slaves had learned in the same way and played their own brand of ball on their side of the tracks. Not until Reconstruction ended, however, did baseball expand and improve.

The game, as had already happened elsewhere in the nation, became dominated by community teams, with sponsorship often supplied by businessmen. Jewish merchants, in particular, funded teams in New Orleans, Macon, Atlanta, Augusta, Mobile, Houston, and Birmingham. In the mid-1880s, when the original Southern League was instituted, organized professional baseball finally set up shop in the region. *Atlanta Constitution* editor Henry W. Grady, in the forefront of the idea of a modern, industrial New South, was key to the establishment of the Atlanta franchise in that league. The team was an obvious example of boosterism.

The Southern League unfortunately led a miserable existence, needing frequent reorganization efforts to prevent its demise. Team rosters had very few players from the South, as locals were not yet talented enough to get contracts with even second-rate minor league clubs. The players who had the contracts performed so poorly that it was believed their ineptness was typical of "northerners sick in the heat."

By the 20th century, the sport was extremely significant in southern culture. Wherever there was a mill or mine, that company fielded a team. Competition in the many industrial leagues that developed was fierce, promoting a notable improvement on the ball diamond. Workers who detested the long days and dangerous conditions of their underpaid employ nonetheless were exuberant when their company team was victorious, especially if a championship was at stake. Community spirit was present, at least on game days. Management recognized this and did its utmost to keep the best players and to add the best from other teams. A winning ball club meant a stable work force. Who would want to leave a mill with a title team to take a job with a competitor that fielded losing nines?

Improved skills drew notice from the major league cities to the north. Community and regional pride was enhanced more than ever as increasing numbers of homegrown players advanced to the "bigs." Ty Cobb roared out of Georgia, Joe Jackson came up from South Carolina, Tris Speaker from Texas, Clyde Milan from Tennessee, and the march was on. Throughout the 20th century, the lineups of major league clubs were dotted with such nicknames as "Dixie," "Reb," "Tex," and "Catfish." The South became and remained a chief stomping ground for big league scouts.

Only since the late 1940s, however, when organized baseball was finally desegregated, has that scouting included blacks. Yet black players in the South had been competing on their own fields since the late 1880s. Most of the black semipro players who toured the United States decades later were from the South. Not surprisingly, their struggle was frequently marred by racist insults, even when their playing ability was held to be superior to that of whites.

As late as 1953 a Jackson, Miss., team in the Cotton States League refused to play against its Hot Springs opponent because the Arkansas squad was going to use a black pitcher. To compound the situation, the league's officers forfeited the game to Jackson. Hot Springs, to their way of thinking, had no right to expect Jackson to play against a black. Their ruling was overturned by the commissioner of minor league baseball, who made it clear that blacks could not be refused the right to play. In 1955, however, a Pine Bluff, Ark., team in the same Cotton States League signed three blacks to contracts and then released them a few days later, citing the pressure placed on it by other league teams.

Southern racial attitude and regional loyalties also gave teams a fan base. Black Southerners became loyal Dodger fans when Jackie Robinson was signed by Brooklyn and cheered for the Cleveland Indians when Larry Doby became the first African American player in the American League. Although white southerners often expressed dismay as more black faces appeared on major league rosters, there is little to suggest that the Boston Red Sox gained many white fans by being the last to integrate (1959). Indeed, southern fan loyalty often had more to do with which games southerners could pick up on radio; because KMOX in St. Louis sent Cardinal games deep into Dixie, listeners responded by becoming Cardinal fans.

The South by the mid-20th century had enthusiastically supported numerous minor league teams, with 43 cities in North Carolina alone actually fielding professional teams in seven separate leagues in 1949. Over the years the South had seen play in leagues with names like Texas, Piedmont, Southern,

Longhorn, Sally, and Appalachian. Their own sons had graduated to the majors by the many hundreds, often stereotyped in scapegoat images associated with the South. When racism was involved, the term "southerner" assumed an extra burden. Today, black and white southerners, such as Dennis "Oil Can" Boyd (Miss.), Ron Guidry (La.), Nolan Ryan (Tex.), and Dwight Gooden (Fla.), remain among the game's best players.

A single major league team declared itself to be "America's Team" in the 1980s. This bold stroke fit nicely into the apparent "southernizing" of the United States. The Atlanta Braves, the only major league baseball franchise ever based in the Deep South, claimed national sovereignty because of its owner's extensive television cable system. Fans in all corners of the nation watched the Braves on WTBS-TV and, familiar with that team's personnel because of its frequent television exposure, became supporters of Ted Turner's organization. The Braves, in essence sole baseball representatives of the South, are owned by a white man, utilize the American Indian as their symbol, and had a black, Hank Aaron, as the best player in their history. If anything tells the story of change in America, and particularly in the South, that is it.

However, the advent of cable and satellite TV, the very thing that made the Braves "America's Team," hastened the decline, and in some places the demise, of the network of minor league franchises that once served as avenues of opportunity for aspiring players and farm clubs for the majors. Although major league teams still have 20 minor leagues with around 240 teams, most are not in the South. Indeed, Dixie does not have a AAA league. However the Southern League and the Texas League are AA and three of the six A leagues are in the South. But the once competitive network of small town teams has disappeared as fans opt to stay home, turn on the TV, and watch "America's Team" and the others. In the meantime, the expansion of college baseball has provided young athletes another way to break into the big leagues.

But while the minors may be declining in Dixie, the majors have arrived. Even before the Atlanta Braves put southern baseball on the map, in 1962 Houston, Tex., got a team, and though it was better known for where it played (the Astrodome) than how it played, the Astros brought the majors to the South. Two decades passed before Dixie got another major league franchise, but in 1993 the Florida Marlins joined the National League, and five years later the Tampa Bay Devil Rays (now the Rays) came into the American. Success soon followed as the Braves won five National League pennants in the 1990s and were crowned world champions in 1995. The Florida Marlins won both pennant and World Series in 1997 and 2003, while Tampa Bay won the American League pennant in 2008 but lost the World Series to Philadelphia.

As far as baseball was concerned, Dixie played second fiddle to no one, no where.

JOHN E. DIMEGLIO
Mankato State University

Charles C. Alexander, *Ty Cobb: Baseball's Fierce Immortal* (1984); Alfred Duckett, *I Never Had It Made* (1972); Harvey Frommer, *Rickey and Robinson* (1982); Donald Gropman, *Say It Ain't So, Joe!: The Story of Shoeless Joe Jackson* (1979); John D. McCallum, *The Tiger Wore Spikes: An Informal Biography of Ty Cobb* (1956); Daniel Okrent and Harris Lewine, eds., *The Ultimate Baseball Book* (1979); Lawrence S. Ritter, *The Glory of Their Times: The Story of the Early Days of Baseball Told by Men Who Played It* (1974); George Vecsey, *Baseball: A History of America's Favorite Game* (2008).

Basketball

"Basketball is a city game," writes Pete Axthelm in his 1970 book, *The City Game*. "Its battlegrounds are strips of asphalt between tattered wire fences or crumbling buildings; its rhythms grow from the uneven thump of a ball against hard surfaces. . . . Basketball belongs to the cities." Indeed, basketball does belong to the cities. However, the classification of basketball as a "city game" overlooks the tradition of basketball in the South, where the game is played in both urban and rural areas, and where it has for years flourished as a rural game. Basketball courts of all descriptions and designs blanket the South. Salvaged stop signs or sheets of metal or wood often make functional backboards for young players who attach a suitable rim, as their desire to play basketball overrules any prescribed notion of a conventional goal or court.

Shortly after the invention of basketball by James A. Naismith in 1891, southerners began to experiment with the game. As early as the 1920s, high school boys throughout the South played on organized school teams and generally on outdoor courts. The indoor gym was a later addition to the southern game, and it was not uncommon at first for a Mississippi team to dress in spiffy uniforms, patterned after the indoor teams, and play on outdoor courts in subfreezing weather. School systems and towns dedicated to the game could perhaps afford the fancy uniforms, but it would be many years before they could afford the big gymnasium. For high schools and colleges in the South, neither of which had as large a budget as their northern counterparts, the cost of football was often prohibitive. Basketball, on the other hand, required a smaller investment and by the 1950s was earning large revenues for colleges such as Kentucky, North Carolina State, and Western Kentucky. In 1946 North Carolina State "imported" Everett Case, a coach from basketball-rich Indiana; by 1950 the school's annual attendance had reached 230,000, the largest in the country. Part of the increased attendance was the result of increasing postwar college enrollment. College athletic facilities could not hold the crowds, and at a University of North Carolina–North Carolina State game the problem reached crisis proportion. A large crowd of followers, frustrated after being denied admission, tore down the doors of the gym, poured in, and stood around the perimeter of the court. The game eventually was canceled as fans continually spilled onto the court. A similar problem canceled a game between North Carolina State and Duke in 1948.

Even before World War II, college basketball in North Carolina was very popular. Beginning in 1933, Raleigh hosted the Southern Conference Tournament with Chamber of Commerce support. In 1947 the tournament was shifted to Duke University's 9,000-seat gym, still in use today and a vivid symbol of the richness of basketball tradition in the South. With the catalyst of a $100,000 donation from the Charles Babcock family, the North Carolina Legislature appropriated money for Reynolds Coliseum, finished in 1951. Not surprisingly, smoking was always permitted in the facility, and R. J. Reynolds tobacco supporters bragged about the ventilation system capable of providing "a complete change of air every 15 minutes." With the new coliseum, North Carolina State dubbed itself the "basketball capital of the South."

North Carolina was also home to a very competitive and successful group of women's basketball teams, led by Hanes Hosiery of Winston-Salem, N.C., the dominant force in the Southern Textile League. Writing about women's basketball in the South in a 1979 issue of *Southern Exposure*, Elva Bishop and Katherine Fulton assert that "high caliber women's basketball wasn't born in the South in the 1970s; it merely got its second wind." Indeed, such teams as Hanes Hosiery and Nashville Business College were very high caliber. By 1947, in large part because of the dominance of Hanes, newspapers in Winston-Salem were hailing the city as the "new women's cage capital." Up until 1947, Hanes had limited competition in the Southern Textile League, made up of company teams formed to induce corporate pride and competition in workers. The dominance of Hanes in that league led the team to compete nationally through the Amateur Athletic Union's (AAU) national playoff. Though Hanes did not win the 1948 tournament, it did reach the quarterfinals where six out of the eight teams were from North Carolina, Georgia, and Tennessee. In 1951 Hanes won the AAU national championship, defeating the Flying Queens of Wayland College, Tex., 50–34.

North Carolina State and Raleigh may have boasted that, with the completion of Reynolds Coliseum, they were the basketball capital of the South, but one school and one state could lay more legitimate claim to such a title. If there is one team and one region of the South that is most noted for its basketball, it is Kentucky. Much of that notoriety, ironically, is because of a basketball sage from Kansas. Adolph Rupp, who coached the Kentucky Wildcats from 1930 to 1971, came to Kentucky from Kansas, where he played under Phog Allen. After 28 seasons at Kentucky, Rupp won his 772nd game, passing the record previously held by Allen, his former coach and teacher. Rupp was to southern basketball what Bear Bryant was to football, though Rupp's longer tenure proved more dominant. A gruff, determined man, Rupp had the image of a country farm boy turned basketball genius. He became known as a Kentucky gentleman, one who loved his cattle and his bourbon. Dubbed "the Baron," Rupp was a strict father to all of his players. Like other teams in the South-eastern Conference (SEC), Kentucky resisted recruiting black players until the late 1960s, and Rupp's paternal callousness made him seem all the more reluctant to integrate his team. Shy he was not, and in a 1929 interview he claimed he took the job at Kentucky on the advice of a gas station attendant, "because I'm the best damn coach in the country." Such remarks were not uncommon from "the Baron," whose superstitious attachment to wearing brown suits led many to refer to him simply as "the man in the brown suit." In his final years at Kentucky, with his program suffering from lesser talent and from Rupp's genuine fatigue and poor health, he made a modest proposal to the press, again reinforcing his well-earned agrarian image: "The legislature should pass a law that at 3 o'clock every afternoon any basketball coach who is 70 years old gets a shot of bourbon. These damned bouncing, bouncing, bouncing basketballs are putting me to sleep."

Not far from Rupp's Lexington is Bowling Green, Ky., home of the Western Kentucky University Hilltoppers and another coach who embodied southern basketball style and tradition. Edgar Allen Diddle, known as Eddie Diddle, began as the coach of all sports at Western in 1922. A basketball pioneer from outdoor court days, Diddle was a native of Gradyville, in Adair County, where he had played and coached. The son of a lumberman, farmer, and livestock trader, Diddle brought a rural wit and savvy to basketball. Always preferring man-to-man defense, Diddle often said his teams "just play by ear." "Attack is our stock in trade," Diddle once said. "And there are three ways to attack: down one side of the floor, down the middle and down the other side. And you don't even need a play if you get a half-step start on the opposing team." His "half-step" approach bred a very successful fast-break style of basketball at WKU, an approach that after 42 seasons at WKU had won him 759 games.

Fast-break basketball was the backbone of both the Diddle and the Rupp game. The success of both of these coaches and schools led many other programs in the South to emulate the "run-and-gun" style of basketball, but not until the mid-1970s could any school approach the success and dominance of Kentucky.

Jim Crow was a member of nearly every major college basketball team in the South, but nowhere was he more visible than in the Southeastern Conference. Perry Wallace of Nashville became the first black player to start for an SEC team when he took the floor for Vanderbilt in 1967. Thinking back on those days, he once remarked, "I heard a lot of racial jokes. At Ole Miss they waved the rebel flag. They yelled a lot of things I'd as soon forget." Until the 1990s, the rebel flag still waved at SEC basketball contests, particularly when the University of Mississippi or Georgia plays, as a vivid reminder of the history of racial inequality in the South.

By the early 1970s all SEC schools were successfully recruiting black players, but in the mid-1960s many episodes clearly reflected the racial conflict and change on the basketball floor. The strangest of tales concerns an all-white Mississippi State team that won the SEC in 1963. As champions of the all-white SEC, State was slated to play Loyola University, which started four black players. Mississippi politicians, particularly Governor Ross Barnett, who six months prior had attempted to block James Meredith's entrance to the University of Mississippi, attempted to make the Bulldogs of State stay home. A *Jackson Clarion-Ledger* editorial said segregationists felt that "if Mississippi State University plays against a Negro outside the state, what would be greatly different in bringing integrated teams into the state? And why not recruit a Negro of special basketball ability to play on the Mississippi State team? This is the road we seem to be traveling." Barnett and his fellow segregationists said no to the trip, but white fans, students, and the Mississippi State president let their basketball pride override racial prejudice, claiming loudly that State should make the trip to Ann Arbor, Mich., to play Loyola. Barnett's next tactic, a court injunction prohibiting the team from traveling, was deflected with the help of a local sheriff, also a State basketball rooter. Legend has it that the Oktibbeha County sheriff failed to serve the injunction and turned his back long enough for the players to board a Southern Airlines plane in Starkville for the trip to the National Collegiate Athletic Association (NCAA) tournament. They went on to lose a close, hard-fought game to Loyola, eventual NCAA champions.

Under segregation, basketball thrived on historically black campuses, and this tradition has continued. The Southwestern Athletic Conference (SWAC), for example, includes schools from Alabama, Arkansas, Louisiana, Mississippi, and Texas and is a hotbed of basketball interest. Since 1979, in the men's division, Alcorn State and Southern University have each won seven conference tournaments, with Jackson State winning five, Texas Southern and Mississippi Valley State winning four each, Alabama State winning three, and Prairie View A&M and Alabama A&M winning once. In the women's division, Alcorn State has been even more dominant than among the men, winning 11 basketball tournaments.

The story of black basketball is told in depth and with stirring documentary reflection in Dan Klores's film *Black Magic* (coproduced by Earl "The Pearl" Monroe, who played at Winston-Salem State University under Clarence "Big House" Gaines), which opens with the story of "the secret game." Played in Durham, N.C., in 1944 between an intramural squad from Duke University's medical school and North Carolina College for Negroes (later North Carolina Central University), the secret game introduces viewers to John McLendon, one of the preeminent coaches to ever head a basketball team and arguably one of the fathers of the fast break. The film goes on to chronicle key players, coaches, programs, and stories that have been integral to the development of the modern sport, many with fundamentally southern origins.

Texas Western College's defeat of Rupp's Kentucky Wildcats in the final game of the 1966 NCAA tournament was a landmark in American sports. Coach Don Haskins started five black athletes who defeated Rupp's all-white team, helping to break the barrier to integration of basketball in the South and indeed to promote a larger role for black athletes in basketball programs across the nation. Texas Western ended the season with a 28–1 record, and Haskins would later take his teams to 14 NCAA Tournament berths. The film *Glory Road* (2006) depicted the 1966 game.

Over the past two decades, college basketball has risen to new levels of interest and achievement. Traditional powerhouses Kentucky and North Carolina may have off seasons, but they continue to be key institutions in the region's basketball culture. The University of California at Los Angeles leads the nation with 11 men's national championships, with Kentucky second with 6, and North Carolina is tied with Indiana for third with 5 each. The Atlantic Coast Conference (ACC) and the SEC, the South's two major conferences, are among the most powerful conferences in the country. Southern teams that have won national championships include Arkansas (1994), Duke (1991, 1992, 2001), Florida (2006, 2007), Kentucky (1948, 1949, 1951, 1958, 1978, 1996, 1998), Louisville (1980, 1986), North Carolina (1957, 1982, 1953, 2005, 2009), North Carolina State (1974, 1983), and Texas Western (1966). Basketball interest is seen in a city such as Memphis, whose University of Memphis (Memphis State) from Conference USA has twice played in the Final Four March Madness NCAA Tournament competition, and in the traditionally football-obsessed state of Texas, where the University of Texas under coach Rick Barnes has become a national contender in the past decade.

College basketball coaches once epitomized regional styles and manners, but since the 1970s coaches, and players too, have come from across the nation. Bobby Cremins of Georgia Tech and Jim Valvano of North Carolina State were two examples of brash "yankee" coaches who recruited in the 1970s and 1980s as easily on the playgrounds of Brooklyn and Atlanta as they did in rural North Carolina or Georgia. Dean Smith, who came from Kansas, coached at North Carolina from 1961 to 1997 and became the "dean" of southern coaches, winning more games, 879, than any NCAA Division I men's basketball coach and took the Tar Heels to the NCAA Tournament 27 times. Roy Williams, who long coached at Kansas, won a national championship in his second year at North Carolina in 2005 and again in 2009. After Rupp's retirement, three Kentucky coaches won national championships: Joe Hall (1978), Rick Pitino (1996), and the school's first African American head coach, Tubby Smith (1998). Coach Mike Krzyzewski came to Duke University in 1981 and made that institution into a premier national basketball program. Duke has been in the Final Four of the NCAA Tournament 14 times and has had a national player of the year 11 times. The North Carolina–Duke rivalry is a preeminent one in the South, with championship programs only eight miles apart. Will Blythe's award-winning book *To Hate Like This Is to Be Happy Forever: A Thoroughly Obsessive, Intermittently Unbiased Account of the Duke–North Carolina Basketball Rivalry*, published in 2006, evokes the tale of place, competition, and the reach of the game. While players and coaches battle for victory on the court, the alumni and university officials try to "beat" each other by building the biggest coliseum. Cameron Indoor Stadium was renovated and expanded in the 1980s to accommodate growing crowds in the contemporary growth of basketball passion in the Piedmont. The "Dean Dome" at Chapel Hill, built in the 1980s and named for Dean Smith, was built just large enough to surpass the capacity of the Rupp Arena in Lexington, Ky.

Southern interest in basketball typically has focused on college and university programs, but professional basketball has also grown in the region during the past three decades. The National Basketball Association (NBA) was established in 1946, but no southern teams were among the original ones. Teams came to the South after 1970, including the New Orleans Jazz, the San Antonio Spurs, the Dallas Mavericks, the Charlotte Hornets, the Miami Heat, and the Orlando Magic. The Vancouver Grizzlies moved to Memphis in 2001, establishing an unlikely mascot for a Deep South river city. The Houston Rockets won back-to-back NBA titles in 1994 and 1995, and the Spurs won in 1999, 2003, and 2007. Some of the greatest NBA players have been from the South, including Charles Barkley, Shaquille O'Neill, and the incomparable Michael Jordan. Jordan grew up in Wilmington, N.C., and played basketball with Dean Smith at North Carolina, where he was ACC freshman of the year in 1981 and helped the Tar Heels win a national championship the following year. He played professional ball with the Chicago Bulls, where he led his team to six NBA championships and was a five-time NBA most valuable player. He helped popularized basketball across the nation in the 1980s and 1990s. A 1990s *Atlanta Journal-Constitution* poll of the 100 Most Influential Southerners listed Jordan among the top-10 southerners in cultural significance.

Women's college basketball in the South took on new prominence after the first National Collegiate Athletic Association (NCAA) Women's Division I championship tournament was held in April 1982. ESPN has broadcast tournament games since 2003, providing new exposure and contributing to growing popularity across the nation. Louisiana Tech has long been a powerhouse, winning the national championship in 1982 and 1988. Other national women's champions from the South include Old Dominion (1985), Texas (1986), Texas Tech (1993), University of North Carolina (1994), and Baylor (1995). The dominant power in not only southern but national women's basketball is the University of Tennessee, which has won eight national championships (1987, 1989, 1991, 1996, 1997, 1998, 2007, 2008). The best Division I women players compete for the Margaret Wade Award, named for Lily Margaret Wade, the long-time coach of Delta State University, where she won three consecutive AIAW Women's Basketball championships in 1975, 1976 and 1977.

Tennessee coach Pat Summitt has won more games than any college basketball coach, man or woman, gaining her 1,000th win in February 2009. Summitt coached many of the greatest women basketball players of the last three decades, many of whom became stars in the Women's National Basketball Association (WNBA), the professional league founded in 1996. One southern team, the Houston Comets, dominated the league's first few years, with coach Van Chancellor (formerly of the University of Mississippi) winning the first four league championships. The Comets' Cynthia Cooper was the league's first star. By the 2000 season the WNBA had doubled in number of teams from the founding eight. As of early 2010, there were teams in Orlando, Miami, and Atlanta.

Fred Hobson grew up in western North Carolina and captures the significance of basketball for the South in his memory of the 1957 North Carolina victory over longtime college powerhouse Kansas for the national men's basketball championship. Looking back on his experience as a 13-year-old boy hearing Tar Heel Joe Quigg hit two free throws to defeat the Wilt Chamberlain–led Jayhawks in triple overtime to win North Carolina's first national championship, Hobson writes that "as all time stopped for an earlier generation of southern boys just before two o'clock on that July afternoon in 1863 when Pickett began his charge at Gettysburg," so did time stop, "or at least subsequently cease to have the same meaning," for him on that Saturday night in March 1957.

TOM RANKIN
Duke University

Pete Axthelm, *The City Game* (1970); Christine A. Baker and Becky Hammond, *Why She Plays: The World of Women's Basketball* (2008); Elva Bishop and Katherine Fulton, *Southern Exposure* (no. 2, 1979); Art Chansky, *Blue Blood: Duke-Carolina, inside the Most Storied Rivalry in College Hoops* (2005); Bill Finger, *Southern Exposure* (no. 2, 1979); Frank Fitzpatrick, *And the Walls Came Tumbling Down: Kentucky, Texas Western, and the Game That Changed American Sports* (1999); Fred Hobson, *Off the Rim: Basketball and Other Religions in a Carolina Childhood* (2006); Mac C. Kirkpatrick and Thomas K. Perry, *The Southern Textile Basketball Tournament: A History, 1921–1997* (1997); Joe Menzer, *Four Corners: How UNC, N.C. State, and Wake Forest Made North Carolina the Center of the Basketball World* (1999); *Newsweek* (6 January 1947); *Newsweek* (12 February 1968); Harry T. Paxton, *Saturday Evening Post* (10 March 1951); Fred Russell, *Saturday Evening Post* (19 January 1957); *Sports Illustrated: The Basketball Book* (2007); *Time* (12 January 1959).

Beaches

Warmed by the waters of the Gulf of Mexico and the Gulf Stream, flanked by barrier islands from Virginia to Texas, southern beaches represent more than sand dunes and salt spray. In fact, southern history begins on the beach. Since the late 15th or early 16th century, when a Spanish soldier or sailor stepped ashore on an unidentified beach on the Florida peninsula or Gulf Coast, each generation of southerners has defined and redefined the beach as a place to escape, invest, define and display social class, and even break barriers.

Once seen as unhealthy and dangerous, the beach later became identified with health and relaxation. In the decades before and after the American Revolution, wealthy South Carolina planters wishing to escape the sickly summer months began to frequent the beach communities of Edisto and Pawley's Island. Families of planters and merchants wishing to escape the summer heat along the Upper Gulf Coast sought the comforts of Mobile, Bay St. Louis, and Biloxi. North Carolinians also began to visit Ocracoke and Portsmouth Island on the Outer Banks in the 1760s. The first hotel at Nags Head appeared in 1838, and by 1858 a three-story hotel appeared at Morehead City on Bogue Sound. In 1870 the elegant Cumberland Hotel opened.

Following the Civil War, the New South ushered in an era of beach resorts. The expansion of a dynamic middle class also created the modern American vacation, and the construction of modern railroads and the availability of steamboat travel allowed travelers to reach once-remote beach communities. Grand hotels and wooden beach cottages came to define the South's Gilded Age, and in no southern state did the emergence of the beach resort help transform the image and economy more than Florida. The future of Florida's resorts pointed toward the Gulf and Atlantic beaches. Keenly aware of this, Henry Flagler extended his rail line, erecting stunning hotels in Ormond Beach, Palm Beach, and Miami. The Breakers, Royal Poinciana, and Royal Palm hotels redefined southern luxury and helped create Florida's Gold Coast. Palm Beach advertised itself as the "Queen of Winter Resorts," while the writer Henry James depicted Palm Beach in February as "Vanity Fair in full blast." Across the peninsula, the masthead of the *Fort Myers News-Press* proclaimed the region as "the Italy of America."

In an era of conspicuous consumption, the upper classes flocked to Cumberland Island and Palm Beach as much to be seen as to restore their nerves. But the South's middle and working classes also enjoyed the sensuous pleasures of salt-air breezes and oyster roasts. In 1886 the *Halifax Journal* described the summer's rage, "surf bathing, a perfectly safe gigantic bathing trough provided by nature." In 1887 the *Pensacolian* predicted "that the day is not far distant when this part of Santa Rosa Island will become the Coney Island of the South." In 1901 the *Florida Times-Union* estimated that perhaps a quarter of Jacksonville's population celebrated the Fourth of July on a local beach. On the barrier islands east of Wilmington, N.C., Wrightsville Beach boasted the famous Lumina pavilion, illuminated at night by thousands of electric lights.

Not all tycoons simply luxuriated in chaise lounges and billiard parlors, though. Southern beaches and bays challenged "the best men" to pursue the strenuous life. Florida's Charlotte Harbor hotels attracted large numbers of sportsmen in the 1880s, determined to pursue America's most glamorous new sporting trophy: leaping tarpon. Shooting waterfowl along the Outer Banks during the autumnal migrations became a popular pastime, and on Georgia's Sea Islands industrialists purchased large tracts of land to be used as hunting preserves. The Canaveral Club, an exclusive fraternity limited to Harvard's graduating class of 1890, purchased 18,000 acres of property adjacent to the Cape Canaveral lighthouse, including several miles of pristine Atlantic beach.

Regardless of the pastime activities, everything about the beach evoked leisure and pleasure: the cooling breeze tempering the warm waters, the smells of fried flounder and smoked mullet, the open-air dance pavilions and wooden bathhouses. By the end of the 1920s, roads funneled motorists to South Carolina's Grand Strand. Horry County, once one of the state's poorest places, capitalized upon budget-minded tourists from the Carolinas headed for a beach vacation. Calabash, N.C., maximized its location as a crossroads for vacationers headed to and from Myrtle Beach. "Calabash-style seafood" became a trademark for fried flounder and shrimp platters. The 1920s also brought tourists across Bogue Sound to the bustling resort town of Atlantic Beach, N.C.

But for all the hoopla and boosterish rhetoric, southern beaches were not so much an escape from reality as a reflection of it. Southern beaches were "for whites only," and the history of the 20th-century southern beach mirrors the struggle for freedom as well as the quest for consumption. In the early years of the 20th century, Jacksonville, Fla., boasted a large black middle class, which expressed frustration over Jim Crow policies enforced at the local beaches. For example, Pablo Beach (later known as Jacksonville Beach) allowed African Americans admission on Mondays only. In 1907, however, nearby Manhattan Beach opened as "all-colored," and by the 1920s and 1930s black beaches had become more common throughout the South. Gulfside Summer Assembly, located along the Mississippi coast, dates from 1923 when light-skinned Robert E. Jones, a Methodist Episcopal bishop, purchased 300 acres to be used as a black religious resort. Similarly, in 1928, white businessman J. Elia Reid purchased property on Chowan Beach, N.C., and marketed the place as a family friendly resort for black professional families. The accommodations included a restaurant, German-made carousel, a dance hall, and cottages. In the 1940s, Dr. William Sharpe donated 4,000 acres of North Carolina shore to create Hammocks Beach, a black park on Bogue and Bear Inlets. The South's most famous black beach, American Beach on Amelia Island, Fla., was developed in the 1930s, when Abraham Lincoln Lewis, one of the owners of Jacksonville's Afro-American Life Insurance Company, purchased the beachfront. By design, American Beach offered blacks "recreation and relaxation without humiliation."

For all of the fascination with southern beaches, though, as late as the mid-20th century astonishingly little of the southern coastline had been developed, but the migration of Americans to the Sunbelt South, especially along the coasts, marked one of the great transitions in American history. Why and how Americans discovered some of the most obscure places on the continent is both simple and complicated. Southerners and northerners had always enjoyed a vacation along the shoreline, but access, time, and money had limited the pleasure. By the 1960s, interstate highways, new bridges, new frontier prosperity, new technologies, a youth culture, a building boom, and new attitudes were re-creating the modern beach. DDT had eliminated mosquitoes, and air-conditioning allowed year-round living. Members of the Lower South's rising middle class took advantage of these changes, headed for the coast, and along the Alabama and Florida Panhandle created the famous (and sometimes infamous) Redneck Riviera.

While southern beaches until the 1960s had been primarily known for attracting families on vacation, by the late decades of the century the now-infamous "spring break" had become a youthful rite of passage, attracting college-age youth from across the country to the South's warm, springtime coastline. What had begun in Fort Lauderdale in the 1930s had blossomed into popular culture, and movies and songs celebrated this coming-of-age ritual event. Early on in the history of spring break and summer beach parties, white and black South Carolinians perfected "the shag" in coastal juke joints and dance floors—most notably Charlie's Place in Myrtle Beach. Evolving from jazz and rhythm-and-blues traditions, the shag became South Carolina's official state dance in 1984. South Carolina's Pat Conroy has written about youthful rebellion and the Lowcountry in *Prince of Tides* (1986) and *Beach Music* (1995). By the 1980s and 1990s, America's youth was flooding into spring-break hot-spots such as Daytona Beach, Panama City, Destin, Gulf Shores, and South Padre Island, making southern beaches places where the elite and the adventurous, young and old, continue to share—and often compete—for space.

Still today the beach continues to be a privileged place. Once some of the South's poorest places, Hilton Head, Amelia Island, Padre Island, and Gulf Shores have become some of the region's most affluent sanctuaries. For many new residents, their beachfront condominiums serve as second homes, and as a result of southern beaches' continuing to be considered privileged space, public access to various beaches across the region remains a contentious issue.

Growth along southern coastal counties, nicknamed "the boom along the edge," has been dramatically higher than the interior. Between 1950 and 2000, for instance, Florida's coastal counties gained 10 million new residents while the state's noncoastal counties added less than three million new inhabitants. When one adds seasonal residents and tourists, the disparity is even greater. Growth has been especially striking in historically undeveloped areas of Florida: Southwest Florida, the panhandle, and the east coast. But Florida represents only a slice of the booming beach population in the South. Texas's barrier islands, a stretch of Gulf Coast between Gulf Shores, Ala., and Panama City, Fla., South Carolina's Grand Strand, and North Carolina's Outer Banks have all registered dramatic growth spurts in the last decades—a reflection of and reaction to the allure of the South's diverse and attractive coastline.

GARY R. MORMINO
University of South Florida at St. Petersburg

"Growth Reshapes Coasts," *USA Today* (21–23 July 2000); Charles Joyner, *Shared Traditions: Southern History and Folk Culture* (1999); Gary R. Mormino, *Land of Sunshine, State of Dreams: A Social History of Modern Florida* (2005); Frank Stephenson, *Chowan Beach: Remembering an African American Resort* (2006).

Beaches, Black, Jim Crow Era

During the first half of the 20th century, and especially in the years following World War II, America witnessed a veritable rush to the sea. Advances in transportation and the changing relationship between work and leisure compelled growing numbers of Americans to venture to the coast for pleasure, relaxation, and extended vacations. Southern states, in particular, experienced a steady growth in tourism-related industries, due in no small measure to hundreds of miles of pristine beaches the region possessed. Cities and states devoted resources to the development and upkeep of public beaches, while private developers turned once-forbidden coastal areas into summertime playgrounds for middle-class Americans. By the 1950s, summertime youth beach culture both reflected and shaped changing concepts of gender and encouraged greater sexual expression.

Not coincidentally, beaches also became one of the South's most racially segregated spaces, where white privilege and black exclusion were most pronounced and where racial boundaries violently policed. As African Americans fought for civil rights (among them, the right to equal access to public beaches), city and state governments employed every tool imaginable to prevent integration and preserve racial privilege. Many of them scrambled to sell coastal properties and public resorts to private, racially discriminatory groups or, when that failed, simply closed public beaches. African Americans' efforts to desegregate beaches led to some of the era's ugliest acts of racial violence, and the proliferation of private clubs and resorts and neglect of public facilities, like the rise of private educational academies, offer a telling reminder of Jim Crow's legacy in the South today.

But the exclusion of African Americans from whites-only beaches tells only part of the story of leisure in the Jim Crow South. Behind the color line, black southerners struggled, often against great odds, to develop and defend beaches of their own. As early as the 1890s, small enclaves of wealthy African Americans worked to develop private, exclusive resorts. In 1892 Charles Douglass, son of the famed abolitionist Frederick Douglass, facilitated the acquisition of a small stretch of shore along the Chesapeake Bay's western shore and founded Highland Beach. In the coming years, many of Washington's and Baltimore's "aristocrats of color" purchased lots and built summer homes there. Many pointed to this and other burgeoning summer resorts, such as Michigan's Idlewild, as symbols of African American initiative and achievement in the face of Jim Crow. "Even such small enterprises as a successful watering resort swells the heart with pride," the prominent black intellectual Kelly Miller said, and "show how earnestly we all long for political, economic, and social structure built upon our own foundation." But these early black resorts also reflected the growing class segregation of black America and the social and cultural alienation of upper-class blacks from the working poor. Highland Beach residents, for example, worked hard to maintain their exclusivity and prohibited beach access to the general public.

Throughout the early 20th century, there remained, for the vast majority of African Americans, few places for relief from the summertime heat. Few southern cities allocated separate beaches or parks for black citizens, and those that did located them in remote, inaccessible, and environmentally hazardous areas, places that often bred crime, confirmed white stereotypes, and reinforced blacks' feelings of inferiority. Enterprising African Americans struggled to fill this void and capitalize on segregation. In the early 1900s, Washington, D.C., African American businessman and shipping magnate Lewis Jefferson purchased a Potomac riverside resort and refurbished it into the modern amusement park Washington Park. This and other, smaller-scale ventures abounded across the South and became popular destinations for families otherwise excluded from white places of public amusement. By the early 1930s, black southerners claimed small stretches of shore as their own across the region, often on black-owned coastal property or in remote, undeveloped areas. Other black beaches developed alongside white resorts and became places of pleasure and rest for the crews of laborers and domestic workers who serviced white vacationers' needs.

But while many black beaches remained shrouded behind the color line and rarely aroused any opposition, others elicited white hostility and inspired efforts to scuttle and suppress. In Norfolk, Va., a city virtually surrounded by water, African Americans were prohibited from swimming on any of the city's beaches. Throughout the 1920s, black leaders petitioned the city to provide them with a beach of their own, but each attempt to designate an area for black recreation was met with vocal and sustained resistance from nearby white residents who deemed African American pleasure seekers a nuisance and a threat to their property value. In 1926 a group of black investors converted a swimming hole near Salem, Va., into a "colored bathing beach" and "first-class resort." The beach aroused considerable opposition from white citizens and county officials, due in part to its close proximity to a popular white resort. Three days before its scheduled opening, an anonymous band of assailants bombed the dam upstream and vandalized the newly built facilities. On Mon Louis Island, in southern Alabama, black coastal property owner Harry L. Moseby rented out his beach to churches and other groups for weekend picnics and barbecues in the summer months. But, by the 1930s, he and other black coastal residents contended with deep-pocketed whites in search of desirable coastal property for summer homes and dedicated to driving—by threat, by courts, or by force—"undesirables" from the coast. A group of white neighbors first intimidated, and then swindled, Moseby into signing away his rights to host parties on his property.

Beach segregation in the Jim Crow era was not unique to southern shores, as evidenced by the 1919 Chicago Race Riot, which was sparked by the drowning death of a young African American boy after he accidentally swam across an invisible color line in the waters of Lake Michigan. Nor was white resistance to the fruition of separate black beaches and resorts a southern phenomenon. In 1925 the Pacific Beach Club in Huntington Beach, Calif., an exclusive resort for African Americans, burned down under suspicious circumstances just months before its completion. Across the country, white strategies to drive African Americans from the beach and monopolize desirable coastal property stemmed not only from fears of interracial sexual intimacy and declining property values but moreover from unease over African Americans' enjoying themselves, by themselves, and over blacks' efforts to lay claim to the cultural currency of leisure. As black Charlestonian Mamie Garvin Fields put it, "Really, certain whites didn't like to think you had leisure to do anything but pick cotton and work in the field. Just generally, if you were black, you were not supposed to have either time or money, and if you did, you ought not to show it."

But in the face of legal and extralegal obstacles, intimidation, and the threat of violence, black southerners continued to circumvent Jim Crow, carve out desirable coastal space for pleasure and entertainment, and utilize leisure in the service of racial uplift and reform. North of Jacksonville, Fla., Abraham Lincoln Lewis, founder and president of the Afro-American Life Insurance Company, founded American Beach in 1935. In the coming years, families purchased lots and built summer homes there, and hotels, nightclubs, and restaurants that catered to the large summer crowds sprouted up. By the 1950s, American Beach became a hub on the rhythm-and-blues summer circuit and a destination for African American celebrities. Numerous other beaches, such as Atlantic Beach, in Horry County, S.C., Riverside Beach, outside of Charleston, S.C., Sea Breeze, in New Hanover County, N.C., and Carr's and Sparrow's Beaches, outside of Annapolis, Md., also attracted growing numbers of African American families in the 1950s and early 1960s, playing host to picnics, barbecues, dances, sporting events, and musical performances and fostering the growth of seasonal businesses such as food stands and do-drop inns.

While visitors to American Beach danced to the sounds of Duke Ellington, James Brown, and Ray Charles, at others they swayed to the sounds of spirituals. In 1923 Methodist Episcopal bishop Robert E. Jones purchased nearly 300 acres of beachfront property along the Mississippi Gulf Coast and founded the Gulfside Summer Assembly, the nation's first permanent African American religious resort. It was rumored that, in purchasing the property, Jones passed as a white man. Regardless, Gulfside's survival in the Jim Crow South was due, in large part, to the slightly more racially tolerant attitudes of Gulf Coast whites and to the seemingly nonthreatening nature of a religious resort. Not simply a place to escape from the hardships of life, the resort became an important center in the racial uplift and interracial cooperation movements of the 1920s and 1930s. Gulfside hosted a variety of groups, including training institutes for ministers and teachers, Boy Scouts and Camp Fire Girls Camps, recuperative retreats for "tired mothers" each summer, and an industrial training school for impoverished young black males throughout the year. Gulfside camps enforced strict regimentation of daily activities and preached the productive and uplifting use of leisure time. Alongside camps and institutes, Gulfside also hosted middle- and upper-class black families from New Orleans and the surrounding area, who vacationed at the resort throughout the summer. In the succeeding years, 30 additional buildings were constructed on the grounds, including cabins, classrooms, and a 1,000-seat auditorium. Each summer, Gulfside hosted an annual Song Fest that brought an interracial (though segregated) crowd to the beach to listen to choirs and glee clubs from black colleges and universities across the South. Indeed, the different types of black beaches that came of age in the mid-20th century both reflected and gave expression to the class and cultural diversity of black southerners as a whole.

Despite the rise of these and other beaches and resorts, southern black communities continued to suffer from dire recreational inequality and a striking absence of safe and healthy places of play. In the 1950s and 1960s, local and national civil rights activists often drew attention to the patterns of white privilege and black exclusion along southern shores, and its deleterious effects on community life and childhood development, to underscore the fiction of "separate but equal." To counter their claims, city and state governments developed "colored" beaches, swimming pools, parks, and campgrounds. The early 1960s witnessed an unprecedented number of black beaches under development in communities large and small, especially in the aftermath of wade-ins at white beaches by civil rights activists. After a group staged a wade-in at a segregated beach in Carolina Beach, N.C., in 1961, for instance, city officials attempted to placate black community leaders with promises of increased funding and upkeep of the "colored-only" Freeman Beach.

Following passage of the 1964 Civil Rights Act, though, governments ceased funding most of these public facilities, some of which had blossomed into important centers of community life, and they quickly fell into disrepair. Beginning in the 1970s and to the present, many historically black beaches and coastal communities have fallen prey to developers in search of property to build golf courses and resorts for middle- and upper-class vacationers and to the skyrocketing property taxes that accompanied the rise of vacationing and tourism along the coast. In places such as Virginia Beach, Va., the sandy soil that had long sustained African American farmers became a valuable commodity, and black property owners were targeted by developers seeking to acquire coastal property at below-market values. The steady demise of American Beach, which as a result of development on all sides is today a shell of its former self, has drawn national attention and calls for preservation. Its residents' ongoing struggle to fend off rapacious developers and their political allies was fictionalized in John Sayles's 2000 film *Sunshine State*.

The fight for safe, attractive, and accessible beaches played an important, if often unheralded, role in African Americans' long freedom struggle. The disappearance of black beaches in the modern South symbolizes the ironic consequences of desegregation, while the persistence of patterns of racial privilege along America's coasts and of recreational inequality in southern black communities speaks to the failure of civil rights reforms to confront a history of economic and environmental injustice.

ANDREW W. KAHRL
Marquette University

Cindy S. Aron, *Working at Play: A History of Vacations in the United States* (1999); J. Michael Butler, *Journal of Southern History* (February 2002); Jeffrey Collins,

"Once-Segregated South Carolina Beach Town Fights to Survive," Associated Press, (30 January 2009); Dianne D. Glave and Mark Stoll, eds., *"To Love the Wind and the Rain": African Americans and Environmental History* (2006); Mark S. Foster, *Journal of Negro History* (Spring 1999); Willard B. Gatewood, *Aristocrats of Color: The Black Elite, 1880–1920* (1990); Charles Joyner, *Journal of Southern History* (February 2006); Andrew W. Kahrl, "On the Beach: Race and Leisure in the Jim Crow South" (Ph.D. dissertation, Indiana University, 2008); Andrew W. Kahrl, *Journal of American History* (March 2008); Earl Lewis, *In Their Own Interests: Race, Class, and Power in Twentieth-Century Norfolk, Virginia* (1991); Russ Rymer, *American Beach: A Saga of Race, Wealth, and Memory* (1998).

Blood Sports

The history of blood sports in the American South is as long as that of the region itself, and its definition just as amorphous. The term "blood sport" is used to refer to a range of geographically and historically disparate social practices that center on the baiting or killing of animals for the pleasure and entertainment of spectators. Such practices were known as far back as the Roman Empire, and remnants of 19th-century British and Irish blood sports, such as the baiting of bears and badgers, fighting of roosters and dogs, and hunting of foxes and hares, survived in the U.S. South and were transformed into folk traditions. In the 20th century, the term has also come to refer to certain high-risk contact sports among humans, such as boxing, wrestling, and mixed martial arts competitions. This essay treats the following blood sports most strongly associated with the American South: bare-knuckle fighting, cockfighting, dog fighting, and "hog-dogging." Although these are by no means the only blood sports enjoyed in the South, they are the most widespread, documented, and clear-cut examples.

It must be noted at the outset that blood sports are not distinctively southern. Southern studies scholars have soundly critiqued the notion of a "savage ideal" as being more characteristic of an imagined South than the complex and varied lives of individuals in the region. Moreover, as animal rights organizations have gained acceptance, blood sports have become increasingly controversial as activists dispute the classification of such practices as "sport" and decry them as exploitative of animals. Indeed, legislation prohibiting these practices and increasing penalties is proliferating across the United States; during the writing of this essay, cockfighting was criminalized in New Mexico and Louisiana, its last two strongholds. Sporting enthusiasts argue that in the context of a society highly dependent on animal exploitation for its products, such legislation may be motivated less by a concern for animals and more by a colonial impulse to police working-class pleasures. In any case, blood sports have been central to the construction and expression of southern cultural identities.

The practice of southern backcountry brawling was traced by scholar Elliott J. Gorn through a review of oral histories and travelers' accounts. Bare-knuckle fighting in the English style (according to Broughton's Rules) was fashionable in the 18th-century South. According to these rules, a "fist battle" continued in timed rounds until one fighter was knocked out or thrown down. Yet in the South, these rules were ignored in favor of a "no holds barred" style of fighting, which came to be known as "rough-and-tumble" or simply "gouging." This style of fighting was not limited to the peasant classes and in fact was popular as early as 1735 among Virginia gentlemen in Chesapeake Bay. As the names suggest, scratching, choking, tripping, and throwing were common elements of these fights, and gouging, with the intent of removing an eye, was considered the *sine qua non* of a tumble. The goal of each fight was the maximum disfigurement of one's opponent, which might include the severing of body parts, but a code of honor dictated that no external weapons be used (although long fingernails, often filed to a point, were fair game). Fights continued until one fighter gave up or was unable to continue.

In the late 18th century, ceremonial dueling gradually replaced hand-to-hand combat among the upper classes, but rough-and-tumble remained alive and well in rural and backwoods areas of the South. A rich oral history of rough-and-tumble speaks of a culture guided by notions of honor and kinship, where small slights might well provoke outrage and violence. Southern backcountry gouging became associated with moral turpitude and degeneracy, but it has been persuasively argued that by embracing violence through actions and legends, southern men were better able to cope with the grief and alienation that surrounded them. By the mid-1800s, as weapons became more widely available, other contests gradually came to replace a rough-and-tumble style of fighting.

Perhaps the most iconic of southern blood sports is cockfighting. Yet, as with the remaining blood sports treated in this essay, this term refers not merely to animals fighting in a wild or domestic setting but to a practice orchestrated by humans. Game fowl are descended from the jungle fowl of India and Southeast Asia but were selectively cultivated for pit fighting in 19th-century England. Unlike many other breeds of farm and ornamental chickens, game-cocks (roosters of game-fowl bloodlines) are typically aggressive toward other roosters and will fight to the death or incapacity of one bird. Cockers, as their human handlers are known, come from a wide range of ethnic and socioeconomic backgrounds.

A cockfight typically involves the matching of two gamecocks, each with a handler, and a referee who enforces the Modern Tournament or Derby Rules that govern the fight. The most common venue for a cockfight is a Derby, or series of fights that take place on a given day or weekend in an arena, or "cockpit," which measures 16 feet across and is surrounded by bleacher seating conducive to spectatorship and betting. Birds are conditioned much like athletes, with special diets and exercise regimes for at least two weeks (a period known as a "keep"), in anticipation of Derby day.

On the morning of a Derby, birds are weighed and paired so that each bird will have an opponent within two or three ounces of his own weight. They are also paired according to fighting style; knives or gaffs are attached to the roosters' legs near their natural spurs. Knives resemble razor blades and can be long or short, whereas gaffs are long spikes. Gaff fighting is a more traditional style and requires more stamina from the chicken, whereas knives, which inflict damage more quickly, have become increasingly popular in the South. Animal welfare advocates condemn the use of these weapons, but cockers insist that the weapons, which facilitate a quick end to a match, actually make the practice more humane.

The cockfight commences when the referee orders the handlers, spaced nine feet apart, to "pit your birds." The birds are released and often "break," or fly up and meet in the air. They peck and strike each other with beaks and feet until a handle is called, when each handler must pick up his bird. A handle is called when one bird is "hung" or caught on a knife or gaff, and a count is called if one does not fight. If a bird is counted out in 30 seconds, or attempts to run away, the other bird is declared the winner. When a fight is prolonged, it is moved to a smaller "drag pit" to keep the action in the main arena moving. The cocker who has won the most matches at the end of the Derby is the victor.

As illegal underground practices, many blood sports are difficult to measure through traditional data-gathering techniques, but a 1970 issue of the trade publication *Grit and Steel* estimated 500,000 cockers in the United States, a figure that has surely declined as legal penalties have increased. Die-hard cockers from around the South attended the 2006 Derby at Sunset Gentlemen's Club at Lafayette, La., one of the few remaining historic cockpits in the United States, to witness one of the final Derbies before cockfighting was declared illegal. Talk of states' rights abounded, along with peach brandy, Cajun French, and high-breaking, spectacular birds. Rather than appearing backward or cruel, hosts at the Derby were full of information and warm hospitality.

Dog fighting has recently burst into public consciousness with the 2007 federal indictment of the Atlanta Falcons' quarterback Michael Vick, but the practice was considered a "national institution" as far back as 1816. Fighting dogs (typically Staffordshire bull terriers) accompanied English and Irish immigrants to the United States and were later imported, primarily into New York and Boston where dog fighting became popular among "sporting men," gentlemen and working-class men alike. The ASPCA mounted a campaign against dog fighting, which resulted in its prohibition in the United States in 1860. However, it was still widely practiced, as demonstrated by the publication by the *Police Gazette* of its own version of rules for dog fighting in 1888.

In the early 20th century, the South became the locus of a particular culture of rural dog fighting built around the concept of the dog's gameness, or perceived desire to fight. The Cajun Rules were developed by G. A. Trahan to govern dog matches, and the American Pit Bull Terrier was bred specifically to excel under these rules. Contrary to popular belief, the Cajun Rules do not require a fight to the death or incapacity of one dog. "Dogmen," as dogfighters are known, argue these rules prevent a match from being inhumane, because they are designed to test a dog's gameness rather than mere fighting ability. According to these rules, a dog that crosses the pit to his opponent and takes hold (known as a "scratch") is seen as potentially game, whereas if a dog turns away from his opponent or shows other signs of hesitancy, time is called. A dog that turns is given another chance to scratch to his opponent, and if he is unwilling, he is branded a "cur," and the match is over. Thus, even if one dog is severely injured and barely able to fight, but keeps scratching, he can defeat a more capable but less willing opponent. The concept of gameness is valorized and frequently applied not only to the dogs in the context of fighting but to the men and their families in their daily lives and struggles.

In the late 20th century, the locus of dog fighting shifted once again to more urban areas as certain inner-city African American and Latino men took up the sport. According to the Humane Society of the United States, these men are more likely to engage in street fights rather than organized fights, where dogs are matched "OTC" (off the chain), without formal rules and without a referee. Old-time southern dogmen define themselves in opposition not only to mainstream American society but also to dogfighters who do not use the Cajun Rules. While dog fighting has historical roots in the South, as well as a high concentration of dogmen in the region, dog fighting according to the Cajun Rules is not uniquely southern, as it is still practiced throughout the United States and abroad.

Hog hunting has taken place for much of recorded human history, but the capture of hogs with dogs has recently developed into a competitive spectator event known as "hog-dogging," or "hog dog rodeos." The hunting of feral hogs and wild boars, abundant throughout the South, has traditionally been accomplished through the use of specially trained "bay" dogs, which chase and corner the hog, and "catch" dogs that take hold of the hog and allow it to be captured. A demonstration called "Uncle Earl's Hog Dog Trials" was organized in 1995 in Winnfield, La., as part of former governor and hog hunter Earl K. Long's 100th birthday celebration. In a series of field trials, judges score the skill with which dogs are able to bay and catch a penned hog. As a spectator sport, this practice has since spread throughout the South and is particularly popular in Alabama. Although hog hunting still appears sacrosanct, hog dog rodeos are a new target of animal welfare legislation.

JERE ALEXANDER
Emory University

George C. Armitage, *Thirty Years with Fighting Dogs* (1935); Alan Dundes, ed., *The Cockfight: A Casebook* (1994); Charles W. Eagles, ed., *"The Mind of the South": Fifty Years Later* (1992); Richard K. Fox, *The Dog Pit* (1888); Adrian Franklin, *Animals and Modern Cultures: A Sociology of Human-Animal Relationships in Modernity* (1999); Elliott J. Gorn, *American Historical Review* (February 1985); Mike Homan, *A Complete History of Fighting Dogs* (1999); Ted Ownby, *Subduing Satan: Religion, Recreation, and Manhood in the Rural South, 1865–1920* (1990); Bob Stevens, *Dogs of Velvet and Steel: Pit Bulldogs; A Manual for Owners* (1983).

Boxing

Modern boxing grew out of the fairs and gambling rooms of early 18th-century England. It was a bloody and violent sport that placed a premium on courage and a low price on human life. It was also a sport that reinforced the class structure of England. Poor men fought and sometimes died for the entertainment of wealthy patrons, who risked only the money they bet on. By the Regency period, boxing had achieved remarkable popularity. It excited the imaginations of Lord Byron, William Hazlitt, and Dr. Samuel Johnson, and it received the patronage of members of the royal family.

Wealthy southerners who traveled to England learned the intricacies of boxing. Lovers of English sports and pastimes, and especially of the English class system, planters sometimes staged impromptu matches between slaves, although there were probably fewer of these matches than once believed. In addition, throughout the 19th century the South provided a moral climate conducive to the growth of boxing.

In part, this moral climate was the result of southern attitudes toward leisure. Even before the Revolution, a leisure ethos was apparent in the South. Whereas

Joe Louis looks for an opening during a boxing match with Max Schmeling, 1936.
(Photograph by staff photographer at New York World-Telegram,
Library of Congress [LC-USZ62-114335], Washington, D.C.)

northerners emphasized the moral importance of work and criticized sport, southerners viewed the enjoyment of leisure as an important aspect of a gentleman's life. Consumption and hospitality, pride and defense of one's honor, were apt to gain more social approval than the pursuit of money and respectability.

The first important American boxer was a southerner. On 18 December 1810 in a field 25 miles from London, Tom Molineaux, an ex-slave from the South, battled English champion Tom Cribb for title of the world's best fighter. Molineaux was backed by another American black, Bill Richmond, who had fought a few matches himself but spent most of his time running a pub. The fight was close and controversial, but in the end Cribb won. Molineaux stayed in England, engaged in several more important contests, and died young and penniless after a serious bout with dissipation.

Molineaux's career stirred little American interest. Organized boxing was practiced seldom in the South until the 1830s. By that time the sport faced troubles in England. Fixed fights, ring deaths, and Victorian piety and moral earnestness all hurt boxing in England. In 1836 English champion James "Deaf" Burke left the Old Country for America, or, as he referred to it, "Yankeeshire." Searching for an area to hold a prizefight, he looked toward the South. In 1837 he fought Sam O'Rourke in New Orleans. The most important result of the fight was to show that New Orleans would tolerate a sport that was barred in most other parts of the country. Even during the opening tense days of the Civil War, patrons of the prize ring were not too busy to journey to Kenner, La., to watch Mike McCool take "the conceit out of big Tom Jennings."

By the time of the Civil War, a pattern in American boxing had emerged. Although promoters staged a number of championship fights in the South, few southerners became important boxers. Most boxing champions came from the cities of the North, and a high percentage of these were immigrants (or sons of immigrants) from England and Ireland. Nevertheless, wealthy southerners enjoyed watching boxing matches and often took lessons in "the manly science of self-defense" at exclusive men's clubs in southern cities.

The golden age of southern boxing occurred in the 1880s and early 1890s. On 7 February 1882 John L. Sullivan defeated Paddy Ryan for the American championship in a bout staged in Mississippi. Sullivan soon attracted a large national following, and boxing momentarily came out of the shadows and saloons into the sun of public acclaim. In this dash for quasi respectability for boxing, New Orleans led the way. The height of 19th-century American boxing occurred during a remarkable three-day period in September 1892. On consecutive days, New Orleans's Olympic Club staged three world championship fights. In the final of the matches, James J. Corbett defeated Sullivan. The triple event was a great critical and financial success.

After 1892 New Orleans declined as the boxing center of the nation. The focus of the ring followed the hands of gamblers, first to the West, then to New York and Chicago, and most recently to Las Vegas and Atlantic City. In the 20th century, the South produced some leading fighters and even a few great champions, but the South was never again the center of boxing.

The South produced two of the 20th-century's greatest boxers—Joe Louis and Muhammad Ali. Louis (1914–81) was born to sharecropping parents on a farm near Lafayette, Ala. The young Louis moved with his mother and stepfather to Detroit, where he became active in amateur boxing and had his first professional fight in 1934. The "Brown Bomber" went on to be a legendary heavyweight champion from 1937 to 1949. He was a symbol of the triumph of the underdog, a popular Depression-era figure for many Americans, but his greatest significance was as a symbol for black Americans. He was a soft-spoken, clean-living, God-fearing man, and southern blacks looked on him as one of their greatest heroes.

Muhammad Ali (Cassius Clay) was the preeminent boxer of the 1960s and 1970s. Born 18 January 1942 in Louisville, Ky., to a close-knit, working-class family, Ali won a 1960 Olympic gold medal in boxing and, after 19 victorious professional bouts, defeated Sonny Liston for the heavyweight championship in 1963. Ali became a controversial champion. His refusal to enter the armed services resulted in the World Boxing Association stripping him of his championship. He later became the first person to regain the heavyweight crown twice. A black Muslim in religion, Ali became one of the best-known and most admired Americans in the Third World. He was a colorful champion with his quick wit, graceful style, and dominating personality. He was an appropriate figure in the turbulent 1960s and became a major cultural symbol for the black pride uniting blacks in the South of his birth, in the nation, and in the world.

Through the last quarter of the 20th century and into the 21st, championships in the lighter weight divisions were taken over by Latino fighters, but the heavier championships continued to be dominated not just by Americans, but by African Americans of southern birth. In the 1960s and 1970s, in addition to Ali, there were "Smokin' Joe" Frazier, born in Beaufort, S.C., Jimmy Ellis (Louisville, Ky.), and Leon Spinks (if you count St. Louis as southern). In the 1980s there was Larry Holmes of Cuthbert, Ga., but like so many other fighters he grew up in the North, and it was there he got his training.

However, in the 1990s the South once again had a champion with a firm regional identity. Evander Holyfield, was born in Atmore, Ala., but made his home in and near Atlanta, Ga. That city's boosters adopted him as their own and, with the Atlanta image makers working full time, Holyfield became a local hero. The fights between Holyfield and Mike Tyson were presented as a contest between the quiet, gentlemanly professional (Holyfield) and the unprincipled street brawler (Tyson, who just happened to be from New York), and when Tyson confirmed that image by biting off part of Holyfield's ear, southern boxing fans, with little sense of irony, lavished praise on their champion as a true son of Dixie. In 1996 he carried the Olympic torch en route to the stadium in Atlanta, where the flame was lit by that other southern boxing great Muhammad Ali.

But of all the southern fighters, the most successful, and arguably the most popular, has been George Foreman of Marshall, Tex. His flag-waving triumph in the Olympics introduced him to a southern audience hungry for patriotic heroes, and when he turned pro he relentlessly fought his way to a 1973 title bout with undisputed heavyweight champion Joe Frazier, whom he beat in what is still considered one of the greatest upsets in fight history. From that point his career lasted more than 20 years and included title defenses, losses (to Ali in the 1974 "Rumble in the Jungle"), comebacks, and the success in 1994, of becoming at 45 the oldest fighter to win the title. Though Foreman was considered aloof and dull when a fighter (and, compared to Ali, he was), once out of the ring he became one of the most successful of boxing entrepreneurs. Selling himself as well as products like the George Foreman Lean Mean Fat Reducing Grilling Machine, he reportedly has earned $240 million—three times what he brought home as a fighter. When so many boxers experience financial difficulties once out of the ring, George Foreman has become as famous as a salesman as he was when he was fighting.

Today there is no Foreman, Frazier, Ali, or Norton to represent, however tenuously, southern boxing. Roy Jones Jr., born in Pensacola, Fla., briefly held the World Boxing Association heavyweight title in 2004, but he fights more comfortably at a lower division. Moreover, with the proliferation of boxing organizations, each of which certifies its own champion, it is unlikely that any fighter, northern or southern, will be able to unify all the titles and dominate the sport the way Dixie fighters did in the past. Nevertheless, if pay-per-view receipts are any indication, boxing is still popular down South, even if the boxers are from somewhere else.

RANDY ROBERTS
South West Texas State University

HARVEY H. JACKSON III
Jacksonville State University

Elliot Gorn, "The Manly Art: Bare-Knuckle Fighting and the Rise of American Sports" (Ph.D. dissertation, Yale University, 1983); Randy Roberts, *Papa Jack: Jack Johnson and the Era of White Hopes* (1983); Dale A. Somers, *The Rise of Sports in New Orleans, 1850–1900* (1972); George Foreman and Joel Engel, *By George: The Autobiography of George Foreman* (2000).

Buck Dancing, Flatfooting, and Clogging

Buck dancing, flatfooting, and clogging are three names for the percussive step dancing of rural Appalachia and the South. Also known as "hoedowning" (in eastern Kentucky) and "jig dancing" or "jigging" (in the Ozarks), this type of dance is characterized by fast, percussive footwork that makes use of the toes, the heels, or the whole foot, with dancers creating a rhythmic accompaniment to the music. The roots of these dances can be traced to the arrival of the earliest settlers in America, beginning a process in which dance steps and styles moved freely from one culture to another. Buck dancing, flatfooting, and clogging are clearly multiethnic blends; they draw on jigs and other step dances brought from the British Isles and northern Europe, the West African dances of those who were enslaved, and the dances of the Cherokee and other Native Americans.

Flatfooting and buck dancing are older terms that are generally used to indicate time-honored styles of idiosyncratic step dancing done by individual dancers. Flatfooting is a style of buck dance in which a dancer's feet stay close to the floor with the heels down, rather than being up on the toes. As early as the mid-16th century, dancers in Scotland used the term "platfute" (flatfoot) to describe a type of dancing. Evidence suggests that the term "buck dance" derives from the word "buck," a demeaning, 19th-century reference used by whites to refer to African American males. Some have argued, however, that buck dance came first. Whichever is the case, the terms are related, and countless references in the narratives of ex-slaves recall "buck dancing" at antebellum "frolics." While these dance styles share some common steps, they have no prescribed footwork. Instead, they encompass a range of steps and styles that invite improvisation and spontaneity as individual dancers interact rhythmically with both the musicians and each other.

Rather than remaining static, rural step dance traditions have evolved over time, constantly adopting new dance steps into local repertoires. Dancers took some steps (e.g., the pigeon wing) from itinerant French dancing masters at the end of the 18th century and borrowed others from stage dancers who performed British hornpipes and clog dances in wooden-soled shoes. Throughout the 19th century, various steps and elements of these urban dance styles became part of the rural southern dance tradition.

It was not until the 1950s that the term "clogging" (a name derived from English clog dancing) came to designate southern Appalachian step dancing. This shift in terminology followed the advent of square dance competitions in western North Carolina during the 1930s and 1940s, and the emergence of a new, performance-oriented square dance style. In 1928 and the years that followed, Bascom Lamar Lunsford invited local square dance groups to compete onstage at his annual Mountain Dance and Folk Festival in Asheville, N.C. Over time, as a direct result of these competitions, a new square dance style evolved that combined individual percussive footwork with group square dance figures. By the 1940s dance groups were wearing matching costumes and tap shoes on stage. By the early 1960s, in turn, clogging teams in western North Carolina were beginning to incorporate synchronized footwork and more performance-oriented choreography into their dance routines. This new style, called "precision clogging," moved the dancing further away from the social context of traditional buck dancing, by placing an even greater emphasis on competition and performance.

Since the 1960s, the popularity of precision clogging has led to the standardization of steps and styles; national clogging organizations now host annual conventions, certify clogging instructors, and sanction contests. This widespread interest has led to the creation of a modern precision clogging style called "contemporary clogging." Although its roots lie in traditional southern Appalachian buck dancing, this modern style incorporates footwork borrowed from tap dance as well as Canadian and Irish step dancing. Dancers memorize prescribed sequences of steps and dance routines that are choreographed by clogging instructors and then perform these to recorded pop music at exhibitions and competitions. While this standardized modern form of clogging is now popular throughout the South, traditional buck dancers and flatfooters still grace the dance floor at rural dances.

PHILIP A. JAMISON
Warren Wilson College

Philip A. Jamison, *Old Time Herald* (November 1993); Mike Seeger, *Talking Feet: Buck, Flatfoot, and Tap; Solo Southern Dance of the Appalachian, Piedmont, and Blue Ridge Mountain Regions* (1992); Susan Eike Spalding and Jane Harris Woodside, eds., *Communities in Motion: Dance, Community, and Tradition in America's Southeast and Beyond* (1995).

Card Parties

Card parties and their corresponding clubs and societies have long been a popular means of recreation for southern women. Although those who have come of age in the past few decades tend to associate card groups with maiden aunts and widows, card party participants come from a variety of social and demographic groups. The one thing they have in common is that these ladies have the leisure time to play. Any Google search will lead to numerous groups dedicated to the turn of a card or to Web sites aimed at improving one's knowledge and skill. Some of these are quite old and exclusive, like Savannah's Married Woman's Card Club, which has been meeting once a month since 1893. Others are relatively new and the membership varies, depending on who is available at the time

Although games such as whist, euchre, 500, and canasta are sometimes played, today bridge is far and away the most popular game for these ladies. With its rigid rules, exacting player requirements, and element of chance, bridge requires skill and, according to bridge players, a great deal of practice. In contract bridge, four players form two partnerships. Each partnership then attempts to take the most "tricks" and obtain the highest score in order to win. Status within a bridge group can be attained by mastering the various recognized levels of the game.

In the southern tradition, ladies have used their card parties and bridge groups for a multitude of purposes. Obviously, playing cards is a form of entertainment. And how much more entertaining is a game accompanied by fabulous fashion statements, delicious hors d'oeuvres, and savory bits of gossip? Card parties have often been a convenient way for southern ladies to meet and exchange information and discreetly "bond" as their husbands do in their private clubs and remote hunting camps. These parties usually rotate among the women's homes; however, as more gentlemen's clubs have opened their doors to women, card parties now take place in many nontraditional venues.

As southerners become more mobile, card groups are a way to establish oneself or one's position in a community. A current resident of Shoal Creek, Ala., tells that everywhere she and her husband have lived, bridge groups have helped her acclimate into new communities and provided the opportunity to make friends across the card table. These groups require a commitment of time and dedication to the game that the other members rely on, building bonds of trust and camaraderie quickly.

Southern women also use their card parties for charitable purposes. Most commonly, this is done through bridge tournaments. Each player must post a required stake to play in the tournament, thus raising money for causes like educational scholarships and hospital auxiliaries. Bridge tournaments then serve a dual purpose, both raising money and providing a social event for those involved.

Longtime bridge player and party hostess, the late Elizabeth Wilkinson Ware Searcy (known to most as "Ludie"), believed bridge to be a game that requires an enormous amount of brainpower and concentration. She believed the game kept her mind sharp and that bridge parties allowed her to maintain the social contacts made over nearly a century of life. What more could one ask, of a game or a party?

CATHY BURROWS
Jacksonville State University

John Berendt, *Midnight in the Garden of Good and Evil* (1994); Charles Henry Goren, *Goren's Bridge Complete: A Major Revision of the Standard Work for All* (1963).

Cheerleading and Twirling

Cheerleading and twirling are found in a variety of forms in the South, ranging from children's informal playground routines to highly formalized and choreographed performances at high school, college, and professional sports and musical entertainment activities. There are rewards for participants in competitions, including trophies, travel, scholarships, prize money, and prestige. Southern cultural spirit and identity are revitalized through these activities.

Formalized cheerleading seems to have originated in eastern and midwestern colleges at the turn of the 20th century. It quickly spread to high schools and colleges nationwide, taking a particularly strong hold in the South. Cheerleading began as a student extracurricular leadership activity tied to athletics and performed by two to five males to inspire school or class loyalties and good citizenship in the student body.

After World War I more women studied at coed institutions and chose to participate in extracurricular events. By the end of World War II cheerleading had become predominantly a female activity. Squads of 5 to 18 girls were selected on the basis of physical or social characteristics, performance skills, and popularity. The entertainment aspect of cheerleading has grown to rival its original focus on school leadership and has broadened the range of performances.

In the last decades of the 20th century, male cheerleaders became more prominent, and by 2009 males represented 50 percent of collegiate cheerleading squads. The popularity of gymnastics, resulting from gymnastic competition in the Olympics, has made cheerleading a true athletic activity and attracted better male and female athletes. Two cheerleading groups—the Garland, Texas–based National Cheerleading Association (NCA) and the Memphis, Tennessee–based Universal Cheerleading Association (UCA)—promote, supply, and generally address the administrative needs of southern cheerleaders. The NCA, for example, trains thousands of high school and college students annually in hundreds of clinics and workshops. It markets cheerleader goods of all sorts— uniforms, megaphones, and pompons. The modern pompon was invented by a southerner, Lawrence "Herkie" Herkimer, a former Southern Methodist University cheerleader, who applied colored streamers to batons. The NCA and the UCA both stage annual nationally televised cheerleading championships.

In 1972 the Dallas Cowboys broke a long tradition of using high school cheerleaders for their games and began the first professional cheerleading squad consisting of seven scantily clad professional dancers. The pattern was soon followed by such National Football League cities as Houston, Atlanta, Washington, D.C., and others in an effort to capitalize on the potent entertainment value of a successful blend of sex with sports. Their style is an extension of the cheerleading and pompon girl traditions, and it helped stimulate a revitalization of amateur cheerleading.

Formalized baton twirling also began as a male activity in the early 20th century, but during the 1930s it evolved into performances by groups of beautiful women dressed in skimpy costumes and using smaller, lighter batons than their male counterparts had carried. Best known as an activity for a marching corps in association with marching bands in halftime shows and parades, baton twirling also features solo and team performances in entertainment and competitive settings. Although batons are the most popular of twirled objects, flags, sabers, and flaming batons are among the specialty items used by experienced twirlers.

The dream of becoming a professional cheerleader or a baton-twirling Miss America has inspired many southern girls. By the age of three or four, some girls have begun to perform publicly as mascots with groups of older, more skilled performers as well as with girls their own age. Many girls eventually take private lessons to strengthen their physical coordination skills and to master specific techniques, but most begin to learn necessary skills by watching friends or siblings and then attempting to execute various maneuvers in the backyard or on the playground. In many urban and suburban neighborhoods, it is common to find girls gathering to play and practice their skills on a daily basis. They bring these street skills to school and recreation center squads and attend camps and workshops where their skills mature and are refined. Terry Southern in "Twirling at Ole Miss" (1962) discusses the Dixie National Baton Twirling Institute, which was held annually at the University of Mississippi and was once one of the largest twirling clinics. Today the camps are conducted twice each summer in conjunction with the Universal Cheerleaders Association and are innocuously referred to as Ole Miss Mid-South Cheerleading Camps.

Elsewhere in popular culture, as a result of a handful of cheerleading movies such as *Bring It On* (2000); its three straight-to-DVD sequels, *Bring It On Again* (2004), *Bring It On: All or Nothing* (2006), and *Bring It On: In It to Win It* (2007); *Sugar & Spice* (2001); and *Man of the House* (2005, starring Tommy Lee Jones and set in Texas), cheerleading took on a much larger profile. A reality television show was seemingly inevitable. Thus, in 2006 *Cheerleader Nation* aired on the Lifetime Television Network. The show followed the dramatic ups and downs of the two-time champion Paul Laurence Dunbar High School cheerleading squad from Lexington, Ky., on its way to a third national championship.

Cheerleading and twirling combine African and European cultural elements. Robert Farris Thompson argues for the African source of "the main baton-twirling pose, with left hand on hip," and he believes that cheerleading, in general, was mainly derived from southern black influences. *Time* magazine noted (11 December 1939) that "some of the most versatile cheerleaders" were "at Southern colleges (notably Alabama and Tennessee)." Swiss flag twirling was another influence, and European-style precision marching provided the context for twirling at football halftimes.

Whatever the origins, African American culture, particularly in the South, has developed these activities into extraordinary art forms drawing on performance principles based in the aesthetics of black American traditional and urban cultures. Syncopation, black dance styles, and soul music have changed the rhythmic character and style of movement for both cheerleading and baton twirling, injecting a new rhythmic energy for black and white performance styles.

PHYLLIS M. MAY
Indiana University

Natalie Guice Adams and Pamela Jean Bettis, *Cheerleader!: An American Icon* (2003); James T. McElroy, *We've Got Spirit: The Life and Times of America's Greatest Cheerleading Team* (2000); Fred Miller et al., *The Complete Book of Baton Twirling* (1978); Randy L. Neil, *The Official Cheerleaders Handbook* (1979); Terry Southern, *Esquire* (February 1963); Robert Farris Thompson and Joseph Cornet, *The Four Movements of the Sun: Kongo Art in Two Worlds* (1981).

Children's Games, Traditional

Children's play was rarely mentioned by observers of the Old South. Sources that do exist suggest that southern children had active play lives and that games occupied a major portion of their time. Assumptions about social roles, human nature, and conduct were expressed in their play. Many old and popular southern games are remnants of significant events in history and common cultural traditions of the region.

Literature on white middle-class children's games may be found in novels, diaries, and artistic prints. Eighteenth-century prints show a number of games, and below each picture is a statement of the moral lesson the game teaches, reflecting the dominant cultural values. Informal ball games included stoolball, cricket, fives, tip-cat, and baseball. Hopscotch, leapfrog, and hide-and-seek, all common to American children today, and imitative games such as playing house are also identified in the prints. Board games included chess, fox-and-geese, and checks, which is similar to checkers.

L. Minor Blackford, in *Mine Eyes Have Seen the Glory*, recorded typical games of the Blackford children of Virginia in the mid-1850s. Examples included Anthony over, hickeme dickeme, blindman's buff, prisoner's base, pullover-the-bat, kite flying, bull-in-the-pen, cutting jacks, stilt walking, knock, and catch out. The boys often played soldier, perhaps resulting from their

Child with kite, location unknown, 1930s (Eudora Welty, photographer, Mississippi Department of Archives and History, Jackson)

awareness of the Mexican War. Additional outdoor play included snowballing, hunting, gymnastics, wrestling, swimming, and skating.

The relationship of play to Old South values was often clear as in the case of representational play or playacting, in which children acted small, real-life dramas or imitated everyday life. The dramatic elements of this play, such as in "playing" soldier, were analogous to social roles in antebellum society. Among the more affluent families of the Old South, games emphasized effort and skill, teaching children that outcomes of situations depended on the amount and quality of effort one expended.

Many historical and contemporary games of black children, on the other hand, are most notable for exhibiting an attitude of resistance and assertiveness on the part of the players. Older game songs that date from the days of slavery express an anger against slave masters. The following example of an old game song demonstrates resistance:

Way go, Lily
Way go, Lily
I'm going to rule my ruler
I'm going to rule my ruler
I'm going to rule him with a hickory
I'm going to rule him with a hickory

This song probably originated during slavery and is rarely heard now except in Charleston and Savannah. Blacks have used creative song games in "talking bad" to their oppressors since coming from Africa, allowing them to say what they needed to say without being perceived as a threat.

Another common African American children's game song, played by forming a ring, is "Little Sally Walker." One of a cycle of ring games with African roots, its lyrics encourage a child to "rise":

Little Sally Walker
Sitting in a saucer
Crying and a-weeping
Over all she has done

Rise Sally Rise
Wipe out your eyes
Fly to the east, Sally . . .

Contemporary games of black children show an inherited oral tradition and simultaneously engage in nonverbal behavior that involves body movement and gestures similar to playacting. Clapping games are popular and are primarily nonverbal. Most of the games are rhythmical and allow for improvisation.

Older game songs common along the Georgia and South Carolina coasts have been recorded by Bessie Jones and Bess Lomax Hawes in *Step It Down*. Jones is a black woman born in an area famed for its rich Gullah culture. The book reflects her efforts to preserve remnants of southern tradition and the African heritage. Many of these older game songs may still be heard in black communities and are often taught within organized play times in an effort to preserve cultural traditions. The renewed interest in the preservation of the multiethnic origins of America has stimulated educators to consider traditional games as an instrument for teaching about cultural uniqueness and historical events.

There is limited documentation of games indigenous to the South in the 20th century, and it is likely that southern children's play has become very much like that of other children in the United States. Changes in game preferences of American children were examined by Sutton-Smith and Rosenberg, who compared four studies on games over a 60-year period from 1896 to 1959. They found that formalized games, such as party games, ring games, acting games, singing games, and dialogue games, were becoming less important while imitative games and chasing games continued their popularity. This shift away from formalized games is especially significant in relation to the South, where games have been traditionally more decorous and formal than elsewhere in the country.

The uniquely southern aspects of children's games that remain represent traces of ethnic diversity within the dominant American culture and are most likely found within the poorer regions as well as among the larger minority groups. Awakened desire to cultivate multicultural heritage is acting as a stimulus to preserve some traditionally southern children's games as a unique folk art.

RACHEL D. ROBERTSON
Arizona State University

L. Minor Blackford, *Mine Eyes Have Seen the Glory* (1954); Ruth F. Bogdanoff and Elaine T. Dolch, *Young Children* (January 1979); Dickson D. Bruce Jr., *Southern Folklore Quarterly* 40 (1977); Jane Carson, *Colonial Virginians at Play* (1965); Bessie Jones and Bess Lomax Hawes, *Step It Down: Games, Plays, Songs, and Stories from the Afro-American Heritage* (1972); B. Sutton-Smith and Bruce G. Rosenberg, *Journal of American Folklore* (January–March 1961).

Civil War Reenactments

Each spring and summer thousands of white southerners don Confederate-style uniforms and civilian wear more or less appropriate to the mid-19th century and drive considerable distances to spend weekends reenacting the bloodiest conflict in American history. The phenomenon is not new, but it has grown considerably in terms of spectators and participants since the early 1990s. Major reenactments such as Gettysburg are hot tickets requiring advance purchase if one wants to catch a glimpse of hundreds of reenactors banging away at each other with Italian-made Springfields and Enfields. Such events reflect continuity and change in aspects of southern culture.

Reenactments emphasize the Lost Cause interpretation of the Old South and the Civil War. One Lost Cause image reinforced at reenactments is that of ill-clad but brave and chivalrous Confederates fighting bravely against overwhelming odds. Many Rebels wear uniforms with patches all over and carry Federal gear (haversack, canteen, cartridge, and cap boxes) almost exclusively, demonstrating that the Confederate government could not supply its poor troops. There is evidence to sustain such ideas and impressions, but like Lost Cause–era interpretations, they are romantic oversimplifications. The issue of slavery rarely, if ever, comes up because it would put a damper on the celebration.

Not surprisingly, with so many people interested in reenactments, vendors (booksellers, artists, sculptors, general souvenir dealers) are in abundance. Many tents display Confederate iconography. Artwork, offered for sale, depicts Confederate officers or celebrates particularly famous Rebel units but gives few renderings of northern officers or units. The Rebel flag is on sale everywhere, and baseball caps, T-shirts, key chains, and license plates emblazoned with the Army of Northern Virginia's battle flag are also readily available. These businesspeople understand very well that there is plenty of money to be made supplying white southerners with all sorts of goods celebrating the Confederacy.

Reenactments may suggest that white southerners remain trapped in ahistorical traditional beliefs about the Old South and the Confederacy, but subtle yet important changes from past ways are at work as well. For one thing, the Lost Cause generation romanticized the institution of slavery, which is not part of reenactments. In fact, Confederate units are generally very scrupulous about informing new members that their use of the battle flag is for historical purposes only and is in no way meant as a racial statement. Another significant change from the past is that earlier generations of white southerners harbored rather serious ill will toward northerners. Today there is a considerable amount of good-natured kidding among modern Yanks and Rebs but very little, if any, simmering bad blood over the war among southerners. In fact, many Confederates routinely spend weekends portraying Yankee soldiers—termed "to galvanize"—an act that would surely have made the Lost Cause generation of the late 19th century give a collective shudder.

Without a doubt, there is still an element in the region that enjoys indulging in romantic notions about the Confederacy and the Civil War, but it would be a hasty judgment to conclude that interest in the war and its mythology illustrates that southerners are "still fighting the war." Too many breaks with past generations can be found at reenactments to allow such a pat conclusion. Few romanticize slavery or lament the war's ultimate conclusion and fewer still are openly hostile toward northerners. So while modern white southerners may buy mountains of Confederate memorabilia at modern Civil War reenactments as a tangible expression of regional pride, their display means little more than that.

JAY GILLISPIE
Sampson Community College

Sam Hodges, *B-Four* (2000); Tony Horwitz, *Confederates in the Attic* (1998).

Cockfighting

The sport, or cultural performance, of cockfighting involves pitting evenly matched pairs of game fowl in competition, in the presence of wagering, often until at least one is dead or severely injured. As such, these events are part of a larger orbit of related sport or gamelike undertakings involving animal participation. In antiquity, such events may have been viewed as modes of mediation with the gods or methods of negotiating with unknown forces. Today, the identical behavior is more likely considered a social pollutant. All 50 states now ban cockfighting, Louisiana being the last state to enact such regulations, doing so in the first decade of this century.

Current theory presumes that the domestication of game fowl took place from wild stock in the Far East before the birth of Christ, and rapid distribution of the sport and the bird followed normal trade lines. Certainly the sport was known among the ancient Romans, for cockfighting and reading cock entrails was commonplace among the legionaries. According to travel narratives and other reportage, cockfighting was endemic throughout Europe, especially in the maritime nations, by the time of expansion to the New World. English and Spanish settlers alike imported the spirited bird to North America, for food and for its noteworthy contesting.

Cockfighting was widespread throughout North America by the early

1700s—laws to regulate the sport were among the first regulations enacted in the New England colonies in the 1600s. Poorly substantiated but hardly unlikely legend tells us that presidents Washington, Jackson, and Jefferson raised game fowl and that Abraham Lincoln's nickname, "Honest Abe," came from his fairness as a referee of cockfights.

In actual competition, gamecocks often use the bony spurs that grow naturally on the back of their legs as their primary weapons in bare-heel bouts. They are rigged out with small, generally tubular or pointed rodlike gaffs (occasionally called harpoons), or they may be fitted with sharp, strong knives. Cockfighters make the attachments from coral, turtle shell, stainless and other steels, space-age alloys cut from recycled turbine engine blades, or chemically treated chicken spurs—all designed to make competition even handed (or legged).

A specialist group within the fraternity of handmade knife craftsmen custom fabricates the blades; a further subspecialty exists in the "edgers," the people who sharpen the cockfight knives. These items are beautifully crafted, as if they constitute jewelry for miniature warriors.

As a form of play, cockfighting offers both a fundamental exit from the everydayness of the "real world" and a trope, or representation, of a community's social values. The animal breeders, owners, or trainers in these animal-surrogate sports tend to feel a strong affiliation with the gaming fowl. They see the cocks as representing the "stuff" of their culture: bravery, courage, honor, and related social markers. Breeders actively seek these qualities in their birds and even breed them for these attributes. Thus, some cockfighters will describe rearing birds for endurance, speed, or stamina; "training" them to bring out these particular qualities; and enacting elaborate programs of development or feeding to maximize the bird's individual potential. There can be no question that emotional connections to outcomes (entirely aside from wagering concerns) run deeply in these contests.

Although cockfighting has been very popular in the American South, the naive notion held by many that the sport is somehow uniquely "southern" or lowbrow and rural does not fit the historic record. For much of its arc of popularity, cockfighting was a middle-class, yeoman, or elite pastime, with great estates, popular pubs, and commercial sport houses playing host to these contests. (Some theorists suggest that today's orchestra pit is the residuum of previous theater designs with the cockpit in the center.) Although cockfighting was popular throughout the South, it was equally popular everywhere in the United States, the bird being well suited for the nation's diverse climates and foodways.

By the middle of the 19th century in the United States and much of Europe, activists and reformers were powerfully bent on eradicating many leisure events supposedly associated with the rough rural roots of working-class men. Tavern sports, such as ratting, badger and bull baiting, goose pulling, and cock-fighting (to say nothing of whoring, drinking, and brawling) fell under the baleful gander of bourgeois authority. The eradication that began in earnest in the late 1800s was completed about a century and a half later.

JON GRIFFIN DONLON
Tokai University, Japan

Jon Griffin Donlon, in *Encyclopedia of American Social Movements*, ed. Immanuel Ness (2002), *Mississippi Folklife* (Summer–Fall 1995), *Journal of Material Culture* (Summer 1993), *Play and Culture* 3 (1990); Alan Dundes, ed., *The Cockfight: A Casebook* (1994); Clifford Geertz, *The Interpretation of Cultures* (1973), *Daedalus* (Winter 1972); Johan Huizinga, *Homo Ludens: A Study of the Play Element in Culture* (1971); Ted Ownby, *Subduing Satan: Religion, Recreation, and Manhood in the Rural South, 1865–1920* (1990); Mark Schneider, *Theory and Society* (1987); Page Smith, Charles Page, and Charles Daniel, *The Chicken Book* (2000).

Debutantes

The social institution known as the debutante season is certainly not a peculiarly southern (or even American) phenomenon, but in the face of the turbulent 1960s and 1970s, it has exhibited more tenacity and vitality in Dixie than elsewhere in the United States or in Great Britain, where the custom began. A number of factors help explain the custom's popularity: the South's pride in its womanhood, a tendency to keep women on a pedestal, a conservative clinging to venerable institutions, social distinctions by status, and belief in a Cavalier heritage.

Although many societies, both primitive and advanced, have had their own rituals to signal the coming of age of men and women, England's Queen Elizabeth I supposedly began the custom of formal presentations of eligible young women at court. However, nearly three centuries later, Great Britain's young Queen Victoria, shortly after she married Prince Albert, gave the ritual much of its present form, when the daughters of the rising haute bourgeoisie of the Industrial Revolution began to be included in court presentations, along with those of nobility and gentry. A century later, yet another British queen, Elizabeth II, ended such events after the last presentations in March 1958.

The custom of debutante presentations spread across the Atlantic when America began to prosper during the late 19th-century Gilded Age. In New York, according to social historian Cleveland Amory, public presentations began in 1870 at Delmonico's. Dixon Wecter wrote 50 years ago how the costly rituals of debutante presentations symbolized the wealth of fathers. On the other hand, in the impoverished postwar South the custom displayed another dimension—emphasizing who had been well born before all was "gone with the wind." The criterion was necessarily not that of wealth but of the family's antebellum status and lineage.

At the turn of the 20th century the most exclusive of the southern debutante seasons was held in Charleston. The St. Cecilia Society began in 1737 as America's first concert society but abandoned that function by 1822 and became a purely social organization. This elite all-male society began to sponsor what has been termed "the ultimate debutante presentation in the South, if not the whole United States." It is so proper and exclusive that any local publicity about either the society or its ball is taboo.

In Montgomery, Ala., Lila Matthews was presented to society with a dance and collation at her parents' house in 1884. The 1900 Social Directory of Montgomery listed 33 debutantes, and the Montgomery Debutante Club began in the depths of the Depression in 1931. Today, young women of Montgomery society are presented at junior, senior, and debutante assemblies and at mystic society balls. Most notable of these are the New Year's Eve Ball given by the men of the Mystic Order of Revelry, the Mardi Gras Ball of the male Krewe of the Phantom Host, and the ball of the female Mystic Order of Minerva, where debutantes are presented in pastel Victorian court dress with plumes, trains, 18-button gloves, and fan bouquets. There are also presentations of military officers' daughters at Maxwell Air Force Base, and since 1970 Montgomery's black debutantes have been sponsored by the local chapter of the national black teachers' sorority of Phi Delta Kappa, founded in 1923.

In Mobile, where mystic societies in America began, the season's leading debutante is queen of Mardi Gras, and she and King Felix III salute merrymakers from the Athelstan Club. Each season's debutantes are presented first at the Camellia Ball at Thanksgiving time. In New Orleans, which is synonymous with Mardi Gras, debutantes reign over the predominantly all-male Krewe festivities and are presented at the Debutante Club and Les Debuts des Jeunes Filles de la Nouvelle Orleans and many private debut parties.

Space permits only a limited listing of the debutante balls in other southern cities. Moving down the Atlantic Seaboard, Baltimore has its Bachelors' Cotillion; Washington, D.C., has its Debutante Cotillion and Thanksgiving Ball; Richmond has the Bal du Bois in June at the Country Club of Virginia; and the all-male Norfolk German Society selects those who will come out in that city. Raleigh's Terpsichorean Club stages the North Carolina Debutante Cotillion,

Savannah features the Cotillion and Parents' Debutante Ball, Atlanta has its Halloween Ball at the Piedmont Driving Club, and Jacksonville has its Presentation Ball at the Florida Yacht Club.

In Birmingham, the Redstone Club Christmas Ball is at the Birmingham Country Club and the Beaux Arts Ball at the Mountain Brook Club. The Mississippi Debutante Ball is in Jackson, while the Delta Debutante Ball is at the Greenville Country Club. In Memphis, the Queen of Cotton Carnival reigns, and there is the ball at the Hunt and Polo Club. West of the Mississippi River at Texarkana there is the Cotillion Club Ball, at San Antonio the German Club Ball, and at Austin the Bachelors Cotillion. Dallas has its Idlewild Ball, where debutantes bow to the floor in all white at the beginning of the season and make their final bow at the Terpsichorean Ball in pastels.

CAMERON FREEMAN NAPIER
Montgomery, Alabama

D. Susan Barron, *Sunday New York Times Magazine* (15 January 1984); Stephen Birmingham, *The Right People: A Portrait of the American Social Establishment* (1968); Lisa Birnbach, ed., *The Official Preppy Handbook* (1980); Bethany Bultman, *Town and Country* (November 1977); Michaele Thurgood Haynes, *Dressing Up Debutantes: Pageantry and Glitz in Texas* (1998); Karal Ann Marling, *Debutante: Rites and Rituals of American Debdom* (2004); *Montgomery Advertiser* (6 February 1884, 4 November 1931, 15 April 1984); Cameron Freedman Napier, *Social Register Observer* (Summer 1998); Mary Ann Neeley, *Alabama Review* (April 1979); *New York Times* (19 March 1958, 21 March 1958); Dixon Wecter, *The Saga of American Society: A Record of Social Aspiration, 1607–1937* (1937).

Drinking

The drinking habits of southerners have oft been the subject of frequent and colorful observation, likely best captured by the ubiquitously cited southern commentator W. J. Cash, who wrote that a southern man's greatest aspiration is "to stand on his head in a bar, to toss down a pint of raw whisky in a gulp, to fiddle and dance all night." Though certainly not an activity exclusive to the southern states, drinking has long continued to play a central role in the cultural and recreational life of the South. The image of the planter casually sipping a cool julep or Faulkner pensively searching a glass of bourbon for inspiration permeates the southern consciousness; while, if asked, many a southerner would likely assert that the pastimes listed in this volume all improve with the addition of an ice-cold beer.

The origins of the alcoholic South date to the early colonial period, where the confluence of frontier loneliness and an abundance of easily distilled grain bred a culture in which alcohol was consumed at a rate hardly imaginable by modern standards. By 1830, on average, Americans were drinking nearly four gallons of pure alcohol annually, with the majority of this ingurgitation concentrated in the adult male population. Southern men relied on camaraderie and consumption to ease the burdens of frontier life, taking any available opportunity to liberally imbibe in both. Drink possessed an egalitarian quality and offered a medium to smooth social tensions and soothe the hard-pressed soul. Thus, at many southern social gatherings, "barbecue law" held sway, compelling any man attending to drink to intoxication, with unconsciousness as the only recourse of the unwilling. Drinking in this manner signified virility and validated masculine bonds of friendship and solidarity. Toast making was also a practice common to both formal and informal settings, offering an occasion for one-upmanship in both eloquence of speech and capacity to consume. For instance, upon his visit to Charleston, S.C., in May of 1791, President George Washington presided over a banquet where 18 separate toasts were drunk, including homages to the useful arts of peace, Louis XVI, and the lady of the president, all of which were recorded for public consumption in the next week's paper.

This egalitarian nature of drink—all men, they say, become equal before the bottle—fit snuggly within the South's emerging democratic political system. Distribution of alcohol brought and perhaps bought votes, as Washington knew well, compelling the Virginian to spend more than 38 pounds sterling on "brandy, rum, cyder, strong beer, and wine" to win his seat in the House of Burgesses. Drinking was not limited to the election process either, with the judiciary creating its own opportunities for impassioned consumption; throughout the South, both before and after the Civil War, court days served as a prime occasion for spirited male drinking. Across the region's vast rural landscape, southern court judges traveled from county seat to county seat, trying civil and criminal cases that had arisen since their previous visit. These court days drew crowds of men from the surrounding countryside, some looking to pursue redress, others looking for opportunities for trade, while still others attended for the mere spectacle. Almost all, though, intended to drink. Thus, court week created an outlet for the monotony of farm life, and many southern men indulged heavily in town's most popular recreation, relieving the tension from business dealings, steeling themselves for an upcoming trial, or simply taking a welcome rest from backbreaking agricultural labor.

Although drinking in the early South appears to be the exclusive milieu of white men, other sections of southern society also sought recreation and relief in the whiskey bottle. In the antebellum era, slaves, too, participated in the drinking culture, albeit in a manner limited by their state of bondage. The Christmas holiday often entailed an extended break period during which masters, in a crafted display of paternalism, bestowed gifts on their slaves. Alcohol proved especially useful, giving slaves a respite from a year of labor and a chance to recharge for the next year of service. Additionally, southern grog shops and roadside taverns offered slaves a place to spend wages earned from extra work, usually on colorfully named varieties of "bust-head" whiskey. In these venues, blacks and poor whites often interacted over a tankard and a card table, if not in a display of egalitarianism, perhaps in companionship bred of repression. These interactions were less than pleasing to elite whites, who saw black drunkenness as a threat to order—a fear that remained strong following the Civil War. Alcohol was believed to enflame black lust, leading to sexual assaults on white women. This fear held significant power, leading rioters in Atlanta, acting on falsified rumors, to focus much of their wrath on drinking establishments frequented by African American customers, and ultimately strengthening the statewide push for prohibition.

Yet, whereas black men, by virtue of their gender, attained limited access to public drinking culture, women in the South did not have many opportunities to drink recreationally before the modern era. Drinking fell squarely in the masculine realm, and Victorian values of propriety and temperance strictly curtailed the social acceptability of female consumption. Still, women were able to imbibe in the form of elixirs and tonics, nominally intended to aid digestion or to perform some other medicinal purpose. These activities, though, were firmly relegated to the home, and in public much of women's relation to southern drinking occurred within the temperance movement. Weak before the Civil War because of its ties to abolition, temperance, and specifically the Woman's Christian Temperance Union (WCTU), gained significant ground in the latter half of the 19th century. Temperance unionism even crossed racial boundaries, as in North Carolina, where black and white chapters of the WCTU worked together to support statewide prohibition. As the moral bedrocks of their respective families, white and black women sought to curtail recreational, and perhaps excessive, male drinking and to revitalize evangelical culture. These movements succeeded, leading to both state and national prohibition by the early 20th century, although they were not able to completely stamp out alcohol consumption.

Following the repeal of prohibition and the postwar economic reinvigoration, southerners, like most Americans, reembraced drinking culture, albeit in new modes dictated by the broader shifts taking place in both American and southern society. Scholar Darren Grem notes that "rising wages, increased leisure time, increased college enrollment, the popularity of automobiles, and the migration from farm to town combined to create a population of drinkers with money and time to spend on a Saturday actively forgetting about the strictures of Sunday morning." The revitalized southern alcohol culture was far more inclusive than the white-man-only customs that had prevailed to that point. Nightclubs, juke joints, dance halls, and fraternity parties became sites where men and women, black and white, could experience new and vibrant opportunities for consumption, while alcohol assumed a more prominent role in southern recreation. In the 20th century's middle decades, clubs and bars offered African Americans sites of community solidarity, where all classes could join together and seek release from hard times through music, dance, and drink. At the same time, southern whites' entertainment tended to stratify along class lines, but now women as well as men were able to enjoy a Saturday night out, mingling at the fraternity house or dancing all night at the local honky-tonk.

More recently, southern drinking has become intertwined with community celebration and public spectacle, such that events commemorating regional or ethnic identity stand out as prime opportunities for spirited communal imbibing. Mardi Gras along the Gulf Coast, celebrating the region's French-Creole heritage, and St. Patrick's Day in Savannah, Ga., commemorating the city's Irish roots, both entreat revelers with fetes, parades, and copious bacchanalian street drinking. Although Savannah's city government ceased dying the Savannah River green several years ago, the knowledgeable reveler will still find green beer on tap in many of the city's overcrowded watering holes. Southern collegiate football provides a similar venue for mass consumption, playing host to decadent displays of pomp and state pride, while offering tailgaters hours of pre- and postgame food and drink. The annual contest between the University of Georgia and the University of Florida, dubbed the World's Largest Outdoor Cocktail Party and attended by tens of thousands of fans ready to bleed red-and-black or orange-and-blue for their teams, and vicariously their states, exemplifies sports ritual as a venue for drinking.

Finally, southern entertaining, of which tailgating represents one of the more bountiful examples, has from the earliest days demanded that a guest's every whim be met and every thirst be quenched. Whether during the month-long visits common to the 18th and 19th centuries, or at modern cocktail parties, barbecues, and debutante balls, southern hospitality's myth and legend are undergirded by the expectation of lavish gaiety, of which drinking now plays a significant part. Consequently, experts on the subject from Paula Deen to

Southern Living Magazine expose their audiences to myriad colorful and sumptuous beverages that celebrate the South; whether an Open-House Punch for the sweltering summer days or a Tennessee Hot Chocolate for the cool Appalachian nights, all are intended to warm the spirit in a distinctly southern manner—which they succeed in doing, if none so well as the region's legendary bourbon, preferably neat.

SEAN VANATTA
University of Georgia

Ted Ownby, *Subduing Satan: Religion, Recreation, and Manhood in the Rural South, 1865–1920* (1990); Jeff Forret, *Race Relations on the Margins: Slaves and Poor Whites in the Antebellum Southern Countryside* (2006); Darren Grem, *Southern Historian* (Spring 2006); Thomas R. Pegram, *Battling Demon Rum: The Struggle for a Dry America, 1800–1933* (1998); Joe Gray Taylor, *Eating, Drinking, and Visiting in the South: An Informal History* (1982).

Fairs

"Step right up! You won't believe your eyes!" Such cries of midway carnies have rung out in the South at state, county, and local fairs, accompanying animal and homemaking exhibitions and a variety of competitions. Southern fairs—like all fairs—have roots in primitive festivities that focused on religious celebrations and bartering. In the Middle Ages, fairs were well-established trade mechanisms, evolving by the 1800s toward the grand-scale educational and commercial expositions known as world's fairs. Evolving also in the 1800s in the United States were the agricultural fairs, with their prizes and competitive displays, which most strongly shaped the nature and growth of fairs in the South.

Merging agricultural society exhibitions and traveling carnivals, southern fairs began as mechanisms for promotion of agricultural societies. Planters' clubs formed in the 18th century for discussion of agricultural problems and stimulation of farm improvements. In 1810 Elkanah Watson organized in Massachusetts the nation's first agricultural fair, and the tradition of annual fairs spread quickly in the eastern seaboard states and more slowly into the South. During the 1840s and 1850s fairs in the livestock states of Kentucky, Tennessee, and Missouri prospered, and by the late 1850s to 1860s most of the southern states boasted annual state fairs. So popular and successful were the fairs that many of the sponsoring agricultural societies—increasingly organized on a statewide basis—purchased permanent fairgrounds and equipment. Georgia's fair in Macon in 1831 stands out as one of the earliest in the Deep South, where fairs were apparently fewer in number than in such states as Virginia and the

Child eating cotton candy at the annual Cotton Carnival, Memphis, Tenn., 1940 (Marion Post Wolcott, photographer, Library of Congress [LC-UCF-33-30905-M3], Washington, D.C.)

Carolinas. In most southern states the legislatures readily supported the agricultural societies and fair associations through allocation of state funds; both the societies and fairs promoted commerce and the planters' interests. Businesses and private individuals also offered support.

Fairs have always lured crowds with the exotic, the new, the exciting. Southern farmers and planters in the early to mid-1800s perused the newly imported Cashmere goats and Berkshire hogs in the exhibition stalls, while their children gawked at the two-headed snakes and miniature horses in the sideshows. Fairs served as important mechanisms for transmission of knowledge about improved breeds of domestic animals and innovations in farm machinery. Not only did farmers learn of improvements through local and state fairs; southerners garnered international recognition at the world's fair level, as did one Tennessee livestock baron with his blue-ribbon Saxony sheep at the London World's Fair in 1851.

The South has hosted its share of large expositions. Eight regional expositions, planned mainly to promote cotton and other southern products, had been held in the South by 1907. The Atlanta World's Fair and Great International Exposition in 1881 attracted some 225,000 people and received considerable financial backing from northerners. In 1883 Louisville's Southern Exposition drew 375,000 people and trumpeted its 15 acres of exhibit floor space. The federal government earmarked approximately $1.3 million in loans and contributions for the New Orleans World's Industrial and Cotton Centennial Exposition (1884–86), which highlighted the South's industrial prospects. Other successful expositions followed. Despite the economic panic and depression in 1893, Atlanta launched the Cotton States and International Exposition and attracted more than 1.2 million attendees. South American and European countries as well as a variety of states contributed buildings and displays. Booker T. Washington played a prominent role in the exposition's efforts to promote racial reconciliation.

More recently, San Antonio, Tex., dazzled the world in 1968 with Hemis-Fair, an international exposition celebrating the city's 250th anniversary. With a theme of "The Confluence of Civilizations in the Americas," this world's fair contained on its 92.6 acres, among other things, a 622-foot-high observation tower, a multimillion-dollar pavilion, a mile-long lagoon, and a mini monorail train. Twenty-two countries and 19 private corporations participated as exhibitors, and Texas's colorful, multiethnic heritage was the focus of several key exhibits. Knoxville, Tenn., served as the South's next world's fair host in 1982. Congruent with the theme "Energy Turns the World," the Sunsphere, a 266-foot-high tower topped by a restaurant and observation decks, punctuated the skyline and rivaled the six-story, cantilevered, prismlike U.S. Pavilion for attention. In addition to major exhibitions by corporations and foreign nations (most notably the People's Republic of China), the fair featured a variety of shows and displays heralding the culture of the state and the region: a Tennessee music revue, the Stokely Folk Life Festival with southern Appalachian musicians and craftspersons, and a two-barge exhibition on the history of the Tennessee Valley Authority.

Just two years later New Orleans hosted the Louisiana World Exhibition, whose theme was "The World of Rivers: Fresh Water as a Source of Life." The 84-acre site contained a 2,300-foot collage, the Wonder Wall, plus a maze of streams and other water conduits. Displays ranged from an exhibition of Vatican art treasures to a full-scale oil rig. Local flavor on a large scale appeared in the form of jazz and Cajun musical performances, twice-a-day Mardi Gras parades, boat parades on the Mississippi River, and the Louisiana/Gulf South Folklife Festival. Both the Knoxville and New Orleans fairs suffered from disappointingly low attendance and major financial problems, coloring the prospects for the 1992 Miami World's Fair.

To most southerners, though, the character of the fair is embodied in the sights, sounds, and smells of the state, county, or local fair. Usually held in September or October, each state fair is held in one of the larger cities, such as Birmingham, Ala., or Raleigh, N.C. Especially in years past, the location allowed for many rural children's first trip to a big city and for many young city dwellers' first contacts with farm animals. Showmanship, competition, recreation, education, social exchange—all have been inextricably entwined in the history of southern fairs. Exhibitions of prize livestock and displays of award-winning jams and pies stand a room or a building away from schoolchildren's science fair entries and artwork. Government agencies' demonstrations show the newest developments in space technology or flood control, and private enterprises promote their wares and distribute literature. Just yards away beckons the other world of the fair—the midway.

Once providing entertainment in the form of horse races, state and county fairs became dependent upon the traveling carnivals that proliferated after the Chicago World's Columbian Exposition in 1893. Within a short time many fairgoers felt that the midway carnival was the heart of a fair. The heyday of the carnival business was in the 1920s, and freak shows were common sideshow entertainment in the 1930s and 1940s. Images of the midways in the 1920s to the 1940s converge with those of today's midways: gaudily and scantily clad women doing a striptease to blaring, bawdy music; carnies shouting "test your skill and win the prize" from booth after booth lined with cheap trinkets and brightly colored stuffed animals; monkeys racing on tiny motorcycles; a tattooed man turning to display a body covered with lines and pictures; children laughing and screaming as they meander through the house of mirrors; teenagers boasting of five turns on the scariest amusement ride; grownups clamoring to lift baubles out of a bin using a toy earth mover. Eudora Welty celebrates these worlds through her photographs of country fairs and in her short story "The Petrified Man."

The excitement of being free of usual social constraints for a few evenings continues to have appeal—if not full approval from the community. Church and civic groups have long protested the lewd shows and gambling practices in carnivals. During the past several decades, northern states cracked down through both legislation and enforcement on gambling and other illegal enterprises at fair carnivals, but southern states were somewhat slower to act and have had the reputation for having local authorities more willing to take bribes to overlook illegalities. For this and other reasons, certain images are frequently associated with southern fairs: the "rube," or country bumpkin, who gets fleeced, and the hotheaded brawler infuriated by losses in rigged carnival games. Although tighter policing now prevails, a certain amount of rigging persists and is considered by some to be part of the risqué character of the fair. The midway dazzle increasingly accompanies performances of musical stars, often country singers, and special events such as car races or tractor pulls.

County fairs often try to emulate the offerings of the state fairs. At county fairs, however, more local color is evident in the activities, the foods, and the participants. Alongside common fair foods such as hot dogs, cotton candy, and popcorn, fairgoers often find special treats, such as hickory-smoked barbecue, peanut brittle, and fried pork rinds. Many county fairs host a local beauty pageant and competitive activities for local youth, often members of 4-H clubs. The Neshoba County Fair in Philadelphia, Miss., is an unusual but excellent example of down-home southern atmosphere at the county level. About 12,000 people descend on Philadelphia and pack into cabins built for the fair and passed down through generations. The 70,000-plus additional daytime fairgoers hear local and state politicians engaged in old-time stump speaking. Horse races, parties, contests, and a carnival midway offer excitement; but a different revelry marks the nightlong songfests, prayer and memorial services, and the hours of play and visiting for scattered family members drawn together for the annual event. Although many county fairs lack the permanent structuring of the Neshoba County Fair and more closely mimic the state fairs, most boast distinctive local touches.

Outstanding among smaller southern fairs are various American Indian celebrations, such as the Cherokee Fall Festival at Scottsboro, Ala., and the Choctaw Indian Fair in Philadelphia, Miss. Traditional American Indian dances, crafts, games, and foods highlight the festivities. Growing in popularity at the local level are festivals with many features of fairs. Various festivals celebrate the European heritage of area residents, as with the Scottish Festival and Highland Games at Stone Mountain, Ga.; the Mexican Heritage Fiesta in Port Arthur, Tex.; and the British Faire in Mobile, Ala. Native products are the focus of countless festivals; for example, the Seafood Festival in Cedar Key, Fla.; the Tobacco Festival in Bloomfield and the Wool Festival in Falmouth, Ky.; the Brushy Mountain Apple Festival in North Wilkesboro, N.C.; the Pumpkin Festival in Pumpkintown, S.C.; and the Sorghum Festival in Springville, Ala. Of note, too, are the festivals and contests centered on southern pastimes, such as the Athens, Ala., Tennessee Valley Oldtime Fiddler's Contest; the Raleigh, N.C., National Tobacco Spitting Contest; the Yellville, Ark., National Wild Turkey Calling Contest and Turkey Trot; the Buford, Ga., Masters Invitational Clogging Hoedown; the Whigham, Ga., Rattlesnake Roundup; and the Jonesborough, Tenn., National Storytelling Festival. And then there are festivals that are focused on regional music, food, and identity, which include Hillbilly Days in Pikeville, Ky.; the Crawfish Festival in Breaux Bridge, La.; the King Biscuit/Arkansas Blues and Heritage Festival in Helena, Ark.; Mayberry Days in Mount Airy, N.C.; various barbecue and catfish festivals; and innumerable other festivals, small and large, based on the blues, zydeco, jazz, and mountain music. Fairs, carnivals, and festivals thrive at all levels in the South, and most actively promote the unique heritage and character of the region.

SHARON A. SHARP
University of Mississippi

Paul Richard Beezley, "Exhibiting Visions of a New South: Mississippi and the World's Fairs, 1884–1904" (Ph.D. dissertation, University of Mississippi, 1999); Rodger Lyle Brown, *Ghost Dancing on the Cracker Circuit: The Culture of Festivals in the American South* (1997); Theodore M. Dembroski, *Journal of Popular Culture* (Winter 1973); Lewis C. Gray, *History of Agriculture in the Southern United States to 1860*, 2 vols. (1933); Melton A. McLaurin, *North Carolina Historical Review* (Summer 1982); Wayne C. Neely, *The Agricultural Fair* (1935); *Newsweek* (5 November 1984); Carolyn B. Patterson, *National Geographic* (June 1980); *Southern Living* (May 1982); Don B. Wilmeth, *Variety Entertainment and Outdoor Amusements: A Reference Guide* (1982); Pat Zajac, *Southern Living* (May 1984).

Family Reunions

"Next week be the fourth of July and us plan a big family reunion outdoors here at my house," says Celie, the main character in Alice Walker's *The Color Purple*. On the day of the reunion family members analyze the custom this way: "'Why us always have family reunion on July 4th,' say Henrietta, mouth poke out, full of complaint. 'It so hot.'" . . . "'White people busy celebrating they independence from England July 4th,' say Harpo, 'so most black folks don't have to work. Us can spend the day celebrating each other.'" Among the other attendees are two women who sip lemonade and make potato salad, noting that barbecue was a favorite food for them even while they were in Africa. The reunion day is especially joyful for the two women, who had been thought lost until their appearance at the reunion, where they are reunited with Celie and the other family members.

Southern family reunions are characteristic of extended and elaborated families, who plan the occasions around celebration, abundant good food, shared reunion responsibilities, simple recreational activities, and, above all, talk.

Although summer is the most popular season and the Fourth of July a popular date for family reunions for both black and white southern families, family reunions can happen at any time. Some families have them annually, others have them on a schedule best described as "every so often," and still others have them only once or twice in a generation's lifetime, depending on some member's initiative in getting the reunion organized.

Like the indefinite date for family reunions, there is an inexactness as to who constitutes "family" for each gathering. Some families invite only the descendants of a given couple and those descendants' spouses and children. Others invite the eldest couple's brothers and sisters and their children plus in-laws and some of the in-laws' relatives. Some gather households that have only a vague bond of kinship—those who are "like family" because of strong friendships. There is inevitably a logic of kinship and affection to each family reunion, and such a party is hard indeed to crash.

The impetus for a family reunion, if it is not an annually scheduled event, may be a late-decade birthday party for one family member, a holiday, a wedding anniversary, or the celebration of an achievement such as paying off a home mortgage. Sometimes a family holds a reunion for a homecoming of one of its members, as in the case of Eudora Welty's novel *Losing Battles*, which is a family reunion story focused around the day a son and husband return from a stay at Parchman, the Mississippi state prison.

Families often gather in someone's home, though summer picnic versions are commonly held in state or city parks. Motels, hotels, or restaurants host them, as do clubhouses or community centers, but by far the most popular settings after homes are churches. "Dinner-on-the-grounds" in the churchyard, with food burdening tablecloth-covered makeshift tables set on sawhorses, is a happy memory of family reunions in the minds of many southerners.

The occasion for catching up on the relatives' news and gossip, perhaps for transacting a little family business, for settling or even stirring up family disputes, a time for generally getting in touch again, a family reunion in the South usually has no program. There might be an occasional game or swim or boat ride, but the main activities are conversation and eating. The time span may be overnight or even several days, but it is most frequently only over one meal.

The food might be barbecue with baked beans and coleslaw or fried fish with hush puppies, fried potatoes, and a salad. A restaurant meal might be ordered, but in a great many cases family reunion food is a large and generous potluck dinner where each participating household brings versions of its best offerings of food and drink—fried chicken, ham, meat casseroles, rice dishes, cooked garden vegetables, fresh raw vegetables, potato salad, gelatin salad, seafood salad, homemade rolls and breads, cakes, pies, cookies, jams, preserves, pickles, watermelons, iced tea, and lemonade. A time for eating, conversing, and sharing each other's company, a southern family reunion is a special occasion for reaffirming family ties.

GAYLE GRAHAM YATES
University of Minnesota

Alice Walker, *The Color Purple* (1982); Eudora Welty, *Losing Battles* (1970).

Festivals

The southern festival of today is the direct descendant of the camp meeting and political barbecue, the Saturday night dance and Sunday's "all-day meeting and dinner-on-the-ground." Those were the gatherings that gave southerners the chance to lay aside the plow and pick up the fiddle. Although some fairs and festivals date to those times, most arose in the decades after World War II, when southerners were more educated, better traveled, and one generation removed from the cotton field. The festivals southerners initiated then, and attend today, reflect either that new urbane sophistication or the heritage of the rural past. Some festivals have brought the region's predominant black and white populations together, but many festivals remain rooted in separate racial and ethnic cultures. The new celebrations of Latino festivals represent dramatic changes in the contemporary South.

Each June in South Carolina, two celebrations, only 80 miles apart in distance but a world apart in content, demonstrate southern traditions. While thousands gather in Charleston for Spoleto Festival with its outpouring of fine arts, thousands of others fill the streets of tiny Hampton for the town's watermelon festival, now more than 60 years old. From late May through June, Spoleto Festival, held in Charleston since 1977, may offer a playwright's world premiere, a New York choreographer's newest creation, or an orchestra's concert of classical music. Celebrants in Hampton, meanwhile, are listening to gospel music and dancing to country bands, picking among the goods of an arts and crafts fair, watching a parade led by a beauty queen, and, most of all, feasting on the traditional southern delicacy. It is not unlikely that some in Charleston, after getting their fill of Balanchine and Bach, hop in their car and gorge on watermelon a weekend or so later in Hampton. If many southerners hunger for fine arts today, just as many yearn for the tidbits of their inheritance.

Southern festivals provide both. The themes of most small-town festivals center on some aspect of their heritage or livelihood. Even in many urban festivals focusing on the fine arts, there are southern features. Spoleto Festival often includes such Dixie-nurtured music forms as jazz and blues, country, and soul and gospel. So does Memphis in May, a monthlong celebration that combines its regional customs of music and food (barbecue) with the cultural characteristics of a different country each year. Heritage Weekends in Louisville, Ky., feature the arts, crafts, food, costumes, and music of Old World ethnic groups that settled in the city.

Southern customs, traditions, and products are most often extolled in the small-town festival. If there is a vegetable that ripens in fall, a plant that blooms in spring, an animal that grazes in pastures, or a food served on local tables, some community has found a way to praise it. Gilmer, Tex., honors the yam; Dothan, Ala., the peanut; Tonitown, Ark., the grape. Towns and cities from Palestine, Tex., to Norfolk, Va., celebrate the arrival of spring in azalea and dogwood festivals. Food festivals often combine cookery with contests. At the Oyster Festival in Leonardtown, Md., the champion of the oyster-shucking contest goes on to international competition. Crawfish races highlight the biannual salute to the local crustacean in Breaux Bridge, La.

Some small-town festivals have helped to preserve a slice of the southern past. In mule festivals, towns such as Columbia, Tenn., Benson, N.C., and Calvary, Ga., trot out the legendary but endangered species that plowed farms, scraped out roads, and built river levees. At these gatherings, younger generations hear for the first time words that once sprinkled southern conversation:

jack and jenny, hames and singletree, or what it means to "bust the middles" or "lay by a crop."

Although the themes of small-town festivals vary widely, they differ little in form and function. Salley, S.C., may be the only town that honors chitterlings, but its Chitlin' Strut, held one November day malodorous from the aroma of five tons of frying chitterlings, incorporates most all the earmarks of a small-town festival. Along with a lunch of chitlins, gobbled with gusto or tossed away after one nibble, celebrants pick among the tacky and tasteful offerings of the ubiquitous arts and crafts display, listen to country music, and watch a parade led by Miss Chitlin' Strut. Some don T-shirts that may read "I got the guts to strut" or "Chitlin Fever—Catch it!," then enter the chitlin' strut contest. The freestyle choreography many create is often determined by the amount of whiskey surreptitiously spiking their soft drinks.

Although most festivals are used for boosterism or fund raising, they nevertheless offer townspeople a chance to get together and renew acquaintances, a by-product of earlier events when the first southerners gathered in a pioneer forest clearing to help a neighbor raise a new barn.

To renew family and friendship ties is still the main reason residents and former residents of Neshoba County, Miss., have assembled faithfully each year since 1889 in the laying-by time of late July. At the Neshoba County Fair near Philadelphia, families live for a week, many in rude cabins their ancestors built. There is harness racing, a carnival midway, and lots of "visiting around," preaching, and political speechmaking at the open-air Founders Pavilion, with its sawdust floor and wooden benches. *National Geographic* described the fair as a place to "join in tribal rites of fellowship" where "a whole way of life finds affirmation." By the 1970s the pavilion provided the last hurrah for old-time southern politicians. As late as 1979 former Mississippi governor Ross Barnett brought the house down with his stump-speaking, gallus-snapping, out-seg-your-opponent brand of rhetoric from a bygone era. The transition to a new South was seen when Ronald Reagan chose the fair as the place to begin his 1980 presidential campaign, which targeted white southerners as a major part of his southern strategy against a native son. The fair has remained mostly a celebration of white southern traditions.

Fairgoers today arrive by Chevrolet instead of mule and wagon, but transportation is about the only ingredient of the fair that has changed since its 19th-century beginning. Certainly, the weather is the same, as afternoon rainstorms turn red dirt to mud, and the white heat of midday sun forces fairgoers to the shade of porches. "If you can't take the heat, mud, and dirt, you oughta stay home," says one fairgoer. But at Neshoba County Fair, as in most southern festivals, few stay at home. Festivals offer them a chance to lay aside their work (the laptop computer now, if no longer the plow); to renew friendships with acquaintances; and, in most cases, to pay homage to a slice of southern life that may be long past.

The increasing numbers of Latinos in the South since the 1990s has introduced a new calendar of festivals, many of them centered around Roman Catholic feast days. The contemporary South celebrates the Latino heritage of its new citizens, for example, through Our Lady of Guadeloupe Day (December 12). In one North Carolina community, Catholic churches stage a procession through the town square and around the Confederate monument, worship at a Holy Mass, and feast on a traditional meal of pork, tortillas, and beans.

GARY D. FORD
Southern Living

Alice M. Geffen and Carole Berglie, *Southern Exposure* (January–February 1986); Jane M. Hatch, *The American Book of Days* (3rd ed., 1978); Carolyn Bennett Patterson, *National Geographic* (June 1980); Beverly J. Stoeltje, in *Handbook of American Folklore*, ed. Richard M. Dorson (1983); Paul Wasserman and Esther Herman, eds., *Festivals Sourcebook: A Reference Guide to Fairs, Festivals, and Celebrations* (1977); Trent Watts, *Southern Cultures* (Summer 2002); David E. Whisnant, *All That Is Native and Fine: The Politics of Culture in an American Region* (1983); William Wiggins, in *Discovering Afro-America*, ed. Roger D. Abrahams and John F. Szwed (1975), *Prospects* 5 (1979).

Festivals, Music

In the South, music and merriment go hand in hand. From huge events that showcase scores of national and world artists like Merlefest in Wilkesboro, N.C., to smaller local affairs like Willie King's Freedom Creek Blues Festival in Pickens County, Ala., southern music festivals offer a fantastic living example of cultural integration, tradition making, and recreation in the South.

Each year, many festivals occur that focus on distinct genres or styles. Two fantastic examples are the Ole Time Fiddlers and Bluegrass Festival held every spring in Union Grove, N.C., and the annual Mississippi Delta Blues and Heritage Festival of Greenville, Miss. Festivals of this type stress specific roots, playing styles, and the contributions of certain artists. By doing so, they function as acts of preservation and usually display idealized characteristics of singular southern regions such as Appalachia or the Mississippi Delta. Other southern music festivals while still maintaining ties to traditional roots include artists from more diverse backgrounds. For example, the New Orleans Jazz and Heritage Festival offers bands that play zydeco, blues, Dixieland, rock and roll, hip-hop, gospel, big band, jazz, and numerous other styles. Similarly, the lineup at Merlefest includes artists who play bluegrass, gospel, old time, alternative country, folk, blues, and a host of other less readily identifiable styles often labeled as Americana. Large multigenre festivals evidence the interrelatedness of all southern music and the vast array of regional and cultural groups it sprang from.

Southern music festivals bring together elements from several centuries of public music making in the South. These range from 19th-century "hush harbor" slave spirituals to the lilting sentimentality of jazz funerals to the powerful, socially conscious gospel of civil rights movement marches. Likewise, festivals echo the sounds of all-day singings with dinner on the grounds, square dances, and political rallies of the early 1900s, and commercial ventures like the Grand Ole Opry. Festival music bespeaks the contributions of both folk and commercial artists. The fame of many folk musicians never spread outside their community. Yet their legacy lives today as part of a tradition that reached the festival through later generations of musicians dedicated to authentic reproduction of traditional styles. Commercial influences on the southern music festival range from the styles of Charlie Patton and Charlie Poole to Bill Monroe, Muddy Waters, and Dewey Balfa to Elvis Presley and Chuck Berry. Ultimately, southern music festivals offer something from most every musical venue in the South. The music hails from the porch, yard, and community, the phonograph record and radio, early concerts at schoolhouses and fairgrounds, and on to the modern festival stage.

One of the southern music festivals with a deep history is the fiddle contest. Fiddle contests represent a rich tradition that dates back at least to Hanover County, Va., in the 1730s. The tradition continues to this day in contests such as the Old Time Fiddlers Convention in Galax, Va., and the Tennessee Valley Old Time Fiddlers Convention in Athens, Ala. Fiddle contests are formal social events centered on instrumental competition. They operate like a musical version of the Olympic Games. From within a set of predetermined criteria, fiddlers choose selections that showcase their instrumental virtuosity. They perform the pieces for an audience and a panel of judges. The judges then rank the contestants on their performance, sometimes taking audience response into account as well. Similar, at least in terms of age, to the fiddle contests are religious singing conventions. Since before the Civil War, groups have convened at churches and public meetinghouses to participate in and be entertained by the singing of Christian hymns from shape-note hymnals. Early gatherings like the fiddle contests and singing conventions evidence traditional practices that, with the help of festival promoters, eventually coalesced into the modern southern music festival.

The modern southern music festival began after World War II at a time when the roots consciousness of the WPA era and industrial-age technological advances blended with postwar economic changes and a renewed regional, social, cultural, and racial awareness spurred by phenomena such as the folk revival and the civil rights movement. As the South progressed, the music festival developed as a means for southerners to express their identity. As festivals repeated, they became invented traditions that served to enforce the component attributes of particular groups' identities. Often, these identities and their representative festivals were anomalies in that they stressed preindustrial folk or rural phenomena like agrarian themes or traditional playing styles through the use of sophisticated modern inventions such as the public address system, dynamic microphone, and electric instruments. The southern music festival, from its genesis, represented the tension between the idealized folk solidarity of the preindustrial South with its enforced racial, social, and economic divisions and the homogenization, commercialization, Americanization, and evolving racial and social climate of the modern South.

The modern festival evidences the precarious balance between reality and southerner's idealized perceptions of the past, present, and future. A clear example is the bluegrass festival. Carlton Haney held one of the first official bluegrass festivals in 1965 near Roanoke, Va. Haney, aided by Ralph Rinzler of Smithsonian Folkways, organized the festival in a manner that allowed it to generate a bluegrass oral history by including a staged event called the Bluegrass Story. The Bluegrass Story traced the creation and evolution of bluegrass music through the career of Bill Monroe. This served to authenticate bluegrass music historically by suggesting an idealized relationship between Monroe, bluegrass music, and preexisting traditional phenomena. The story proclaimed Monroe carried on older traditions while simultaneously functioning as the progenitor of a new tradition. Likewise, it brought the audience into the bluegrass oral tradition by simulating a personal relationship with Monroe and by offering a story for the audience to pass on. The Bluegrass Story, along with the jam session community that developed in the parking lot and campground, helped create communal bonds and a type of bluegrass language and etiquette between festival-goers based on the invented bluegrass tradition. Ultimately, the bluegrass tradition and its festival evidenced a desire on the part of a certain element of bluegrass musicians, fans, historians, and promoters to control the past, or the way people remembered the music, and the future, by attempting to implement and maintain a form of bluegrass orthodoxy. Today, bluegrass music, though steeped in myth, tradition, and controversy over stylistic variations and authenticity, is very much alive largely because of the festival.

The southern music festival is also inextricably tied to the process of cultural change. Today, some festivals function as celebrations of cultural integration. For the past several years, Manchester, Tenn., has hosted the Bonaroo Festival, which presents music ranging from the classic bluegrass of the Del McCoury Band to the experimental style and avant-garde theatrics of the Oklahoma band the Flaming Lips. Though Bonaroo occurs well below the Mason Dixon, its contemporary theme, which can be approximated as a combination of Woodstock and Burning Man, draws bands and fans from just about everywhere. In a sense, southern music festivals like Bonaroo evidence a modern South, no longer an antiquated "other" in America, but a rich, ever-evolving amalgamation where the limitations of the past have been cast aside for an idealistic, youthful, musical egalitarianism.

Other festivals, such as Mamou, Louisiana's annual Mamou Cajun Music Festival, function as a means of coping with cultural integration. In the early 1970s, several Mamou residents started the festival because they felt their culture slipping away. This preservationist stance is widespread throughout many southern music festivals, though it evidences the work of northern folk revivalists like Alan Lomax and Mike Seeger as much as it does the ardent dedication to heritage of many southern musicians. The act of putting traditional musicians on stage and charging attendees admission fees creates an interesting situation where southern folk music is simultaneously preserved, introduced to new listeners, and commoditized. Thus, within the festival atmosphere, music exists as a cultural artifact, a viable means of creative expression, and as a source of capital.

Like organized sporting events, southern music festivals bring together people from all walks of life. The old and young, rural and urban, conservative and liberal, southern and nonsouthern are all represented in countless festivals each year. Oftentimes, they mingle together. Not only does this indicate the immeasurable importance of music and musical heritage to southern culture, but it also suggests the importance of recreation to southern life. The festival provides a chance for folks to get away from everyday stress. Festival-goers often celebrate this temporary escape through merrymaking. Festival behavior ranges from the ordered group participation of southern gospel singing conventions to the "anything goes" atmosphere of Bonaroo or the New Orleans Jazz and Heritage Festival to feats of unrestrained all-night jamming in the parking lot of most bluegrass festivals. Likewise, the music and celebration are usually paired with offerings of regional crafts, food, and sometimes alcohol. Thus, the festival provides people a space where the many limitations of the outside world diminish in importance. People attend with the intentions of letting their hair down, reinventing themselves for a weekend, catching up with their festival friends, or just relaxing and taking in a bit of music, history, and culture. Combine this with the preservation of traditions, and the whole experience emerges as an educational party.

The southern music festival is where the rivers of regional and traditional culture meet the sea of the homogenized modern South. In this place, where the old and new collide, a rich sustenance of music, community, and recreation are churned together producing a veritable feeding frenzy in the attending population. It is one of the many scenes where the phoenix of southern identity dies in a burst of expressive flames and then emerges anew, solidified and authenticated by tradition and softened and given relevance by the solvent of cultural integration.

CLAYTON WISNER
Rainbow City, Alabama

Gavin James Campbell, *Music and the Making of a New South* (2004); Robert Cantwell, *Bluegrass Breakdown: The Making of the Old Southern Sound* (1984); Steve Cheseborough, *Blues Traveling: Holy Sites of the Deltas Blues* (2004); James C. Cobb, *Away Down South: A History of Southern Identity* (2005); Eric Hobsbawn and Terence Ranger, eds., *The Invention of Tradition* (1983); Lawrence W. Levine, *American Historical Review* (December 1992); Bill C. Malone, *Southern Music-American Music* (1979); Neil V. Rosenberg, *Bluegrass: A History* (1985).

Fiddle Contests

These days, most active American fiddlers attend several fiddle contests every year. Indeed, because dances accompanied by live fiddling have become uncommon in most parts of the United States, and because no major alternative opportunities for public performance have emerged, contests have become the main public venue for fiddling. These events build social and musical alliances, inspire practice, and help shape repertoires and styles. But every fiddler has mixed feelings about each contest that he frequents and, indeed, about whether competition is good for him or healthy for fiddling in general. In fact, many fiddlers and other musicians who attend contests regularly never compete. Some of the most avid performers concentrate exclusively on what most musicians do when not on stage: jam and socialize. Nevertheless, the competition itself, pernicious or not, is indispensable; without it, fiddlers and their fans would seldom gather and interact in numbers comparable to those we see at contests.

Fiddling is vernacular violin performance, drawing mainly on repertoires based on traditional dance music genres. Related fiddle repertoires—and congruent fiddle contest traditions—reach from Scandinavia across the British Isles to North America. In the American South, performers and, to a slightly lesser extent, audiences are composed largely of white, blue-collar, often rural individuals. In many cases, the best fiddlers are intelligent, very energetic men (still mostly men, though the rising fiddle world of children and teenagers is gender balanced) who don't thrive particularly well in formal educational situations.

In the southern United States, contest formats correspond to a region's dominant fiddle styles. In the Southeast, fiddle "conventions" center on ensemble performance, specifically on old-time music and on bluegrass. Old-time fiddle bands supplement the fiddle-banjo duo inherited from blackface minstrelsy, with a guitar and string bass furnishing harmonic support. The fiddle and banjo play in heterophony, that is, not quite in unison, because each musician plays a given melody in a way idiomatic to his instrument. Bluegrass bands are a little bigger than their old-time counterparts, averaging a half-dozen musicians. Like old-time bands, they tend to be groups of friends and/or family members. But bluegrass performances are different: most members of bluegrass ensembles get brief chances to step into the musical foreground in many tunes, by taking solo "breaks." Most southeastern fiddle contests reserve their important contest brackets for old-time and bluegrass bands; they also have divisions for individual instruments (often plus an accompanying guitar) and for folksong.

In marked contrast to southeastern fiddle contests and conventions, Texas fiddle contests concentrate nearly exclusively on solo fiddling in an exciting, linear style packed with variation that is less rhythm-oriented and more harmonically governed than that characteristic of older styles. One or several guitarists accompany the Texas contest fiddler with crisp, jazzy chords. In these contests, separate brackets are nearly all defined by the ages of the contestants. We hear the oldest and the youngest players earlier in a given contest, and then the prime-of-life (and thus most expert) fiddlers. The best fiddling per capita in this style takes place in contests in Texas, though this style now dominates in most of the United States Indeed, the so-called national contest in Weiser, Idaho, features the northwestern take on Texas style (though a handful of true Texas fiddlers also attend).

Between the Southeast and Texas, especially in the Tennessee Valley and in the Deep South, many contests are in hybrid formats. For instance, the well-regarded Tennessee Valley Oldtime Fiddlers Contest in Athens, Ala., starts off on an October Friday evening like a southeastern contest, with competition brackets defined by performance medium (harmonica, mandolin, finger-picking guitar, etc.). Then, during Saturday, those brackets gradually yield to age-defined groupings of Texas-style fiddlers, one of whom will be crowned "Fiddle King" late that night. This and several other contests in this part of the United States (and as far north as Minnesota!) also reserve a bracket for old-time fiddling.

Although fiddle contests are built around staged, structured competition between individual fiddlers or between fiddle-based bands, they must include much more than the competition itself to be considered satisfactory and to survive over time. These annual, small to medium-sized festivals are typically set in small towns, in part to have room for camping, lots of jamming (which most fiddlers say is more fun and more important than the official competition), craft sales, and homespun fast food. These aspects of fiddle contests, like the music itself, are believed to hearken back to an earlier time, which, in the way of nostalgia, is willfully considered to have been simpler and overall better. Historic small-town values of community and family frame how the fiddle community chooses to remember the past and become the focus for values expressed by behavior in all spheres in this regularly reconstituted weekend subculture.

CHRIS GOERTZEN
University of Southern Mississippi

Chris Goertzen, *American Music* (Fall 1996), *The World of Music* (2003); Sharon Poulson Graf, "Traditionalization at the National Oldtime Fiddler's Contest: Politics, Power, and Authenticity" (Ph.D. dissertation, University of Michigan, 1999).

Field Trials

A field trial is essentially a mock bird hunt in which the bird dogs, rather than the birds themselves, are the main attraction. The object is to show off a dog's exemplary training and breeding by allowing it to compete against others in locating game for the hunter.

Though modeled on the sport of bird hunting, field trials have not been recognized as a sport in their own right for very long. Begun in the 1860s in England, they were introduced to America in the 1870s. The first recorded American field trial took place in October 1874 near Grand Junction, Tenn., home today of the Field Trial Hall of Fame and the national field trial championship, the sport's most prestigious event. Since then, field trials have become increasingly popular throughout the United States and wherever bird hunting is practiced. As a cultural institution, however, field trials are a legacy of the Gilded Age, when wealthy northerners vacationing in the South took the sport of bird hunting to new heights of luxury and sophistication. Today, the pedigree of the dog is more important than the pedigree of the hunter, but field trials have retained some of the character of high-society entertainment.

In the United States, field trials are divided into several classifications according to dog breed (pointers, retrievers, beagles, spaniels, and hounds) and further subdivided by game bird (everything from prairie chickens to Hungarian partridges). But the most popular field trial competitions by far, particularly in the South, are those for pointing breeds used in hunting quail.

Bobwhite quail spend most of their time on the ground. During a field trial, dog pairs, called "braces," are tested in 30-minute heats. To find the birds' scent, the dogs thoroughly and rapidly cover an area until one of them stops, its body frozen stiff, on-point. The dogs' handlers, competition judges, officials, and a gallery of spectators follow on horseback. When a dog points, the judges verify the point and the handler dismounts, walks over to the dog, flushes the quail, and shoots blanks into the air to demonstrate the dog's steadiness under the sound of the gun and the frenzied flight of the birds. The judges rank the dogs according to their bird-finding ability, speed, style, handling, and staunchness under shot and wing. After a number of elimination rounds, the best dogs run in a final heat, and the trials end with the presentation of trophies and cash awards to the dogs' owners.

In the first half of the 20th century, the most prestigious field trial events—those officially sanctioned by the American Kennel Club or the sporting journal *American Field*—became more than competitions to determine bird dog bragging rights. They grew into major social events where the best of southern hospitality, fine cuisine, and wealth were on display. The national field trial championship, the national amateur free-for-all, and the various American field futurities all regularly attracted politicians, movie stars, famous athletes, and foreign dignitaries to private hunting reserves throughout Tennessee, Alabama, Mississippi, and Texas. This was the heyday of plantation-style quail hunting, when northern millionaires—taking advantage of cheap land prices in the economically depressed South—converted thousands of acres of former cotton fields into private hunting reserves for their own recreational use. Many of them kept professional dog trainers on hand year-round (though the quail hunting season ran only from October to February) to tend to their purebred English pointers and setters, often valued at hundreds, sometimes thousands, of dollars.

In 1954 the Field Trial Hall of Fame was established in Grand Junction, Tenn., as a way to honor the winningest field trial dogs as well as noteworthy individuals who have made significant contributions to the sport of field trials in America. Each year since, two dogs and two people have received the sport's highest honor: induction into the Hall of Fame. Dogs are nominated on the basis of their entire careers. (Among the more legendary dogs, ranked according to the number of winners subsequently beget, are names like Riggins White Knight, Paladin's Royal Flush, Air Pilot's Sam, Sport's Peerless, and Ariel.) People, living and dead, are nominated for their service and the length of time they devoted to field trialing.

Today, the number of field trials held annually across the United States—more than 4,000—indicates that the sport has gone mainstream. Modern field trial enthusiasts hail from all walks of life, and women participate almost as frequently as men. However, the southern origins and popularity of field trials in the South remain evident in the number of Hall of Fame dogs, dog handlers, and dog owners who hail from southern states. Some areas in particular have produced more than their fair share of champions. In 1996 the town of Union Springs, Ala., unveiled a life-size bronze statue of an English pointer topping an eight-foot granite pillar bearing the names of the 11 local residents inducted into the Field Trial Hall of Fame. Because of its long list of field trial notables, the town declared itself the "Field Trial Capital of the World."

AARON WELBORN
Washington University in St. Louis

William F. Brown, *Field Trials: History, Management, and Standards* (1977); George M. Humphrey and Shepard Krech, eds., *The Georgia-Florida Field Trial Club, 1916–1948* (1948).

Fireballing

Over the past 15 to 20 years, a unique southern folk tradition has been revived in a few communities in Alabama and perhaps other rural areas of the South. This unique game is variously called "kerosene ball" or "Hail E-Over" or is simply referred to as throwing "fireballs." Sometimes referred to as the "poor man's fireworks," this game was practiced in Alabama and Georgia on a regular basis 50 to 150 years ago. It involves tossing or throwing a flaming, kerosene-soaked cotton or wool ball between players in an open field or over the roofs of tin-clad houses.

The Gibson family in Monroe County, Ala., and the Strickland family in Barbour County, Ala., have resurrected this unusual ritual, which is usually planned around the Christmas or New Year's holidays. Some heat-tolerant players also practiced this game around the Fourth of July. In an interview sev-

A time-lapse photo of a fireballing scene in Barbour County, Ala.
(Photograph courtesy of Tim Chitwood, Columbus, Ga.)

eral years ago, Hank Williams Jr. recalled playing with fireballs at Christmas as a young boy.

Fireballs are tightly woven cotton or wool balls, about the size of a softball, which are soaked in kerosene for a few weeks before their use. Three variations· of the fireball game have been reported to researchers. One involves the tossing of fireballs in an open field to players in random locations or at different ends of a large cleared field. Once the fireball is lit, it is tossed back and forth to participants who try to catch it with gloved or bare hands. More often than not, the fireball hits the ground with a swooshing "thump" and is then picked up and quickly thrown to another person. Sometimes two or more balls are in play at the same time. Another interesting variation is called "Hail-E-Over," which is similar to a game called "Annie-Annie-Over." In this game, the players are on opposite sides of a tin-roofed house and the flaming sphere is thrown over the house where the other team attempts to catch it. The final version involves the enclosure of the fireball in wire netting, which is then twirled on a wire by a player at night.

The origins of the game are lost to history but a similar ritual, known as "swinging the fireballs," was played in Stonehaven, Scotland, at midnight on New Year's Eve. Participants used wire-netting globes that were packed with rags and other paraffin-soaked combustibles. The globe was then attached to long wire "ropes" and swung around the heads of young fireballing enthusi-asts. Some say the game was enjoyed as a way of burning the old year out while others believed that fireballs would help ward off evil spirits and witches. Still others thought that fireballing would help ensure prosperity.

Does cartoon character Snuffy Smith's expression "Balls of Fire" or Jerry Lee Lewis's song "Great Balls of Fire" have anything to do with fireballing? This interesting question remains unanswered.

DOUGLAS CLARE PURCELL
Historic Chattahoochee Commission

Tim Chitwood, *Columbus (Ga.) Ledger-Enquirer* (6 January 1994).

Fishing

More than one-half of the contiguous U.S. coastline is in the South. Within these limits are the most prolific estuarine complexes in the nation—Chesa-peake Bay, Pamlico Sound, and the Gulf of Mexico. The rich waters of the Gulf Stream pass closest to land in the South, and the barrier islands that shelter the mainland South from the ocean are rich breeding grounds for fish. The rivers draining the southern highlands offer fishing of a different kind. There are few natural lakes in the South, but hydroelectric, flood-control, and irrigation im-poundments have created a unique inland fishery.

Fishing thus offers an integral form of recreation and livelihood in this re-gion. Its popularity is part of the legacy of agrarian small-farm existence where every farm needed and often constructed a reliable water source. Fishing fol-lowed as a matter of course. Pond fishing today is one of the great pleasures of the region. Fishing is a predominantly masculine activity, passed along from one generation to the next. It fulfills a need to provide; it is a private chal-lenge—success or failure is the individual's alone; and, most important, failure can quickly be attributed to outside circumstances, beyond the individual's control. Fishing can be relatively inexpensive, but the more you fish, the more likely you are to spend to fish.

The South is one of the most important fisheries in the nation. Louisiana, Virginia, North Carolina, and Mississippi are traditionally among the nation's leaders in live catch. Louisiana and Mississippi are among the top fishing ports. Shellfish caught in southern waters include clams, blue and golden crabs, oys-ters, surf clams, spiney lobsters, and shrimp. The latter is the largest category of shellfish in the region. In 2002 the South Carolina shrimp industry alone registered 3.3 million pounds of catch valued at $9 million. Finfish found in the South include bluefish, drum, croacker, mackerel, monkfish, red snapper, sea bass, summer flounder, tilefish, and tuna. Recreational and commercial fishermen in Texas catch more than 12 million pounds of finfish annually, valued at $700 million.

Each regional fishery of the South has a cultural heritage comprising unique boat styles developed for local waters. The character of these fisheries is based on the available harvest of the offshore waters as well as distinctive cuisine and social customs. Several regions have unique products: Chesapeake Bay blue crab, Lynnhaven oyster of Virginia, Bon Secour oyster of the Gulf, red snapper from Florida, and Georgia and Louisiana shrimp. (President William Howard Taft consumed seven dozen Lynnhaven Oysters at one sitting.)

Through their culture and cuisine, the Cajuns of Louisiana, the Lowcountry people of South Carolina and Georgia, the watermen of the Chesapeake, and the Downeasters of North Carolina have maintained and reinforced a clear identity. These individual groups are clannish and sustain tradition from one generation to the next. They are not open societies—the vehement opposition to Mexican and Vietnamese immigrants and to religious cult–related fishermen by traditional groups bears witness to their strong emotions and fears of economic and social change. Outsiders are warily watched, seldom welcomed, and even when accepted as "fellow fishermen" still remain outsiders.

Sea Grant Research in North Carolina reveals a very precise social network, which distributes fishing information in one typical small coastal North Carolina village. Information and innovation become legitimate only when certain accepted and admired fishermen advocate or legitimize them. This would seem to indicate a traditional subculture, rigidly set in its ways. Nevertheless, commercial fishing has been forced to change because of circumstances beyond the control of fishermen. Fuel prices, declining and polluted fisheries, and the substantial cost of a vessel have altered regional patterns. Since the 1990s, imports have reduced market prices and diminished profits for the South's fish industry. Fishermen have shifted from local water, seasonal fishing to open-water, year-round fishing. It is simply not possible to make fishing pay on a local basis unless a monopoly exists, such as legal rights to rich oyster grounds. Fishermen must follow the catch to make ends meet, and this, along with foreign competition, is gradually altering the traditional commercial fishing industry. The explosive growth of private boat ownership has created conflicts with recreational fishermen, leading at times to bans on the use of nets, without which some commercial fishermen cannot profitably operate.

Southerners are serious about fishing for fun, and no other region works so hard to have a good time at recreational fishing. State wildlife agencies issue fishing licenses in the hundreds of thousands. Across the South, fishermen sustain a fishing publication, *B.A.S.S.* (the magazine of the Bass Anglers' Sportsman's Society) and regional editions of *Field and Stream* and *Sports Afield*. The region has a professional fishing circuit, saltwater fishing rodeos, tournaments, invitational fish-offs, derbies, and contests with substantial prizes. Every southern city of any size has an outdoor commercial show, highlighting the latest in outdoor gear and equipment, which includes fishing necessities.

State wildlife agencies actively work to develop the fisheries resource through the construction of fishing attractors, artificial reefs, boat ramps, and docking facilities—all funded by licensing revenue. Good fishing has a constituency in the South: public works projects as noncontroversial as the Blue Ridge Parkway have been sidetracked because of potential fishing stream pollution by the completion of the roadway as originally proposed.

The two major categories of southern recreational fishing are saltwater and freshwater—everything else is derivative. Within these categories are curious subcategories, many of which are identified by either the technique they use or the species of fish they pursue. Anglers fish from piers, shallow wading areas, private boats, and charter boats. They fish on rivers, large lakes, bays, creeks, ponds, and marshes and in the Atlantic Ocean and the Gulf of Mexico. The three most popular means of catching saltwater game fish are by boat, private or rental; pier fishing; or surf-casting. The U.S. Commerce Department statistics confirm that the greatest number of saltwater fish landed are caught within three miles of beachfront, the distance corresponding most frequently to pier fishing, surf casting, and both private and charter (or rental) boating.

Sixty percent of the South's population lives within two hours' driving time of saltwater, so it is not surprising that saltwater fishing is extremely popular. Saltwater fishermen are willing to catch anything and do not simply pursue one species of game fish to the exclusion of others. They spend extravagant sums of money to achieve their goals. A properly equipped surf fisherman can spend as much as $25,000 for a recreational vehicle that will negotiate the sandy stretches of barrier islands such as the Outer Banks of North Carolina and Padre Island in Texas. In addition to the vehicle cost, there are substantial expenses for tackle and clothing. A serious surf fisherman can justify all of the expense, for only with such equipment can he or she achieve the mobility needed to properly fish the beaches. The expense may make this sport seem an improbable one, but it is commonplace.

There is a definite camaraderie among surf fishermen as opposed to private boat owners who fish open and sound waters. A community is created by a shared experience of testy weather conditions and successful fishing "runs."

Many fishermen return to the same beaches year after year—indeed, so established are the routines that an element of superstition seems to govern the planning of annual surf-fishing trips. On the Outer Banks of North Carolina, the surf-fishing mecca in the South if not the nation, motel owners have booked the same rooms to the same fishing parties for many years—often because of the success of a past trip. In 1984 a world record Red Drum, the prized surf game fish weighing 94 pounds, was landed near Avon, N.C. That catch alone doubtlessly brought fishermen to the Outer Banks in droves, and there is always another season of Hatteras Island sunrises, silhouetting shoulder-to-shoulder anglers, and vehicles bristling with poles and as chock-full of equipment as any tackle shop. They will want to better the record of the unfortunate angler, who, if he had waited a week later to land his drum, would have pocketed $50,000 during the annual Red Drum Tourney.

Freshwater fishermen tend to pursue one game fish more than others. The fish may be either native or naturalized trout, hybrid and striped bass, crappie, bream and other sunfish, catfish, or the king of all freshwater game fish, the large-mouth bass. The method may be fly rod, spinning tackle, ultralight spinning tackle, bait casting, or cork or bobber fishing with natural bait. There seems to be a correlation between the economic and social stature of fishermen, the game fish they pursue, and the method they prefer to use. At the bottom of the economic scale, the preferred fishing is catfish/bream by cork or bobber fishing/bait casting, bass/spinner fishing is the choice of blue-collar families, bass fly-rod fishing of white-collar workers, and artificial fly fishing for native trout is the preserve of upper-income professionals. This observation is grounded in economic realities. The expense required for bream and catfish fishing is substantially lower than that for trout fishing. Bream and catfish may be caught from the edge of a lake—a boat is not required; bass fishermen need a boat to fish large impoundments, and trout fishermen must have the means and time to travel and stay in the remote highlands where trout are found.

The large-mouth bass is a southern institution. The fish is widely distributed, easily caught, and a dependable fighter. Bass is also good to eat. Its following is fanatical, almost cultic in devotion. The large-mouth bass may have been placed in the waters of the South so that fishermen have a preordained reason for idleness and spending money. Bass is frequently used as a verb—"bassin." This is not the same as fishing but refers to the pursuit of the large-mouth bass with the fire of a crusade. "To bass" is to spend money—on a bass boat with a swivel chair and an outboard motor that could power an aircraft carrier, on a trolling motor, on a fish finder, temperature gauge, fishing maps, boat trailer, docking fees, a suitcase full of tackle, membership in the Bass Anglers' Sportsman's Society (and subscription to its magazine), on beer, on a "gimme cap," but never on suntan lotion. Bass fishermen are always sunburned to the "gimme cap" line. Magazine articles are devoted to fishing the remote corners of one lake for bass, professional bass fishermen cast for prizes up to $50,000, and substantial multimillion-dollar industries produce equipment for bass fishing. No other fish has such a following in the South, and no other group of fishermen spends so much money as does the bassers. Indeed, the name is almost synonymous with fishing.

Although smaller in numbers, trout fishermen are equally devoted to their fish. Trout are confined to the pure running water streams and rivers of the mountains and to a few mountain impoundments. This restricted range places the fish out of reach of much of the region's population but does not diminish its popularity. Trout are wary fish, caught by stalking, rather than fishing. Much of the appeal of trout fishing is in the enjoyment of the fish's environment, and so, to a greater degree than perhaps other game fish, there is an "aesthetic" to trout fishing. The value of catching the fish is often surpassed by the quest for it. This is not a hard-and-fast rule. For every trout fisherman arduously using an artificially tied fly at the end of a $500 pole, there is a mountain native working the stream with canned corn or worms. Trout fishermen write most often about one single issue: the threatened destruction of a prime trout stream. Indeed, so fragile are the southern waters supporting trout, and so limited is the number of fishable miles, it could very well be the South's most tenuous outdoor recreation.

One further aspect of recreational fishing should be noted—the active stocking of created fisheries funded by wildlife revenues. Money from the sale of licenses has gone to provide a number of "unnatural" prime fishing opportunities, such as inland striped bass fishing on lakes such as the Santee-Cooper in South Carolina. Normally an ocean species, striped bass have adapted very nicely to the all-freshwater habitat of certain reservoirs. This has resulted in a superb inland recreational fishery of an endangered native ocean species. In addition, extensive artificial hybridization has developed cross-specific game fish, which are more readily adapted to the growth conditions of inland impoundments.

Inland fishing is enormously popular in the South. This is a region where the first bream on a worm-baited hook marks a rite of passage in its own way and means passing the love of angling from one generation to the next.

GLENN MORRIS
Durham, North Carolina

Havilah Babcock, *My Health Is Better in November: Thirty-five Stories of Hunting and Fishing in the South* (1985); Tina Bucuvalas, Peggy A. Bulger, and Stetson Kennedy, *South Florida Folklife* (1994); Larry S. Chowning, *Harvesting the Chesapeake: Tools and Traditions* (1990); William Elliot, *Carolina Sports by Land and Water* (1846); Patrick Mullen, *Southern Exposure* (Summer–Fall 1977); Glenn R. Parson, *Sharks, Skates, and Rays of the Gulf of Mexico* (2006); Lance Robinson et al., *Trends in Texas Commercial Fishery Landings, 1972–1993* (1993); Louis D. Rubin Jr., *Southern Living* (March 1983); Frank Sargeant, *Outdoor Life* (March 1981); Southeastern Association of Fish and Wildlife Agencies, *Proceedings of Annual Conference* (annual); *Southern Exposure* (May–June 1982); U.S. National Oceanic and Atmospheric Administration, *Fishery Statistics* (annual); Dianne Young, *Southern Living* (July 1983).

Football, College

More than any other sport, college football has a long and noteworthy place in the history of the South. Not long after the inaugural Princeton vs. Rutgers game of 1869, Washington and Lee played Virginia Military Institute in the first official football game in the South. The year was 1877, and by 1895 John Heisman had instituted the innovation of using offensive guards as blockers for running backs at Auburn University. The infamous, outlawed formation referred to as the "flying wedge" was used by Vanderbilt University as early as 1892 in a game against North Carolina. Southern football's contribution to modern-day football continued with the advent of the forward pass as an offensive weapon in 1906. The well-known "Heisman Shift" was introduced by John Heisman at Georgia Tech. Beginning in the 1920s General Bob Neyland introduced the "single-wing" formation at the University of Tennessee. The contributions of these early southern teams, coaches, and players to football were critical for establishing the game as it is played today.

In addition, the South has provided college football with some of the most outstanding coaches in the history of the sport. In 1899 Herman Suter coached the famous "iron men" of the University of the South. The national attention generated by Coach Suter at Sewanee was continued through Daniel E. McGugin's coaching achievements at Vanderbilt. In his 30-year career at Vanderbilt, McGugin's teams won 13 titles and 196 games. Following McGugin's accomplishments, John Heisman, the person for whom the Heisman trophy was named, succeeded McGugin as the outstanding coach in the Deep South. Heisman's Georgia Tech teams won four straight national titles from 1915 to 1918. His 1916 Georgia Tech team set the record for most points in a game when they defeated Cumberland University 222–0.

Many other coaches in the South made outstanding contributions to the

Tim Tebow, University of Florida star quarterback and Heisman trophy winner
(Photograph courtesy of University of Florida Communications)

game of football in the early 1900s. Dana X. Bible, in 12 seasons at Texas A&M, won five Southwest Conference titles and posted a winning percentage of over .77 (1917–28). Frank Bridges of Baylor, who has been characterized as "one of the most original and inventive football coaches who ever lived," experimented with innovative formations during the early 1920s, and Wallace Wade's records at Alabama and Duke were outstanding during the late 1920s and early 1930s. However, with the emergence of General Robert Reese Neyland as head coach of the University of Tennessee, one of the first coaching legends of the South emerged. Neyland won 173 games, and his coaching career at Tennessee spanned from 1925 to the modern era of big-time football. The Atlantic Coast Conference provided football in the South with one of its most colorful and witty coaches in Frank Howard, whose teams won a total of 165 games. In the Southwest Conference, the names of Frank Broyles and Darryl Royal echo legendary achievements on the gridiron from 1959 to the early 1970s. Broyles's teams recorded 74 Southwest Conference victories during his tenure at Arkansas, while Royal's Texas teams won 80 conference games.

The most legendary southern collegiate football coach, however, was Paul William "Bear" Bryant. Coach Bryant not only established himself as the winningest coach in the history of collegiate football but also became a charismatic symbol of success to football fans throughout the world. Bear Bryant's coaching career and incredible record as a major-college coach of 323 victories, 85 losses, and 17 ties spanned 38 years and four southern universities—Maryland, Kentucky, Texas A&M, and Alabama. A true modern hero in the South, Bear Bryant influenced football in this region and throughout the United States in ways that will remain as long as the game is played. The continuing achievements of numerous former players of Coach Bryant in professional football, as well as in collegiate coaching, reflect not only his coaching genius but also his personal charisma.

Grambling State coach Eddie Robinson broke Bryant's record for wins in 1985, an important symbol of the accomplishments of a separate black football tradition in the South. Historically Black Colleges and Universities (HBCUs) have sponsored outstanding players, coaches, and programs that still thrive. The Southwestern Athletic Conference (SWAC) headquartered in Birmingham, Ala., was founded in 1920, and its football teams participated in Division I-AA competition, now the Football Championship Subdivision (FCS). The conference does not participate in the postseason FCS tournament competition but stages its own conference championship game. Recent winners of the SWAC championship are Grambling State (2000, 2001, 2002, 2005, 2008), Southern University (1999, 2003), Alabama State (2004, 2006), Jackson State (2007), and Prairie View A&M (2009). Nationally HBCUs also hold 42 classic football matchups (35 of them in the South), which display the pageantry, tradition, sportsmanship, and sheer entertainment that black college football epitomizes. Among the most prominent of these classics are the Bayou Classic (Grambling State vs. Southern University) and the Turkey Day Classic (Alabama State vs. Tuskegee).

In 2004 one of Bear Bryant's former players at Alabama, Sylvester Croom, became the first African American head coach in the Southeastern Conference when he was hired at Mississippi State. Croom earned himself several coach-of-the-year honors in 2007 when he led the Bulldogs to an 8–5 record (after a 3–9 record in 2006) and a trip to the Liberty Bowl.

While Bear Bryant once held the title of winningest coach in the history of collegiate football, that honor has since been earned by another successful coach who put passion into southern football, Florida State's Robert C. "Bobby" Bowden (389–129–4). Bowden is only one of five NCAA Division I coaches to win 300 games and one of two still actively coaching today. The honor alternates annually between Bowden and Penn State's Joe Paterno.

The regional and community interest in high school football in the South provided a rich pool of talent for the development of this sport at the intercollegiate level. The Associated Press National Polls, which began in 1936, reveal the following southern college teams claiming the title of national champion: Texas Christian University (1938); Texas A&M University (1939); Tennessee (1951, 1998); Auburn (1957); Louisiana State University (1958, 2003, 2007); Alabama (1961, 1964, 1965, 1978, 1979, 1992, 2010); Texas (1963, 1969, 2005); Georgia (1980); Clemson (1981); Miami of Florida (1983, 1987, 1989, 1991, 2001), Florida (1996, 2006), and Florida State University (1999). In terms of overall winning percentages, 10 southern teams are ranked in the top 25 all-time winners, and 19 players from southern schools have received the Heisman trophy as the outstanding college football player in the United States for each year of competition, beginning in 1935. Southern football players who have achieved such distinction are Davey O'Brien (TCU, 1938), Frank Sinkwich (Georgia, 1942), Doak Walker (SMU, 1948), John David Crow (Texas A&M, 1957), Billy Cannon (LSU, 1959), Steve Spurrier (Florida, 1966), Pat Sullivan (Auburn, 1966), Earl Campbell (Texas, 1977), George Rogers (South Carolina, 1980), Herschel Walker (Georgia, 1982), Bo Jackson (Auburn, 1985), Vinny Testaverde (Miami, 1986), Andre Ware (Houston, 1989), Gino Torretta (Miami, 1992), Charlie Ward (Florida State, 1993), Danny Wuerffel (Florida, 1996), Ricky Williams (Texas, 1998), Chris Weinke (Florida State, 2000), Tim Tebow (Florida, 2007), and Mark Ingram (Alabama, 2009).

The past decade has seen an increase in the number of bowl games, particularly in the South, where there are now more than 20 bowl games, an increase of at least 10 since the mid-1990s. At the end of the 2008–9 football season, the South hosted most of the nation's bowl games. To whom much is given, much is expected, and nowhere is this more evident when one considers the tremendous increase in coaching salaries. In 1964 Vince Dooley was making a total of $12,500 annually as Georgia's head coach. By 1982, Texas A&M offered Jackie Sherrill $1.7 million over the course of seven years, the equivalent of $240,000 per year, making him the highest paid coach in college football. Most offensive and defensive coordinators make more than that today. In the 1990s Bobby Bowden and Steve Spurrier became two of the first coaches to make $1 million per year. When Nick Saban became the head coach of Alabama in 2007, he signed a contract worth $4 million per year.

KRISTI M. FONDREN
University of Southern Mississippi

DUANE A. GILL
Oklahoma State University

J. STEVEN PICOU
University of South Alabama

Tony Barnhart, *Southern Fried Football: The History, Passion, and Glory of the Great Southern Game* (2008); *Birmingham News* Staff, *Remembering Bear* (1983); Clyde Bolton, *Unforgettable Days in Southern Football* (1974); D. Stanley Eitzen and George H. Sage, *Sociology of American Sport* (1978); Wilbur Evans and H. B. McElroy, *The Twelfth Man: A Story of Texas A&M Football* (1974); Lawrence Goodwyn, *Southern Exposure* (Fall 1974); Marty Mule, *Sugar Bowl: The First Fifty Years* (1983); Richard Scott, *SEC Football: 75 Years of Pride and Passion* (2008); Mark Yost, *Wall Street Journal* (6 December 2008); Alexander M. Weyand, *The Saga of American Football* (1955); Geoff Winningham and Al Reinert, *Rites of Fall: High School Football in Texas* (1979); Don Yeager with Sam Cunningham and John Papadakis, *Turning of the Tide: How One Game Changed the South* (2006).

Football, High School

High school football in the South today is characterized by a passion unrivaled in other regions of the United States. Because the South was predominately a rural area throughout the first half of the 20th century, community identity with high school teams fostered intense competition. Increased industrial and urban development over the past 50 years may have changed the demography of the South, but high school football still remains the most popular Friday night activity across the region, sustaining a very real and vibrant component of southern culture. For example, H. G. Bissinger's book, *Friday Night Lights*, which inspired a motion picture and a television series, explores the emotional investment of a Texas town in its local high school football team, the Permian Panthers. Devoted crowds of more than 20,000 flock to the stadium on Friday nights with the hope of watching the Panthers crush their opponent. In addition to the game itself, southern high school football remains an important source for a variety of social activities that include pep rallies, band performances, and drill teams.

At the end of the 2008 football season, the Valdosta Wildcats, dramatized in the film *Remember the Titans* (2000), were the winningest high school football team in America, with a record of 838 wins and 191 losses. Besides winning more high school games than anyone else in the country, the Wildcats have also won 23 state titles and six national titles, which is only one of the reasons this area has been referred to as "TitleTown." And, it is not unusual for a Friday night game in Valdosta to draw a crowd of 10,000 people when two teams meet to play in "Winnersville," Ga.

The Valdosta Wildcats are not the only impressive high school football team in the South, though. In 2008 the undefeated Lake Travis Cavaliers of Austin,

Tex., were the only team that could make the claim that it started and finished in the No. 1 spot in Texas Class 4A Division I Football. The Lake Travis Cavaliers, who went 16–0 in 2008, were ranked fourth nationally and outscored their playoff opponents by an average score of 55–20. Led by University of Texas-bound quarterback Garrett Gilbert, the Cavaliers won the Class 4A Division II state championship game two years in a row (2007 and 2008).

In Alabama, the Hoover High School Buccaneers gained national recognition as the center of MTV's *Two-A-Days*. The Buccaneers have won the state championship a total of seven times, five of them since 2000. For many in Alabama, the Hoover High Buccaneers are synonymous with state champions. Many former players at Hoover have gone on to play football at Auburn University or the University of Alabama, and some have continued on to the National Football League. The talent at Hoover, as well as that of John Curtis High in River Ridge, La., has been highlighted recently on ESPN's high school sports network.

Located in Batesville, Miss., South Panola High School has been referred to as the University of South Panola because of the physical domination of the football team, the South Panola Tigers. The Tigers once owned the record for the nation's longest winning streak in high school football at 89 wins until being defeated in the state championship game in 2008 by the Meridian Wildcats. A powerhouse in Mississippi, the Tigers have won five Mississippi 5A state championship games.

Along with producing highly competitive high school football programs, the South has provided high school football fans with some of the most outstanding coaches in the history of the sport. In 2004 the winningest high school football coaches were South Carolina's John McKissick, with 531 wins, followed by John Curtis Jr. (427) of River Ridge, La., and Larry Campbell (389) of Lincolnton, Ga. In terms of overall winning percentages, John Curtis Jr. had the highest winning percentage of high school coaches (.902) followed by Larry Campbell (.854), and Carlton Flatt (.853) of Brentwood, Tenn.

The most legendary coach in the history of high school football is South Carolina's John McKissick, also known as the "Baron of Summerville." He has been the head coach of the Summerville Green Wave since President Harry Truman was in office, coaching three generations of players since 1952. Coach McKissick is the only football coach at any level—high school, college, or professional—to pass the 500-win mark.

John Curtis Jr. is the second winningest high school football coach of all time, finishing with a record of 443–46–6 in 2006. The John Curtis Patriot football team has made 34 state playoff appearances, of which 32 have been consecutive appearances. The Patriots have had 11 undefeated seasons and earned the title of state champions a total of 21 times out of 27 appearances, the most appearances ever in Louisiana history. The Patriots faced Evangel in the 2008 state championship game and won, making this the fifth consecutive state championship for the John Curtis Patriots.

Built from scratch in 1970, Brentwood Academy's program, coached by Carlton Flatt, is another premier football program in the South. In the 1990s Brentwood Academy was ranked fifth in the nation by Sports Scholastic America. Coach Flatt has made 20 appearances to the state championship game, winning on 10 occasions. Coach Flatt retired from coaching in 2007 and remains Tennessee's winningest football coach with a record of 355 wins, 67 losses, and 1 tie game.

KRISTI M. FONDREN
University of Southern Mississippi

DUANE A. GILL
Oklahoma State University

J. STEVEN PICOU
University of South Alabama

H. G. Bissinger, *Friday Night Lights* (1990); Clyde Bolton, *Unforgettable Days in Southern Football* (1974); Allison Danzig, *The History of American Football* (1983); D. Stanley Eitzen and George H. Sage, *Sociology of American Sport* (1978); Lawrence Goodwyn, *Southern Exposure* (Fall 1974); Alan Ross, *Football's Biggest Winner* (2004); Alexander M. Weyand, *The Saga of American Football* (1955); Geoff Winningham and Al Reinert, *Rites of Fall: High School Football in Texas* (1979); Wayne Wood, *Hoover Football: Buccaneer Football History* (2008).

Football, Professional

Professional football arrived in the South when both the Dallas Cowboys and the Houston Oilers began National Football League (NFL) play in 1960, and the teams that emerged since have been very competitive. Often referred to as "America's team," the Cowboys gained wide television coverage in the South during the first six years of their franchise. Today they are still one of the most popular teams in the NFL, with the most recognized cheerleaders in the league.

Professional teams in Atlanta and Miami were established in 1966, and the New Orleans Saints franchise had its first season in 1967, followed by the Tampa Bay Buccaneers in 1976. The Miami Dolphins experienced their first winning season in 1970 with new head coach Don Shula. In 1972 the Dolphins became the first team to make it to the Super Bowl two consecutive years in a row, where they first lost to the Cowboys but then defeated the Washington Redskins the following year. In 1973 the Dolphins would return to the Super Bowl yet again to defeat the Minnesota Vikings, making them the first team in the NFL to go to the Super Bowl three consecutive years in a row.

Twenty years later, the South would gain two new teams and see one southern team relocate. In 1995 the Carolina Panthers and the Jacksonville Jaguars played their first seasons in the NFL, and at the end of the 1996 season the Houston Oilers became the Tennessee Oilers, having moved to Memphis for the 1997 season and then on to Nashville. In 1999 the Tennessee Oilers became the Tennessee Titans and went on to experience two of their best seasons (1999, 2000), and made it to the 1999 Super Bowl but were defeated by the St. Louis Rams. Six years after losing their football team, the city of Houston found new life in the Houston Texans, the 32nd team in the NFL (2002).

On 29 August 2005, Hurricane Katrina hit New Orleans, and damage to the city and the Superdome made it impossible for the Saints to play the 2005 season at home. As if Hurricane Katrina were not enough, the Saints finished the 2005 season with a 3–13 record. In 2006, the Saints were back in New Orleans and became a symbol of renewed hope for the Crescent City. Led by the likes of Drew Brees, Deuce McAllister, and Reggie Bush, the Saints finished the season with a 10–6 record, landing first-year head coach Sean Payton coach-of-the-year honors. This was the first year the Saints made it to the NFC championship game, but their season came to an end with a loss in frigid, snowy conditions to the Chicago Bears in Chicago. In 2010, however, the New Orleans Saints rebounded, winning the Super Bowl, against the Indianapolis Colts, for the first time in their 42-year history.

At the end of their turbulent 2004 season, the Miami Dolphins hired LSU's Nick Saban as head coach. Although Saban continued to say that he was committed to rebuilding the Dolphins, rumors about a move back to the NCAA to coach the Alabama Crimson Tide grew stronger as the season progressed. After repeated denials, Saban signed a multimillion-dollar deal and became Alabama's head coach at the end of the 2006 season. What followed would be the Dolphins worse season ever in 2007 with a 1–15 record. At the same time, the Michael Vick era came to an end for the Atlanta Falcons when he pleaded guilty to illegal dog fighting and was sentenced to 18 months in prison. Vick's future in the NFL remains uncertain.

Five southern teams (Tampa Bay Buccaneers, Tennessee Titans, Atlanta Falcons, Carolina Panthers, and New Orleans Saints) have made it to the main event in professional football—the Super Bowl—on one occasion, while the Dallas Cowboys and Miami Dolphins have made multiple appearances, eight

Reggie Bush of the New Orleans Saints (Photograph by Michael C. Hebert, courtesy of the New Orleans Saints)

and five, respectively. Collectively, these teams have made 18 Super Bowl appearances, winning a total of nine Super Bowls. The Cowboys have played in the most Super Bowl games in NFL history, winning five of their eight meetings. New Orleans and Miami have been the most frequent venues for the Super Bowl, each hosting the event nine times. In February 2011 the Dallas Cowboys will host Super Bowl XLV in their new stadium, which will seat 80,000–100,000 fans.

These teams have been very competitive in the NFL. In terms of overall winning percentages, the Cowboys (.577) and the Dolphins (.576) are ranked No. 1 and No. 2 respectively of all NFL teams. In addition to overall winning percentage, the Dolphins and the Cowboys also take top honors and hold the top two positions for highest winning percentage (.580 and .578) during the regular season. Although the Carolina Panthers (.667) have the highest winning percentage during postseason play, the Dallas Cowboys have the most postseason wins of all NFL teams with 32 wins.

The South has provided professional football with some of the most outstanding coaches in the history of the sport. Legendary coach Tom Landry was with the Dallas Cowboys for nearly three decades since their beginnings in 1960, where he recorded a total of 270 wins, 178 losses, and 6 ties over the course of 29 years. Following Landry's retirement, a new era began in 1989 with head coach Jimmy Johnson. Although he was with the Cowboys only four years, Johnson coached the team to the Super Bowl and won two consecutive years in a row (1992, 1993).

The most outstanding coach in the South was Don Shula of the Miami Dolphins. Shula posted the sixth highest winning percentage of all coaches in the NFL (.665) when combining regular and postseason play. Shula's ultimate achievement as Miami's head coach came in 1972, when the Dolphins compiled the first unbeaten and untied record (17–0) in the league's history. At 33 years of age Shula was not only the youngest coach in the NFL, but also the youngest to compile 100 victories. If one included his record while at Baltimore, Shula's six Super Bowl appearances as head coach remain an NFL all-time record. Before he retired following the 1995 season, Shula became the winningest head coach in the NFL by setting a record for most career victories (347). In July 1997 Shula was unanimously elected and inducted into the Professional Football Hall of Fame for his record-setting accomplishments.

KRISTI M. FONDREN
University of Southern Mississippi

DUANE A. GILL
Oklahoma State University

J. STEVEN PICOU
University of South Alabama

Clyde Bolton, *Unforgettable Days in Southern Football* (1974); Allison Danzig, *The History of American Football* (1983); D. Stanley Eitzen and George H. Sage, *Sociology of American Sport* (1978); Lawrence Goodwyn, *Southern Exposure* (Fall 1974); Alexander M. Weyand, *The Saga of American Football* (1955).

Football Traditions

More than any other sport, football seems to reflect cultural characteristics of the South. It has a long and noteworthy place in the history of the region. The pre- and postgame rituals of tailgating (eating, drinking, socializing) are a tradition, if not an art form, in the South. In many southern towns, tailgating and game-day traditions are something close to magical. Louisiana State University (LSU), named best tailgating scene in 1996 by ESPN, celebrates game day with a Cajun twist that includes crawfish, shrimp, and jambalaya. Ole Miss, often listed in the top five of college football traditions, has the Grove, a 10-acre piece of land shaded by oak trees located in the middle of campus. When walking through the Grove on game day, it is not unusual to see white-linen tablecloths held in place by silver candelabras amid a complete buffet of southern cuisine. While Auburn and Alabama fire up the barbecue grills well before kickoff, a common scene at Clemson and South Carolina is the Lowcountry Boil—a combination of shrimp, potatoes, corn, crab, and sausage all cooked in one pot. Regardless of the locale, no tailgating scene in the South is complete without one common staple—fried chicken.

Tailgating is not the only game-day tradition surrounding southern collegiate football. Each college town has its own set of game-day traditions that make football season unique. Auburn has Toomer's Corner, the official gathering place after home football games for fans, students, players, and, at times, coaches. When celebrating a huge victory, it is not unusual for Toomer's Corner to be "rolled" with toilet paper. While fans at Clemson come together at the Esso Club, a converted gas station and one of the area's most popular game-day attractions, Alabama is home to the Quad and Dreamland, both popular spots where generations of fans congregate before and after home games. At Georgia teams face off "between the hedges," a reference to the English privet hedge surrounding the field at Sanford Stadium. Vaught-Hemingway Stadium is filled with the sound of Ole Miss fans yelling the "Hotty Toddy" cheer, while Tennessee fans sing along to "Rocky Top" as players battle between orange and white checkerboard end zones. Before taking the field on game day, Clemson players touch Howard's Rock seconds before running down a grassy hill leading directly into Memorial Stadium. Although they are ostensibly banned from use during conference games, it is not uncommon to see determined Mississippi State fans cheering on the Bulldogs with their favorite noise-making device—the cowbell. At South Carolina, fans cheer their team as they run onto the field to the tune of *2001: A Space Odyssey*, while onlookers at Georgia Tech watch as their team is led onto the field by the Ramblin' Wreck, a restored 1930 Model A Ford Sports Coupe. Although George Edmundson retired in 1998, Florida's infamous Mr. Two Bits still returns, sign in hand, for special Florida games, such as those against Tennessee and Florida State. LSU's Mike the Tiger is housed north of Tiger Stadium in a glass-enclosed area with pool where fans can view him on game day before he is placed in a cage and rolled outside the locker room of the opposing team. While Georgia has perhaps the most recognized mascot in all of college football, the English bulldog UGA (pronounced "Ughguh"), Florida State has Chief Osceola and Renegade as part of its pregame highlights and traditions.

Along with great southern traditions come great rivalries during football season pitting brother against brother, friend against friend, and husband against wife, at least for a weekend. Each rivalry has its own history of triumphs, disappointments, and controversies. The longest continuous football rivalry in the South is Auburn versus Georgia, played every year since 1894. One of the greatest rivalries, however, occurs each year when Georgia and Florida battle on the gridiron in front of dedicated fans who make the pilgrimage to Jacksonville. Because of the festive atmosphere, this social event was once nicknamed "the world's largest outdoor cocktail party" until two Florida students died in alcohol-related incidents. Other noteworthy out-of-state rivalries include Alabama-Tennessee, Alabama–Georgia Tech, and LSU–Ole Miss (recently named the Magnolia Bowl in 2008). However, some of the greatest rivalries in the South include the in-state rivalries of Alabama-Auburn (the Iron Bowl), Ole Miss–Mississippi State (the Egg Bowl), Clemson–South Carolina, Florida–Florida State, Georgia–Georgia Tech, Miami–Florida State, and Texas–Texas A&M.

KRISTI M. FONDREN
University of Southern Mississippi

DUANE A. GILL
Oklahoma State University

J. STEVEN PICOU
University of South Alabama

Tony Barnhart, *Southern Fried Football: The History, Passion, and Glory of the Great Southern Game* (2008); Clyde Bolton, *Unforgettable Days in Southern Football* (1974); Allison Danzig, *The History of American Football* (1983); D. Stanley Eitzen and George H. Sage, *Sociology of American Sport* (1978); Wilbur Evans and H. B. McElroy, *The Twelfth Man: A Story of Texas A&M Football* (1974); Lawrence Goodwyn, *Southern Exposure* (Fall 1974); Richard Scott, *SEC Football: 75 Years of Pride and Passion* (2008); Alexander M. Weyand, *The Saga of American Football* (1955); Don Yeager with Sam Cunningham and John Papadakis, *Turning of the Tide: How One Game Changed the South* (2006).

Fox Hunting

Southerners love their horses, their hounds, their land, and their pedigrees, both family and livestock. Fox hunting incorporates all of these passions. Southern culture has a rural heritage that borders on a religious devotion to stewardship of the region's way of life, including hunting with horse and hound.

Fox hunting exists today in much the same way as it has for hundreds of years, dating back to its United Kingdom origins. The first firm record of importation of English fox hounds was by Colonel Robert Brooke, arriving in Prince George's County, Md., 30 June 1650, with his wife, 10 children, 28 servants, and a pack of hounds. Those bloodlines are still to be found in the foxhounds of today. Hounds were brought from Maryland to Virginia starting in the 1660s. The number of horses was rapidly increasing at this time in Virginia, with the colony starting to export horses by 1668.

Hunting was either for meat or for vermin. The favored vermin quarry was the wolf until its virtual extermination. Early in the 18th century, fox became the principal game. The importation of the red fox from England replaced the gray fox, which was indigenous to the southern forests. The gray fox is not much of a runner, tending to circle back around and tending to climb trees like a cat. The red fox is more doglike and will take hunters for a merry run, using his renowned cunning to give the hounds the slip if he can. In the harsh winter of 1779–80, the Chesapeake Bay froze over, allowing the red fox to cross over into Baltimore. From here, the red fox spread rapidly down through Maryland and Virginia starting a new era in American fox hunting.

After visiting his cousin William in Virginia in 1746, Lord Fairfax moved from England to live at the family estate, Belvoir, bringing with him hounds to improve his cousin William's pack. Hunting was a favored pasttime for the entire family. William's daughter, Anne, married Lawrence Washington of Mount Vernon. Upon his return to Virginia, Lord Fairfax avidly began to hunt, having Lawrence's half brother, George Washington, as a frequent visitor and pupil. George Washington inherited Mount Vernon in 1752. By 1767 George had his own pack of hounds that were admired for their speed, bottom, and cooperative hunting style. George was often joined in the hunt field by his wife, Martha, and Thomas Jefferson.

In the early 1700s, horses in southern colonies were small and lacked the stamina needed for fox hunting. In 1730 Bulle Rock, son of the Darley Arabian, was the first thoroughbred stallion to be imported. Shortly thereafter, more thoroughbred stallions were brought in, allowing liberal crossbreeding with the local mares. By 1770, there were quality hunters available to fill the hunt field's need for fast and courageous mounts.

By the mid-19th century, fox hunting was considered a southern sport. Throughout Maryland, Virginia, and the Piedmont sections of North and South Carolina, most counties had at least two or more private packs of hounds, with untold numbers of farmers having several couples (hounds being counted in twos called couples). The old southern hound, known as Penn-Marydels, was well suited for the varied terrain of the colonies, being tall, long-eared, and deep-voiced with a splendid nose. They are still found throughout the packs of today.

Fox hunting has a culture of its own, with vocabulary, traditions, and protocols plus great passion and beauty. For hunters, nothing compares to an early winter morning on the back of a trusted mount, breath steaming from his nostrils, waiting for the pack to sound off. Everyone is alert, all dressed in the black coats of the field and the scarlet coats of the staff. The horse's ears follow the hounds, for they know the game as well as the hunters. First one hound bays, followed by the others, and then the hunters are off, galloping after the hounds on the hot scent of fox. It truly is a glorious experience. Devotees hope that this legacy can continue in the face of today's urban sprawl and animal rights activism.

BEVERLY PURSWELL
Virginia Polytechnic Institute and State University

Michael Clayton, ed., *The Glorious Chase: A Celebration of Foxhunting* (2005); Roger Longrigg, *The History of Foxhunting* (1975).

Gambling

Wagering on games of chance has been a recurrent feature of southern social life from the colonial era to modern times. In the 1700s, for example, it offered clues as to social status in the early South. When colonial planters gathered, especially in Virginia, they typically played cards and backgammon or rolled the dice. Wealthy tobacco growers, living in a society with fewer restraints than Puritan New England, were willing to risk much of their wealth on anything involving chance. George Washington kept a list of his gains and losses at gaming and typically preferred large stakes. Above all, southerners bet on horse racing. After 1730 quarter horse racing was popular, and then at midcentury English thoroughbreds were introduced into the colonies. Races were held in conjunction with fairs, which also brought occasions for gambling. Historian Timothy Breen has argued that gambling on horse racing identified one as a member of the gentry. Honor was gained through victory over one's peers, and this was a safety valve for planters, nurturing structured competition within the group without endangering its hegemony.

The inhabitants of the Old South, proclaimed a foreign visitor, "are universally addicted to gambling." Betting during the antebellum period in the Northeast was "about as common as in England," reported an Englishman, but in the South it was far more prevalent. New Orleans was a major center of gambling, but even rural southerners bet on cards, dice, dominoes, billiards, lotteries, cockfights, horse races, and many other activities. Southerners were such inveterate gamblers, claimed one eyewitness, that many "lost in a night their all."

Professional gamblers frequented riverboats and bars; some got rich and a few got lynched—five in 1835 in Vicksburg alone. But many gamblers considered themselves respectable members of southern society. A Yankee, induced to share his bed at a crowded tavern by the assurance of a landlord that his bedfellow was a gentleman, grew concerned when his heavily armed roommate placed a bowie knife and a pistol by the bedside and a pistol under his pillow. "I shuddered," admitted the Yankee, "having never slept with pistols," but he raised no objection until his bedfellow announced that he was a "gambler by profession." Horrified, the Yankee leapt from bed and exclaimed: "The landlord assured me that you were a gentleman, sir, but had he told me of your profession, I would not have consented to share my bed." The gambler, who failed to understand such squeamishness, "entered into an elaborate argument to prove that his profession was as honest and honorable as that of the physician."

New Englanders, in keeping with their Puritan heritage, were much less tolerant of gamblers and gambling than were southerners, who were as fond of wagers and risks as their Scottish, Irish, and Welsh ancestors were. Expressing his objection to horse racing, a Yankee wrote from South Carolina: "Curiosity induced me to go once, which will satisfy me for life." President Timothy Dwight of Yale College boasted: "In New England horse racing is almost and cockfighting absolutely unknown." Both activities enjoyed widespread popularity in the Old South, where spectators frequently gathered at cockpits and racetracks and wagered large sums. Whole seasons were devoted to racing, which so appealed to southerners, noted an observer, that "they have race-paths near each town and in many parts of the country." If gambling was not quite a universal pastime, it had far more adherents, among planters and plain folk alike, in the Old South than in the Old North.

Georgia gentlemen playing cards and smoking, 1918
(Georgia Department of Archives and History, Atlanta)

After the Civil War, organized, big-time gaming was rationalized in some southern states as a way to generate money for depleted treasuries or worthwhile charities in hard times. Legal lotteries had existed earlier in some areas, and these were revived. Civic and charitable groups were formed to raise money through lotteries for orphans, widows, crippled Confederate veterans, museums, libraries, schools, and various artistic activities.

The Louisiana Lottery, the largest in the South, was chartered in 1868 in New

Orleans, with a 25-year charter. It held daily drawings, with prizes up to $5,000, plus monthly drawings and a six-month drawing, which awarded a grand prize of $600,000. A popular referendum in the 1890s turned down the proposed renewal of the lottery's franchise, but southerners continued, illegally at times, to take part in lotteries of various sorts. New Orleans remained a gambling center, with its activities tied in with boxing promotion and, especially, red-light-district prostitution.

Southerners continued in the postbellum era to gamble on horse racing at tracks in places such as New Orleans, Memphis, Nashville, Montgomery, and Little Rock. They won and lost at fairs, carnivals, and circuses, as professional gamblers descended on communities where these shows appeared. They could not resist wagering on cockfighting, dog fighting, and other sporting events, either.

By the 1880s, however, a rising moral consciousness among the South's religious people led to restrictions on gambling. New laws were passed outlawing horse racing, which earlier had been the sport of the southern gentleman. Large-scale gambling activities, and particularly wagering on horse racing, came to be concentrated in resort areas, such as Hot Springs, Ark., and in coastal towns such as Galveston, Tex., and Miami, Fla., as well as continuing in New Orleans. Though sometimes hidden, gambling continued in other regions of the South. Even where illegal, gambling houses were still found.

Gambling has been celebrated in southern culture from Mark Twain's portrayal of the riverboat gambler on the Mississippi to country music singer Kenny Rogers's 1970s hit song "The Gambler." The early Mississippi country singer, Jimmie Rodgers, who knew the world of small-town gambling as a traveling railroad worker and later as a musical performer, sang such songs as "Gambling Bar Room Blues," "Those Gambler's Blues," and "Gambling Polka Dot Blues."

The image of the sharp-dressed, successful gambler has been a recurrent one in southern black literature and music, especially in the blues. Lack of economic security and their low social status surely encouraged poor blacks to risk gambling as a way to temporary economic betterment. Stuck in oppressive jobs or in the boredom of unemployment, many of the southern poor, black and white, found excitement and thrills in the risk taking of gambling. Blues performers sang the "Poker Woman Blues," "Gambler's Blues," "Dying Crap Shooter's Blues," and "Gambling Man." Card games such as Georgia skin and cooncan are associated with black gamblers, as well as "skin-ball" and shooting craps (the popularity of the latter in the South shown by southerners calling it by such names as Memphis dominoes or Mississippi marbles).

The modern era of casino gambling in the South began in 1989 when Mississippi's state legislature approved the first in a series of bills authorizing local-option dockside "riverboat" gambling in counties bordering the Gulf Coast and the Mississippi River. Plagued by the chronic poverty of its citizens and significant state budgetary shortfalls, Mississippi followed an increasing national trend toward the adoption of casino-style gambling for the purpose of generating desperately needed revenue. Passage of gambling legislation opened a public debate that brought religious, state, and community leaders into conflict. Opponents of gambling in the Bible Belt argued that moral decay, gambling addiction, and the spread of governmental corruption would accompany the new casinos. Boosters promised a panacea for the state's economic ills and job growth in counties dogged by high unemployment. By the mid-1990s, the new casinos around Tunica and Biloxi had indeed produced a dramatic increase in both state and local revenue and had generated many jobs. Unfortunately, they also brought some of the negative aspects that detractors had warned about, most conspicuously crime. Moreover, contrary to promises made by pro-gambling forces, the advent of gambling in Mississippi has yet to significantly ameliorate the low wage levels of the state's sizable minority population.

Critics of legalized gambling received more ammunition when neighboring Louisiana sought to adopt competing "riverboat" casinos. While Mississippi avoided government corruption scandals, Louisiana did not. Federal authorities would ultimately convict Louisiana governor Edwin Edwards on charges of bribery and racketeering for his role in awarding state casino licenses to a host of shady characters. Further, most Louisiana casinos have failed to live up to the economic success of their Mississippi counterparts. While casino gambling as an economic solution for southern state governments has had a mixed record of success, its impact on the region's culture is profound. The legalization of these establishments reflects a seemingly widespread acceptance of an activity once considered a criminal vice into a legitimate industry. The presence of casinos in the South also highlights the paradoxical relationship between Bible Belt evangelical Christian values and Sunbelt economic pragmatism.

JOHN NYSTROM
University of Georgia

GRADY MCWHINEY
Texas Christian University

Herbert Asbury, *Sucker's Progress: An Informal History of Gambling in America from the Colonies to Canfield* (1938); Timothy Breen, *William and Mary Quarterly* (April 1977); Tyler Bridges, *Bad Bet on the Bayou: The Rise of Gambling in Louisiana and the*

Fall of Governor Edwin Edwards (2001); Dee Brown, *The American Spa: Hot Springs, Arkansas* (1982); Henry Chafetz, *Play the Devil: A History of Gambling in the United States from 1492 to 1955* (1960); George Devol, *Forty Years a Gambler on the Mississippi* (1887); Ann Fabian, *Card Sharps, Dream Books, and Bucket Shops: Gambling in 19th Century America* (1990); John M. Findlay, *People of Chance: Gambling in American Society from Jamestown to Las Vegas* (1985); Paul Oliver, *Blues Fell This Morning: The Meaning of the Blues* (1960); Ben C. Toledano, *National Review* (7 April 1997).

Gardening

In the South, as Jack Temple Kirby has noted, "the garden is home, another room, as it were, extending from kitchen and hearth." Flower and vegetable gardens in the region have long been popular sites of recreation. Many southerners, black and white, have turned to gardens for pleasure, relaxation, and exercise.

Creating and tending ornamental and vegetable gardens were popular pastimes among wealthy southern planters. Colonial and antebellum plantation owners, such as Noble Jones of Georgia and Thomas Jefferson of Virginia, planted elaborate flower gardens, experimented with exotic food crops, and enjoyed corresponding with fellow gardeners and entertaining visitors among their plantings. During the 18th century, Jones cultivated oranges, apricots, pomegranates, and century plants for profit and entertainment on his Lowcountry property, while Jefferson experimented with every variety of fruit and vegetable he could acquire at his Piedmont estate, Monticello, in the decades following the American Revolution. Expounding the importance of escaping to his garden, Jefferson wrote in 1811, "No occupation is so delightful to me as the culture of the earth, and no culture comparable to that of the garden." Open on occasion to guests and neighbors, these and other expansive private gardens were precursors to modern public gardens and botanical parks.

Gardening was an equally popular activity among poorer southerners. Slaves raised small kitchen gardens for subsistence and as a diversion from the strictures of plantation labor. Popular vegetables included traditional African staples such as eggplants, okra, arrowroot, benne (sesame), rice, peanuts, yams, and collards. Garden produce supplemented slave diets, but the garden was also a place of temporary escape. Richard Westmacott has stated that "working in the garden was often considered recreation rather than work." In these small plots slaves could govern their own labor, manage their own plantings, and, if lucky, exchange produce with neighbors or sell excess on neighboring plantations and in town. Poor white tenants and sharecroppers similarly relied on gardening for both food and recreation before and after the Civil War. For southerners lucky enough to own or rent a patch of land, gardens provided both entertainment and insurance against hard times.

In the postwar South public gardens and botanical attractions became popular vacation destinations. Throughout the 20th century southern tourists flocked to admission-charging gardens such as Callaway in Georgia, Williamsburg in Virginia, Magnolia and Middleton in South Carolina, and Biltmore in North Carolina. In a number of cases these public attractions were outgrowths of earlier private gardens established by wealthy individuals. Many of the others were funded by regional colleges and universities. Urban botanical plantings, such as the azalea trails and parks in Mobile, Savannah, and Charleston, also drew thousands of tourists annually. By the early 21st century, well over 100 botanical gardens open to the public dotted the southern states.

Backyard gardening remains a popular avocation throughout the South. Each year gardens across the region fill with classic southern vegetables such as okra, sweet corn, hot peppers, sweet potatoes, mustard greens, and purple-hull peas and flowering plants such as camellias, old-fashioned roses, daffodils, and jasmine. These outdoor spaces reinforce connections between southerners, their agricultural past, and the present. Southern companies have also developed to meet the needs of the recreational gardener, from the expansive outdoor departments of the megachain stores Lowe's and Home Depot (based in Mooresville, N.C., and Atlanta, Ga., respectively), to online and mail-order seed and plant companies, such as Park Seed in Greenwood, S.C., and Bonnie Plants in Union Springs, Ala.

DREW A. SWANSON
University of Georgia

Edwin M. Betts, ed., *Thomas Jefferson's Garden Book, 1766–1824: With Relevant Extracts from His Other Writings* (1944); E. Merton Coulter, *Wormsloe: Two Centuries of a Georgia Family* (1955); Jack T. Kirby, *Mockingbird Song: Ecological Landscapes of the South* (2006); Elizabeth Lawrence, *Beautiful at All Seasons: Southern Gardening and Beyond with Elizabeth Lawrence*, ed. Ann L. Armstrong and Lindie Wilson (2007); Philip D. Morgan, *Slave Counterpoint: Black Culture in the Eighteenth-Century Chesapeake and Lowcountry* (1998); Richard Westmacott, *African-American Gardens and Yards in the Rural South* (1992).

Golf

William Faulkner's *The Sound and the Fury* (1929) begins with the idiot Benjy Compson and his young black companion retrieving golf balls. Faulkner himself frequently played golf in the 1920s at the nine-hole University of Mississippi golf course and even acted as chairman of a tournament committee. Faulkner regarded himself as a sportsman, and his interest in golf reflected the South's changing sports scene in the early 20th century. Golf has not traditionally been regarded as a sport particularly associated with the South, yet the region has produced great athletes in that field and established an extensive network of courses and tournaments. Since World War II it has increasingly become a part of the life of middle-class southerners.

The popularity of golf in the United States reflects the British influence on American sport. Golf came to this country from Scotland, and Scottish merchants set up the South Carolina Golf Club as early as 1786. The first extensive American play was in New York, where country clubs were organized in the 1880s. The U.S. Golf Association appeared in 1894 to provide institutional direction, but at the turn of the century few golf courses had appeared in the South. Galveston, Tex., chartered Texas's first country club with a professionally designed course in 1898. Before 1900 golf had an elitist air to it and was mainly a pursuit of the leisured classes. The Southern Golf Association dates from 1902 and is one of the oldest such regional associations, now serving 500 member clubs in 14 states. Chicago and other cities of the Midwest led in building public courses in the early 20th century, but the appearance of amateur championship golf tournaments and celebrity golfers in the 1920s, along with the prosperity and consumerism of the people of that decade, helped to popularize golf. The South lagged in these developments, although Georgia and Texas were leaders; Georgia Technological Institute, for example, from the 1920s on fielded successful intercollegiate golf teams, while Texas produced a number of prominent professional golfers.

The country club appeared in many southern communities in the 1920s, although its widespread popularity in the region was a post–World War II phenomenon. Country clubs were organized for social activities, such as dancing, dining, card playing, and drinking, in addition to athletics. Members joined in order to meet influential people and to promote their business interests. The young in small towns especially had a new focus for combining athletic activities and courting. Golf was a social sport well designed to these ends. Unlike urban athletic clubs, country clubs were for both men and women, and golf proved early to be popular among both sexes.

The South has produced some of the most prominent amateur and professional golfers. In a 1980s survey of the 70 greatest players of all time, 16 were from the South, including 7 from Texas. Prominent golfers have included Jimmy Demaret, Ben Hogan, John Byron Nelson, and Lee Trevino, all from Texas; Cary Middlecoff from Tennessee; and Betsy Rawls from South Carolina. Robert Tyre

"Bobby" Jones Jr. from Atlanta is recognized as one of the game's greatest performers. The media of the 1920s and 1930s nurtured his image as the modern southern gentleman and helped make him a nationally popular hero. Sammy Snead of Hot Springs, Va., cultivated an image, according to *Golf* magazine, as "a hillbilly type who always had a vast storehouse of pungent jokes." "Slammin' Sammy," who won more than 100 tournaments, claimed he had his earnings buried in tin cans back in the hills of home. During the 1930s and 1940s Texan Byron Nelson dominated professional golf, victorious in 18 tournaments.

Mildred "Babe" Didrikson Zaharias, from Port Arthur, Tex., is referred to in virtually all surveys as the greatest American woman athlete. She excelled in every sport she attempted, was a star of the 1932 Olympic Games, and dominated women's golf in the 1930s. Outstanding Ladies Professional Golf Association golfers from the South include Beth Daniel, Sandra Haynie, and Kathy Whitworth.

Figures from the Professional Golf Association in 1967 showed that southerners continued to play a prominent role in the game. Of the top 100 money winners for the previous year, 35 were southern natives, with 15 of them coming from Texas. Dallas's Lee Buck Trevino became golf's first Latino star, winning the U.S. Open championship in 1968 and other championships in the 1970s.

The South's interest in golf can also be seen in its premier courses. The Augusta National Country Club in Georgia, the Pinehurst Country Club in North Carolina, the Seminole Golf Club in Palm Beach, Fla., the Dunes Golf and Beach Club in South Carolina, and the Ocean Course at Sea Pines Plantation in Hilton Head, S.C., are among the South's nationally recognized courses. Robert Trent Jones (1906–2000) designed 500 golf courses throughout the nation and 35 other countries including many in the South. Born in England, he would retire to Florida. His first significant commission was designing, with Bobby Jones Jr., the Peachtree Golf Club in Atlanta in 1948. Alabama established the Robert Trent Jones Golf Trail in 1992. The Atlantic shore of the Southeast has been referred to as "The Golf Coast of America." Florida and South Carolina are particularly well known for the number and quality of resorts built around golfing for the region's, and indeed the nation's, vacationing elite. The Grand Strand area of coastal South Carolina has more than 100 courses, and a 2009 survey of the top 100 public golf courses in the United States listed 11 from South Carolina alone. Almost half of the professional tournaments in the United States take place on southern courses. The Senior PGA tournament began in Austin in 1978 as the Legends of Golf Tournament and hosted golfers over 50 years of age.

The Masters Tournament at the Augusta National Country Club is one of the game's four most significant professional championships (along with those of the U.S. Open, the British Open, and the Professional Golf Association). Georgian "Bobby" Jones retired in 1930 from competitive golf, then conceived the idea of creating the Augusta course. Wall Street banker Clifford Roberts became his development partner and Scotland's Alistair Mackenzie was the designer of the course. Its site was 365 acres of rolling Georgia pinelands, which had for a hundred years been a nursery. A Belgian baron named Prosper Jules Alphonse Berckmans moved to Augusta in 1857 and established the first nursery in the South. He disseminated hundreds of species of flowers, shrubs, and trees; in his catalog of items in 1861 were 1,300 varieties of pears, 900 of apples, 300 of grapes, and more than 100 each of azaleas and camellias. This natural background has made the Augusta course famed for its beauty, with long lines of magnolias, brilliant colors from azaleas, redbuds, and white dogwoods, and a chorus of sounds from the mockingbirds and cardinals. The architecture at Augusta adds to the stereotypical southern ambience. People sip mint juleps at café tables under huge magnolia trees on the front lawn of the sedate, Georgian-styled clubhouse, which could be from the *Gone with the Wind* film set. Despite the southern setting, the Augusta Country Club is a national institution. When the club was organized, only 30 members from Augusta itself were allowed. Most members have always been from outside Georgia, including many outside the South.

As Associated Press sportswriter Will Grimsley has noted, the Masters Tournament "has been called autocratic, arrogant, snobbish, and racist." At the same time it has been lauded as the best organized, most relaxed, and most pleasant of the professional tournaments. As Florida golfing great Gene Sarazen says, "It's the only tournament with class." Tournament directors carefully regulate the players and spectators, prohibiting cans, tents, and the sale of junk food and programs. CBS television has been televising the tournament since 1956, but even television trucks must be covered in green for camouflage. The key word at the Masters is "tradition," a word not unknown in the South. This emphasis led to conflict in the 1960s, however, when strong press criticism was directed at the tournament directors for never having invited a black to compete. A rule was soon adopted so that any winner of a professional golfers' association tournament could compete, and Lee Elder, winner of the 1974 Monsanto Open, became the first black to receive a bid from Augusta, playing in 1975 without incident. Controversy also appeared in 2003 when Martha Buck organized a protest to pressure the Augusta club to admit women members; law enforcement officials marginalized protestors away from the course and Buck did not mount a subsequent challenge.

Under Jim Crow segregation, middle-class blacks built a golfing structure parallel to the whites-only public facilities and the "Caucasian"-only role of the Professional Golf Association (PGA), which kept black golfers out of its tournaments until 1961. The PGA formed in 1916, and the United States Golf Association (UGA) appeared in 1926 to direct development of the sport among black amateurs and professionals, sponsoring the annual Negro National Open championships. The black caddie was a familiar figure in the segregated South, expected to serve in this traditionally deferential and submissive service role. The Robert Redford film *The Legend of Bagger Vance* (2000), set in 1930s Georgia, mythologized the black caddie (played in the film by Will Smith) as a wise guardian angel of a white golfer. In any event, because many black men learned to play golf while working as young caddies, they were most significant for promoting golf in the black community in the early 20th century.

Washington, D.C., established the first black golf club in the 1920s. The earliest, black country and golf clubs in the South were Acorn (Richmond, 1924), Lincoln (Jacksonville, 1927), and Lincoln (Atlanta, 1932). Atlanta's club hosted the first Southern Open championship in 1934; among the club members that year was scholar and activist W. E. B. Du Bois. The 1940s saw new clubs in Houston, Miami, and Atlanta. Atlanta's Howard Wheeler was a leading UGA professional golfer, winning titles over three decades from 1933 to 1958. Asheville's John Dendy was a three-time UGA champion while attending Morehouse College. Black golfers in the 1940s included Calvin Searles and Ben Green (both from New Orleans), Solomon Hughes (Gadsden, Ala.), and Zeke Hartsfield (Atlanta). Nashville's Theodore Rhodes won the Joe Louis Tournament in Detroit four times beginning in 1946.

CHARLES REAGAN WILSON
University of Mississippi

Marvin P. Dawkins and Graham C. Kinloch, *African American Golfers during the Jim Crow Era* (2000); Frank DeFord, *Sports Illustrated* (7 April 1986); William Price Fox, *Golfing in the Carolinas* (1990); John M. Ross, ed., *Golf Magazine's Encyclopedia of Golf* (1979); Curt Sampson, *The Masters: Golf, Money, and Power in Augusta, Georgia* (1998); Alan Shipnuck, *The Battle for Augusta National: Hootie, Martha, and the Masters of the Universe* (2004); *Southern Living* (August 1967); Dawson Taylor, *The Masters: An Illustrated History* (1973).

Holidays

Sunday has been the most frequently commemorated holiday in the South. Originally kept with some solemnity, it has now become largely a celebration of the cessation of work, although it is still a *dies non* in law. Once there was also a weekly half holiday, usually Wednesday or Thursday, but a tendency to slacken work on Saturday has recently appeared. Banks have generally transferred most of their holidays to a Monday.

The only total holiday is Christmas and perhaps the day following. New Year's Day shares in some of the Christmas festivities, but it has become mainly an occasion for viewing football bowl games. Newspaper stories still remind southerners to eat black-eyed peas on New Year's Day for good luck. The popular meaning of Memorial Day is that it is the beginning of summer and vacation season. Early in the 20th century, the South began observing it for the first time since the Civil War as a memorial to veterans of the Spanish-American War. In many southern states 26 April is the special Confederate Memorial Day; in others it is 3 June; still others combine it with the national Memorial Day. The Fourth of July Independence Day was observed by southern blacks, although whites showed more interest in it after southerners fought for the nation in the Spanish American War. Still, through much of the 20th century, whites mainly viewed it as a nonworking day or picnic day. The 1976 bicentennial commemoration revived its significance, and it has grown in popularity. Labor Day used to be marked by a parade and baseball game, but now it generally marks the end of summer and vacation time. Thanksgiving in the South never had quite the importance it held outside the region. It is a time of hunting and feasting, and also the date for special football games.

The preceding holidays are of primary regional importance, but southerners, like other Americans, celebrate a variety of additional special occasions as well. St. Valentine's Day (14 February) is an occasion promoted by gift and stationery shops. The George Washington observance is a bank and post office holiday. Mardi Gras (Shrove Tuesday) is a major festival in New Orleans, Mobile, and Pensacola, the culmination of a season of Carnival preceding Lent. St. Patrick's Day (17 March) has grown from an ethnic Irish commemoration to a more extensive observance, once again promoted by gift and stationery shops. Easter Sunday is a high religious festival but, being a Sunday, is somewhat less commercialized than Christmas. Both Easter and Christmas celebrations tend to be only daylong rather than season-long events. The Jewish days of Rosh Hashanah, Yom Kippur, and Hanukkah are quietly recognized by the news media and stationery shops. Halloween (31 October), especially the night, is a party festival and a time of pranks by children and some adults, many of them now staged in churches and community centers to ensure safety.

A third group of holidays are, as yet, minor days to be noted. The birthdays of Robert E. Lee (21 January), "Stonewall" Jackson (22 January), and Matthew

Fontaine Maury (24 January) are observed by organizations of descendants of Confederate veterans. Groundhog Day (2 February) is noted by news media and schools. St. Joseph Day (19 March) attracts major attention in New Orleans and some other Roman Catholic communities, and Good Friday is a legal holiday in Louisiana. May Day evokes some school attention. Flag Day (14 June) is a legal holiday. The days of St. John (the baptizer, 24 June, and the evangelist, 27 December) are occasions for Masonic lodges (picnics in summer, banquets in winter). There is a sentimental Francophile notice of Bastille Day (14 July) and a school recognition of Columbus Day. All Saints' Day (1 November) is a legal holiday in Louisiana. In nearby states it is an occasion for decorating cemeteries, although the latter practice belongs more aptly to the following day, All Souls' Day. Armistice Day (11 November) used to be a widespread observance, but under the designation of Veterans Day it has become a day noted by veterans' organizations of all wars from World War II onward.

Four holidays—Christmas, New Year's, the Fourth of July, and Thanksgiving—are times when most institutions of a community are closed. Memorial Day and Labor Day are also nonworkdays for many; they serve to signal the opening and closing respectively of resort areas and vacation spots. Other holidays attract less attention (except for Easter), but they are nonetheless generally commemorated. The Jewish high holy days have gradually become more significant, especially because of the prominence of Jewish merchants and Jewish academics, many of whom celebrate Rosh Hashanah and Yom Kippur.

Among blacks there used to be extensive, if informal, commemoration of Emancipation Day (variously 8 May, 19 June, and perhaps others); businesses did not close, but blacks frequently did not report for work. Blacks in Texas celebrated the distinctive Juneteenth holiday. More recently other events, as, for instance, those of the civil rights activities of the 1960s, as well as disillusionment with the progress of emancipation, have pushed it into the background. The late Martin Luther King Jr.'s birthday (15 January but celebrated the third Monday in January) won approval in 1983 as a federal holiday. Kwanzaa is a weeklong celebration of African history and culture, December 26 to January 1, characterized by lighting of candles, pouring of libations, giving of gifts, and feasting.

The rapid growth of the Latino population in the recent South has resulted in celebrations of new holidays regionwide. Newspapers increasingly take note of Mexican Independence Day (16 September, Diez y Seis), when Mexicans proclaimed their independence from Spain. More popularly known is Cinco de Mayo, which recalls Mexico's independence from French occupation in the 19th century and is occasion for Mexican restaurants and bars to celebrate.

More important is Our Lady of Guadeloupe Feast Day (December 12), which honors the story of an Indian, Juan Diego, who saw the Virgin Mary on a hill near Mexico City. Our Lady of Guadeloupe is the patron saint of Mexico, and Latinos in the South celebrate the holiday at churches, in homes, and with community processions following banners proclaiming her image.

ALLEN CABANISS
University of Mississippi

Hennig Cohen and Tristram Potter Coffin, eds., *The Folklore of American Holidays* (3rd ed., 1999); Jane M. Hatch, *The American Book of Days* (3rd ed., 1978); Robert Lee, *National Forum* (Summer 1982); Robert J. Myers, *Celebrations: The Complete Book of American Holidays* (1972); William E. Woodward, *The Way Our People Lived: An Intimate American History* (1944).

Horses

The distinctive role of horses in the South began in the antebellum era. The plantation economy created sufficient wealth to permit the development of a gentry class and the breeding of horses for pleasure and sport. This resulted in three native American breeds, all developed in significant part in the South: the American Quarter Horse, the American Saddlebred Horse, and the Tennessee Walking Horse.

Before the Civil War, the Old South was the center of thoroughbred breeding and racing. Williamsburg, Va., and Charleston, S.C., each claims to be the first community of established racing in America. Virginia was the early center for thoroughbred breeding. Andrew Jackson established an important center for racing at Nashville, Tenn., and for a long time this area was second only to Virginia in thoroughbred breeding. Kentucky became the dominant breeding area in the early 19th century and is still so, although thoroughbreds are bred in other parts of the South, most notably Florida, Virginia, and Maryland.

Horse racing ceased during the Civil War. It came back strongly after the war, but without the dominance of the Old South. Racetracks were widespread, and many were disreputable. The establishment of the Jockey Club with legislative, judicial, and executive functions in 1894 commenced the process of cleaning up racing. Racing, nevertheless, declined in the period immediately preceding World War I, probably because of its bad reputation and moral objections of the public to betting. A slow and steady renaissance was led by men of integrity and substance. Since World War I, flat racing has steadily increased in popularity and acceptability and is now the largest spectator sport in the United States. The most significant southern tracks operate in Florida, Mary-

The 83rd Annual Pony Swim in Chincoteague, Va., 2008
(U.S. Coast Guard photo/Petty Officer 3rd Class Mark Jones)

land, Kentucky, Arkansas, and Louisiana. Other states in the South either have or are about to adopt active racing programs.

The classic three-year-old thoroughbred races (the Triple Crown) were all instituted in the decade following the Civil War, one in the North and two in border states: the Belmont Stakes (New York), in 1867; the Preakness Stake (Maryland), in 1873; and the best-known horse race in America, the Kentucky Derby, in 1875. These races are regularly contested by southern-bred horses.

Fox hunting (riding to hounds), a natural for the plantation class, developed in the colonies as it was developing in Great Britain and became the principal sport of the planter class before the Civil War. (The first pack of hounds was probably imported to southern Maryland in 1650 by Robert Brooke.)

The destruction of the South in the Civil War almost destroyed fox hunting. After the war, the sport was revived and is now very active, with Virginia and Maryland generally considered to be its center. However, almost every state in the South boasts at least one recognized hunt, and the Deep South has produced one of the outstanding fox hunters of all time. Benjamin H. Hardaway III, master of foxhounds and huntsman of the Midland Fox Hounds, Midland, Ga., is a keen student of fox hunting and a worthy successor to Peter Beckford, an early pioneer of modern fox hunting. The world famous Midland Fox Hounds, developed entirely by Hardaway, are deer proof, big mouthed, and aggressive and will effectively drive a fox. The Midland Hounds hunt continuously in Georgia and Alabama and regularly in Pennsylvania, Maryland, and Virginia.

Hunting is a direct ancestor of steeple chasing. The introduction of jumping horses in the hunt field led to races across the countryside from one landmark to another, usually the steeples of village churches. Early American jump racing was much like the British counterpart. The sport developed in the South, where most of the races are still held.

The horse, necessary for a civilized existence and important for recreation, was an indispensable partner in war. Aside from the mundane, but essential, matter of supply, the horse provided the mobility needed for intelligence gathering and communication, and in battle the horse made the difference. Mounted infantrymen, who rode to battle and fought on foot, appeared in frontier conflicts of the prerevolutionary period. These frontiersmen penetrated deep into enemy territory and appeared where least expected. Horse soldiers flourished in the Revolutionary War, especially in the South where irregular cavalry contributed significantly to the American war effort. Cavalry was a primary factor in the South's early successes in the Civil War and permitted the conflict to last as long as it did. The Confederacy had a brilliant array of cavalry chieftains. Two of the best known of these gifted horse soldiers were the almost invincible Nathan Bedford Forrest and the colorful and dashing James Ewell Brown "Jeb" Stuart.

Today, the cavalry is gone, and mules no longer plod the cotton rows or pull the freight and cotton wagons. Churchyards and town squares are not filled with wagons, buggies, and saddle horses. Human existence, with a high level of material comfort, can be maintained without a horse. Nonetheless, the bugle call to the post and the hunting horn are still heard. The Walking Horse and the American Saddlebred Horse are not necessary for plantation management, but throughout the South ringmasters at horse shows are heard to say, "Let your horses walk on" or "Let your horses rack on."

Racing and the breeding of racehorses are large industries. Horse shows range from small one-breed shows to weeklong events in large urban centers such as Dallas, Houston, Atlanta, New Orleans, Memphis, Raleigh, and Louisville. Lengthy affairs are devoted to selecting the best of a breed, such as the Tennessee Walking Horse National Celebration in Shelbyville, Tenn., and its counterpart for the American Saddlebred in Louisville, Ky., where annually the champion of the breed is chosen. Many of the contestants at the annual Quarter Horse World Congress in Ohio come from the South. The return of draft horses and mules has led to shows devoted entirely to these animals.

Although a product of the West, the rodeo has become one of the most popular of the horse sports or shows in the South. The roots of rodeo are in the work of the 19th-century cowboys of the West. Ranch life was demanding and tough. Cattle herds were brought in each spring from winter pasture and tended until the autumn trail drives. Each cowboy required a string of horses, and no one could afford the time to train them. Therefore, green and sometimes freshly caught wild horses were roped and ridden. At the end of annual trail drives, when the cowboys gathered in the railroad towns, conversations, particularly with the aid of liquor, soon turned to boasts of prowess with lariat and horse. Impromptu riding and roping contests resulted. Thus, the rodeo was born. Two of the five standard rodeo events, calf roping and saddle bronc riding, grew out of practical cowboy work. The three remaining events, bareback bronc riding, bull riding, and steer wrestling, rose from bragging.

The subject of horses in the South cannot be left without a reference to polo. Polo, a stick-and-ball game that originated in the Orient more than 2,000 years ago, was introduced into the United States in 1876 and reached its golden age during the 1920s and 1930s. Once considered the province of the very rich in areas outside the South, it is now played by many people throughout the region on courses ranging from cow pastures to the well-appointed clubs of the wealthy. Polo has been slow to catch on as a collegiate sport in the South, but several southern schools have polo teams, including the University of Georgia, the University of Virginia, and the University of Texas. In 2009 the University of Virginia won both the men's and women's National Intercollegiate Tournament championship with the number-one ranked men's team defeating two-time national champion Texas A&M. The number-two ranked women's team beat first-ranked Cornell.

In addition to serving as domesticated animals for work and play, horses have increasingly become sought-out objects of tourism. Along the Atlantic Coast, on various islands off the coasts of Virginia and Maryland and on the Outer Banks of North Carolina, feral herds of horses and ponies draw visitors year round. North Carolina's Cape Hatteras National Seashore and Assateague and Chincoteague islands off the coasts of Virginia and Maryland are popular tourist destinations for sightseers eager to watch horses roam in a natural environment. Practically every summer since 1925, the Chincoteague volunteer fire department has herded ponies from Assateague Island across Assateague Channel to Chincoteague Memorial Park in an annual "pony swim." The first pony to come ashore at the park is crowned King or Queen Neptune and given away at the carnival that follows the return of the remaining ponies to Assateague Island.

Not to be overlooked is the just plain horse of dubious pedigree and faulted conformation found on farms and in backyards. An experienced horse fancier would pass him by, but he can turn a child into a gallant knight, a Wild West marshal, or a reincarnation of Jeb Stuart or Nathan Bedford Forest. Perhaps his real value exceeds that of the blooded horses of the racetracks and show rings.

FRANK HAMPTON MCFADDEN
Pike Road, Alabama

Robert Denhardt, *The Horse of the Americas* (1975); Nan Devincent-Hayes and Bo Bennett, *Chincoteague and Assateague Islands* (2000); J. Frank Dobie, ed., *Mustangs and Cow Horses* (1940); Kent Hollingsworth, *The Kentucky Thoroughbred* (1976, 2008); Robert W. Howard, *The Horse in America* (1965); Kitty Slater, *The Hunt Country of America* (1973).

House Parties

Musicians and partygoers across the South regularly gather at house parties for long evenings of conversation, dancing, and music. The crowds may be white, African American, Cajun, Latino, or American Indian; the music, in turn, may be blues, country, jazz, Cajun, or hip-hop. Mouth-watering food is a constant (gumbo, fry bread, chicken stew, fried catfish), as is liquid refreshment and a spirit of revelry. Some parties set out a hat or guitar case for tipping the musicians; others charge at the door to catch up on back rent, cover the musicians' fees, or perhaps raise funds for a neighbor in need; still others rely on the sale of food and drink to raise a bit of extra cash. Southern house parties fueled country music creativity in the 1930s and 1940s, and country music scholar Bill Malone calls them "one of the great seedbeds of country music." They also launched the careers of generations of blues musicians, and today they provide fertile ground for hip-hop emcees and Cajun rock and rollers.

While southern house parties have long been associated with grass-roots music making, the association is nowhere stronger than in the Mississippi Delta, where these gatherings have provided a home for the blues for more than a hundred years. Every Friday and Saturday night for most of the 20th century, African American audiences gathered to hear guitarists or piano players—often accompanied by a harmonica player and a drummer—play and sing. Sometimes a musician would rub a broom handle across the floor to provide rhythm; other times, a partygoer would "pat" rhythms on his or her body to accompany a buck dance. Once the music began, those in the audience would join in with their own verses and verbal encouragement.

Stories, jokes, and music are all part of the blues performance at a house party. As small rooms fill with smoke and the smell of alcohol, couples talk, dance the slow drag, and sing with the performer. As the music continues, the dancers speak to the singer, and he, in turn, responds to their words with his music. The blues singer learns to "talk the blues" with his audience, deftly integrating the conversation between his blues verses. When a verse ends, the musicians keep playing, turning the extended moment into a time for talking. The singer then sings another verse, giving the audience a chance to recall rhymes and jokes to tell at the next verse break. The partygoers thus influence the length and structure of each blues, as they force the singer to integrate his song with their response. Experienced bluesmen know that audience response is a measure of their musical skill; a successful blues session is filled with comments and jokes that partygoers tell as the music unfolds. This "call and response" exchange between the blues performer and his audience finds its counterpart in African American church services, where a similar pattern develops between the preacher and his congregation.

The constant verbal interplay at blues house parties means that the role of "performer" constantly shifts from the singer to his audience and then back again. After a partygoer tells a joke, the performer recaptures his audience by changing the musical beat or striking louder chords. While he allows the center of attention to shift to members of the crowd, the performer nonetheless maintains overall control through his music.

This pattern of back-and-forth interplay is well illustrated by the talk and singing at a 1968 blues house party in Clarksdale, Miss. The exchange begins when pianist Pine Top Johnson declares to Jasper Love, "You know one thing, Boy? I'm drifting." Love replies, "He's trying to drift outta Mississippi. I know what he's trying to do." Then Johnson sings a verse:

> You know I'm drifting, and I'm drifting, just like a ship out on the sea.
> Well, I'm drifting, and I'm drifting like a ship out on the sea.
> Well, you know I ain't got nobody in this world to care for me.

Pine Top thus introduces "Drifting Blues" by integrating both storytelling and music into his performance. Throughout the party, Pine Top and Jasper Love "talk" through the music. Pine Top sings a verse, for instance, and then says, "You know what I'm talking about." Later, Jasper Love encourages Pine Top with the phrase, "Talk to them, Pine." The performer "talks" through his music; to play it well is to talk clearly. So when Pine Top finishes a verse, Jasper Love replies, "Now it's talking to me."

The distinction between music and talk blurs as blues talk mixes with verses, at times even becoming the focus of the performance. Such talk can take the form of short phrases or lengthy conversations. Brief phrases like "Play the blues, Pine" frequently punctuate the musical breaks after each line. (This same pattern of inserting phrases during instrumental breaks also marks the on-air commentary of blues disc jockeys, who often talk "over" recorded tracks.) Lengthier blues talk, in contrast, can pull the center of attention away from the verses, focusing it instead on the conversation between the singer and the audience. Such conversations can unfold like a verse within the song; they can include obscene tales, toasts, and dozens, all performed to the musician's instrumental accompaniment.

Localization is another way that house party performers engage their audiences. Mississippi Delta artists, for instance, often insert the names of local towns in their verses. Hence, when Pine Top performs "Dust My Broom" at a Clarksdale house party, he sings, "I'm going to find me a Clarksdale woman if she dumb and crippled and blind." Later, in "Santa Fe Blues," he sings:

I say Mobile on that Southern line, Jackson on that Santa Fe.
You know I got a woman in Tutwiler, I got a woman in Sumner too.

The state of Mississippi itself is an important point on the musical compass at Delta house parties. Pine Top tells Jasper Love, "I'm down in Mississippi, and I got to play the blues." To be "down in Mississippi" is both a geographic and an emotional state. Hence, when Pine Top and Jasper Love both declare their plans to move "up" to Chicago, they are not only talking about escaping from Mississippi. Jasper makes this pointedly clear when he tells Pine Top, "I'm glad we up here on Seventy-ninth and Cottage Grove, where we can be *free* . . . in Chicago, Illinois."

Jasper locates Mississippi on the "down" side of the blues map in both a literal and an emotional direction; he suggests that to leave Mississippi is to move *up* to a better life. "I'm a Mississippi boy, but I done skipped from it now." In this world of talk and song, Mississippi becomes the land of tribulation and misfortune. Thus, when Pine Top sings the blues line "Love, I've had my fun if I don't get well no more," Jasper replies, "Long as you stay in Mississippi, you never will get well." Later Pine Top sings that he is dying and plans to ship his body back home: "On the next train south, Love, look for my clothes back home." Jasper Love responds by arguing that you shouldn't send even a corpse back to the South: "You don't want to go south. Tell him to go west or north. But don't go south."

Exchanges like these reveal how house party performers embrace their audiences through music. Performer and audience merge in the unfolding drama, as the blues—like the old hymns that Jasper often invokes—"pitches sound backwards and forwards."

Though the popular heyday of the blues has long past, blues house parties remain common in the Mississippi Delta. They now find a vibrant complement in hip-hop house parties, with the two sometimes even unfolding together. In other regions of the South, where house parties feature different musics and different cultural norms, the mix of music, merriment, and dance still remains much in demand. When a musician finds an audience and a comfortable room where he or she can play, the party begins early in the evening and will last "into the wee, wee hours."

WILLIAM FERRIS
University of North Carolina at Chapel Hill

William Ferris, *Blues from the Delta* (1984), *Give My Poor Heart Ease: Voices of the Mississippi Blues* (2009), *Mississippi Delta Blues* (film, 1974); Bill C. Malone, *Country Music, U.S.A.* (2002); Eudora Welty, *The Collected Stories of Eudora Welty* (1980).

Hunting

During the South's colonial and antebellum periods, the pursuit of wildlife provided settlers with both a diversion from their ordinary work routines and a supplement to their sometimes-meager stocks of food. Settlers also hunted to control the numbers of larger mammals in their vicinity, for their crops were vulnerable to grazing by deer and by flocks of birds, while their free-roaming livestock fell prey to wolves.

During this period, some wealthy planters sought to emulate the privileges and refinements of European aristocrats. In some areas, hunting certain wild game became identified with the prerogatives of power and status; as such, it emerged as an important social activity for influential, wealthy individuals. The elite hunting narratives of the antebellum years offer detailed descriptions of the hunt, the chase, and the shoot. Although claiming to be factual, these narratives are actually standardized accounts whose recurrent themes provide insights into the ideology of affluent planters and the ways in which they sought to distinguish themselves from other social classes.

Many planters believed that hunting enabled them to understand nature and man's place in the world. Southern hunters loved nature for its supposed order and stability, which their own organized social life (based in a hierarchical arrangement of people and contingent upon the judicial application of force) could only approximate. For these planters, hunting was a socially sanctioned

John A. Taylor hunts quail with bird dogs Speck and George in Monroe County, Ala., 1966.
(Photograph by Fred Eddins, courtesy of Mary Amelia Taylor)

expression of power; they saw its violence as a requirement for participating in the natural world and appreciating its indestructible order. This perspective allowed planters to differentiate their modes of hunting from others on the basis of presumed motive and purpose. If most whites and blacks in the South hunted out of necessity, planters did so for sport and for amusement. While other classes pursued wild animals for meat and tangible trophies, planters saw the process itself as the most important part of the chase. For them, the end was both unimportant and inconsequential. Hunting conventions (sportsmanship) became prerequisites for membership in polite society, and they provided its participants the opportunity to learn the important lessons of self-discipline and control.

Plantation-style hunting, of course, was not for everyone. Outside the restricted circles of gentility, most men hunted wildlife for food and for profit. The majority of these hunters subsisted on the land and sold skins and game meat whenever they found buyers.

After the Civil War, the processes of urbanization and industrialization gradually concentrated many southerners in towns and cities. Leisure and wealth for growing numbers of these urban dwellers made a return to nature and the land increasingly attractive. This "escape" to nature became possible for those who owned or leased large tracts of land; outside of these tracts, however, city hunters came into increasing conflict with rural landowners, market hunters, and game dealers over the declining stocks of wild game. State trespass laws and federal game regulations became a solution to these conflicts; to legislators, they seemed the most democratic way to handle access to wildlife for those aspiring to hunt. By 1910 most southern states had joined the rest of the nation in enacting trespass and game laws and providing cadres of officers to enforce them. With these legal structures in place, market hunting and the sale of wild animals became illegal. State legislatures, in turn, gave wildlife agencies the power to monitor the populations of species now defined by law as "game" and to determine the ways and means by which these species became legal to hunt. Hence, as a direct result of legal processes initiated by city dwellers, states across the South restricted the variety of hunted species and formalized many hunting norms. These statutes and regulations still provide the ground rules and boundaries determining what, where, when, and how species are hunted. Although many southern hunters continue to hunt for food, most hunting in the South is now for sport and recreation.

Most of the current initiatives affecting field sports have come not from the South's rural populations but from organized groups in the cities; these groups include antihunting leagues and such hunting and conservation organizations as Ducks Unlimited, the National Turkey Federation, and the National Wildlife Federation. These organizations and their many counterparts publish their own journals, solicit contributions, and maintain lobbies that seek to influence legislation favorable to their causes. From these journals, contemporary hunters glean the latest tips, techniques, and technologies for tracking their game; find out about what to wear while pursing it; learn about the big ones that escaped; and read about current fads in men's games.

Modernizing developments have influenced some types of hunting more than others. Particular varieties of dogs and hounds are bred, trained, and certified for specific types of hunters. National organizations focus on these particular breeds, keep breeding records, and sponsor annual series of field trials and bench shows to authenticate their products. The trading, purchase, and breeding of hounds and dogs are a big business in many rural areas of the South, particularly in those that host the various field trials.

The influences of technology and the changing patterns of landownership are also apparent in the organization of hunt clubs. Hunt clubs began in colonial days when neighbors joined together for game drives. At that time, their organization was informal, often spontaneous, and involved no fees or formal membership. Later, when the large estates were divided or sold, individuals joined together to lease land for game and to alleviate the costs of maintaining hunting dogs throughout the year. Formal hunt clubs began about 1900. These clubs had a paid and limited membership and set specific times for hunting. In the latter decades of the 20th century, agribusiness—with its mechanized operations on large tracts of land—dramatically reduced game habitat on the better lands; most of the marginal lands, which had previously been occupied and tilled by tenants, reverted to pine plantations and scrub. With this secondary growth, deer returned to these marginal lands; so too did hunt clubs, now frequently headquartered in refurbished tenant shacks.

Today, precision firearms have largely replaced the muskets of former times (although many purists still prefer to stalk their deer with muzzleloaders or bows and arrows). Four-wheel-drive vehicles have superseded horses and wagons, dirt roads the foot trails, and cell phones and loudspeakers the hunter's horn. Yet the informal, intimate rituals between hunting buddies and the traditions of time and place continue to make the hunt club a seasonal feature of southern life.

The distinctiveness of southern hunting stems from a peculiar combination of traits found in the region. The myth of the plantation lifestyle continues to inform the traditions of those who can afford to live the image of this lifestyle and to influence others. Its reality persists in the hunting plantations for quail and deer (many of which were purchased and maintained by northern wealth in the late 19th and early 20th centuries), and in the colorful pageantries of the exclusive hunt clubs located throughout the South. Extensive landownership, wealth, power, and leisure sustain these plantations and clubs, luring some to join and many others to observe their seasonal rituals. Still others read about them or participate in regional or national field trials for fox, quail, and coon— species associated with earlier plantation life.

Most hunting in the rural South lacks the pretentiousness of the plantation tradition; nonetheless, it continues to reflect regional traditions of gender, racial, and socioeconomic stratification. More than two-thirds of southern hunters come from small towns or live in rural areas. Most are whites and Indians. Among these groups, youngsters typically learn to hunt from their fathers or close relatives. Guns are often heirlooms passed between generations. African Americans are proportionately underrepresented in the ranks of southern hunters; in contrast to the other cultural groups, they learn to hunt later in life and tend to learn from peers rather than from their fathers. Most southern hunters come from the working classes and are generally under 40 years of age. Although the expressed motivation for hunting varies, most hunters say that they hunt for sport rather than for food; nonetheless, they eat most of the game they take.

Hunting is still very much a masculine domain. Historically, most women who hunt have come from the far ends of the economic spectrum; this pattern seems to be shifting, however, as more southern women in the middle economic class take up the sport. Yet, hunting remains an activity dominated by men, and it is to them that the cleaning, cooking, and serving of game meat usually falls.

Socialization as a hunter begins at an early age, guided by fathers or an intimate circle of friends. In these close groups, young boys learn lessons about masculinity and their identity within a given community, together with skills useful in their transitions to manhood. Coming of age rituals (aptly described by William Faulkner in *Go Down, Moses*) celebrate their maturation and accomplishments. Most boys' initial kills are small game such as squirrels and rabbits, which make relatively easy targets. Youngsters generally pursue a variety of mammals and birds as their time allows, but as they mature, they tend to specialize in one or a few species, depending upon their associations with other men, their jobs, and the costs of maintaining trained dogs.

Men who hunt together are also influential in other areas of community social and political life. Increasingly, however, family and work commitments disrupt these male hunting fraternities. Although jobs outside of the local community may temporarily dislodge these networks, many men return home religiously for the fall hunting season.

The types of game that southern hunters pursue reflect stratification along socioeconomic and racial lines. Ownership of trained dogs and the availability of extensive tracts of land are prerequisites for game that many count as the most "prestigious," including quail, deer, fox, and turkey. Access to these species remains difficult for many, although they may be hunted on public lands. Dove shoots, which usually open the fall hunting season, are generally open to most people because the shoot requires guns positioned in as many places as possible around a recently harvested field to keep the birds flying. (In many northern states, doves and quail are classified as songbirds and thus not hunted.) Many African Americans and working-class whites hunt squirrels, rabbits, raccoons, and possums, species that are normally avoided by other, more specialized sportsmen.

As a region, the South still retains an edge over other areas in the number of households that include a hunter. In 1959, Gallup Polls revealed that slightly more than half of southern white households contained a hunter, compared to one-third for the rest of the nation. Fifty years later, these percentages have dropped dramatically. A cumulative tabulation of survey data from 1972 to 2006, compiled by the University of Chicago's National Opinion Research Survey, showed that the number of southern households with hunters now barely edges above 25 percent. This still suggests that one of every four households in the South includes a hunter—a figure that continues to lead most other regions of the country.

Every five years the U.S. Fish and Wildlife Service publishes a national survey of wildlife-associated outdoor recreation. Its 2005 surveys in North Carolina estimated that 277,000 hunters spent 4.6 million days afield. That year, these hunters reportedly spent $512 million on their pursuits within the state, a sum that contributed to 8,800 jobs. The majority of these sportsmen (8 out of 10) say that a political candidate's position on hunting-related environmental issues is an important factor in determining for whom they cast their votes. Sportsmen and sportswomen have powerful voices in legislation through the Congressional Sportsmen's Foundation and the National Assembly of Sportsmen's Caucuses.

STUART A. MARKS
Durham, North Carolina

Dickson D. Bruce Jr., *Violence and Culture in the Antebellum South* (1979); William Elliot, *Carolina Sports by Land and Water* (1859); William Faulkner, *Go Down, Moses*

(1942); C. Gondes, ed., *Hunting in the Old South* (1967); Stuart A. Marks, *Southern Hunting in Black and White: Nature, History, and Rituals in a Carolina Community* (1991); Nicholas W. Proctor, *Bathed in Blood: Hunting and Mastery in the Old South* (2002); Robert Ruark, *The Old Man and the Boy* (1957); U.S. Fish & Wildlife Service, *National Survey of Fishing, Hunting, and Wildlife-Associated Recreation* (2006).

Juke Joints and Honky-Tonks

Southern roadhouses, which are usually called "juke joints" and "honky-tonks," had their origins in the antebellum "groggeries," or taverns, that were found throughout the South. In these establishments, groggery keepers dispensed questionable liquors to local customers and travelers. Consisting of little more than a room for drinking and a room for gambling, these groggeries were the haunts of white farmers, who exchanged their hard-earned cash for "bust-head" whiskey, and black slaves, who traded produce for "red-eye" rum.

Following the Civil War the integrated camaraderie of the antebellum groggeries gave way to racial segregation. In much of the New South, whites claimed the roadside taverns as their own, leaving the newly freed blacks to find their own recreational sites. In response, some rural blacks opened their homes to the public, selling homemade liquors to friends and strangers alike. To entertain their customers, the owners of such houses employed local musicians, who played "jump-ups" and blues for dancing couples and gambling men. Offering entertainment as well as refreshments, these black-owned houses were invariably known as "jukes" or "juke joints."

"Juke" is the common pronunciation of "joog," a word meaning disorderly, which is found among Gullah-Geechee blacks of coastal South Carolina and Georgia. "Joog," in turn, may ultimately derive from "dzugu," a Bambara African word meaning wicked. The term "juke" is applied to black roadhouses throughout the South, but it can also refer to white taverns, especially in Florida and Georgia. It is not uncommon in those states to hear whites speak of "going jukin" after work.

Most southern whites, however, refer to their roadhouses as "honky-tonks." The etymology of this curious word is unknown; but "honky-tonk" first appeared in print in 1894, when a correspondent for the *Daily Ardmoreite* (Ardmore, Okla.) wrote the following: "The honk-a-tonk last night was well attended by ball-heads, bachelors, and leading citizens." Whatever its origins, the term "honky-tonk" was applied to the roadside taverns that dotted the outskirts of oil boomtowns in Oklahoma and Texas. The "honky-tonks" contained little more than a bar, a dance floor, and a tiny stage for the musicians (in some instances shielded by chicken wire to protect the performers from flying objects when the fights broke out). Amid these small but noisy honky-tonk crowds, musicians amplified their guitars and Dobros, overcoming the sounds of shuffling dancers and gambling men to play their mournful ballads about drinking, divorce, and downfall.

Honky-tonks remained a phenomenon associated primarily with the Southwest until 1935, when the Texas-born musician Al Dexter recorded his popular "Honky-Tonk Blues." Within a few years white roadhouses throughout the South were known as "honky-tonks" or "honkies." In the Southwest, it was not uncommon for whites to attend black jukes and for blacks to visit white honky-tonks. But in the Southeast the racial barriers proved more rigid. Although intermingling was not unknown there, black jukes and white honky-tonks remained segregated by custom. Even today southeastern jukes and honky-tonks are segregated at a time when racial integration in public places has become commonplace.

"Honky-tonks" and "juke joints" continue to provide rural southerners with music, recreation, and, all too often, violence. The commercial success of middle-of-the-road country music has given "honky-tonks" a heretofore undreamed of commercial popularity, but even in the midst of commercial boom the rural "honky" survives. The urban migration of blacks has likewise taken its toll on the southern "jukes," but they too remain a part of the southern rural landscape. Today popular bars like the beachfront Flora-Bama (which calls itself "the last American roadhouse") seek to give their clientele at least some of the "honky-tonk," "juke joint" atmosphere associated with the name. At the other end of the scale, customers who visit a Nashville-based restaurant chain's "Logan's Roadhouse," take one look at its antiseptic décor and traditional menu and know that it is a roadhouse in name only—even with the complementary bucket of peanuts, whose shells you can throw on the floor.

JOHN S. OTTO
AUGUSTUS M. BURNS
University of Florida

William Ferris, *Blues from the Delta* (1988); Daniel R. Hundley, *Social Relations in Our Southern States*, ed. William J. Cooper Jr. (1979); Birney Imes, *Juke Joints: Photographs* (1990); Bill C. Malone, *Country Music U.S.A.: A Fifty Year History* (1968); Mitford M. Mathews, *Americanisms: A Dictionary of Selected Americanisms on Historical Principles* (1966); Paul Oliver, *Savannah Syncopators: African Retentions in the Blues* (1970); John S. Otto and Augustus M. Burns, *John Edwards Memorial Foundation Quarterly* (Spring 1974); Nick Tosches, *Country: The Biggest Music in America* (1977).

Line Dancing

Line dancing is a popular form of social dance in which individuals dance side-by-side and repeat short sequences of steps choreographed for a particular song or group of songs. Line dancing has become indelibly associated with country music, a connection that was forged in the early 1990s during the enormous increase in that music's popularity. The dance's roots and its current forms, however, extend far beyond the borders of country music.

The precursors of contemporary line dancing hail from many folk traditions, the most commonly cited being the tap steps in 1930s swing and lindy dances (such as the Shim Sham) and the traditional dances of West Africa. Modern line dancing finds its direct origins in the disco craze of the 1970s, when fans appropriated the stage choreography in soul, Motown, and rhythm-and-blues performances and organized it into dances such as the Bus Stop and the L.A. Hustle.

During the 1980s two broad changes occurred in line dancing. The first was the rise in popularity of music videos (MTV was launched in 1981), which frequently included lines of backup dancers moving in choreographed unison. Michael Jackson's hit video for "Thriller," for instance, imprinted the idea of line dancing on millions of viewers. The second major change was the popular decline of disco and the simultaneous popular rise of country music, and the attendant creation of countless, cavernous country music dance halls. Line dancing and country music became convenient bedfellows, as these new dance halls had lots of space for dancing. At the same time, recent country fans were eager to learn a way of dancing that did not involve the complicated partnering or "leading and following" of more traditional country dances. The result was a slow but steady incorporation of line dancing into country fan culture, with dances such as the Tush Push and Slappin' Leather quickly taking hold.

The event that transformed line dancing into a veritable phenomenon was choreographer Melanie Greenwood's creation of a new line dance for country singer Billy Ray Cyrus's recording of "Achy Breaky Heart" in 1992. Cyrus's record label cleverly donated copies of an instructional video (and step sheet, or notated instructions) to country dance halls, so that local dance instructors could teach fans the same dance that they saw in the popular music video. Soon thereafter, country fans across the nation were line dancing to the number-one hit record.

The marketing blitz of record-plus-video-plus-dance propelled "Achy Breaky Heart" to legendary status and established a business model adopted by countless new songs. Choreographers increasingly created individual dances for specific country songs, prompting country nightclubs to hire local dance instructors to teach fans new dances each week as new songs were released. Fans, in turn, kept coming back to learn more dances. At the height of line dancing's popularity, fans readily knew 70 to 80 complete dances, while magazines such as *Country Dance Lines* and *5678* disseminated new dances and helped create a sense of community among the dancers.

A basic line dance typically involves 24 to 64 beats of choreographed steps, consisting primarily of walking steps, turns, kicks, and sideways travel. Dancers arrange themselves on the dance floor in lines, all facing the same way. In many venues, a DJ or self-appointed dance leader will call out "5–6–7–8" to cue the start of the dance. Dancers then perform the sequence of steps, repeating it until the end of the song. The last step in the choreographed pattern often involves rotating either a quarter or a half turn, so that dancers begin the next iteration of the pattern while facing a different direction in the room, or "wall."

While several of the perennially favorite line dances (such as the Watermelon Crawl) are directly linked to country music, with its predominantly white fan base, a parallel tradition of soul (sometimes called "urban") line dancing also thrives in African American communities. Across all line dance communities, choreographers and participants draw heavily from many different genres of popular music. For instance, the Electric Slide—traditionally done to Marcia Griffiths's reggae-flavored "Electric Boogie"—has become a line dance classic, frequently commanding the floor at house parties, informal social gatherings, and nightclubs. The techno-pop record "Last Night," recorded by Chris Anderson, fuels an extremely popular line dance called "Chill Factor" in both country bars and top-40 nightclubs. DJ Casper's hip-hop "Cha Cha Slide," whose lyrics offer instructions for the dancers, has become a favorite of both fitness instructors and nightclub goers. And Atlanta hip-hop DJ Unk's "Walk It Out"—a song that started as a regional hit—became a southern and national hip-hop sensation as both song and line dance after it was featured in the Hollywood film *Stomp the Yard*.

Line dancing's social appeal comes from its combination of prescribed movement and individual freedom of expression. Its fixed choreography allows individuals with relatively little dance experience to participate, while inviting more advanced dancers to add stylized elaborations that set them apart from the crowd. Because line dancing lacks the conventional male-female partnering of couples' dances, it has become popular among friends who want to avoid both the social pressures and the technical difficulties of dancing with a partner. The lack of partnering also makes line dancing an extremely popular form of exercise and social entertainment among women's social clubs, church groups, and gay and lesbian organizations. Throughout the South, middle-school gym teachers have added it to their syllabi as a way of introducing formalized dancing to young teens.

Although one can learn to line dance from courses, commercial videos, books, and instructional materials, most line dances are transmitted casually from friend to friend. This process invariably yields differences between communities in how a particular dance is done. But the speed and accuracy with which many line dances move through fan communities testifies to the centrality of line dancing within many cultural spheres, as does the sight of old, young, black, white, graceful, and awkward participants gamely crowding the floor at a wedding reception to dance the Electric Slide.

JOCELYN R. NEAL
University of North Carolina at Chapel Hill

Christy Lane, *Christy Lane's Complete Book of Line Dancing* (2000); Jane A. Harris, Anne M. Pittman, Marlys S. Waller, and Cathy L. Dark, *Dance a While: Handbook for Folk, Square, Contra, and Social Dance* (2000); Shawn Trautman, *Line Dance 101: A Quick-Start Guide to Line Dancing* (DVD, 2005).

Marching Bands

"As the players tried to take the field, the marching band refused to yield." Don McLean penned these words to "American Pie" more than 30 years ago, yet the spirit found within them pulses mightily with every beat of the drum in the world of southern marching bands today. Every fall, high schools and colleges across the South give these unique ensembles fertile ground to plant their creative roots and flourish. While southern marching bands evolve exponentially in their artistic genealogy year after year, they remain firmly established on the ageless principles of tradition, honor, and pride that first gave them life. Regionally, marching bands in southern high schools and colleges lead the charge in musical excellence and pageantry. Such success is a direct result of their respective southern heritages.

The New South Creed, in addition to providing a guideline for the general way of life in post–Civil War South, set forth what was appropriate behavior for the specific social types in southern society. Among these social types were the southern lady and the southern gentleman. From this idealized social class of people came the men and women who, through the passages of generation to generation, found their way into various college music departments and subsequently founded marching band programs. These people grew up with a southern traditionalist mentality of honesty, integrity, and the belief that hard work was the key to success. Notable college marching bands such as the Pride of the South from Ole Miss, the Million Dollar Band from the University of Alabama, the Sound of the South from Troy University, the Redcoat Band from the University of Georgia, and the Marching Southerners and Ballerinas from Jacksonville State University all found their humble beginnings in the able hearts and minds of men and women who, being raised in the South, dedicated themselves to preserving their identity through the pageantry and art of the marching band.

Nationalism is a trait near and dear to many southerners' hearts. Before the Civil War and Reconstruction, this nationalism among whites was, of course, to the southern nation, evolving into the national spirit of Americans today. Early southern marching bands, particularly at the university level, frequently were under the leadership of directors who had previously served in the military, and the discipline fostered in military service provided a powerful catalyst to these young ensembles. From the military tradition came concepts such as the band uniform and overall attention to detail. John T. Finley, the first director of the Jacksonville State University Marching Southerners in Jacksonville, Ala., noted that the kinship felt among his early band members mirrored the brotherly kinship he had experienced in the military.

Military experience, in addition to molding the mentality and social fabric of these early ensembles, also contributed greatly to the development of the present-day drum corps style of many of the South's notable marching bands. Principally, the military drill commands of attention, dress center, ready front, and the company front have evolved into the current precision drill movements featured today. Moreover, marching bands frequently utilize the company front for its ability to yield powerful and exiting impact moments. Military bands are notable for their musical excellence and sterling performance quality, and southern marching bands warmly embrace this standard of achievement today. Additionally, many universities across the South have school fight songs that originated in a military band, either directly or in general style.

The repertoire of southern marching bands continues to expand and mature from year to year. Many college bands feature the works of great classical composers such as Tchaikovsky, Beethoven, and Stravinsky. Additionally, many modern marching band performances incorporate popular contemporary works of 20th-century composers. While the productions have matured greatly, southern marching bands remain true to their roots in many ways. Many college pregame shows incorporate traditional southern favorites. The Jacksonville State University Marching Southerners perform standards such as "Stars

Fell on Alabama" and "Aunt Dinah's Quilting Party" on a regular basis. "Dixie," the unofficial theme song of the New South Creed, remains a popular number among many southern marching bands. Musicians incorporate the familiar tune in subtle instances into a great portion of their modern repertoire. The marching band halftime tradition, just like other phenomena that showcase southern music and drama, demonstrates the tenuous but ever-present melding of southern heritage and progress that is necessary to the longevity and identity of southern culture today.

The art of the marching band is at an all-time high. From small high schools to the largest university, the South boasts some of the finest marching ensembles in the nation. Every year, thousands of young men and women dedicate hours of time, great sums of money, and even more emotion to this unique craft. Modern performances are frequently large-scale productions, utilizing effects such as elaborate props, electronics, and even fireworks. Directors and staff plan year-round to ensure that every detail is in place. Rehearsals are frequent and grueling, often taking place in the punishing heat of the South's brutal summer temperatures. The result is a powerful exhibition of earnest passion and sterling musicality. The level of dedication incumbent on the participants is sometimes difficult to understand by individuals outside the marching band microcosm. Closer observation of the history of southern marching bands reveals that this allegiance to the highest artistic and creative attainment is a direct result of the southern tradition and heritage of these ensembles.

Many of the most prominent southern marching bands are composed ironically of large numbers of young men and women from outside the South. The quality and national recognition of these organizations make them very popular among students from all areas of the country. This is no doubt a reflection of the notion that a fragment of southern culture has infiltrated the channels of a national art form. The world of the southern marching band is alive and well. Its tradition is nurtured by its history and developed by its heritage every year on clear, crisp autumn days in schools across the southeastern United States.

JUSTIN WILLIAMS
Rainbow City, Alabama

Bill C. Malone, *Southern Music, American Music* (1979); Christopher Pavlakis, *The American Music Handbook* (2006); James C. Cobb, *Away Down South: A History of Southern Identity* (2005); Bertram Wyatt-Brown, *Southern Honor: Ethics and Behavior in the Old South* (1982).

Marching Bands, HBCU

Throughout the South, the football fields and stadiums of Historically Black Colleges and Universities (HBCUS) host some of the most elaborate and competitive musical performances presented to the public on a regular basis, as the schools' marching bands offer exciting spectacles of showmanship, pageantry, and performatory excellence. The performance traditions that we observe today on the campuses of southern HBCUS—traditions that frame and sustain game day as a vital, distinct, and dynamic cultural event—have deep roots in a variety of American marching band traditions. Drawing upon the discipline of black military bands, the spirit of provincial and municipal brass bands, the pageantry of minstrel bands, and the showmanship of concert jazz bands, HBCU marching band performances are firmly grounded in a rich history of African American outdoor music making.

Blending musicality, pageantry, and theatrics, HBCU marching bands have nurtured and developed a dynamic performance tradition whose innovative style and competitive spirit promote an emotional intensity that is unparalleled in non-HBCU marching band performances. Perhaps referencing the marching band's military roots, or drawing parallels with the football contest, HBCU marching bands often refer to their performances as "battles." With the field as its main stage, the stadium becomes as much a site for confrontation and competition between the bands as it does for the football teams. As the home and visiting bands vie for the audience's support, the competitions fuel passionate rivalries between schools and conferences.

These competitions neither begin nor end with the traditional halftime field shows. During the game, sections from each band (trumpets, trombones, tubas, and drums) take turns playing short musical pieces back and forth across the field in competitions known as "sectional battles." Following the game, the bands engage in a musical duel of their own, appropriately referred to as the "fifth quarter." Before, during, and after the game—whether the football players are on the field or not—the stadium is inundated with the sounds of horns, woodwinds, and percussion instruments playing tunes in a manner designed to both please and engage the crowd.

HBCU band members' goal is to win the most "house"—the audience's loud, energized participation. To win "house," a band must invest its music and movements with meanings that the crowd both understands and appreciates. With audience members as key players in the performance equation, bands strive to keep their performances fresh, creative, and engaging, while always embodying a shared sense of cultural values and aesthetics.

Collegiate marching band traditions in the United States have developed into two distinct presentational and cultural styles: corps style (as in drum corps) and show style. Early collegiate marching bands drew on the European aesthetic principals of precision, uniformity, and restraint. Evoking their military heritage, their music and movements were both restricted and carefully controlled. In this Eurocentric model known as corps style, marching, for example, utilizes either a walking step or some variation of a low gliding roll step from heel to toe that limits the torso's movement and emphasizes straight angular forms. Most of the corps style bands' repertoire draws from traditional European marches, chorales, and overtures. Show style, in contrast, blends precision drills with flashy high-step marching (90-degree knee lifts), natural upper-body swing, and popular music so as to highlight the performance's entertainment value and excite the audience.

Dance "breaks" or "breakdowns" are one of the core features that distinguish HBCU marching bands from their predominately white counterparts. While marching bands in the Big Ten conference claim to have originally popularized high-step marching and natural upper-body swing, it was not until the predominately black colleges and universities in the South began adding dance steps to their field show routines, parades, and processionals that the *show* style marching came into being.

Just as the show style's freedom of movement appeals to many African American band and audience members, so too does the musical repertoire. Although HBCU performance repertoires include classical and traditional marching music, they also dip into the rich pool of African American contemporary music, encompassing jazz, gospel, funk, soul, rhythm and blues, and hip-hop. Marching band performances become celebrations of African American aesthetics, featuring foregrounded percussion, the off-beat phrasing of melodic accents, overlapping call-and-response patterns, and pervasive polymeter.

Most HBCU marching bands memorize all of their music. This allows both band director and band to accommodate any last minute changes in the field shows and to challenge the other team's band in the improvisational postgame band competition. These "fifth quarter" competitions are unique to HBCUs. Led by the band directors, these musical battles pit the opposing schools' bands against each other, with each playing full musical scores back and forth across the field until one band acquiesces and leaves its bleachers. Reminiscent of the jazz band battles at Harlem's Savoy Ballroom in the 1930s and 1940s, fifth-quarter competitions unfold as collective improvisations as directors choose tunes that challenge the opposing band's depth, technique, sound quality, and ingenuity. The band that plays the loudest, sweetest, and longest—drawing on the widest repertoire and performing the songs flawlessly—"wins" the competition.

Deeply emblematic of diaspora expressive traditions, HBCU band performances unfold as bold public declarations of what it *means* to be African American today. Through their musical choices; their dance routines; their treatment of public space; their commitment to evaluation; and their penchant for pageantry, competition, originality, adaptability, rhythmic complexity, and performer-audience conversations, HBCU marching bands embody aesthetics that transcend band membership and embrace values belonging to time-honored traditions of African American expressivity. Given that the bands are always assessing the crowd's response and designing future performances accordingly, their performances become occasions to express, mediate, and challenge social issues, political ideas, and cultural values.

HBCU football fields stand apart as one of the few places where tens of thousands of African Americans regularly gather and celebrate—before, during, and after the game—artistic excellence. Adding to the symbolic power of the bands' performances is the fact that these proud, young, talented artists are college educated and thus excellent role models for their community. Band members are keenly aware of this responsibility. They know that they are staging one of the largest artistic performances presented to African American audiences on a regular basis. They also know that their performances reaffirm a vibrant spirit of community and perpetuate shared cultural values. With this knowledge in hand, HBCU band members lift their knees a little higher, dance a little harder, and blow a little louder—giving it their all and leaving it on the field.

WILLIAM LEWIS
Piedmont Council of Traditional Music
Raleigh, North Carolina

Jaqui Malone, *Steppin' on the Blues: The Visible Rhythms of African American Dance* (1996); Robert E. Foster, *Multiple-Option Marching Band Techniques* (1991); Laurie Dunivant Sneiderman, *Black Issues in Higher Education* (27 April 2000); Richard Alan Waterman, in *Mother Wit from the Laughing Barrel: Readings in the Interpretation of Afro-American Folklore*, ed. Alan Dundes (1973).

Mardi Gras

The celebration of Mardi Gras along the central Gulf Coast portions of Louisiana, Mississippi, and Alabama marks the region's historical and cultural difference from the rest of the South. Mardi Gras ("Fat Tuesday"), or Carnival ("fleshly excess"), is celebrated with costumed float parades, neighborhood marches, informal parties, and formal balls in New Orleans, Biloxi, and Mobile among other Gulf Coast cities. In contrast, a rural Louisiana Cajun and black Creole *courir de Mardi Gras* or Mardi Gras run is carried out by horseback-mounted revelers in more than a dozen French-speaking communities of southwest Louisiana.

Mardi Gras is historically associated with French and Spanish populations along the Gulf Coast. However, many ethnic groups now join in the traditional festive occasion, which falls in February or March before Ash Wednesday and 40 days before Easter. It has been speculated that the Mediterranean-Latin roots of Mardi Gras are to be found in the pre-Roman rites of spring and later Roman festival or ritual occasions such as Bacchanalia, Lupercalia, and Saturnalia. Over time such occasions became part of the Catholic liturgical calendar. Thus, the Gulf Coast Carnival season officially begins on 6 January, the Epiphany and Feast of Kings. On this date in New Orleans, "King Cakes"—with a plastic miniature baby (representing the Baby Jesus) inside each and adorned in Mardi Gras colors of gold, purple, and green—are consumed in celebration. The season may be as short as three and a half weeks or as long as two months, depending upon the date of Easter. The culmination of Carnival is Mardi Gras day or Shrove Tuesday (referring to a time to be "shriven of one's sins"). The festive eating, dancing, and drinking associated with Mardi Gras are followed by the relative austerity and penitence of the Lenten period.

Just as Roman Catholicism absorbed earlier pre–Roman Carnival elements, so too the worldwide variations on Carnival now reflect regional cultural diversity. Thus, Gulf Coast Carnival, like Carnival in related societies of the Caribbean and Latin America, represents a syncretism of French/Spanish, Native American, and African/Afro-Caribbean performance styles and structures. That the earliest European settlers of the Gulf Coast celebrated Mardi Gras is verified by the explorer D'Iberville's naming of Mardi Gras Bayou along the Mississippi in southern Louisiana. Informal parades and festive masquerades are reported to have occurred in major centers, including Mobile (where the first Mardi Gras parade in the United States occurred) and New Orleans throughout the early 19th century; and by midcentury (1857 in New Orleans) officially sanctioned parades began.

The early public parades in New Orleans and Mobile were founded by the Anglo and Creole (French/Spanish) elites of both cities. In New Orleans, such "krewes" as Comus, Momus, Proteus, and Rex continue from the 19th century into the present. Some krewes still utilize smaller antique floats depicting mythological scenes crafted in papier-mâché. These floats were origi-

Cajun Mardi Gras celebrant, Church Point,
La., 1978 (Photograph by Philip Gould,
Lafayette, La.)

nally drawn by mules, which were eventually replaced by tractors in the 1950s. The artwork found on newer floats is made of plastic.

Today as many as 60 different krewes parade in the roughly two-week period before and including Mardi Gras day. Some, such as Arabi and Argus, are quite recent and represent suburban neighborhoods. All parades throw doubloons (introduced in the early 1960s) and other plastic trinkets to the crowds that line such primary parade routes as St. Charles Avenue and Canal Street. The varied krewes both reflect and invert the social structure of New Orleans on a day when the upper classes play at being kings, fools, and mythological beings. Suburban middle classes may likewise assert their right to be royalty for a day. Elite old-line krewes maintain an aura of secrecy about the selection of their royalty and invitation to their balls and affiliated social events. The newer krewes such as Bacchus, on the other hand, charge admission to their open gatherings in the Superdome and elsewhere at the end of parades.

The Zulu parade of New Orleans's black middle-class and elite community, founded in 1909 as a reaction to white stereotypes of blacks as "savages," is a Carnival activity rivaled only by the Rex Parade on Mardi Gras day. Zulu members dress in grass skirts and "wooley wigs," put on blackface, and throw rubber spears and decorated coconuts to the delighted crowds. Working-class blacks, particularly those of Creole (French/Spanish) ancestry, also invoke white stereotypes of "wildness" by masquerading pridefully in stylized Plains Indians costumes.

The black "Mardi Gras Indians" are hierarchical groups of men with titles such as Big Chief, Spyboy, Wildman, and Lil' Chief who dress in elaborate bead and feather costumes weighing up to 100 pounds. After months of time and money invested in sewing costumes and practice sessions at local bars, a dozen or more "tribes" appear early on Mardi Gras day to sing, dance, and parade through back-street neighborhoods. Some of these black Indians, with "tribe" names such as "Creole Wild West," "White Cloud Hunters," "Yellow Poca-hontas," and "Wild Tchoupitoulas," do in fact have partial Native American ancestry and speak in mythological fashion about Indian spirits and customs. Their performance style, however, is essentially Afro-Caribbean, as expressed in competitive dance and song and the call-and-response chants that mark their foot parades. These chants are often based on a secret code language consisting of a group leader's call and responses such as "Hey pocky way" and "Ja ca mo feen non nay." They also use standard tunes such as "Lil' Liza Jane" and "Shoo Fly" to improvise tales of their daring and exploits as they "go to town" on Mardi Gras day.

While the Mardi Gras Indians and the Zulu parade utilize Mardi Gras to make statements about group pride through inverted stereotypes of Indian and African tribes, many blacks also work at the service of whites on Carnival, thereby reflecting the postcolonial social structure of New Orleans. Some, for example, lead horses for major white parades such as Rex and Momus. Others dress in pointed white hood and cloaks and carry torches called "flambeaux" that light the way for night parades of old elite krewes such as Comus.

Although smaller in scale and less widely known than New Orleans Carnival, Mardi Gras in Mobile has been celebrated in various ways since the beginning of the 19th century. The Cowbellions, an early parading group using cowbells and other noisemakers, formed in the 1830s and later ordered their costumes from Paris. During the Civil War Mobile's public Mardi Gras ceased. It was revived in 1866 by a veteran named Joe Cain, who dressed that year as a mock Chickasaw Indian chief called "Slacabamorinico" and drove through the then-occupied city in a decorated wagon. On Sunday before the Mobile Carnival Joe Cain is now commemorated with a jazz funeral procession. Various other Mobile krewes such as the Comic Cowboys, a comedic and satirical krewe, and the Infant Mystics date to the 19th century. The Order of Myths, the oldest krewe (1867), was modeled after the early Cowbellions. The symbol of the Order of Myths, which is the last krewe to parade on Mardi Gras, is Folly chasing Death around a broken neoclassical column and flailing him with a golden pig bladder. Although this imagery symbolizes a general Mardi Gras theme of mirth's triumph over gloom, some suggest that the broken column originally alluded to the broken dreams of the Confederacy.

The large float parades in the Mardi Gras celebrations of Mobile and New Orleans represent Mediterranean and Caribbean traditions. In contrast, the Cajun and black Creole *courir de Mardi Gras* of rural southwest Louisiana reflects country French traditions brought by Acadians of Nova Scotia who came to Louisiana in the latter part of the 18th century. In a manner not un-like Christmas mumming in Europe and the West Indies, a band of masked male revelers goes from house to house on the open prairie land of south-west Louisiana. The men, on horses or flatbed trucks, dress as clowns, thieves, women, and devils. Some wear the traditional pointed capuchon hats with bells and streamers. The group is led by a capitaine, who may wear an elegant silk costume in the Cajun bands or simple work clothes in some black Creole Mardi Gras bands. The Mardi Gras bands come as quasi vigilantes and clowns in search of charity, in the form of live chickens, rice, spices, grease, sausages, and other ingredients for a gumbo supper. The capitaine, standing apart from the group as a keeper of the law, tries to prevent the men from getting too dis-orderly or drunk and sees that they carry out their agreed-upon rounds for the day. At each visited farmstead the capitaine or a flagman will visit ahead of the band to see if the household will receive the Mardi Gras. There is usually an af-firmative response to the courtly request "Voulez-vous recevoir cette band des Mardi Gras?" (Do you want to receive the Mardi Gras band?), whereupon the clowns are waved on to charge the house on horseback. After dismounting and dancing together (which men do only on Mardi Gras), a competitive chase is often held for a live chicken. (This chase is usually preceded by a song of request to the man or lady of the house.) The chicken chase involves a designated bird, or one tossed into the air, and is a hilarious spectacle as men in costume pursue elusive birds through the muddy rice fields of early spring, leaping fences and crossing pigsties. After a chicken is caught, it is killed and put with other spoils in a sack, which is sent back to town where the cooking begins at midday. As the Mardi Gras runners depart a house, they sing a word of thanks and invite the householders to the dance and communal supper to be held in town or at a rural club late in the night.

The Mardi Gras song is especially significant because it is sung in a minor modal style reminiscent of medieval French folk music, generally not found in Cajun music today. The song also contains a description of the Mardi Gras band's activities. Sung in French, the song is usually performed by musicians who ride in a sound truck. The translated song is as follows:

The Mardi Gras Dance

The Mardi Gras riders come from everywhere
All around, around the hub.
They pass once a year
To ask for charity
Even if it's a potato.
A potato and some cracklins.
The Mardi Gras riders are on a long voyage
All around, around the hub.
They pass once a year
To ask for charity
Even if it's a skinny chicken
And three or four corn cobs.
Captain, captain, wave your flag.
Let's go to the other neighbor's place
To ask for charity.
You all come meet us.
You all come meet us.
Yes, at the gumbo tonight.

By the end of the afternoon the band heads back toward "the hub" or its starting point in rice- and soybean-growing and cattle-raising towns, such as Mamou, Church Point, L'Anse Maigre, and Swords. The riders on horseback may enter at a gallop. Those who are sober enough entertain waiting crowds with stunts and various acts of bravado. The gumbo from the day's catch is served to the riders and the general public, followed by a large dance ending at midnight and the beginning of the Lenten season.

The parallel black Creole Mardi Gras bands are often located near the Cajun towns in tiny rural settlements established in the 19th century by manumitted slaves and other people of color. The black Creole Mardi Gras celebrations are usually smaller (10–20 men), more intimate, and more traditional than today's Cajun courirs. The cowboy style of Cajun Mardi Gras has not taken hold in the black Creole community. For example, the black bands take great care not to trample house gardens or urinate in public while pursuing the fowl. Elders are helped down from their flatbed trucks by younger men, and the bands present themselves more as polite beggars than as vigilantes. The older Creoles especially take great stock in such details and are critical of young men who do not behave or sing properly. The Creole Mardi Gras song is similar to that of the Cajuns but is often performed in a call-and-response manner showing Afro-Caribbean influences. The usual response line to the leader's song is "Ouais mon/bon cher camarade" (Yes my/good dear friend).

While old traditions and Carnival groups continue, new Mardi Gras events and locales have emerged in recent years to meet current social concerns. In New Orleans, for example, gay krewes and their French Quarter costume contests have become highly visible. In New Orleans and Baton Rouge, the Krewe de Vieux and the Spanishtown Mardi Gras, respectively, have emerged as hipster satires on Carnival itself and on a variety of Louisiana and national topics, including sexual and financial scandals, corrupt politics, and pollution. In New Orleans, two single-gender krewes of mostly professional men (Krewe D'Etat, led by an unnamed "Dictator") and women (Muses, whose Queen rides in a 15-foot tall, sparkling electric high heel) host popular night parades that are filled with carefully crafted political and sexual innuendo. Many Uptown residents with children shy away from these nighttime revels and focus instead on catching fluffy animal toys thrown from less satirical and more family-friendly daytime parades. A range of suburban Mardi Gras celebrations, like Family Gras, have also emerged, with children included and excessive drunkenness or sexual suggestiveness excluded.

In the period after Katrina in 2005, many questioned whether New Orleans and Gulf Coast Carnival would happen at all, because of imperiled local logistics and a diminished population. Luckily, Mardi Gras—in this region where play is a serious cultural and historical tradition—came back strong in 2006. Some floats addressed the tragedy with self-parodying comedy; some attacked FEMA and other agencies' incompetence; other floats were dark and empty to honor those lost in the waters. The annual celebration has since become an agent of cultural and social return and recovery. Mardi Gras continues to express a sense of feast, fantasy, and social transformation through costumes and masks, performance and play, and krewe themes related to the life situations of the participants, all before Ash Wednesday's penitent rituals and Lenten mood are invoked by the remaining believers in this Catholic-dominated region of the Gulf South.

NICHOLAS R. SPITZER
Tulane University

Roger D. Abrahams, Nick Spitzer, John F. Szwed, and Robert Farris Thompson, *Blues for New Orleans: Mardi Gras and America's Creole Soul* (2006); Barry Jean Ancelet, *Capitaine Voyage Ton Flag: The Traditional Cajun Country Mardi Gras* (1989); Les Blank, director, *Always for Pleasure* (film, 1978); Margaret Brown, director, *The Order of Myths* (film, 2008); Frank de Caro and Tom Ireland, in *Mardi Gras, Gumbo, and Zydeco: Readings in Louisiana Culture*, ed. Marcia Gaudet and James C. McDonald (2003); James Gill, *Lords of Misrule: Mardi Gras and the Politics of Race in New Orleans* (1997); Arthur Hardy, *Mardi Gras in New Orleans: An Illustrated History* (1997); Lisa Katzman, *Tootie's Last Suit* (film, 2008); Samuel Kinser, *Carnival American Style: Mardi Gras at New Orleans and Mobile* (1990); Carl Lindahl, ed., *Southwestern Louisiana Mardi Gras Traditions*, special issue of the *Journal of American Folklore* (Spring 2001); Pat Mire, *Dance for a Chicken: The Cajun Mardi Gras* (film, 1993); Rebecca Snedeker, *By Invitation Only* (film, 2007); Nicholas R. Spitzer, in *Creoles of Color in the Gulf South*, ed. James Dorman (1996); Carolyn E. Ware, *Cajun Women and Mardi Gras: Reading the Rules Backward* (2007).

Noodling

Noodling is the practice of catching catfish by hand. Predominantly practiced in the South and Midwest, noodling is otherwise known as grabbing, grabbling, graveling, hogging, stumping, tickling, cooning, and dogging. Its name varies by locale, but the practice follows a pretty standard pattern. Noodlers usually fish in waist-deep water in groups of three or so. One of them reaches into a hole in the bed of a river or lake, wriggling his fingers, while the others block off the space through which the fish could escape. Meanwhile, the fish—typically an adult male flathead catfish—takes the wriggling finger bait. The human lure then struggles to grab the fish by its gills, and the entire team frequently helps to wrestle it to the surface. Once the fish is caught, someone threads a stringer through the gills of the fish to secure it.

Though noodling may sound as simple as reaching into a hole and pulling out a catfish, it is an art. Like any art form, it does have some variations. First is the issue of equipment. Noodling requires going underwater, and some noodlers use diving equipment to enable safer deep-water dives. Others consider this method cheating. Thus, the world's most popular noodling event, the Okie Noodling Tournament, divides competitors into SCUBA and natural divisions. Gloves are another piece of optional equipment. Other noodlers use sections of cane to probe likely catfish holes. Although proponents of these forms of protection consider them commonsense responses to the painful bites of catfish, some barehanders insist that gloves and probes prevent them from accurately identifying and locating the inhabitant of a given hole. Others characterize these innovations as substitutes for toughness. Most noodlers have a few favorite fishing holes, but some set up artificial nesting containers such as barrels to provide more efficient, ready-made sites.

Some experts categorize noodling as an extreme sport, and it does present some extreme dangers. Drowning is a serious threat because hauling large catfish (some exceeding 100 pounds) to the surface is a struggle, and if it happens to prove impossible, releasing oneself from their jaws sometimes takes a while. Snakebites are another serious danger because water moccasins often haunt underwater holes. Less lethal—yet seriously frightening—hazards include bites from snapping turtles, beavers, muskrats, and nonvenomous snakes. Beyond these unintended threats to one's well-being, even the successful noodling catch usually involves at least a moderate amount of pain. This is caused by the catfish's sharp, curved maxillary teeth. Agitated fish often lock down on noodlers' arms and proceed to barrel roll in the style of a crocodile killing its prey.

The sport's danger to noodlers is obvious, but noodling may also present a serious threat to flathead catfish populations. In 2007, this threat led to the banning of hand fishing in Missouri. Some conservationists argued that the vast majority of catfish occupying burrows are protecting eggs and that removing them from these nests exacts a disproportionate blow to catfish populations. This stance came two years after Noodlers Anonymous, an advocacy group, successfully lobbied for a trial noodling period, making Missouri the 13th state to legalize noodling. This argument and safety concerns frame the ongoing legalization debate.

Noodling is commonly associated with lower-class whites from states throughout the South. In the poem "Grabbling in Yokna Bottom," James Seay muses about noodlers: "The well-fed do not wade this low river." This poem's inclusion in *White Trash: An Anthology of Contemporary Southern Poets* is also a testament to noodling's association with the working class. Interestingly, if the videos on YouTube are any indication, women as well as men enjoy the sport.

Although noodling's fame is limited and relatively new, its roots are deep. Burkhard Bilger dates it back to an American Indian practice described by James Adair in 1775, and during the Great Depression many Americans relied on noodling for a significant part of their diets. Many—probably most—noodlers still eat their catches for supper. In fact, the Okie Noodling Tournament's festivities include a catfish cook-off.

Nonnoodlers frequently denigrate the sport as crazy or deny that it is a sport at all, but noodlers tend to take pride in being tough enough to do something so crazy. This pride is not solely the property of grown men; a significant number of women also noodle. Some are featured in the films *Girls Gone Grabblin'* and *Girls Gone Grabblin' 2*. Furthermore, one of the sport's earliest spokespeople was Kristy Addis, a Mississippian who professed her love for noodling en route to the 1987 Miss Teen USA crown. Because noodling tends to run in families, most hand fishermen (and women) get started at an early age. Some begin around the age of seven.

Shortly after noodling began grabbing national publicity, Jerry Rider became its most famous face. Numerous news outlets featured him, and he even appeared on *Late Night with David Letterman* in 1989. Rider's style is daring even by noodling standards. He forsakes not only line and lure but fishes alone and without gloves. He probes for catfish in riverbank holes as well as in crevices of inundated highways, a practice that claimed the life of one of his friends. He is featured in *Okie Noodling*, Bradley Beesley's 2001 documentary film about hand fishing, although his unofficial title as the world's best noodler slips from his grasp during the course of the film.

Frequent victims of criticism from "real fishermen," the noodlers in Beesley's film voice their desire for a fishing tournament of their own. Thus, he organizes the Okie Noodling Tournament in Pauls Valley, Okla. Possibly owing to high water in his usual noodling haunts, Rider comes up empty handed in the tournament. Lee McFarlin, a plumber who also figures prominently in the film, fared better. He finished third in the Biggest Stringer category and won the 2005 tournament. The McFarlins are noodling's most famous family today. They noodle the tournament together, and Lee's daughter Misty won the title Okie Noodling Queen in 2005.

Jerry Rider seemed to regard his 2001 loss as bittersweet. On one hand, he conceded that he was not definitively the world's best noodler. But on the other hand, he said he was glad that other skilled noodlers are out there. Perhaps most noodlers value the niche sport's survival more than having the largest catfish on hand at a given tournament. Professor Mark Morgan observed noodling's transition to a macho trophy sport paralleling the transformation of bass fishing and NASCAR, a trend that bodes well for its future. Indeed, the Okie Noodling Tournament has grown over the past decade. One hundred seventy noodlers competed in the 2009 installment, and the level of competition has increased along with the number of noodlers. Jon Bridges grabbed the largest fish (68.6 pounds) of the tournament's 10-year history en route to the 2009 tournament championship.

MILES LASETER
University of Mississippi

Burkhard Bilger, *Noodling for Flatheads* (2000); Carolee Boyles, *Mississippi Game and Fish* (June 2006).

Passing the Time

The Andy Griffith Show presents appealing television images of southerners "passing time" by presenting small-town characters at rest in usually tranquil settings. Sheriff Andy Taylor sits and talks in Floyd's barbershop. He plays his guitar and dispenses wisdom on the front porch of his house. Ellie takes time to chat with customers and offers advice in the drugstore when not serving up sodas, and Gomer and Goober not only pump gas and fix tires but also swap gullible gossip and gawk at tall tales told by other more worldly types. The show is an idealized version of the rhythms of the small-town South, one that does not capture realities of a biracial population beset by class hierarchies and that portrays tensions in the society with gentle humor that does not suggest the latent violence that could come to the surface. Nonetheless, Andy Taylor and his friends offer a snapshot of the centrality of simply passing time as a recreation in southern culture.

According to a 1978 Harris Poll, southerners spent more time than other Americans fixing things around the house, helping others, enjoying the company of family and kin, resting after work, getting away from problems, napping, and "just doing nothing." Many of these are embodiments of passing time in the South, and the poll supports the idea that hanging out, or loafing, has been an intentional recreational choice of southerners and ties in with central themes of southern life. In particular, passing time in semipublic places is a long tradition, with its own expectations and ground rules about behavior in such settings and representing a particular form of community. Hanging out was associated with certain specific locations. Southern rural and small-town people knew each other, living in a face-to-face society. They gathered around the courthouse square or crossroads store. Crop cycles, community life, and church worship structured daily activities. It was a deferential society, with a hierarchical class system rooted in wealth, gender, and skin color. Orthodoxy ruled, yet it allowed for eccentricity as long as the foundations of the society were not challenged. The household was a common space for men and women, but when away from the home they often gathered in separate gendered spaces that provided distinctive venues for hanging out.

Talking was an important part of hanging out. Writer Allen Tate noted the importance of "passing the time of day" in the South and that involved a regionally specific form of conversation. In other parts of the nation, he said, talk was often about ideas, whereas "a typical southern conversation is not going anywhere; it is not about anything. *It is about the people who are talking.*" Young ladies mastered the language of small talk to be used when visiting or courting; women exchanged local news and speculations on childrearing and neighborhood doings at quilting bees; and men swapped tall tales, freely told off-color stories, and cursed when in pool halls. African American men and women placed a high value on verbal dexterity and used occasions when they were together in segregated settings to converse freely about both the black community and whites for whom they worked. Zora Neale Hurston immortalized what she called the "lying sessions" that took place on the porch in the all-black town she grew up in, Eatonville, Fla., and the same institution would have been found throughout black communities throughout the South.

If talking was an essential component of passing time, so was drinking alcoholic beverages, at least for men. Before bars and taverns dotted the landscape in the 20th century, men bought whiskey at town general stores, which often sold more liquor than any other commodity. Men spent much time hanging out at storefronts leading into these stores. But they sometimes got jiggers of whiskey in the backrooms of the blacksmith shop. A north Georgian looking back on the 1880s recalled that men "imbibed from a stone-crock jug while lounging near the dusty hardware or pungent horse collars in the back of a store." Drinking created a sociable mood, but could also promote a lowering of inhibitions in an intensely competitive society. As historian Ted Ownby notes, "the camaraderie of the barroom always contained a strong element of personal conflict." Men associated gambling with drinking, and the combination could lead to rivalries and long-standing grudges that could easily erupt into brawls.

One prime location for men, mostly, to hang out was the country store at the rural crossroads. Houses were far apart in the countryside, life was lonely and often harsh, and the crossroads store offered the best hope for socializing. Once you were there, you probably stayed awhile passing the time before setting out on the long road home. In cold weather, men gathered around the stove, played cards or checkers, talking all the while. When the weather allowed, they generally sat on the store porch, participating in the same activities as in the winter. Young men and boys gathered at the crossroad stores for tests of strength, racing horses, playing horseshoes, testing skills in marble or croquet, or simply sitting and loafing. The store was sometimes open late, serving as an informal male community center. Blacks and whites mingled together on the porch, but whites would be served before any blacks when purchasing goods inside the store. The store represented a place for male cross-racial passing of time in the rural countryside, possible because women were often not around. Emmett Till's alleged "wolf whistle" at a white woman in a country store in

Money, Miss., and his subsequent murder by whites showed the tragic boundaries of the informalities of behavior while passing time. Passing time could be punctuated by random violence on short order, among whites and/or blacks, with a word or gesture that violated norms of behavior, upsetting racial etiquette or codes of honor.

The general store was one institution in town street life that represented a major setting for passing the time. Ownby notes that loafing in town had "morally questionable connotations" and was a concern for evangelicals. The small-town street was a male sanctuary, the site for rough talk, competitiveness, and enjoying small confrontations. As at the country store, black men were present and participating in its life. Black men and white men intermingled on town streets, and sometimes they interacted directly in drinking, gambling, or just talking. Passing the time had dangerous meanings for African American men, as loitering in town could be a crime leading not only to the county jail but also to forced labor for planters who paid their bail and then compelled their work.

The barbershop and the beauty parlor were 20th-century institutions that brought people of differing social classes and occupations together for not only hair work but also conversation and simply visiting. They were informal civic forums where people went to discuss public issues and private concerns. They were racially segregated, and the black institutions were critical embodiments of a separate black community. They were one of the few semipublic spaces where blacks could gather away from the oversight of whites and swap local news, confirm or deny gossip, or conduct business. The film *Barbershop* (2002) captures the black barbershop culture. One character in that film suggests the social meanings invested in black barbershops when he says that the shop was "the black man's country club."

Passing time on the street took on added significance on special days. Saturday was the one day of the week that could be dedicated to leisure. Town employers often gave workers a half day off, and farmers poured into towns from the countryside for business and hanging out. People would buy and sell, often having money to spend on drinking, eating out, gambling, shooting pool, getting a haircut, or other attractions of the towns. Barbershops, beauty parlors, cafés, grocery stores, movie theaters, and other businesses would be open late into the night on a day when people had money and the inclination to spend it in town before heading back into the countryside.

Court week afforded even more opportunities for passing the time in exciting circumstances. Circuit court judges typically came to county seats for four to five days once a month or so. The sheer size of crowds gave opportunities to sit or stand and observe a range of experience around them. Ped-dlers came to town to serve the crowds. Horse trading added excitement. A country man could gain honor from a wise trade but shame could appear if he bargained poorly. People passed the time not only buying and selling but also simply watching. It was entertainment. Christmas was a season of rela-tive leisure in this agrarian society that validated passing the time. But it meant even more license for men to drink and pass the time with such violent activi-ties as shooting guns, fireworks, turkey shoots, bearbaiting, and dog fighting.

Strictures on the role of evangelical women and that of the southern white lady prevented women from participating in many passing-the-time activities. But they were central to a ritual in this regard — visiting. An Alabamian in the 1920s described visiting as "happy recreation" but one that southerners took "very seriously." Society page stories, small-town newspaper columnists, and church newsletters documented the pervasiveness of this form of hanging out. As members of families, men also visited kin and neighbors, but this ritual was preeminently one for women. They visited to relieve the humdrum quality of rural and small-town life, to nurture ties beyond the household, and to enjoy the company of others. Church was one setting for visiting. Men often stood around outside the church building before and after services. Women visited in church parlors and fellowship halls before and after services as well, often while preparing or cleaning up after meals. Weddings, funerals, and revivals offered ample occasion for talking, joking, swapping gossip, networking with neighbors and extended kin, and otherwise passing the time. Women com-pared notes on community needs — including how to help friends in need and how to discipline those whose moral failures sullied the community. Women who were members of elite families visited to nurture connections with other such families.

The porch ranked as a key spot for passing the time, for women and men, blacks and whites, rich and poor. Mississippi poet and planter William Alex-ander Percy remembered the porch as a center of male political power, as his father, Mississippi senator Leroy Percy, gathered his cronies together in early 20th-century Greenville, Miss., to drink bourbon, smoke cigars, and plot po-litical strategy. Zora Neale Hurston remembered the porch as a place with a different kind of talk and behavior from that, a spot where African Americans who were voiceless during the day could relax and share their feelings and be-liefs in a free context among other blacks. The porch's passing of time nur-tured a tradition of creativity, through storytelling, and of community. More recently, Clifton Taulbert has written of the "porch people" of his Mississippi Delta youth — adults who sat on the porches looking out for everyone's children as though they were their own. The region's heat for much of the year was a reason for the porch's popularity, as southerners waited in the evening for their hot houses to cool off and filled the time by talking with other family members and neighbors passing by. Women were on the porch shelling beans or peas in the morning getting ready for the main meal at noontime. Elderly men and women sat on the porch to stay out of the way of hectic goings on inside the house, and children developed games to be played on the porch.

Passing the time is a cultural principle not unique to the South but embodied there in ways that reflect regional concerns of race, religion, gender, rurality, and other aspects of southern culture. "Life's center flows with time being passed," writes folklorist Henry Glassie, a South Carolinian who studied the phenomenon in one community in Northern Ireland. "On the inactive side of the center lie the misery of 'boredom' and the necessity of 'rest.'" But he notes that people rest to work, "so the best rest is filled with 'entertainment,' with food and chat to carry you on, enabling you to work again." Entertainment converts rest "into time-passing action." Passing the time, he adds, can have an element of danger as well, as recreational competition can be "ripped by violence out of the tissue of communal reciprocity," whereas "the middle path" can lead into "the gentle action of passing the time." The southern landscape, like that in Northern Ireland, was marked by the furniture of passing the time—chairs set everywhere outdoors, benches in front of the courthouse, swings hanging from porches.

The context of southern life has changed drastically in the past decades, but people in the region find new ways to pass the time in semipublic ways. The men's coffee clubs have moved to McDonald's restaurants but the same political discussions and communication networks for local news still operate among their members. People take their laptops to coffee shops, where they sit for hours passing the time online but also conversing with friends they see. Electronic hanging out is surely a major activity of young people in the South as elsewhere. Twitter with its fast-paced communication does not resonate much with older regional habits, but one can imagine the southern DNA responding to the "doing nothing" dimension of Facebook. Electronic games can be purely individualistic but can also be played with people in other places also passing the time. The big shopping mall is the equivalent of the 20th-century small town, with young people spending time in the food court and in electronic stores and older people using mall space for walking, drinking coffee afterward, and just sitting on numerous benches provided.

CHARLES REAGAN WILSON
University of Mississippi

Pete Daniel, *Standing at the Crossroads: Southern Life in the Twentieth Century* (1986); Jocelyn Donlan, *Swinging in Place: Porch Life in Southern Culture* (2001); Henry Glassie, *Passing the Time in Ballymenone* (1995); Trudier Harris, *Southern Cultures* (Fall–Winter 1996); Melissa Harris-Lacewell, *Barbershops, Bible, and BET: Everyday Talk and Black Political Thought* (2004); Zora Neale Hurston, *Mules and Men* (1935); Jack Temple Kirby, *Rural Worlds Lost: The American South, 1920–1960* (1987); Ted Ownby, *Subduing Satan: Religion, Recreation, and Manhood in the Rural South, 1865–1920* (1989); Joel Williamson, *Crucible of Race: Black-White Relations in the American South since Emancipation* (1984).

Pets

Keeping domestic animals as pets and as companions is a widespread, almost ubiquitous, pattern in human societies. Pets are of several types: (1) the pet animal kept for pleasure or amusement predominantly, but with no utilitarian function; (2) the food animal, hand- and/or house-raised, which enjoys pet status during some or all of its lifetime; and (3) the companion animal, fulfilling multiple overlapping roles, ranging from comrade to such other roles as work assistant, recreational partner, or surrogate family or household member, any of which meets the key elements already described. In addition, tamed wild animals are sometimes kept as pets.

Earliest evidence of pet or companion animals in the South comes from a site in North Carolina dating to A.D. 1100. The special pet or companion status of a dog is inferred from a burial site, where careful arrangement of remains indicates a close relationship between the animal and a person or the community. Both pets and companion animals have persisted within southern culture, as have careful burials and memorials for companion animals. Franklin County, Ala., has an elaborate coon dog graveyard, complete with a monument said to cost $5,000.

Southern pet-keeping practices must be viewed within the larger context of general attitudes toward animals more characteristic of southern culture than of other regions: southerners are more likely to express concern for the practical and material value of animals or their habitat. They are less likely to express concern about the right and wrong treatment of animals or to strongly oppose exploitation or cruelty toward animals. On the other hand, while expressing indifference or incredulity toward the idea of "loving" animals, many southerners form strong affectional attachments to individual animals. This is best expressed in the rural South through the ambivalent relationship between a man and his hound. Other southerners report no such ambivalence in their relationships with their pets and companion animals, readily expressing strong and enduring attachment to them and mourning their loss, whether these companions are household residents or working companions.

The importance of the animal as working companion is reflected in the emergence of several regional dog breeds. The breeds usually derive from stock registered by national breeding registries, but offspring are no longer registered with national bodies. They are identified with the region and local area and are a source of great community pride. Examples are the multiple varieties of coonhounds (many locally recognized as separate pure breeds, with strong local sanctions against breeding back to nonregional stock), the Boykin Spaniel (a variety of Field Spaniel, developed as a hunting spaniel but also suitable as a household companion), and the Catahoula Leopard Dog (a stock dog prized for working ability and companionship, developed from several breeds of stock dogs). Few of these are known or seen outside the South. Small mixed-breed dogs are still routinely referred to as "feist" or "fice" and within local areas may be so similar to one another in appearance and ancestry as to be recognized as the "feist" of a particular area. William Faulkner celebrated the bravery of a "fice" in "The Bear."

The species of pets and companion animals in the South do not differ notably from those in other regions of the United States, especially in urban areas. Dogs are most common, with a greater proportion of the regional purebred and mixed breeds than found in other regions. Some patterns of the dog-human relationship do differ. Individuals and household members develop strong attachments to individual dogs and, while treating them with affection, evaluate them on the basis of their working ability. Once unable to work, however, they still retain a special status within the household. Because their primary function is that of working animal, the special status within the household does not necessarily mean the animal resides inside. This is true for many pets and companion animals in southern culture: the key elements of companion animal status are frequently fulfilled without inside residence for the animal. This remains true when people migrate or obtain animals of other species or breeds. When the need for an animal to assist with work is no longer present, many southerners select an animal solely for companionship purposes. Special status is earned on the basis of satisfaction with fulfillment of companionship function. Country musicians sing sentimental songs of dogs, such as "Old Shep." Writer Willie Morris wrote of the companionship and death of his dog Pete in *The Courting of Marcus Dupree* (1984) and of another boyhood companion in *My Dog Skip* (1995).

Cats are kept as pets less frequently than in other areas. Most cats kept as pets or companions live in urban areas. In rural areas of the South many barn cats are kept to control rodent populations, with attachments to the territory on which they live and hunt, rather than to people. Breeding cats for companionship functions has occurred only recently. The recency of this practice is not peculiar to the South, however. Although selective breeding of the dog has occurred for more than 2,000 years, selective breeding of cats in most areas of the world has occurred only within the past 100 years.

As in other areas, horses have risen in popularity as companion animals. Previously kept primarily as performance animals by members of the upper and upper-middle classes, they are increasingly acquired for companionship and pleasure riding by members of the middle class. Frequently, a strong mutual attachment develops between horse and owner, and the horse spends an entire lifetime with a single owner, rather than being regularly sold and replaced as are many performance animals.

Southerners also keep their share of "pocket pets," guinea pigs, rats, mice, rabbits, gerbils, ferrets, birds, amphibians, and fish. Patterns of keeping these species do not differ notably from other regions of the United States; they are more popular in urban areas.

Another common practice in the South persists even among those who express a utilitarian attitude toward animals: hand raising food animals and selecting an occasional food animal to be kept as a pet. In the past this practice has involved very few animals but has included hogs, dairy and beef cattle, sheep, and poultry. As southern animal agriculture shifts from small operations to large agribusiness, the practice persists, but the types of animals change: goats have become increasingly popular, as have pigs. Both provide food and animal by-products. Both species are also social animals, a fact that increases the probability of becoming a successful companion.

The practices of raising orphaned and keeping tamed wild animals as if they were pets are far more common in the South than in other regions. In many southern towns and rural areas, these are long-standing customs, often considered as much a part of southern culture as nurturing regional breeds or lines of dogs. In the past most of the tamed wild animals have been small and native to the South—raccoons, skunks, possums, squirrels, and birds. They frequently fulfilled some marginal companionship function. Recently, however, there has been a marked increase in the keeping of exotic or endangered animals, including pot-bellied pigs, cougars, wolves, buffaloes, wolf-hybrids, parrotlike birds, monkeys, and large snakes. The last-named species are kept largely for amusement or as status symbols rather than for utility or companionship. Such practices are currently being actively discouraged in many southern communities as lawsuits against owners of animals that kill or injure people are successfully prosecuted, as the incidence of rabies among wild animals increases, as zoonotic diseases are transmitted from animals to people, and as existing laws that prohibit keeping such animals are more strictly enforced. Efforts to discourage keeping wild animals as pets are usually met with strong resistance and are viewed as attempts of outsiders to interfere with southern rights. In the summer of 2009, wildlife officials in Florida allowed permits to hunt nonnative pythons in the Everglades because for years snake owners have used the area to release the pets when they became too large to keep. Wildlife officials are unsure of how many of the large snakes live in the area, but they estimate the number reaches into the tens of thousands and are concerned that the snakes will disrupt the preserve's fragile ecology and eventually migrate north.

Patterns of keeping companion animals in the South are similar to those in other areas of the United States in many ways. Dogs are still the most popular companion animals, with cats, birds, and other small domestic animals becoming more popular, especially as urbanization increases. But the South has several notable differences from patterns in other regions. Companion animals in the rural South are more likely to be employed actively in some work-assistant role, and they are more frequently kept for herding, hunting, or controlling pests, while enjoying special status within the household or farmstead.

Ownership patterns also differ. The use of the companion animal in its work function is frequently shared by various members in the community; however, the primary figure for attachment, loyalty, affection, and care is an individual rather than a group. Other animals are kept primarily as household companions or working companions during most of the year and employed in communal work-recreational functions (such as raccoon or bird hunting) at intervals throughout the year. In addition, in the South, human companions to companion animals are less likely to be legal owners of the animals than in other regions.

Residence patterns of companions and pets differ from other regions. In the South, many animals are sheltered outside the house. In other regions, most are housed in the same structure as their owners. Types of pet animals vary. More wild animals are kept as pets, as are more farm animals. Regional breeds are more highly valued, and animals are more likely to be evaluated on performance of their companionship function than on their status as pure or mixed breed.

MARGARET SERY YOUNG
University of North Carolina at Chapel Hill

David S. Favre and Murray Loring, *Animal Law* (1983); Katherine C. Grier, *Pets in America: A History* (2007); James W. Jordan, *Appalachian Journal* (Spring 1975);

Stephen R. Kellert, *Transactions of the 45th North American Wildlife and Natural Resources Conference* (1980); Willie Morris, *My Cat Spit McGee* (1999); Margaret Sery Young, *Veterinary Clinics of North America: Small Animal Practice* (March 1985).

Picking Sessions

If it's after eight o'clock in the morning or within an hour or so of midnight, somewhere around the South—in Virginia or Kentucky, Alabama or Tennessee, Florida or Louisiana—very likely a picking session is under way. Virtually every night, most afternoons, and on many more mornings than you might expect, musicians gather together in groups ranging from 3 to 30 or more to make music. They convene at community centers, inside cafés, at fast-food joints, in the back rooms of barbershops, under the shade trees and pavilions of public parks, on somebody's back porch, in a friend's living room, beside dirt-road country stores, and at music shops. Once gathered, they sit or stand for hours on end, instruments in hand, as they pick and sing their favorite traditional old-time, bluegrass, and gospel tunes. They do it with great fervor, and they do it just for the fun of it.

Generally speaking, picking sessions are public events to which all comers are welcomed, either as musicians or as listeners. Players range from the oldest and most skilled to rank beginners and youngsters. For the most part, participants allow only acoustic instruments and frown upon amplified ones. And while the form of picking sessions may (and often does) vary from place to place, in general the musicians arrange themselves into loosely defined circles, typically with the acknowledged leaders or best players situated closest to the center, and the novices, beginners, and less skilled players toward the outer fringes.

The basic or lead instrument for most picking sessions is the guitar, although fiddles and banjos will also take the lead. Fiddles, five-string banjos, guitars, and mandolins are almost always present at picking sessions. Less essential (but often seen) additional instruments include double-bass fiddles, mountain dulcimers, and harmonicas. In addition, tenor banjos, mouth bows, banjo-lins, washboards, accordions, bongo drums, hammered dulcimers, spoons, jugs, kazoos, dobros, musical saws, bowed psalterys, bodhrans (traditional Irish drums), triangles, and a variety of other acoustic instruments appear from time to time, especially at old-time jam sessions. On rare occasions, a piano, if available, will be included. The human voice is virtually always an essential part of the musical mix. So is dancing. Dancing is especially prevalent in the Appalachian regions of the South, where a picking session would seem a bit odd if there weren't a flatfoot dancer or two (or more) on the floor and dancing to the rhythm of every nongospel tune that's played. The same is true for jam sessions in French Louisiana, though there you'd substitute the two-step or waltz for flatfooting.

Several noteworthy items differentiate traditional old-time picking sessions from bluegrass sessions. The instrumentation in bluegrass sessions is usually much more restrictive than in their old-time counterparts. Bluegrass sessions typically allow only guitar, five-string banjo, fiddle, double-bass, mandolin, and voice. Old-time players enjoy picking sessions that form a circle. From within that circle they play toward and to each other. Old-time players generally sit or stand with their backs to any listeners who may be present; listeners at such sessions are expected to politely remain outside the circle of players while the jam is in process. Bluegrass players, on the other hand, are much more likely to be audience-centric and will often pay a great deal of attention to the performer-listener relationship. Bluegrass music is, by its very nature and history, a performance-based genre, and this characteristic is not usually discarded when community-based bluegrass jam sessions are under way.

"Thou shalt not forsake the beat!" is the first "commandment" of "The Ten Commandments of Jamming," a set of rules of etiquette that are adhered to by most musicians who get together to play communal music. While picking sessions are typically friendly, laid-back affairs, they follow an informal code of behavior that is sometimes spoken, sometimes written, yet always understood—sooner or later—by those who participate. The commandments of jamming—which have many variations, and many competing claims of authorship—generally go something like this:

The Ten Commandments of Jamming
1. Thou shalt not forsake the beat.
2. Thou shalt always play in tune.
3. Thou shalt arrange thyselves in a circle so thou mayest hear and see the other musicians and thou shalt play in accord with the group.
4. Thou shalt commence and cease playing in unison.
5. Thou shalt stick out thine own foot or lift up thine own voice and cry, "This is it!" if thou hast been the one to begin the song, this in order to endeth the tune, which otherwise wilt go on and on forever and forevermore.
6. Thou shalt concentrate and not confound the music by mixing up the A part and the B part. If thou should sinneth in this, or make any mistake that is unclean, thou mayest atone for thy transgression by reentering the tune in the proper place and playing thereafter in time.
7. Thou shalt be mindful of the key of the banjo, and play many tunes in

that key, for the banjo is but a lowly instrument, which must be retuned each time there is a key change.

8. Thou shalt not speed up nor slow down when playing a tune, for such is an abomination.

9. Thou shalt not noodle by thine ownself on a tune which the other musicians know not, unless thou art asked or unless thou art teaching that tune, for it is an abomination and the other musicians will not hold thee guiltless, and shall take thee off their computer lists, yea, even unto the third and fourth generations. Thou shalt not come to impress others with thine own amazing talents, but will adhere to the song, which shall be the center around which all musicians play.

10. Thou shalt play well and have fun.

Many of the seemingly impromptu picking sessions that take place around the campgrounds and backstage areas of large annual musical gatherings such as the Old Fiddler's Convention at Galax, Va., or the Bluegrass and Old Time Fiddlers Convention at Mount Airy, N.C., will often diverge from the friendly and inclusive pattern of community picking sessions. Within the participant areas at these large music events, where hundreds or even thousands of skilled musicians are gathered, a different kind of picking session frequently occurs— one in which participants discard the usual standards of inclusion and openness, and exclusivity becomes the rule. The prevalent sense of competition at such events seems to take over the mind-set of many of the musicians in attendance, yielding scores of small, exclusive picking sessions beside, inside, and between the many tents and RVs that line the festival grounds. These sessions often last way into the night and beyond. Many such sessions are restricted to the four, five, or six musicians who have been expressly invited to join them; other players are not encouraged to participate, although listeners are usually welcome to gather around. The posture of the included musicians will very often signal their exclusive intent. Direct eye contact with potential intruders is clearly avoided, lest outsiders mistakenly assume that they've been invited to join the session. Newcomers often misunderstand this phenomenon, particularly when they're accustomed to the cordial friendliness and welcoming openness of community-based picking sessions.

Picking sessions manifest themselves in a number of distinctive ways, depending on the geographic location, participants, physical surroundings, local traditions, time of day, musical preferences, and so on. The following four events typify many of the hundreds of picking sessions that occur every week across the southeastern United States.

At the weekly, Thursday night jam session at the Silvermont Mansion Community Center in Brevard, N.C., musicians set up chairs in a large circle and place a single microphone on a stand in the center. Each musician in the circle takes his or her turn leading a song and, when finished, passes the microphone to the next person, moving in a clockwise direction. The music played at Silvermont ranges from bluegrass to old-time to country to gospel. This mixed session is truly open to all who want to participate, with even an occasional jazz or classical player joining the lineup.

Every second and fourth Saturday (or whenever there's a special event), pickers gather to play acoustic instruments at Old Alabama Town, a living history museum in the heart of downtown Montgomery, Ala. From 20 to 40 players participate on a typical Saturday afternoon, depending on the weather and whether an important Auburn or Alabama football game is being played that day. Most of the musicians are regulars, and many have been participating in the session for years. The main jam takes place at the historic Rose House, but side jams often break off from this group and play elsewhere on the grounds, usually beneath a certain shade tree or on the front porch of an adjacent building. Montgomery-area musicians have been congregating here ever since 1988. The musicians usually, but not always, situate themselves in a circle. Breakaway groups will often play with those whose particular style they share. Generally speaking, the participating musicians play to each other, seldom acknowledging the presence of any audience members.

Picking sessions that lie a bit outside the traditional community mainstream of old-time or bluegrass jams—like those in French Louisiana—often have their own culturally specific jamming etiquette and procedures. Every Saturday morning, the Savoy Music Center near Eunice, La., hosts an acoustic jam session that invites all comers to join in and play. They have just one very emphatic rule: no more than ONE triangle player is allowed to participate at a time. Not surprisingly, the beautifully handcrafted accordions of local master instrument maker and National Heritage Award recipient Marc Savoy are an integral part of almost every session.

On Florida's Space Coast, picking sessions happen every Sunday at Trailhead Park in the small town of Malabar. All players—including rank beginners—are welcome to participate in these sessions, which present a mixture of old-time, country, and bluegrass numbers. Newcomers to the event usually hold forth around the outer edges of the picking circle, at least until they feel comfortable playing along with the core group. The session can include as many as 25 pickers and 35 "grinners" (audience). This Sunday jam began in 1975 at the Castaway Point Tavern beside the Indian River Lagoon, where it happened every Wednesday evening. When a recent hurricane destroyed the tavern, local musicians reincarnated the jam at Trailhead Park. The mostly seated musicians who play here position themselves on a raised wooden floor beneath an outdoor pavilion. Audience members gather nearby, sitting in lawn chairs pulled to the edge of the stage on cooler days, or resting in the shade of a large nearby oak tree on warmer ones.

In recent years picking session participants have made effective use of the Internet to communicate with each other about music-related matters. Several online mail lists share information about specific regions and the picking sessions that happen there, and numerous Web sites announce and espouse community picking sessions. For example, Pickin' in the Park—a trademarked entity licensed by Pickin' in the Park, LLC—is a national membership organization of community-based picking sessions. With headquarters in Georgia, Pickin' in the Park offers guidance to communities that want to establish their own locally based acoustic picking sessions. They offer a handbook with tips for getting started and a companion CD-ROM with standard artwork and templates for signage, posters, stationery, press releases, sponsor pitches, and even Web site design. Currently active Pickin' in the Park chapters exist in Americus, McCaysville, and Summerville, Ga.; North Augusta, S.C.; and several locations outside the South.

Anyone interested in observing or participating in a community picking session should have little trouble finding one. A good place to start is a local music store, particularly the kind that sells stringed instruments. An inquiry here will almost always provide one or more leads to local picking sessions.

FRED C. FUSSELL
Buena Vista, Georgia

Timothy Duffy, in *North Carolina Folklore Journal* (Winter–Spring 1990); Fred C. Fussell, *Blue Ridge Music Trails: Finding a Place in the Circle* (2003); North Carolina Arts Council, the Virginia Commission for the Arts, and the Blue Ridge Institute and Museum of Ferrum College, "Blue Ridge Music Trails," www.blueridgemusic.org; "Pickin' in the Park," www.curmudgeoncafe.com/pickinthepark.

Pool Checkers

Pool checkers remains the board game of choice for many African American men in the South and beyond. It is often played in clubs, barbershops, and community centers, sometimes under shade trees and viaducts. Play occurs on a 64-square board (eight squares by eight squares), as in English draughts or American checkers, known to pool checker players as "straight" checkers. Pool checker partisans consider their game more exciting, because pieces can move forward or backward, and kings are "flying kings," empowered to move and capture all along a diagonal, like a bishop in chess.

The history of pool checkers and how African Americans came to play it is a matter of speculation, though veteran players believe the game derives from European forms of checkers and may have been learned from immigrants several generations ago, perhaps in slavery days. An important early text was *The Secrets of Spanish Pool Checkers*, and older players remember when the game was called Spanish pool checkers in the United States.

Tournament play—locally and beyond—goes back at least to the early 20th century, but the American Pool Checker Association (APCA) did not form until 1961, holding its first national tournament five years later in Detroit. Since then, the APCA has had annual national tournaments. Carl "Buster" Smith emerged as a dominant player in the early years and joined a few other African Americans in traveling to Europe for tournaments. In the 1970s and 1980s two Soviet émigrés, Vladimir Kaplan and Iser Kuperman, enlivened and strengthened APCA play, with Kuperman winning the annual tournament from 1984 to 1989. In recent years, Calvin Monroe and Al "East Point" Barnett—both of the Atlanta area—have been the strongest tournament players, often battling one another for the title. Along with putting on tournaments, the APCA recognizes clubs. The first club was the Georgia Pool Checker Association in Atlanta. Other southern cities with clubs include Baltimore; Durham, N.C.; Memphis; Winston-Salem, N.C.; and Jacksonville, Fla.

In tournament play, quiet is encouraged, but otherwise pool checkers tends to be a loud game, with players slapping checkers on the board and teasing one another. The term "ham," for example, is commonly applied to a player who is easy to beat. Player nicknames too are common, such as "Ham Killer" and "Schoolboy."

These days, pool checkers can be played on the Internet, and YouTube offers videos that demonstrate the game and repeat television news coverage of tournaments. Still, participation in tournaments and clubs is down. Ervin Smith, president of the APCA, said young people today prefer flashier entertainment, such as video games. He laments that trend, believing pool checkers is a wholesome pastime that also improves thinking and discipline. Smith said, "I'm convinced that if they could sit down and learn the game of checkers, the number of people who do stupid stuff would be cut significantly."

SAM HODGES
Dallas Morning News

Sam Hodges, *Orlando Sentinel* (4 September 1986); Douglas Martin, *New York Times* (14 October 2002); Paul Schwartzman, *Washington Post* (1 April 2005); Anthe Mitrakos, *Chicago Sun-Times* (19 July 2008).

Porch Sitting

Scholars generally agree that southern culture is as much about talking as it is about hot weather, cotton, mosquitoes, and mules. Historically, most of this talking has taken place on porches, especially front porches. If there is any place in the United States where architecture has determined a part of the culture, that would be the South and the talking that has been shaped in part by porch sitting. With its tradition of storytelling, the South has institutionalized the porch as a site of creativity, and porch sitting as the activity through which this creativity emerges. Until the mid-20th century and before the widespread use of air-conditioning, families gathered on front porches in the early evening to wait until hot houses cooled off. The waiting process provided time for sharing the day's events as well as for storytelling. Members of the extended family and neighbors were often incorporated into the latter events.

Porch sitting, in spite of the second word in the phrase, is indeed an activity. Although it usually includes groups of people on a porch, in its minimal form it may involve a single individual. A lone figure sitting quietly on a porch and staring off into space is probably not as idle as he or she may seem. Porch sitting allows for engagement with passersby, interaction with neighbors, and reconnaissance. That individual may yell out greetings, chastise children, note what the postman or delivery men are doing, and observe the comings and goings of just about everybody in the neighborhood. A person sitting alone on a porch, therefore, probably knows more about what is happening in a neighborhood than many others who are rushing to and from their daily activities.

In its more interactive form, porch sitting is an activity that allows for tellers and listeners, for performance and audience. The exchange might be as simple as discussing the day's dinner (among women, for instance, who are on a porch late in the morning shelling peas or beans and preparing for the day's meal) or as formalized as a storytelling contest. As late as the 1960s, it was not unusual to eavesdrop on tales of Brer Rabbit and John and other traditional folk heroes as they traipsed across the imaginations of persons bringing them to life on southern porches. As Zora Neale Hurston points out in her various discussions and representations of activities on porches, reputations could be made or destroyed in these open-air competitive exchanges.

In the storytelling dynamic as well as the visitor factor, porch space is the semipublic arena where one can entertain and engage with visitors (who at times might be unwelcome) without having to invite them into the more private space of the home. While the porch might in some ways have been an extension of the home (for persons coming from the inside out), it could also place boundaries on the home (for persons coming from the outside in). Porch sitting could take the place of entertainment in a living room or family room. In terms of competition, porch sitting could also be a miniature playground for children in their games or a miniature playing field for adults who may have argued about everything from whether Jack Johnson or Joe Louis was the better fighter to whether astronauts actually landed on the moon.

In public settings in the South, porch space could be the democratic space in otherwise segregated environments. As Lewis Nordan makes clear in *Wolf Whistle*, blacks and whites mingle and engage one another on the porch of the store in his little southern town, even as they separate and are served hierarchically inside the store. Elderly men of both groups migrated to southern porches to get out of the way of activities going on in their homes. (Nowadays, restaurants such as McDonalds allow for that option.) They could wile away the hours with talk or board games such as checkers.

As the architecture of the South has changed, so too has the widespread phenomenon of porch sitting. Decks at the backs of houses, along with side porches, have altered some of the interactive nature of porch sitting. Alteration, however, has not meant extinction. The tradition continues in its vibrancy on porches that are available, as it does in the literary representations and documentations of these porches. Just as southern talk followed the trail from shade trees during plantation days to porches, so too has it moved to decks and side porches to remain one of the most practiced leisurely activities in the South.

TRUDIER HARRIS
University of North Carolina at Chapel Hill

James Agee and Walker Evans, *Let Us Now Praise Famous Men* (1941); Jocelyn Donlon, *Swinging in Place: Porch Life in Southern Culture* (2001); Trudier Harris, *Southern Cultures* (Fall–Winter 1996); Zora Neale Hurston, *Mules and Men* (1935), *Their Eyes Were Watching God* (1937); Lewis Nordan, *Wolf Whistle* (1993).

Quail Hunting

The northern bobwhite quail (*Colinus virginianus*) is native to much of the eastern United States. It is found as far north as Massachusetts and Wisconsin, as far west as Colorado, and throughout the South. It was the first species of quail encountered by European settlers, as well as the smallest (typically less than 10 inches long), and the one with the largest geographic range. Unlike most western species of quail, which dwell in remote sage-covered slopes and wild bottomlands, the bobwhite sticks relatively close to human habitation. It prefers the weedy grasslands, cultivated fields, and hedgerows typically found around small farms.

Because of the bird's abundance and close proximity to agricultural settlement, quail hunting became a natural part of life in the early colonial South. It also evolved into a much-anticipated form of entertainment from October to February—peak quail hunting season. Though not strictly a sport for the wealthy, quail hunting today is rooted in a tradition of privilege and refinement that stretches back to the days when landed southern gentry sought to emulate European aristocratic fashions and customs.

Bird hunting has a long history in England as a gentleman's sport, and quail hunting in the South takes its character and conventions from English hunting culture, particularly in its emphasis on dog breeding. Wherever it is done, quail hunting relies on the close, cooperative relationship between humans and dogs. With no dog to locate the birds, one might as well not even try to find them. An untrained dog will not be of much help. But a dog that has been selectively bred and trained to locate game turns quail hunting into a kind of collaborative sport.

In outline, quail hunting involves following a pair, or "brace," of dogs (typically English pointers or setters) that have been trained to point, with muzzle aimed forward and body frozen stiff, when they come upon quail in a field. When a dog points, the hunter approaches, flushes the covey, and shoots the birds on the wing. The quails' swift and unpredictable flight patterns are one of the reasons they are considered especially sporting game. The dog retrieves the kill, and the hunt resumes. Hunters and dog handlers typically follow on foot or horseback. The use of a mule-drawn wagon (sometimes known as a "Georgia shooting wagon") for transporting spectators, dogs, and equipment appears to be a uniquely southern convention—although 21st-century quail hunters are just as likely to drive ATVs instead.

To the hunter of modest means in the preindustrial South—who looked upon his quarry as food, rather than the object of a noble chase—the amount of money, labor, and gunpowder involved in killing such a small fowl might have seemed extravagant. (Netting was a far more economical, if unsportsman-like, method of catching the birds, and 19th-century sporting literature is full of disparaging accounts of netters.) Among quail hunting enthusiasts, however, the costs were outweighed by the value placed on dogs of exceptional breeding and the status that could accrue from a dog's outstanding performance in the field. In certain circles, then as now, owning a fine bird dog could enhance one's reputation almost as much as accumulating money or land. Individuals who owned accomplished bird dogs were respected by their hunting peers, as were expert dog handlers.

However, the most important factor that popularized southern quail hunting as a stylish, high-society pastime came from outside the South. That factor was northern money. Around the turn of the 20th century, owing to the decline of the old plantation economy and changing agricultural practices, many farming families in the Deep South migrated to industrialized cities such as Birmingham and Atlanta, or further north to Chicago and Detroit. At the same time, wealthy northern industrialists, looking for a place to spend the winter, descended on the region and bought up large tracts of land at reduced prices. On these plots they built lavish winter retreats, which they called "plantations" after the manner of their antebellum precursors, and whiled away their days at their favorite sport—hunting quail.

In some places—notably the regions around Tallahassee, Fla., and Thomasville, Ga.—the shift in land use from agricultural production to private quail hunting reserves was especially pronounced. According to one historian, between 1900 and 1950 more than 100,000 acres of prime cotton farming land in Leon County, Fla., were consolidated into large quail hunting plantations owned by a handful of northern families, which then became the de facto landlords of more than 90 percent of the county's tenant farmers.

Ironically, the rise of the southern quail plantation as a rural playground for the rich and famous coincided with the dramatic loss of habitat for the quail itself. As cornfields, pea patches, and fencerows around small farms disappeared, so did the bobwhite's natural environment. In its place came pine forests, industrialized cattle ranches, and creeping urbanization. As a result, wild bobwhite populations have dwindled to a fraction of their former numbers, and quail hunters today primarily hunt birds raised in pens on plantation grounds.

While the northern industrialists have largely died, moved on, or sold out, many of these plantations remain in the form of commercial hunting retreats. Quail hunting has become big business in some parts of the South. According to the U.S. Fish and Wildlife Service, in 2006 more than 75,000 quail hunters in Georgia spent an average of $950 per person each time they went hunting. Such numbers are hard to ignore, and modern quail-hunting plantations cater to business executives and exclusive clientele, offering haute cuisine, fully appointed conference facilities, golf courses, and luxurious amenities—as well, of course, as an assortment of purebred dogs and an atmosphere of old-fashioned gentility.

AARON WELBORN
Washington University in St. Louis

Johnson J. Hooper, *Dog and Gun* (1992); George M. Humphrey and Shepard Krech, eds., *The Georgia-Florida Field Trial Club, 1916–1948* (1948); Clifton Paisley, *From Cotton to Quail: An Agricultural Chronicle of Leon County, Florida, 1860–1967* (1968); Ben O. Williams, *Hunting the Quails of North America* (2001).

Quinceañeras

Young Latinas traditionally celebrate their 15th birthday with a religious and semisecular event called a *quinceañera*; the term refers both to the young woman being honored and to the celebration. The essential components of the *quinceañera* are a religious celebration (usually a Catholic mass) and a dance. Other elements of the celebration testify to deep roots in European and indigenous ritual; the *quinceañera* includes vestiges of both the Spanish court's presentation of the daughters of the nobility and the menses rituals of indigenous groups such as those found in the Lipan Apache. These references to life's passage find contemporary expression in objects that the young woman carries and wears during the celebration, signifying her transition from childhood to adulthood.

Like baptisms, confirmations, and weddings, the *quinceañera* is a life-cycle celebration that relies on the resources of the full community—the family, neighborhood, *compadres/comadres*, and others—and tends to survive across class and (im)migrant status. The celebration's structure reflects the many ways that the community comes together to make the fiesta happen. In the South, the celebration also fulfills a desire to reproduce the rituals of the past, and—in the case of immigrant groups—those of their places of origin.

Traditionally, the *quinceañera* marks the young woman's special day by wearing a frilly dress (usually lavender or white) that resembles a wedding gown, and a *diadema*, or tiara. Sometimes she also sports long formal gloves and special jewelry.

In a very stratified fashion, the honoree selects 14 young women—either friends or family—to be her *damas*; they in turn select their *chambelans*, or escorts. This *corte de honor*, or court of honor, accompanies the *quinceañera* during the religious ceremony, and then performs at the dance. The ceremony is usually a Catholic mass, though it can also be a Protestant service. Whatever the religious setting, the *corte de honor* enters before the young woman, who is escorted in by her parents. The family and friends gathered at the service then usually hear a sermon or homily admonishing the young people to be chaste and to be grateful for their parents' sacrifices and love.

For several weeks before the event, the *corte de honor* members rehearse a choreographed dance that they perform at the *salón de baile*, the dance hall, on the day of the celebration. Traditionally, they danced to a time-honored waltz, such as "Sobre las olas"; increasingly, however, the court's members are dancing to U.S. or Latino pop music, recorded by such artists as Whitney Houston or Shakira. In some cases, they dance to both a traditional waltz and a contemporary number. Alternately, the *quinceañera* may dance the waltz with her father, and then join her *corte de honor* for the pop music. The family sometimes chooses the celebration's music to coincide with a particular "theme." For example, the court may dance to "Cotton-Eyed Joe" in a celebration with a country and western theme.

Older family members and the family's circle of friends offer support and participate in the celebration as *madrinas* and *padrinos*, or sponsors, to make the whole event happen. In effect, these sponsors subsidize the cost of the *quinceañera*, often footing the bill for the music, cake, and other celebratory elements. The immediate family does not, however, necessarily choose sponsors on the basis of their ability to help shoulder the costs (even though some of the objects of a more ritualistic nature would encourage this practice). Some sponsors are chosen for sentimental or for personal and social reasons. The "last doll" sponsor, for example, is usually a young aunt or cousin of the honoree. Her job is to present the *quinceañera* with a doll (often dressed in a gown identical to the honoree's) at some point during the formal ceremony—an obvious symbol of the young woman's transition from dolls and childish things to the adult world. In like fashion, while various sponsors may give the honoree pieces of jewelry (a watch, earrings, a ring), it is usually a close family member who gives her the religious medal—la Virgen de Guadalupe in Mexican tradition, or la Virgen de la Caridad del Cobre in Cuban tradition.

As an intergenerational event, the *quinceañera* includes children (often the younger siblings or cousins of the honoree), teenagers in the *corte de honor*, and elders in the roles of sponsors. At the center of the celebration, however, is the honoree; she is clearly the focus of the group's attention.

Over time, the *quinceañera* tradition has changed and evolved. It now allows a young woman, for example, to select a nontraditional color for her dress, or to choose a celebratory theme that fits her personality. The major changes, though, seem to revolve around the dress; while the celebration now includes contemporary features and variants that offer ample room for breaking with the traditional format, it nonetheless holds onto the core elements of the traditional *quinceañera*. Testifying to the power of ritual, it remains embedded in the social fabric of Latino communities, even while some young women choose to forgo a *quinceañera* and opt instead for a major gift from their parents (a car, a European vacation, a cruise). Cruise packages designed for and marketed to *quinceañera* celebrants have recently become available for those choosing to celebrate in this manner.

As a folk religious celebration, the semisecular *quinceañera* exists in communities throughout Greater Mexico (folklorist Américo Paredes's term for all those places where people of Mexican origin reside in the United States). Latina teens in Chicago, Los Angeles, Phoenix, and Dallas—as well as in Charleston, Knoxville, and Atlanta—continue to celebrate this rite of passage. It has become increasingly popular in the South over the past few decades, as the region comes to host growing numbers of immigrants from Mexico, Central America, and the Caribbean.

NORMA E. CANTÚ
University of Texas at San Antonio

Julia Alvarez, *Once upon a Quinceañera: Coming of Age in the USA* (2007); Norma E. Cantú, in *Chicana Traditions: Continuity and Change*, ed. Norma E. Cantú and Olga Nájera-Ramírez (2002).

Rafting and Canoeing

From the time the first white man saw an American Indian paddling a canoe, he wondered, "Can you fish from that?" Thus, a fascination with river-going watercraft in the South was born. From lazy inner-tube floats of the Suwannee and the Chattahoochee to the raging whitewater torrents of the Chattooga and the Ocoee, rivers of the American South have drawn outdoor enthusiasts to the lure of downriver paddling. In the early days, freshwater rivers tumbling down from the Appalachian Mountains into the Piedmont and Coastal Plains provided material for song, story, and sustenance. More recently, such locales have become weekend destinations for outdoor adventure and even Olympic-level venues of competition.

The modern history of river recreation harkens back to a simple time of aluminum canoes, fiberglass kayaks, and army surplus black-rubber rafts. Stealthy early river runners employed these low-tech craft to make their way downriver, all for the thrill of making it from put in to take out. Then came *Deliverance*, the James Dickey novel turned blockbuster 1972 film featuring Burt Reynolds, Jon Voight, Ned Beatty, and Ronny Cox. River running, AD (After *Deliverance*), was transformed. Outfitters and adventure companies sprang up like RV parks in the mountains and began to capitalize on the river experience, and a whole new tourist industry was born.

As with most modern outdoor activities, technological advances have played a huge role. In the late 1980s, roto-molded plastic supplanted aluminum, fiberglass, and Kevlar kayak predecessors and ABS (Acrylonitrile Butadiene Styrene: plasticcore sandwiched between two layers of vinyl) became the industry standard in canoe construction. Tire rubber rafts have evolved into fiber-infused, self-bailing, polymer-created crafts resistant to ubiquitous rock and sand wear. Gone are the late-night duct-tape and epoxy repair sessions. Durable, high-tech materials are now standard river gear.

The rivers themselves have evolved in their recognition as true natural resources. The 1968 Congressional Wild and Scenic Rivers Act set in motion binding legislation to provide buffers for development and watershed protection in the nation's ecologically sensitive waterways. Rivers running through national and state forests have been afforded protection and set apart as particular recreational treasures. Fisheries and flow levels are monitored carefully as bellwether indicators of ecological health.

All the while, the volume of whitewater river traffic has increased exponentially. It is not uncommon for recreational parking lots to be crowded with so-called weekend-warrior, roof-rack-encrusted vehicles, pulling up to unload at popular park and play sites. Particularly active and accessible river rapids crawl with whitewater play boats paddling upstream for repetitive surfing and end-over-end acrobatics. While downriver paddlers and raft trips have the right of way, mid-rapid collisions at such sites are not uncommon. Downstream, quieter waters are far less crowded and provide ample opportunity for fishing, birding, and hunting.

Rafting and canoeing in the South are participation sports. The paddler flows with the power of the river and becomes a part of its dynamic. Whether in trout and smallmouth bass streams and deciduous forests or the swampy cypress groves in the Okefenokee, there is no other recreational activity that so thoroughly envelops its participants. On the river, the observer becomes the observed and the distinction between man and nature is blurred.

JOHN TALIAFERRO THOMAS
Saint Andrew's–Sewanee School

Whit Deschner, *Does The Wet Suit You?: The Confessions of a Kayak Bum* (1981); Bill Mason, *The Path of the Paddle: An Illustrated Guide to the Art of Canoeing* (1989); William Nealy, *Kayaking, the New Frontier: The Animated Manual of Intermediate and Advanced Whitewater Technique* (1986); John Ross, *Trout Unlimited's Guide to America's 100 Best Trout Streams* (2005); Bob Sehlinger, *Appalachian Whitewater: The Southern State* (2004).

Resorts

The color photographs in brochures publicizing southern resorts portray romantic luxury in magnificent scenic settings. Handsome couples frolic in the wash of surf, ride bicycles along moss-draped live-oak-lined paths, and play golf on green barbered fairways. They dine by candlelight and enjoy a leisurely breakfast on the terrace of their room, overlooking a sweep of mountains or an expanse of sea. The point of such literature, of course, is to coax the reader to make reservations for a few days in paradise.

Essentially, resorts are rooms with a view, a combination of lodging and nature where the natural beauty of the outdoors, like room service, is offered as an amenity. Resorts are the rich relatives of the poor-cousin interstate motel, inhabiting their own little world on barrier islands and mainland coast, beside lakes and warm springs, in the mountain valleys and in the folds of piedmont. Their guests are mostly middle- and upper-class couples and families that escape home and work for a weekend, a week, even a season to find rest and recreation.

Lodging in most resorts may include both hotel-type rooms for rent and individually owned units, such as condominiums. Through lease agreements, owners permit the resort to rent the property to other guests most of the year. Increasingly popular are timeshare vacation units. In this arrangement, the guest buys a space of time, say a week in June, and the vacation home is theirs for that period each year.

The first southern resorts appeared as early as the late 18th and early 19th centuries and were built around the waters of warm springs. The Greenbrier in White Sulphur Springs, W.Va., and the Homestead in Hot Springs, Va., trace their origins to those times. Early lodging conditions were often no better than the common ordinary (tavern) of that day. A minister from Charleston in 1838 described White Sulphur Springs as "decidedly the meanest, most nasty place in point of filth, dust, and every other bad quality." Yet, despite the fleas in his bed and the grunting hogs outside his window, the minister paid his money to rub shoulders with the elite of the South and the nation. Southern resorts drew the rich and famous. One of the last photographs of Robert E. Lee, sitting among his Confederate general comrades, was taken at White Sulphur Springs in 1869.

Although white southerners used health as an excuse to spend a season at

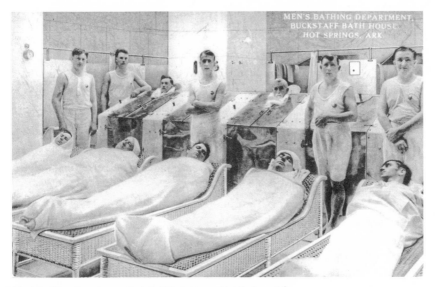

Men's bathing department, Buckstaff Bath House, Hot Springs, Ark.,
postcard, 1900s (Ann Rayburn Paper Americana Collection, Archives
and Special Collections, University of Mississippi Library, Oxford)

a resort, the purpose of their visit was also pleasure. The resort season glittered with balls, sumptuous meals, music, and gambling. In the late 19th century, northerners were also checking into southern resorts and resort towns, not only to bathe in springs but also to drink the mineral waters. Travel guidebooks, such as *Health Resorts in the South*, published in 1893, were a mixture of boosterism and scholarly treatise, praising the towns and resorts and listing the medical benefits of each locale's water and climate.

Many towns were considered beneficial for specific ailments. Consumptives often headed for mountain towns such as Asheville, N.C. Grove Park Inn, still in operation there today, was built in 1886 by a St. Louis businessman who first came to the area seeking relief from his bronchial ailments.

Railroad transportation provided easier access to resorts and encouraged the building of new ones. In the early 20th century, northerners rode the rails further down the southern coastline as these resorts opened. At Jekyll Island, Ga., it is said that one-sixth of the world's wealth gathered each winter on this barrier island. In Florida, Henry Morrison Flagler, the Standard Oil Company magnate, welcomed wintering northerners to a string of coastal resorts he built along his railroad from Jacksonville to Miami.

In the decades after World War II, when the upper class preferred jet travel to Europe, many old resort hotels fell into disrepair. Others, however, survived as oases of grandeur in the neon desert of the chain motel. Such properties as the Breakers in Palm Beach, Fla., the Greenbrier, the Homestead, and Grand Hotel in Point Clear, Ala., constantly upgraded facilities and kept service standards high. For example, in 2009, Sea Island Resorts on Sea Island, Ga., which opened its doors in 1928, earned an unprecedented four Mobil Five-Star awards for its accommodations, its spa, and its fine dining. In 2004 Sea Island Resorts hosted the G8 Summit, the most significant annual gathering of the leaders of the free world. These resorts continued to pamper guests with afternoon tea, chamber music, carriage rides. In dining rooms, ladies and gentlemen dressed for meals prepared by European chefs.

Where the upper class goes, the middle class will scrimp and save and surely follow. Middle-class Americans took their overseas vacations, too, but they also trekked to old resorts and to newer ones that began to arise around the early 1960s. These stretch along beaches and huddle in mountain valleys, offering units with kitchens for guests. Families also bought property on which they built vacation or retirement homes.

As stepchildren to the grand old hotels, these nouveau riche resorts attempt to buy instant tradition and class. Many hire European chefs to prepare continental cuisine and offer afternoon tea. They pay handsome sums to top golf course designers to lay out their 18 holes and hire professional golfers and tennis stars, who represent the resort as "touring pro." These stars drop by for cameo appearances to teach clinics and play exhibition matches. At these new resorts, vacationers may still rub elbows with the rich and famous.

Nearly all offer golf and tennis, water sports, bicycling, and shopping. But despite the similarities, each resort attempts to produce a distinctive ambience. On Greers Ferry Lake, in the foothills of the Arkansas Ozarks, two resorts stretch along opposite shorelines. One, Fairfield Bay, moves with a snappy urbane flair, with rooms as plush as city hotel suites and with entertainment in its nightclub. Red Apple Inn, on the other hand, is flavored with a warm, winesap scent and is as comfortable as worn tweeds. Its rooms are filled with European antiques, fireplaces, and fresh apples. Guests are expected to dress for dinner, which is served with a view of the sunset over the lake.

To build resorts with views from rooms unencumbered by signs of civilization, developers often shouldered into empty pockets of yet-untouched wilderness. Many were gentle invaders. They attached strict building codes to blend vacation structures with natural surroundings, stilted boardwalks above sacred dunes, and left portions of their property in its natural state. On South Carolina's Hilton Head Island, for example, at least 75 percent of Sea Pines Plantation remains in forest and marshland.

One resort in Pine Mountain, Ga., was built specifically as a caretaker of its land. In the early 1950s Cason Callaway, a retired textile magnate, nursed 2,500 acres of eroded cotton fields into a paradise, Callaway Gardens, which is run by a nonprofit foundation for horticultural and environmental research and preservation. In greenhouses and formal gardens, along woodland paths, or bordering an inn, cottage, condominium, tennis court, or golf course, Callaway Gardens blushes with floral color each season.

Traffic sometimes backs up three miles from Pine Mountain as motorists come in spring to see some 700 varieties of azaleas in bloom. The garden's horticulture and education staffs conduct research in plant life and the local environment and pass that knowledge on to guests in nature walks and seminars. At Callaway Gardens the resort is a backdrop to the land and the flowers that grow upon it.

The land itself is a resort's most important asset, groomed and cared for as meticulously as its rooms and restaurants. Guests come for a resort's outdoor features, first for health and later for recreation. Nature—a woodland path, a sunset-kissed curl of golden beach—comprises the main ingredients visitors need "to get away from it all." Visitors still trek to resorts for their health, if not necessarily for the body, at least for peace of mind and of the soul.

GARY D. FORD
Southern Living

George H. Chapin, *Health Resorts of the South* (1893); Robert Conte, *History of the Greenbrier: America's Resort* (1989); Marshall Fishwick, *Springlore in Virginia* (1978); Jeffrey Limerick, Nancy Ferguson, and Richard Oliver, *America's Grand Resort Hotels* (1979); Donald E. Lundberg, *The Tourist Business* (1974); *Southern Living* (September 1979, August 1982, February 1984).

Restaurants

From the colonial period through Reconstruction, southerners did not rely upon commercial hospitality. Except in the large cities such as New Orleans, restaurants were relatively unheard of. The word, derived from the French, was not in general use until late in the 18th century, and the word "hotel" was not used until the 19th century. Even in the larger cities, most eating places were operated in conjunction with lodging.

When southerners traveled, they frequently stopped with friends or relations. Roadside taverns and inns were intended primarily for convivial drinking rather than eating. Food that was supplied was meager and often unappetizing; some of it, travelers discovered, was tainted or spoiled. However, some of the inns were run by widows or private families wishing to supplement their incomes, and in such establishments the traveler fared better.

The food on the eastern seacoast tended to be more appetizing. As the traveler moved westward through the frontier areas, the quality of the food, as defined by outlanders, deteriorated rapidly. In Mississippi and Louisiana (other than New Orleans), food was chased down with whiskey. Available food was generally wild game, chicken, or pork served with locally grown vegetables, fruits, and berries when they were in season.

Spas and resorts, which later became popular in the South, did little to improve commercial dining. Food and accommodations at such hotels as Gray Sulfur Springs, Red Sulfur Springs, and White Sulfur left much to be desired. The Englishman J. S. Buckingham commented with some amazement in his study *The Slave States of America* that most Americans accepted bad accommodations and worse food without complaint.

As the southerner traveled to cities such as Mobile, Charleston, and New Orleans, his chances of finding good food served well in commercial settings improved. Buckingham, for example, ate in the dining room of the Saint Charles Hotel in New Orleans, which accommodated some 500 guests—300 men at one table and 200 women at another. Many immigrants brought with them the more sophisticated knowledge of cuisine from Europe. The Creole and French influences in New Orleans cuisine are still strongly felt.

One area of interest regarding commercial hospitality of the time was the river steamers. Here southerners could find food that frequently equaled the quality of that served in the cities. On one such steamer, the cabin passengers dined first, followed by the ship's officers, white deck passengers, white waiters, black passengers, and black waiters, in sequence. Steamers seemed to offer more beef and less pork and, when they departed from New Orleans, frequently served seafood, especially shellfish.

The manners and eating habits of southerners of the time were born of rough-and-tumble frontier life. Meals were eaten quickly, the knife seemed to be the main utensil, and coffee seemed to be the primary beverage.

The old frontier ways of commercial dining in the South began to change by the middle of the 19th century. More attention was paid not only to the preparation and service of food but also to the environment in which it was served. The Saint Cloud Hotel in Nashville in 1866 had, for example, separate tables for diners, clean and well-appointed surroundings, and more refined food. The great restaurants continued to appear in the cities, and their reputations spread throughout the area.

In the 20th century, urbanization has been perhaps the most notable change

Not everything is guaranteed to still fit after a meal at one of New Orleans's many memorable restaurants. Antoine's in the French Quarter is perhaps the most famous, but it has plenty of challengers. (Courtesy of the Louisiana Department of Tourism)

in southern life affecting foodways. As late as 1920, only nine southern cities had populations of over 100,000 people; in 1980 there were that many or more with populations over a million. Many of the poorest southerners have migrated to cities in the North and West, and this change has affected their eating habits. Modern conveniences, such as electric refrigeration, have also affected the eating habits of southerners. Mass production of meats such as chicken has forced quality down but increased availability. Fast-food shops have changed the eating patterns of southerners, although many of those fast-food shops were founded in the South. Colonel Sanders's Kentucky Fried Chicken began by marketing traditional southern fare. Increasing urbanization has also resulted in a broader palate for southerners, many of whom now eat out more often than they did in the past.

Great restaurants from the past continue to flourish in New Orleans—a city that remains unique within the region. Antoine's, founded in 1840 and reputed to be the oldest continuously operated restaurant in North America, serves its famous oysters Rockefeller (an original), soufflé potatoes, steak, and seafood dishes in both its public front and its plush private dining rooms in the rear. Galatoire's, also in the French Quarter and also one of New Orleans's oldest restaurants, offers shrimp remoulade, oysters Bienville, and trout Marguery. The city is also home to other grand establishments (old and new), such as the famed Commander's Palace and Restaurant August.

Outside the Crescent City a number of restaurants have also achieved national recognition. In the 2000s, chefs at FIG and at Hominy Grill in Charleston, S.C., won James Beard Awards for excellence in cookery. In Atlanta, chefs including Linton Hopkins of Restaurant Eugene and Scott Peacock of Watershed have earned acclaim for modern riffs on traditional southern recipes. In Oxford, Miss., John Currence of City Grocery, also a James Beard Award winner, has revived such traditional dishes as country captain and braised rabbit.

Culinary pilgrims, in search of honest food in humble surroundings, may also visit Doe's Eat Place, a Greenville, Miss., cinderblock restaurant featuring hand-cut steaks and hand-tied tamales. In Nashville, Tenn., at Arnold's Country Kitchen, a bunkhouse of a restaurant set in an industrial area near downtown, midday diners sit down to a feast of fresh vegetables—of crisp fried green tomatoes, sharp stewed collard greens, and gooey macaroni and cheese. Such enduring institutions are just two among dozens of aggressively unpretentious restaurants that have become regional landmarks.

CURTIS C. WHITTINGTON
McNeese State University

John T. Edge, *Southern Belly: The Ultimate Food Lover's Companion to the South* (2007); John Egerton, *Southern Food: At Home, on the Road, in History* (1987); *Food and Wine* (May 1983); Jane Stern and Michael Stern, *Goodfood: The Adventurous Eater's Guide to Restaurants Serving America's Best Regional Specialties* (1983), *Roadfood: The Coast-to-Coast Guide to 700 of the Best Barbecue Joints, Lobster Shacks, Ice Cream Parlors, Highway Diners, and Much, Much More* (rev. ed., 2007); Joe Gray

Taylor, *Eating, Drinking, and Visiting in the South: An Informal History* (1982); *Washington Post* (26 January 1975).

Ring Shouts

The ring shout is a distinctive African American religious practice that involves singing, circular marching, and a focused devotional intensity that invites the Holy Spirit's active participation in the worship proceedings. In their important book *Folksong USA* (1947), folklorists John and Alan Lomax—who had witnessed many regional variations of this worship practice—suggested that ring shouts might best be defined by the following set of characteristics. The shout is not just sung, but is danced, and danced with the entire body. The dancers always move counterclockwise around in a circle. During the shout, the dancers and singers always sing a song that takes a call-and-response form, with numerous repetitions that foreground the cooperative nature of the singing. These repeated passages favor rhythm over melody in a way that emphasizes the collaborative nature of the event. Finally, the worship continues for a long period and escalates in intensity. As this intensity mounts, the shouters feel the presence of the Spirit in their midst. The ring shout, properly speaking, becomes a physical, aesthetic, and spiritual expression of communion. Eyewitness observers of early ring shouts frequently reported that the shouts took place after the close of formal church services. Most of these observers additionally contended that the shouts were of West African origin.

Scholars of African American culture have long associated ring shouts with the tidewater areas of South Carolina and Georgia. This association arose, in part, from the fact that the earliest published accounts of ring shouts came from South Carolina's Sea Islands, where Union soldiers, journalists, and educators who came to the area to help with Reconstruction observed and wrote about such shouts during and after the Civil War. Struck by this dramatic and singular form of worship, they maintained that the shouts had no analogue further north. Ring shouts, however, also thrived in the Chesapeake area of the upper South, particularly in Maryland and Delaware. The shouts of these two areas take a somewhat different form. Accounts of shouts in the coastal Southeast, for instance, consistently describe a counterclockwise ring dance, with a small group of singers off to the side keeping time. Reports from the upper South, in contrast, often portray a circle of singers with a leader in the middle and commonly describe shouters jumping, leaping, and springing into the air as a manifestation of spiritedness, rather than marching in a counterclockwise fashion.

Today, many scholars consider the ring shout to be the central form of worship developed by African American slaves and first-generation freedmen. Scholars have also noted that a general principle of circularity seems to underlie much African American expressive culture. The ring shout gives a religious underpinning to this principle of circularity.

Recent ethnographic work with ring shout groups in the tidewater areas surrounding the Chesapeake and Delaware bays suggests that the centrality of circularity in African American culture perfectly corresponds with patterns of mutual aid that underlie rural African American social life. Since the early 19th century, rural community members maintained the cohesiveness of their communities by enacting patterns of social and economic reciprocity. When one family needed to kill a hog, for example, others in the area would come and help. The family that received this aid would then return the favor to those who had helped them.

This pattern of mutual aid extended into the realm of religious organization. When one church held a camp meeting that featured ring shouts, for instance, leading members of ring shout groups from other churches would come to the host church and sing and shout. (These ring shout groups, which had built a stronghold for themselves in their home churches' prayer meetings, came to call themselves singing and praying bands.) The singing and praying bands of the church that had hosted the camp meeting would then travel and assist the prayer bands and churches that had helped them at their services. The cultural imperative of reciprocity and the attendant principle of circularity underlie this system of fellowshipping.

· More abstractly, this tradition of mutual aid has both an aesthetic and spiritual dimension. Aesthetically, worshipers articulate mutual aid in the call-and-response shout songs and in their collective circular movement, both of which embody an active spirit of cooperation. Spiritually, ring shout worshipers enact this tradition in their belief that the Holy Spirit "runs from heart to heart and breast to breast." The collective experience of the Spirit's in-filling in the ring shout is the culmination of these traditions of grass-roots social solidarity.

Though the ring shout came to be practiced semisecretly at the end of more standard, institutional church services, this African-derived worship practice remained central to early African American Christianity. Its ethic of mutual aid and social solidarity proved highly adaptive to conditions in North America and has remained at the heart of African American culture.

JONATHAN C. DAVID
Philadelphia, Pennsylvania

William Francis Allen, Charles P. Ware, and Lucy McKim Garrison, eds., *Slave Songs of the United States* (1867; 1951); Harold Courlander, *Negro Folk Music, U.S.A.* (1963); Jonathan C. David, with photographs by Richard Holloway, *Together Let Us Sweetly Live: The Singing and Praying Bands* (2007); Samuel A. Floyd Jr., *Black Music Research Journal* (Fall 1991); James Weldon Johnson and J. Rosamond Johnson, eds., *The Books of American Negro Spirituals* (1925; 1977); John A. Lomax and Alan Lomax, *Folksong U.S.A.* (1947); Lydia Parrish, *Slave Songs of the Georgia Sea Islands* (1942); Willie Lee Rose, *Rehearsal for Reconstruction: The Port Royal Experiment* (1964); Art Rosenbaum and Margo Newmark Rosenbaum, *Shout Because You're Free: The African American Ring Shout Tradition in Coastal Georgia* (1998); Sterling Stuckey, *Slave Culture: Nationalist Theory and the Foundations of Black America* (1987).

Ring Tournaments

Usually called lancing tournaments in South Carolina and Georgia and ring tournaments elsewhere, these displays of equestrian skill represent survivals in the South of ancient medieval tourneys. Traditionally held on holidays, particularly Independence Day, and sometimes at agricultural fairs in antebellum times, in the New South tournaments lost most of their quality as spectacle and remained largely an entertainment at planter-class family outings. Extant today in their natural form only in much-simplified versions and in a few localities, they have become essentially folk practices, occasionally retaining some hint of their original pageantry.

Originating in France in the mid-11th century, medieval tournaments—exhibitions of military prowess by horsemen in mock battles—were introduced by the Norman Conquest into England, where they flourished for more than 300 years. Though the introduction of gunpowder and small arms in the 14th and 15th centuries made knightly skills obsolete in warfare, the popularity of tournaments as spectacle continued through the first half of the 16th century. But after the death of Henry VIII, the necessity to economize put such costly shows out of fashion in England, and in 1559 the killing of the French king, Henry II, in a tournament accident blighted the practice everywhere.

Royal tournaments disappeared altogether, but local noblemen in England continued the practice, on a much-reduced scale, as private entertainment. In the course of the 17th century, the tradition was transplanted to England's American colonies. While in 18th-century England tournaments died out, in the colonies, particularly in the South, they survived.

Still intact in the South at the opening of the 19th century, the tournament tradition got a new lease on life from the romantic movement and the Gothic revival. Tournaments were incorporated into the southern ideal of chivalry and achieved phenomenal popularity in the Old South. Five thousand people attended an 1856 tournament in Fredericksburg, Va., for example, and 6,000 were at one in Jackson, Miss., in 1859.

Typically, mounted tournament contestants, often military cadets and officers, styled themselves knights—the Knight of the Old Dominion or the Knight of the Black Prince. Each carried a pointed "lance," a long wooden dowel or, in less polished versions, a small pole from which the bark had been carefully stripped. Contestants in turn "ran the rings," charging down a course of 100 or so yards, along which a series of three or more rings, in diameters diminishing from about three inches to half an inch, were hung on wire hooks suspended from bars fixed to the tops of posts lining the course. After finishing the course, each contestant rode before the judges who counted the rings he had collected on his lance and calculated his time. The winner became the tournament king and crowned a queen.

Tournaments in the New South often lost their medieval trappings and became associated with hunts, particularly with fox hunts. Hence, they were often played out in traditional red, white, and black hunting clothes. Very few tournaments in that form remain today, having lost virtually all elements of pageantry.

JERAH JOHNSON
University of New Orleans

Esther J. and Ruth W. Crooks, *The Ring Tournament in the United States* (1936); John Hope Franklin, *The Militant South, 1800–1861* (1956).

Rock Climbing

When someone mentions sports in the South, most people immediately think of Southeastern Conference football, bass fishing, deer hunting, or mud riding on four-wheelers. Yet every year thousands flock below the Mason-Dixon line to compete in a sport that few others associate with the South: rock climbing. In his *Dixie Cragger's Atlas: A Climber's Guide to Tennessee*, Chris Watford claims that the amount and variety of climbable rock in the South, especially in Tennessee, is so great that choosing where to climb is difficult. In less than two hours, a climber can drive from Birmingham, Atlanta, Chattanooga, Nashville, or Knoxville to one of nearly 50 climbing areas full of challenging possibilities.

Together, the Cumberland Plateau and the southern leg of the Appalachian Mountains encompass an area of land from the upper third of Alabama, north through the eastern half of Kentucky, east into the western half of Virginia, and south through western North Carolina into north Georgia. These two gigantic geological formations are covered with sandstone boulders and sandstone-walled gorges. Climbers began directing their attention to these treasures of the southeastern United States more than 50 years ago. In the early 1960s, John Gill, one of the most noted and influential American climbers, developed his skills on Alabama's Shades Mountain and Desoto Canyon. Gill is often called "the father of bouldering." Bouldering is climbing short technical routes without using a rope. The groundbreaking techniques John Gill established are now a professional sport, complete with a specific grading system, judges, and renowned athletes. Today, the South is a bouldering mecca.

In the fall, three competitions, collectively known as the Triple Crown, occur at Horse Pens Forty near Steele, Ala., Stone Fort near Chattanooga, Tenn., and Hound Ears, N.C. Together, these form one of the largest bouldering competitions in North America. The Triple Crown attracts some of the strongest climbers in the world. It also draws a crowd with an almost unparalleled diversity. A Triple Crown event looks like an amalgamation of Talladega infield rednecks, Telluride ski bums, Grateful Dead concert hippies, dance club ravers, European vagabonds, and skateboard park punks.

Yet the competition and atmosphere of the Triple Crown are only part of the draw that brings climbers from all over the world to match their finger strength against southern rock. The South has become one of the most popular places to climb in the world because it offers almost limitless challenges to climbers of every skill level. Look in any climbing magazine and likely as not there will be adjacent pictures of a European alpinist hanging from an ice-covered Himalayan pinnacle and a chalk-covered teenage kid sprawled out on a boulder in north Alabama.

In addition to those in the Triple Crown competition, the South has numerous other pristine boulder fields, including Texas's Hueco Tanks, Tennessee's Lilly Boulders, Georgia's Boat Rock, and Alabama's Moss Rock Preserve. For climbers that use rope, Alabama has fantastic crags at Little River Canyon, Cherokee Rock Village, and Jamestown. Georgia offers challenging climbs in places such as Tallulah Gorge, Rock Town, and Lost Wall. In Tennessee, the Big South Fork, Foster Falls, and Tennessee Wall represent only a small percentage of the quality pitches available.

Because of the popularity of climbing in the South, concerned climbers created an organization called the Southeastern Climbers Coalition (SCC). The SCC seeks to foster positive relations with climbing-area landowners. It also works at attaining and maintaining public access to privately owned bluffs, gorges, and boulder fields. It organizes cleanup events, hosts competitions and fund raisers, and donates money to help preserve southern climbing for future generations. Because of the efforts of the scc and other climbing organizations like the Access Fund, climbing areas once closed to the public, such as Jamestown, Ala., are now open and accessible. Certainly, climbers will continue to enjoy these challenging ascents on southern rock for years to come.

CLAY WISNER
Rainbow City, Alabama

Pat Ament, *John Gill, Master of Rock: A Lighthearted Walk through His Life and Rock Climbing* (1998); Eric J. Hörst, *Training for Climbing: The Definitive Guide to Improving Your Climbing Performance* (2003); John Sherman, *Stone Crusade: A Historical Guide to Bouldering in America* (1994); Tim Toula, *Rock 'n' Road: An Atlas of North American Rock Climbing Areas* (2003); Chris Watford, *The Dixie Cragger's Atlas: A Climber's Guide to Tennessee* (2005), *The Dixie Cragger's Atlas: A Climber's Guide to Alabama and Georgia* (2005).

Rodeo

Rodeo was born on the open range of the American West. *Vaqueros* had long staged riding and roping contests, and the word "rodeo" derives from the Spanish *rodear* referring to the gathering together of cattle and horses for branding and drives. It was not, however, until the late 19th century that such informal events evolved into organized rodeos that charged admission for spectators and awarded prizes to the contestants.

Rodeo is still concentrated in the West, defined for purposes of this entry to include Texas and Oklahoma. In fact, the wide popularity of rodeo as a participant and spectator sport in the Lone Star and Sooner states offers a clear manifestation of the often-discussed regional transition that classifies those states as partly southern and partly western. For example, of the 20 rodeo cowboys identified as "legends" in a recent book, six hailed from Texas and two called Oklahoma home; but none was from the rest of the South. No non-Texas-Oklahoma southerner has been named "all around" champion cowboy, and of all national champion bull riders from 1929 to 1999, only one (Jerome Davis of Archdale, N.C., in 1995) was from the non-Texas-Oklahoma South. All of the major rodeos with big purses are in the West, with the biggest rodeo in Houston and the national finals in Las Vegas.

Rodeos, however, are not confined to the West. The cowboy myth, nurtured first by dime novels and Wild West shows and later by motion pictures and television, created a national taste for things western. In the 1940s and 1950s at the height of the Hollywood Western, one of the country's biggest rodeos was held annually at Madison Square Garden in New York City. But outside the West, rodeo is most popular in the South. Perhaps cowboy individualism is especially appealing to southern audiences. Annual rodeos are staged at the Louisiana state prison at Angola and in many cities and towns including, just for example, Pendleton, S.C.; Huntsville, Ala.; Perry, Ga.; and Pontotoc, Miss.

Two organizations, the Professional Rodeo Cowboys Association (PRCA) and International Professional Rodeo Association (IRPA), sanction virtually all multievent professional rodeos in the United States. The PRCA is the larger and more prestigious of the two, and some southern rodeos are PRCA sanctioned. However, many rodeos in the South are affiliated with the Oklahoma City–based IRPA, which appeals more to the part-time cowboy characteristic of the South. Specialized bull-riding-only circuits, especially the Professional Bull Riders (PBR), became popular in the late 20th century. As with traditional rodeo, bull riding is more popular in the West, but it has some following in the South. Of 33 events in the highest level of the PBR, 8 are in southern (including Maryland and Missouri) cities, and many southern cities host lower tier tour stops.

In the West, including Texas and Oklahoma, rodeo evokes a way of life from the region's own past—a bygone life of cattle drives, open ranges, and ranches along and west of the 98th meridian. In the South, rodeo evokes the same image; but it is a borrowed one not of its own past.

BRADLEY R. RICE
Clayton State University

Gavin Ehringer, *Rodeo Legends: Twenty Extraordinary Athletes of America's Sport* (2003); Wayne S. Wooden and Gavin Ehringer, *Rodeo in America: Wranglers, Rough-stock, and Paydirt* (1996); Gail Hughbanks Woerner, *Cowboy Up: The History of Bull Riding* (2001).

Running

One would think that in the "lazy South" recreational running would have little attraction. Kenneth S. Greenberg (*Honor and Slavery*) has suggested that in the 19th and into the 20th century, upper-class southerners did not engage in competitive sports that involved running because "men of honor did not run away from anything." W. J. Cash wrote of how southerners "ran spontaneous foot races" but his observation was in reference to frontier folk whose sense of personal honor did not prevent them from enjoying the exhilaration of competition with their own kind. One suspects that both the men of honor of whom Greenberg wrote and the "stout fellow, full of blood" who was Cash's southerner would have been surprised, even shocked, to see a host of their countrymen out on a sweltering Fourth of July morning in the city of Atlanta, scantily clad but wearing expensive running clothes, getting ready to run 6.2 miles (10 K) for only a T-shirt.

But that is what has been happening on Peachtree Street every summer since 1970 when the Atlanta Track Club and the local Carling Brewery sponsored the run that would become a prototype for scores of southern road races that followed. From 110 runners that first year to 55,000 today (at least half of whom, some say, claim to have been among the first 110), running in the Peachtree Road Race has become something like Mecca to southeastern runners—a pilgrimage that must be made.

The T-shirt—evidence that you entered, ran, and finished—is a status symbol in a city obsessed with status and symbol. Although there are trophies and cash rewards, the T-shirt is a goal most can reach. Having one matters.

The Peachtree Road Race began just as the jogging/aerobic fad was evolving into running—according to running expert George Sheehan, "the difference between a jogger and a runner is an entry blank," and the Peachtree had one. The first race was, early participants recall, a haphazard affair, with the organizer getting the runners started and then jumping into his car to drive to the finish to award the prizes, which weren't much because the entry fee was only $2, from which came a 15¢ bus fare so runners could get back to their automobiles to go home. The event's popularity soared after 1976, when the *Atlanta Journal-Constitution* became the sponsor and started promoting it. In 1979 more than 20,000 took part, and the route became so congested that the next year a cap was set at 25,000. However, only nine days after registration was opened, every slot was taken. The protest from those left out was so great that the organizers (there was a professional director now) redesigned the course, especially the start and the finish, and began to increase the number of entries.

The organizers also divided participants into groups based on previous personal bests, a move designed to put the fastest out front and prevent bottlenecks. Even though some entrants lied about their times and there was congestion, it was nothing like it had been in the past. Other events—a 3K fun run for children, a wheelchair division—were also added. In the race held just before the 1996 Atlanta Olympics, a number of Olympic runners took part and shattered course records.

Although the race has become more "professional," with monetary prizes for top finishers, the bulk of the participants are the sort of recreational runners that southerners are not supposed to be. But perhaps the popularity of the Peachtree Road Race and other similar "contests" comes less from the fact that they are "races" than from the fact that they are "experiences," shared by sweaty participants who do something for the fun of it. Being held on the Fourth of July makes it part of the city's Independence Day celebration, so runners often take part in costume. Nonrunners turn out along the route to cheer participants on and enjoy the moment with them. The finish in the meadow of Piedmont Park takes on a carnival atmosphere with booths and displays, first-aid tents, water trucks, and beer. It is all the Fourth of July celebration most Atlantans want, or need.

Although today the Peachtree Road Race is one of many similar races held throughout the South, it remains the largest in the region—and the second largest in the world. The Vancouver Sun Run was bigger in 2008, by 4,000 runners. However, the race is also important for it served as an inspiration and a model for many smaller contests, often held to raise money for worthy causes. At the height of the jogging-running craze, some southern track clubs had "hot lines" that runners could call to find out where the closest race was.

Today www.runtheplanet.com lists 111 yearly "running races." Forty-four of these are in the South. Of all the states listed, Florida has the most with 19 (nearly twice as many as California, in second place). Add to these the host of races held but not listed, and in the lazy South a lot of folks are running. And mostly for the fun of it.

HARVEY H. JACKSON III
Jacksonville State University

Jim Fixx, *The Complete Book of Running* (1977).

Shopping

In the South, shopping is not just about the acquisition of needed items like groceries and gasoline; it is a recreational sport in which some of the participants can be very competitive. Word of caution: do not attempt to take the last cashmere sweater off the rack at a half-off sale; if you do, you might find yourself minus a limb. Within southern culture, shopping is a form of recreation that crosses class and gender lines, allowing everyone an opportunity to participate. No matter the economic status or gender of the participants, there is always a recreational shopping opportunity available and, in the South, these opportunities are abundant.

Those in an economic position allowing them to spend with impunity can find much satisfaction with the shopping opportunities available in the South. Of course, there are the shops that cross all geographic boundaries such as high-end department and chain stores, but throughout the South the wealthy are more attracted to small boutiques specializing in a wide range of high-priced items, ranging from baby needs and lingerie to books and housewares. Within the artistically painted walls of these specialty shops lie hundreds of items that many would classify as "overpriced" or "pretentious," but for many recreational shoppers who frequent these establishments, such qualities are precisely what attracts them. Recreational shoppers of the wealthy sort often find satisfaction in purchasing items that are not necessities at prices they know to be inflated. This satisfaction can be attributed to the simple knowledge the purchaser has that they do indeed possess the extra cash (or credit card) to purchase items that others cannot afford. For them, the purchase can represent something greater than merely handing over a debit card and receiving a monogrammed christening gown in exchange; it can tell them something about themselves, something they need to know. While helping to reassure consumers—and others—of their status in society, specialty boutiques offer those with unlimited funds the opportunity to dispose of it, a niche that boutiques, and their owners, are delighted to fill.

For the recreational shopper with a more modest income, there are myriad choices available in the South. Purchasing a single item from a high-end boutique can be quite satisfying, but many recreational shoppers of more modest means prefer quantity over quality. Enter outlet malls. Although not strictly limited to the South, these megacenters of bargains call to the southern recreational shopper with their promises of half-price china and two-for-one socks more so than other regions—a result of the increasingly overwhelming consumer culture that predominates the South. Southerners like "stuff." They like to have their "stuff" on display in their homes, their driveways, and on their person. Outlet malls allow southerners to obtain "stuff" in great quantities on a single outing in a single location, explaining its unavoidable draw. The discussion of the quantity aspect of outlet malls is not to say that there are not high-end items available at outlet malls. Quite the contrary. Many high-end designers have stores in outlet malls where overstocks and slightly damaged merchandise are sent to be sold at varying degrees of lower price than those same items would be found in a traditional department store or specialty boutique, thus allowing recreational shoppers of limited means the opportunity to own and display luxury goods that they otherwise would not be able to afford.

Another popular option for budget conscious shoppers in the South is the department store, an entity that has added much to the culture of the South throughout the past century. For much of the 20th and 21st centuries, southern department stores such as McRae's (founded in Mississippi), Stein Mart (Mississippi), Pizitz (Alabama), Belk (North Carolina), Dillard's (Arkansas), Goldsmith's (Memphis, Tenn.), Maison Blanche (New Orleans), and Goudchaux's (Baton Rouge) have helped to fuel the heavy consumerism prominent in the South. Among different department stores there has existed a great range in the quality and prices of goods available. Recreational shoppers of all income levels can find a department store to suit their needs in the South. Offering items ranging from clothing to cosmetics, furniture to fragrances, the department store serves as the foundation for recreational shopping.

Department stores have not only influenced the recreational culture of the consuming public but have also greatly influenced the recreational shopping potential of their employees. Many department stores offer an employee discount that allows employees to purchase goods that they otherwise might not be able to afford. Offering such a discount increases the stores profit margins as well as allowing the employee a chance to shop recreationally. Imagine the possibilities of working in a department store every day, seeing new items arrive, later go on sale, and then choosing just the right moment to make your purchase utilizing the employee discount. What better definition of recreational shopping can be found? For the employee the recreation begins weeks, perhaps months, in advance, watching an item as it moves through the store and eventually onto sale racks, and culminates with the purchase of the item. From this perspective, shopping is truly an important form of recreation for the employee of the department store.

Even though the tendency might be to classify recreational shopping as a singularly female pursuit, in the South this certainly is not the case. Not only do men routinely engage in recreational shopping through the aforementioned avenues, but they also participate in the consumer culture by shopping recreationally at stores designed to cater to a predominantly male customer base. Supersized outdoors stores, such as B.A.S.S. Pro Shop and Edwin Watts Golf, as well as smaller boutique-sized shops, such as independent hunting retailers, cater to a predominantly male clientele by offering items for the outdoorsman, the sportsman, and the athlete, among others. Such stores provide men with the opportunity to participate in the consumer culture typified by recreational shopping within parameters that men can define as separate from the recreational shopping spheres of women. Even though it is clear that certain stores and departments within stores cater to either a male or female clientele, it is also clear that both sexes have ample opportunity in the South to participate in recreational shopping.

In so many small towns, Wal-Mart (another southern store) has become the main retail outlet and therefore the heart of recreational shopping. Like a mall, Wal-Mart has everything under one roof. Shoppers begin arriving before 8:00 A.M. and buy a biscuit and coffee at whichever café is allowed to share that space (once exclusively the domain of McDonald's, now Subway dominates that market). Women meet friends, men meet friends; they wander, shop, talk, take a coffee break, wander and shop some more, then have lunch where they had breakfast or at a nearby restaurant. It is a community experience.

Throughout the South recreational shoppers have many opportunities to engage in their favorite hobby. From high-end boutiques to outlet malls to department stores, the southern shoppers have the opportunity to find virtually any consumer good they desire at a wide range of prices. For many, the draw of recreational shopping is the hunt—the hunt for the desired good at the lowest price available. In the South, recreational shoppers have more than enough opportunity to indulge their favorite pastime. Whether enjoying shopping on a budget or spending without regard to financial restriction, the recreational shopper in the South is engaging in an incredibly popular pastime available to members of all races, classes, and genders.

ERIN JONES SCHMIDT
University of Alabama

Marianne Conroy, *Social Text* (Spring 1998); Kuan-Pin Chiang and Ruby Roy Dholakia, *Journal of Consumer Psychology* 13:1–2 (2003); Pasi Falk and Colin B. Campbell, eds., *The Shopping Experience* (1997); Robert Prus and Lorne Dawson, *Canadian Journal of Sociology* (Spring 1991); Edward M. Tauber, *Journal of Marketing* (October 1972); Sharon Zukin, *Point of Purchase: How Shopping Changed American Culture* (2004).

Soccer

Within the past 30 years, soccer, which for generations had been eclipsed in popularity within the South by the dominant sports of football, basketball, and baseball, has emerged as an increasingly popular sport. Formally organized in England during the early 19th century, soccer (or football, as it is known outside of the United States) spread dramatically across the globe in the following century, becoming the world's most popular team-based sport by 1950. In the United States, however, soccer was slow in gaining popularity, owing partially to the game's late entry into the national sporting culture and lingering perceptions of American isolationism. Within the South, the game's popularity was even slower in developing. With few European, Asian, or Latin American immigrants arriving to the southeastern states between 1850 and 1950, the growth of soccer was markedly slower in the South than the North or West, where the game thrived in urban immigrant enclaves.

Soccer first established a foothold in the urban South, where amateur leagues began to organize small tournaments in the 1920s and 1930s. By the late 1950s several universities were fielding men's teams, including Duke, Emory, and the University of North Carolina, which competed against one another in regional conferences. The formation of the North American Soccer League (NASL) in 1968 further boosted the game's popularity, especially when the Atlanta Chiefs became a leading team in the early 1970s. But it was only with the post-1970 "Sunbelt" boom in suburban development that soccer began to grow at an explosive rate, and it was here that the game attained its enduring reputation as a youth sport. For thousands of northern and western white-collar professionals who moved to the suburbs of cities like Atlanta and Charlotte, soccer was a game they had played as children, a safer alternative to the often-bloody game of football. In affluent suburban communities across the Southeast in the 1980s and 1990s, therefore, soccer would quickly grow to challenge the old trinity of baseball, basketball, and football, and by the turn of the 21st century tens of thousands of southern children were playing regularly in intramural, school-sponsored, and private soccer leagues.

While the expansion of soccer as a suburban youth sport was successful in introducing the game to a wide new audience, equally dramatic was the soccer boom that has accompanied the South's recent surge in immigration. After a century of relative homogeneity in its white and black population, the Southeast since 1980 has attracted a diverse new wave of immigrants, most notably from Mexico and Central America, China, South Korea, and various West African nations. This unprecedented demographic transformation has wrought tremendous cultural change, and the growth of immigrant soccer leagues is a prominent example. Especially for Latin American immigrants, whose reverence and dedication to the game is legendary, participation in Latino soccer leagues in urban, suburban, and rural settings has become a crucial avenue of recreation, community formation, and even career networking in their newest home.

Such change has not been without conflict or controversy, however, and many Latino newcomers have encountered hostility and resentment from native southerners, in which public recreational spaces often became a key arena of contention. As immigrant soccer leagues grew in popularity and began to compete with traditional southern sports for the use of public space, unsympathetic city and county governments during the 1990s and 2000s initiated campaigns to restrict immigrant access to public parks, and signs proclaiming "NO SOCCER ALLOWED / NO PERMITE EL FÚTBOL" appeared on football fields and baseball diamonds across the South, in both small towns and large cities.

It was not until the 1980s and 1990s that soccer became a popular sport among southern schoolchildren, but the game has been a collegiate sport in the South since the 1950s. (Photograph by Bill Mathews, courtesy of Judson College, Marion, Ala.)

For Latin American residents, this symbolic attack on their culture and belonging has engendered considerable bitterness and protest, and while negotiation and compromise have led to solutions in some communities, the conflict over immigrant culture and public space continues to plague much of the South.

The growth of soccer, therefore, has become symbolic of the enormous transformation of the South since the civil rights movement. Suburban youth teams and Latino immigrant leagues, while playing the same sport, are clearly the products of different phenomena, yet each represents an important trend in recent social and demographic change.

TORE OLSSON
University of Georgia

Marie Price and Courtney Whitworth, *Hispanic Spaces, Latino Places*, ed. Daniel Arreola (2004); Rory Miller and Liz Crolley, eds., *Football in the Americas: Futbol, Futebol, Soccer* (2007); Andrei S. Markovits and Steven L. Hellerman, *Offside: Soccer and American Exceptionalism in Sport* (2001).

Square Dancing

Square dancing has long been a part of the traditional culture of the rural South. Square dances, for groups of four or more couples, have their roots in popular European social dances of the 18th and 19th centuries (French cotillions and quadrilles, English country dances, and Scots-Irish reels); they also show the influence of African American and Native American dances. The earliest detailed account of southern square dancing comes from English folk music and dance scholar Cecil Sharp, who—with his colleague Maud Karpeles—observed dances at several locations in eastern Kentucky in 1917. Sharp interpreted these rural southern dances (which he called "The Running Set") as survivals of 17th-century English country dances. He mistakenly believed that these old dances had remained intact and unchanged for many generations and that the remoteness of the mountains had kept them free from the contaminating influences of modernity. The southern square dance, however, is a distinctly American dance form, one that did not exist until the 19th century when European social dances merged with elements of African American and Native American dances in the America South.

Before the 20th century, dancing was a common recreation in Anglo-American, African American, and Native American communities. Square dances often accompanied such community work gatherings as corn shuckings, molasses makings, and barn raisings; they also occurred at weddings and other festive occasions, particularly during the Christmas season. Most often held in private homes, such dances also took place in barns, taverns, or even outdoors on the bare ground. By the 1930s, square dances had lost their association with work parties and special occasions and had become public events serving a wider region and held in large community halls on a regular basis throughout the year. While these public dances are now relatively rare, they still happen in some rural communities, with dancers of all ages sometimes traveling several hours to attend on Friday or Saturday nights.

Although the name "square dance" implies a square formation for four couples, southern square dances are often done with any number of couples in a big circle set. Today, the four-couple square is more common in northern West Virginia, Arkansas, and Missouri, while the big circle is the dominant form elsewhere. Southern square dances are characterized by visiting couple figures (where each couple takes a turn leading the figure); a verse-chorus structure (such that the visiting couple figure performed by two couples alternates with a chorus or ending figure involving all of the couples); the presence of distinctive southern dance figures (such as "Bird in the Cage"); fast paced music; and improvisational dance calling that guides the dancers through the figures.

The practice of dance calling appears to have emerged in African American communities in the early 19th century as a way to lead dancers who were not trained in the formal figures of French cotillions and quadrilles through the dances. The first documented dance caller was an African American musician at a formal New Orleans ball in 1819. By the mid-19th century, dance calling had become a common practice throughout the rural South. Such calling was the key element that transformed the earlier European dances into a distinct American dance form, in a process that paralleled the way that the African American banjo transformed European fiddle styles to become southern dance music. Without the African American practice of dance calling, southern square dances would not exist in their present form.

Following World War II, a new form of square dancing, called "Modern Western Square Dancing," developed from the traditional square dances of the western United States. With standardized dance calls, professional callers, recorded music, and western costumes, this new style of square dancing became popular across the country, competing with and displacing many of the older community-based rural dances. Today, Modern Western Square Dance clubs can be found throughout the South.

PHILIP A. JAMISON
Warren Wilson College

S. Foster Damon, *The History of Square Dancing* (1957); Philip A. Jamison, *Journal of Appalachian Studies* (Fall 2003); Richard Nevell, *A Time to Dance* (1977); Cecil J. Sharp and Maud Karpeles, *The Country Dance Book, Part V* (1918); Susan Eike Spalding and Jane Harris Woodside, eds., *Communities in Motion: Dance, Community, and Tradition in America's Southeast and Beyond* (1995).

Stepping

African American step teams throughout the South dazzle audiences with their dynamic, synchronized stomping and clapping and their choreographed dancing to hip-hop tunes. A complex performance involving synchronized percussive movement, singing, speaking, chanting, and drama, stepping developed in the early part of the 20th century as a ritual of group identity among African American college fraternities and sororities. Stepping reflects the African and African American heritage of those who pioneered its development, as well as the verbal and movement traditions prominent among blacks in the South.

Every year in late November, at the Bayou Classic in the Louisiana Superdome, Grambling State University and Southern University compete in one of the largest historically black college football competitions in the United States. There, also, the best college step teams compete in the Bayou Classic Greek Show. Other competitive step shows take place throughout the South, as collegiate step teams vie for bragging rights while raising money for social causes. While such shows are the most public venue for collegiate stepping, most fraternity and sorority stepping happens on campus, where members of the nine historically black Greek-letter societies that compose the National Pan-Hellenic Council celebrate their organizations through probate (or neophyte) step shows that present new members to the public. They also sponsor competitive step shows to support scholarships and other social causes.

Stepping is a dynamic and vital performance for expressing and celebrating African American and other group identities. Popularized in films such as such as *Stomp the Yard* (2007), *Drumline* (2002), and *School Daze* (1988), and in TV programs such as *A Different World* (1987–93), stepping is now also performed by multicultural, Asian, Latino, and occasionally white fraternities and sororities, as well as by community, school, and church step teams. As other ethnic groups form step teams, they incorporate their own ethnic dance traditions into their stepping, while retaining signature African American features.

Stepping routines are orally composed and transmitted. When the stepmaster or leader is older than the steppers being taught, he or she may teach the routine by "breaking it down" into smaller rhythmic units that are imitated until everyone masters them. Composition is often collaborative in groups in which everyone is the same age. Circulating videotapes and DVDs of step shows (often available for sale online) aid in the transmission process; so also do video clips that are readily available on YouTube and other Web sites. Regional and national competitions, as well as regional and national meetings of the nine historically black Greek-letter societies, further help to disseminate steps. A striking example of oral composition can be seen in the way steppers use the words and tune of Omega Psi Phi's song, "All of my love, my peace and happiness, I'm gonna give it to Omega," as an oral formula, borrowing and modifying it as they incorporate it into various step routines. While preserving the same tune, a high school step team substituted the words "I'm going to give it to my people," and a church step team sang, "It's all our love and praise and honor, we want to give it to our savior—Jesus Christ."

Each of the nine black Greek-letter societies has "trade" or "signature" steps that are performed by college chapters throughout the nation and convey the character and style of the organizations. These signature steps have names, and members within the black Greek system recognize them as belonging to particular organizations by their visual and oral patterns. When a group performs the signature steps of another organization, it does so either to pay tribute to the originating group (called "saluting") or to mock it by performing the step in an inept or comic manner (called "cracking" or "cutting"). Some well-known signature steps include Alpha Phi Alpha's "The Grand-Daddy" and "Ice, Ice"; Alpha Kappa Alpha's "It's a Serious Matter"; Zeta Phi Beta's "Sweat" and "Precise"; Phi Beta Sigma's "Wood"; and Iota Phi Theta's "Centaur Walk."

Stepping may have grown out of the popular drill team traditions of African American mutual aid and Masonic societies; it certainly reflects the same kind of emphasis on synchronized clapping and stomping. Interestingly, the founders of the first black college fraternity, Alpha Phi Alpha, were closely associated with black Masonic societies and held their first initiation in 1906 at a Masonic Hall, where they borrowed Masonic costumes for their ritual. The earliest written reference to what may be stepping appears in 1925, when an article on "Hell Week" in the Howard University newspaper describes Alpha Phi Alpha and Omega Psi Phi pledges "marching as if to the Fairy Pipes of Pan."

Stepping may have also grown out of the black Greek ritual of "marching on line," in which pledges expressed their brotherhood or sisterhood by walking in a line across campus, displaying their group's colors and symbols. Over the years, groups added singing, chanting, and synchronized clapping and stomping to their marching. Early step shows often had the brothers and sisters moving in counterclockwise circles; as stage performances for audiences became more common in the 1960s, however, line formations became prevalent. Terms for stepping vary among campuses and change over time, and they include such designations as "demonstrating," "marching," "bopping," "hopping," "blocking," and "stomping."

Stepping reveals its continuity with African American dances that originated in the South during slavery. The most well-known dance of this period, "patting juba," may have originated in an African dance called *guiouba*; it grew in popularity after slaveholders outlawed drums among the enslaved, for fear that they would use them to communicate and plan slave revolts. Without drums, slaves used their hands and feet to create the rhythm for their dances. Recalling this practice among enslaved dancers in Louisiana, Solomon Northup described "patting juba" as "striking the hands on the knees, then striking the hands together, then striking the right shoulder with one hand, the left with the other—all the while keeping time with the feet, and singing." Along with this percussive movement, dancers would sing and chant, often voicing a critique of slavery in coded language. When performing in a group setting, dancers would usually step juba in a counterclockwise circle, with both the words and the steps in a conversational, call-and-response form; the dancing relied on improvisation, low-step shuffling, and clapping, all of which are time-honored features of African American dance performance.

African American dancers on the minstrel stage also performed the juba dance. The most famous such dancer of the 19th century, William Henry Lane, was called "Master Juba" because of his extraordinary step dancing. In the 1840s, Lane held dance duels in the Five Points district of Lower Manhattan with Irish step dancers, including the white minstrel dancer Jack Diamond; in these duels, he freely blended African dance elements with Irish jigs. The frequency of such blending may well account for the widespread white adoption of the term "jigs" to describe African American step dancing, according to dance historians Marshall and Jean Stearns. Thus, stepping may reflect Irish as well as African influences.

Just as the early circular routines of fraternity and sorority steppers suggest the influence of patting juba, so too may they reflect another early African American dance form, the "ring shout." Developed in black Christian churches during slavery, ring shouts feature counterclockwise movement, hand clapping, foot patting, stick beating (to foreground the rhythm), and call-and-response singing. Though ring shouts were primarily acts of worship, they also took place in some 19th-century secular contexts, such as house parties and gatherings of black soldiers in the Civil War. Ring shouts still occur among some church communities in the South and along Maryland's Eastern Shore.

Stepping also embodies aesthetic features common in Western and Central African dances. The counterclockwise circular movement of early step routines recalls not only patting juba and ring shouts but also a common dance pattern in Kongo culture that symbolizes the sun circling the Earth, according to art historian Robert Farris Thompson. One of the most striking stances of African

American stepping—the "get-down" position, in which steppers bend deeply from the waist, or step with knees deeply bent—is common in Africa. Other characteristic features of African dance, according to Thompson, include call and response, dances that convey derision, the use of striking moralistic poses, an emphasis on correct entrance and exit, personal and representational balance, the establishment of clear boundaries around dances, looking smart, the mask of the cool, and polyrhythm (multiple meter). African American steppers exhibit all of these features, demonstrating the strong continuity of stepping with African culture. Indeed, steppers often claim that stepping originated in Africa. One AKA sister, for instance, said that stepping "goes all the way back to African culture," when different tribes competed through dance, and a Christian step team in Detroit, Mich., chanted, "Africa is where stepping began, from the beat of the drums to the sound of our feet."

Since the early 1990s, stepping has grown in popularity and spread beyond college campuses and African American fraternities and sororities to new practitioners, audiences, and venues. Latino, Asian, multicultural, and occasionally white fraternities and sororities around the country now step, as do many school, community, and church groups. Alpha Phi Alpha brothers from Howard University stepped for President Bill Clinton's inaugural festivities in 1993, and the opening pageant of the 1996 Summer Olympics in Atlanta, Ga., featured stepping. African American fraternity and sorority members have played key roles in spreading stepping to new groups and contexts by teaching others to step, starting school, church, and community step teams to mentor youth, and participating in arts organizations such as Washington, D.C.'s Step Afrika, which uses stepping as a tool to promote education and intercultural dialogue.

At the University of Texas at Austin, the Epsilon Iota Chapter of Alpha Phi Alpha sponsors two different stepping shows for non-Greeks. The Non-Greek Step show in the fall is the largest in Texas and includes high school and community step teams from across the state. In the spring, it sponsors "Step for Hope," in which the fraternity members teach students of different cultural backgrounds how to step and then perform on the main mall in front of a large audience. Participating in this step show led sisters of Sigma Phi Omega, an Asian-interest sorority, to start stepping in 1998. Another Asian-interest fraternity at the University of Texas, Omega Phi Gamma, has sponsored a Unity talent show since 1995, in which the brothers perform their special step routine. The first intercollegiate Latino Greek step show on the East Coast, and perhaps in the nation, took place in the Bronx in July 1999. By 2006, Latino step shows were common on college campuses throughout the nation and the South.

Thus, increasingly throughout the South, one can find step shows flourishing in many contexts and among social groups quite different from the historically black fraternities and sororities that invented stepping. Despite the addition of salsa movements by Latino steppers, *raas* and *garba* dance movements by South Asian steppers, or Christian chants by church steppers, the stepping of these new groups retains many characteristic African American features. Stepping has proved to be a highly malleable tradition, able to incorporate new performers and styles as it functions to demonstrate group identity through its complex, synchronized percussive movements.

ELIZABETH C. FINE
Virginia Polytechnic Institute and State University

Carol D. Branch, in *African American Fraternities and Sororities: The Legacy and the Vision*, ed. Tamara L. Brown, Gregory S. Parks, and Clarenda M. Phillips (2005); Elizabeth C. Fine, *Soulstepping: African American Step Shows* (2003, 2007); Walter M. Kimbrough, *Black Greek 101: The Culture, Customs, and Challenges of Historically Black Fraternities and Sororities* (2004); Jacqui Malone, *Steppin' on the Blues: The Visible Rhythms of African American Dance* (1996); Marshall Stearns and Jean Stearns, *Jazz Dance: The Story of American Vernacular Dance* (1968); Robert Farris Thompson, *African Art in Motion: Icon and Act* (1979).

Stock Car Racing

Stock car racing is a form of racing with automobiles that resemble standard production passenger cars. Stock car racing has become especially popular in the South where in its most developed forms it takes place in specialized amphitheaters using expensive, powerful, and carefully made machinery.

Automobiles were initially more plentiful in the industrialized parts of the nation, so much early automobile racing was done in the North and Midwest. Informal races were soon moved from the streets onto existing horse racing "tracks," which were surfaced with dirt. Starting around the turn of the century, the brick-surfaced oval track at Indianapolis, Ind., served as a new focus for racing activity.

It took longer for the automobile to reach rural areas, and not until the 1930s did stock car racing as it is known today become popular in the rural Midwest and South. Mass-produced automobiles gave working-class rural southerners more personal mobility than had been provided by horses. Farmers used cars for speedier delivery of their crops to more distant markets. In some cases, they distilled crops into liquor and transported the liquor to market as part of a long-standing family business. Liquor was a compact means of transporting crops and provided a greater return. This trade was opposed by governmental authorities, because most home-liquor makers ("moonshiners") did not pay taxes on their sales. In their efforts to outdistance law officers, some of the liquor runners skillfully modified their cars for greater power and higher speeds. The drivers of these vehicles also participated in informal races between themselves and others interested in automobiles. Liquor runners, although a small minority of those who entered early races, included many of the most famous and proficient drivers and race organizers. Some of them became legends.

With the greater affluence and hence more widespread automobile ownership that followed World War II, racing became more popular than before, especially in the South. However, the rules under which the racing was conducted and the administration of the tracks were often uncertain. A concerted effort to standardize the rules and the administration of racing resulted in the formation in 1947 of the National Association for Stock Car Auto Racing, Inc. (NASCAR). NASCAR has become the largest and best known of such sanctioning organizations in the United States, with wide media coverage of its activities.

Virtually ignored by the national media, the first major paved amphitheater ("superspeedway") built in the South especially for auto racing opened in 1950 in Darlington, S.C. As a result of its success, tracks opened in other parts of the South. At present, stock car races are held from New England to California, although most of the big speedways are in the South. The Carolina Piedmont has the largest concentration of tracks, major races, driver home bases, and driver folk heroes. The heartland goes from central Virginia down to Talladega, Ala.

During the 1950s and 1960s, automakers noticed that successes of a make of car in the races led to increased sales. The auto companies and other sponsors poured money into the sport as a form of advertising. Support for racing has also come from other large corporations. For instance, a cigarette company sponsors several major race series. Individual racers and racing machines also are sponsored by small businesses and individuals.

Throughout its history, stock car racing has been identified with rural white southern males. Blacks and women, although occasional participants, have never made it to the top. Racing has become an accepted way (along with others, including singing and athletics) for a rural white male to achieve fame, money, and the trappings of success. Successful participants in the sport, such as Richard Petty, Junior Johnson, and Cale Yarborough, keep aspects of their southern heritage while they develop an ability to work with big business. Many of the best racers have, along with driving skill and a mechanical genius, a razor-sharp business acumen. They base their racing activities in their hometowns and maintain close family ties. Their "pit crews" tend to be drawn from the local population. They build closeness to their fans through personal appearances and project a "good old boy" image by expressing an interest in such male activities as hunting, fishing, and, of course, tinkering with automobiles. They are folk heroes with which the average southern male can identify. Stock car racing, with its noise, dirt, powerful cars, and consumption of alcoholic beverages, has become a symbol of the southern way of living.

Stock car racing combines a fascination with technology and a spirit of competition. It has become identified with the South, where it has served both as a sport and as a way for participants to leave rural poverty. At first glance, the cars appear to be like those available to the average person. However, the cars are in fact highly specialized technical accomplishments. The cost of the machinery keeps it from being a widely popular participant sport. As a result, there is mass popular support for a relatively small number of athletes. The drivers epitomize the successful southern male who has managed to retain his "down-home" manner. The average southern male can identify with the racers, both because he drives a car that looks like theirs and because he shares their identification with things southern. At present, many of the prominent drivers are in their 40s, an age by which athletes in many other sports have retired. A few younger drivers are beginning to gain recognition in Winston Cup racing, often through their successes in local competition. Winston Cup racing is the most publicized form of stock car racing.

There are different kinds of racing, varying with the scale of the effort and the technical details of the cars. Categories often are based on the age of the cars and their construction, especially their power plants and wheelbase lengths. Rules also vary with the track where the races are run.

There is a continuum of size and complexity in racing tracks. At the amateur level are small tracks (usually oval in shape and a quarter to a half mile long), which draw spectators and participants from immediately surrounding areas. In these races, older passenger cars are modified for increased safety and speed. As in other sports, there are many participants in local-level, dirt track races, which require less money and effort.

At the professional end of the scale are Winston Cup (formerly called Grand National) races on larger speedways. Contestants come from all over the nation. Media reporters jockey for position to interview the winning drivers. At this level, vehicles are usually constructed by specialty builders solely for racing and have little relation to production cars beyond outward appearance.

At all levels of racing, each vehicle has one or more mechanics who build and maintain the vehicle. The "pit crew" services the car during races by refueling, replacing tires, cleaning the windshield, and giving the driver refreshments.

Sponsors are individuals or businesses that provide money to support the racing effort. Their names are painted on the sides of the cars (along with each car's number) so that the fans will be encouraged to buy their products. Some drivers have consistently used particular makes of automobiles, endorsing the manufacturer. Fans are fiercely partisan toward particular drivers. Many fans wear clothing and other items imprinted with the car number and name of their driver and belong to fan clubs boosting their favorite.

Track officials work to ensure that the race goes smoothly. There are often also officials from the organization ("sanctioning body") that writes the racing rules. Although NASCAR is the best known of these organizations, smaller, local sanctioning bodies organize most racing events. These bodies write rules to promote safety and competition.

"Technical inspections" of cars are made to ensure that cars conform to the rules. Nevertheless, clever racers try to interpret the rules to their advantage. The emphasis on technical sophistication in the preparation of the vehicles is one of the excitements of the sport, and fans and racers alike are constantly alert to innovations that increase the cars' speeds.

Each driver is involved with several kinds of competition simultaneously. Competition for winning the race by being the first to complete the required number of laps around the track is the most visible. Winning is a combination of driver skill and chance. Winning is also dependent on the speed and efficiency of the pit crew and the ability of the machinery to last up to 500 laps at speeds up to 200 miles an hour. Behind the scenes, drivers compete for the best sponsors and mechanics.

Before the race, drivers compete in trials designed to see which car can go fastest around the track. The faster a car runs in the trials, the closer it is placed to the front of the pack of 30 to 40 starting cars. The fastest car gets the most advantageous position (the "pole" position) at the front. Drivers compete to accumulate the most "points" over a season from various accomplishments, such as the position of their car in comparison to the winner's at the end of each race, the number of races entered, and the number of laps completed.

DAVID M. JOHNSON
North Carolina Agricultural and Technical State University

Patrick Bedard, *Car & Driver* (June 1982); Jerry Bledsoe, *The World's Number One, Flat-Out, All-Time Great, Stock Car Racing Book* (1975); Pete Daniel, *Lost Revolutions: The South in the 1950s* (2000); Peter Golenbock, *American Zoom* (1993); Handbook of American Popular Culture, vol. 1, ed. M. Thomas Inge (1979); Tom Higgins and Steve Waid, Brave in Life: Junior Johnson (1999); Ed Hinton, Daytona: From the Birth of Speed to the Death of the Man in Black (2001); Mark Howell, From Moonshine to Madison Avenue: A Cultural History of NASCAR's Winston Cup Series (1997); Jim Hunter, Official 1982 NASCAR Record Book and Press Guide (1982); Bill Libby with Richard Petty, "King Richard": The Richard Petty Story (1977); Bob Nagy, Motor Trend (June 1981); Dan Pierce, Southern Cultures (Summer 2001), Atlanta History (no. 2, 2004); Richard Pillsbury, Journal of Geography (no. 1, 1974); Don Sherman, Car & Driver (June 1982); Southern MotoRacing (biweekly newspaper about stock car racing, Winston-Salem, N.C.); Sylvia Wilkinson, in American South: Portrait of a Culture, ed. Louis D. Rubin Jr. (1980); Tom Wolfe, Esquire (March 1965).

Storytelling

Storytelling—a means of description, entertainment, and teaching known in all cultures—has played a rich role in the South, where Native American, European, and African storytelling traditions have intermingled and enriched each other for four centuries. Despite its great age, storytelling is always new when it unfolds as part of a living tradition, because the teller shapes the tale while interacting with an audience whose tastes and values inform the performance. Without the listeners' interest and approval, the tale dies on the teller's lips. Because tales always emerge in the moment, we cannot know the exact styles and stories of the earliest southern storytellers; nonetheless, written records give some idea of the tales' content and how they were performed.

Southern storytelling began with the region's native peoples, including the Cherokee, who once inhabited the Appalachian Mountains from Alabama to West Virginia. As in all storytelling communities, the Cherokee recognized (formally or informally) certain individuals as narrative specialists. Around 1750 some of these specially trained narrators recited a long legendary history of the Cherokee, beginning with their divine creation and then tracing their migrations across North America. Nearly 150 years later, when James Mooney made the first comprehensive study of Cherokee storytelling, no one could remember this story; tribal elders did recall, however, that in the 1840s boys chosen to learn the sacred stories would sit all night around a ritual fire listening to their teachers and then would strip and bathe in a stream to purify themselves. By the end of the 19th century, the Cherokee no longer observed this ritual, though tribal elders still specialized in the most sacred stories. Of course, most Cherokees knew and told many other types of stories, including local legends, tales of notable hunts and battles, and animal tales that featured a trickster rabbit (some of which resemble the African American tales of Brer Rabbit, a fact that perhaps reflects contacts between Cherokees and African Americans stretching back to colonial times).

When Europeans first reached the South, they brought with them long-standing narrative styles with which they described both the Indians and their stories. Through their writings, Europeans introduced the New World and its people to the Old. Explorers such as the German John Lederer, who traveled through North Carolina in 1670–71, learned Indian history from traditions "delivered in long tales from father to son" that the tellers had memorized as children. Indians also taught Lederer about the natural environment—how, for example, snakes would hypnotize squirrels in trees to lure them to the ground and eat them. Although Lederer did not believe this particular tale, he nonetheless repeated it in his *Discoveries* (1672).

Southern explorers, following a European tradition dating to medieval times, also told stories of their personal adventures, some of which were retold through succeeding centuries. For instance, Captain John Smith—who helped establish the colony of Jamestown, Va., in 1607—often told of his capture by the Powhatan tribe and how the young Pocahontas intervened to prevent his execution. Later historians dismissed this and other Smith narratives as fiction, though recent research supports the accuracy of some of these stories. Regardless of their historicity, explorers' stories seized the popular imagination and blended into the tradition of the tall tale—a form that became the signature genre of the American frontier.

Tall tales were so popular that they long dominated America's periodical literature; as early as the 18th century, and throughout the 19th, almanacs and weeklies were rife with tall tales celebrating southern wilderness heroes, both famous and nameless. Tall-tale performances became features of public life: just as John Smith told explorer tales for self-promotion, political celebrities, including Tennessee congressman Davy Crockett (1786–1836) and Louisiana governors Huey P. Long (1893–1935) and Jimmy Davis (1899–2000), used tall tales to advertise themselves. A successful narrator's tall tales sometimes even outlived him, as in the case of the Crockett almanacs, which were published for two decades after the hero's death at the Alamo.

Usually told in the first person and always presented as true, the tall tale typically begins with a credible situation in a recognizable natural environment and then adds a series of escalating exaggerations, ending as an unbelievable fiction. A plot known to folklorists as "The Lucky Shot" neatly characterizes this genre. A man starving in the wilderness is down to his last bullet; he must kill game or die. Spying ten ducks perched on a branch, he tamps a bullet into his double-barreled, muzzle-loading rifle. But at that very moment, a bear charges him head-on, a panther leaps toward him from his left, and a boar charges from his right. With the ramrod still stuck in one barrel, he pulls both triggers at once. His one bullet kills the bear; the gun's left hammer flies off and kills the panther; the right hammer, in turn, kills the boar. Meanwhile, the ramrod flies to the ducks, pinning their feet to the branch. The once-starving hunter collects his game; he now has food for a year.

"The Lucky Shot" captures some of the most common themes of southern tall tales: the wilderness is filled with both terrifying dangers and life-sustaining abundance; and given one last chance, a lone man—through either resourcefulness or dumb luck—secures abundance from danger's jaws. Versions of this plot have been documented in English in performances by African American John Jackson in Virginia and Anglo Jimmy Wilson in Arkansas, as well as in French by Louisiana Cajun Adlai Gaudet and in Spanish by numerous narrators along the Gulf Coast—testimony to the fact that southern storytelling readily crosses the most rigid boundaries of culture, language, region, and race.

In contemporary southern settings, the tall tale is sometimes a large-scale affair; many county fairs and local festivals feature "liars' contests" in which performers strive to tell the most preposterous tales. But more typical narrative communities are small, all-male groups that congregate at hunting camps, country stores, or courthouse squares. The teller usually speaks in a soft monotone of feigned sincerity, as if unaware that there is anything incredible about his story. Audience members who are "in" on the joke also betray no hint that the narrator is telling an outrageous lie. The ideal is to perform in such a low-key fashion that eavesdroppers believe they are listening in on a normal conversation. (In the Ozarks in the mid-20th century, for example, storytellers in general stores would exchange everyday news until a tourist approached. Just before the visitor reached the store, they would start telling their tall tales—about, for instance, how one of their children rode to school on the back of a friendly bear—to keep the visitor from suspecting that he was witnessing a joke at his expense.)

If the tall tale draws its power by deftly walking the line between fact and fiction, other stories—such as *Märchen*, or magic tale, the oral equivalent to the literary fairy tale—present an unvarnished fantasy world. The Europeans who settled the South may have carried only a few books, but they did bring a significant repertoire of Märchen. Joseph Doddridge recalled that on the West Virginia frontier, around 1770, "Dramatic narrations, chiefly concerning Jack and the Giant, furnished our young people with [a] source of amusement during their leisure hours. Many of those tales were lengthy, and embraced a considerable range of incident. Jack, always the hero of the story, after encountering many difficulties, and performing many great achievements, came off conqueror of the Giant." Such tales as "Jack and the Beanstalk" and "Jack the Giant Killer," beloved in 18th-century Britain, were equally popular in the southern colonies.

More than two centuries later, the hero of the southern Märchen is still typically named Jack, and the Märchen are often called Jack Tales (or Jack, Tom, and Will tales, after the three brothers featured in many versions). Like the tall-tale hero, Jack—the youngest, smallest, and least promising of the three—relies upon resourcefulness and luck to outperform his brothers and save them from menacing giants, evil witches, and fierce animals.

The performance settings for southern Märchen are generally more intimate than for tall tales. Märchen telling typically takes place at home, within the family. The specialists tend to be the oldest family members, and the listeners the youngest. Maud Long of Hot Springs, N.C., recalled how, around 1900, her mother told Märchen at night to soften the children's labor: "after supper, all of us were gathered before the big open fire, my mother . . . sewing or carding . . . ; the older girls were helping . . . and all of us little ones would have a lap full . . . of wool out of which we must pick all the burrs . . . , and to keep our eyes open and our fingers busy and our hearts merry, my mother would tell these marvelous tales." Märchen telling also sometimes accompanied outdoors work. North Carolinian Frank Proffitt Sr., for instance, used tales to both goad and reward his son's labor as the two worked together in the fields. When they finished hoeing a row, the elder Proffitt would tell a tale; then when the two resumed working, the boy would hoe quickly so that he could hear another tale upon reaching the next row's end.

By the mid-20th century, Märchen were probably best known in the bedroom, told one-on-one by elders to their children and grandchildren; such sessions were often inventively personalized. In the 1940s, for instance, Kentucky Märchen teller Sydney Farmer entertained her granddaughter Jane Muncy with nightly tales as the two shared the same bed. Though Sydney told Jack Tales, she changed the hero's name to Merrywise to help her granddaughter identify with the hero and to subtly teach her that small, vulnerable people could triumph in life through wisdom and positive thinking. Sydney's tales so influenced her granddaughter that Muncy—now an adult psychologist—retells them to her clients to foster the same resiliency and hope that her grandmother's tales had given her.

African Americans in the South brought with them vast repertoires of tales from West Africa; they also learned many Märchen from Europeans. Through household situations in which black elders entertained white children, they passed on to European Americans many of their animal tales, most famously those revolving around the character Brer Rabbit. As a boy, white Georgia journalist Joel Chandler Harris (1845–1908) learned many such tales from older blacks and later published them in his Uncle Remus books (named after a fictional slave who personified the oral tradition that Harris had tapped). These books brought Harris widespread fame, though readers soon recognized that their art lay in Harris's ear rather than in his imagination.

Long before and long after Harris wrote, rich African American narrative traditions thrived in households and at communal work and play settings. The wealth of this repertoire is exemplified in J. D. Suggs (1887–1955), a storyteller who shared 175 tales with folklorist Richard Dorson in the 1950s. Born in Kosciusko, Miss., to sharecropper parents, Suggs learned his first tales from his father at home. As he grew, he traveled widely before settling down to raise a family in Arkansas and eventually moving north to Chicago and Michigan. Throughout his adult life, he shared his family tales (and ones he learned during his travels) with friends and coworkers. Suggs's narrative style, like that of many African American storytellers, was dramatically expressive, marked by constant variations in pitch and rhythm as he impersonated story characters, imitated animal sounds, and interjected snatches of chants and song. He specialized in many genres, including animal tales, tall tales, witch legends, magic tales, traditional historical stories, and anecdotes revolving around the competition between a wily slave named John and his white master.

Since the mid-20th century, the normally small-scale art of storytelling has acquired an increasingly public and professional face through the formation of storytelling societies and festivals. The largest venue for such performances is the National Storytelling Festival—held every October in Jonesborough, Tenn., which explicitly seeks to bring together traditional and professional narrators. At Jonesborough, in public library storytelling hours throughout the South, and on "ghost tours" (regularly conducted in New Orleans, La.; San Antonio, Tex.; Savannah, Ga.; and many other southern cities) master storytellers attract crowds of mutual strangers to experience together, in new ways, the power of one of the world's oldest art forms.

CARL LINDAHL
University of Houston

John A. Burrison, ed., *Storytellers: Folktales and Legends from the South* (1989); Richard M. Dorson, ed., *American Negro Folktales* (1967); Carl Lindahl, ed., *American Folktales from the Collections of the Library of Congress* (2004); William Bernard

McCarthy, Cheryl Oxford, and Joseph Daniel Sobol, eds., *Jack in Two Worlds: Contemporary North American Jack Tales and Their Tellers* (1994); Leonard W. Roberts, ed., *South from Hell-fer-Sartin: Kentucky Mountain Folk Tales* (1955); Vance Randolph, *We Always Lie to Strangers: Tall Tales from the Ozarks* (1951); Joseph Daniel Sobol, *The Storyteller's Journey: An American Revival* (1999).

Tennis

Lawn tennis in the South shares much of the same general history as golf. Lawn tennis originated in the United States in New York in the 1870s and soon spread through the Northeast, Middle West, and the Pacific Coast. The United States Tennis Association (USTA), founded in 1881, soon governed the sport of tennis. A few southern cities such as New Orleans promoted the sport, but it was not a popular one until well into the 20th century. It lost many of its aristocratic trappings in the 1920s and became a middle-class game. Tennis celebrities such as Big Bill Tilden and Suzanne Lenglen became popular in the South as well as elsewhere. In the South the game was a country club sport, but the 1930s saw an increase in the building of public courts, as with the building of community golf courses.

Tennis did not lose its country club image until the 1950s and 1960s. The game became more popular in those years with the emergence of appealing young stars, television coverage of major tournaments, large money payoffs to tournament winners, and the establishment of an open system of competition between amateurs and professionals. The Southern Tennis Association, based in Norcross, Ga., is the largest of 17 regional sections of the USTA, with over 180,000 members in 2009. Major tournaments are now held in the South. In 1970 Texas millionaire Lamar Hunt financed World Championship Tennis, which sent professional players on tours around the world. Tennis can now be found as an activity at southern resorts, and it can be played on public courts in cities and small towns throughout the region. The South, however, has produced surprisingly few of the game's great players. Chris Evert from Florida is one of those, winning 157 professional singles titles on a 1,309–146 won-lost record in her career from 1969 to 1989. Tennis has not drawn the attention of many southern writers, but Rita Mae Brown's *Sudden Death* (1983) and Barry Hannah's *Tennis Handsome* (1985) have tennis players as the central characters.

The black community supported a vibrant tennis culture in the days of Jim Crow social segregation, with the South at the center of a network of institutions and coaches that produced some of the game's historic figures. The American Tennis Association is the oldest African American sports organization, founded in 1916 and holding its first national championships at Baltimore's Druid Hills Park in August 1917. The organization now consists of member country clubs throughout the nation and the Caribbean, and it provided until recently the only courts where blacks could play tennis and compete for championships. Coaches, both professional and amateur, worked to develop talent. Walter Johnson, a physician in Lynchburg, Va., opened his home and backyard court to young black players every summer, helping to produce two of tennis's greatest players, Althea Gibson and Arthur Ashe. Gibson, at age 23, was allowed to play in the 1950 U.S. championship, the first African American to do so, and she won the singles championship there in 1957. She would win five of the prestigious Grand Slam championships, including twice at Wimbledon. Ashe had an equally successful career, winning both the U.S. Amateur and the U.S. Open championships in 1968. In an 11-year professional career cut short by an early death, Ashe won 33 singles titles, including defeating Jimmy Connors to win the singles championship at Wimbledon in 1975.

CHARLES REAGAN WILSON
University of Mississippi

E. Digby Balzell, *Sporting Gentlemen: Men's Tennis from the Age of Honor to the Cult of the Superstar* (1995); Will Grimsley, *Tennis: Its History, People, and Events* (1971); Cecil Harris and Larryette Lyle-Debose, *Charging the Net: A History of Blacks in Tennis from Althea Gibson and Arthur Ashe to the Williams Sisters* (2007).

Tourism

Tourist. The word evokes images of Hawaiian shirts and Bermuda shorts, Instamatic cameras and sun-reddened skin, a clay-streaked station wagon, laden with luggage and sacks of Florida oranges. Those millions of wayfarers who hurdle along interstates to bake on sunny beaches and see Rock City pump billions into the southern economy each year.

Tourism has become as much a part of life for Americans as work in the week and church on Sunday. The modern burst of tourism began in the late 1940s. Veterans, who could not be kept down on the farm after they had seen the world during the war, earned their two weeks of vacation and hit the highways for recreation, relaxation, and entertainment. Nearly every family now marks days off its calendar for a vacation, even two or three a year. Despite oil shortages and the recessions of the 1970s and early 1980s, Americans winced at gasoline prices, dipped into savings, and pointed their cars and campers South.

A century and more before, the purpose of most travels in the South was for health. By the late 1700s travelers eased into hot springs baths to unlimber muscles. Modern-day resorts such as the Greenbrier in West Virginia and the

Homestead in Virginia trace their origins to those times and still offer bathing facilities.

For more than a century, Carolinians who lived along the coast traveled to save their lives. Spring through fall, or "frost to frost," they fled the malarial, soggy low country for the spice of mountain air. Hendersonville, N.C., is still called "Little Charleston in the Mountains," and many of the summer cottages, dating back to the mid-1800s and handed down through the generations, still stand.

In the decades after the Civil War, northerners invaded the South again, but this time as tourists in a campaign for their health. The mineral waters of southern springs and the salubrious southern climate were touted for their curative benefits. Physicians prescribed winter vacations in towns like Thomasville, Ga., which once boasted 15 hotels, 25 boardinghouses, and 50 winter cottages.

From the late 19th century to the mid-20th, pleasure travel evolved from a privilege of a wealthy few to an affordable luxury for the average family. A growing economy was partly the reason, but so also was the increasing ease of transportation—from carriages on dirt roads to railroads to family cars on interstates.

Of all southern states, Florida best symbolizes the rise of tourism. To see Florida in the mid-1800s, when much of the state was still wilderness, travelers had to go by boat. Honeymooners took romantic excursions along the Suwannee River, the St. John's, and the Oklawaha to Silver Springs. Often the land alongside was scented with orange blossoms in spring, and, at night, the light from burning pine knots played on the overhang of cypress and Spanish moss. By the 1890s railroads were skimming the shoreline of both coasts; Henry Flagler linked Jacksonville to the squat settlement of Miami, building alongside his railroad such palatial hotels as the Ponce de Leon in St. Augustine and the Breakers in Palm Beach.

Down Flagler's railroad came the very rich. But along the increasing miles of paved highways came the families of average means that, in the flush times of the 1920s, could afford pleasure travel. They fashioned homemade campers on Model-T's, ate store-bought food from tin cans, and camped beside the roads. These "tin-can tourists," as Floridians called them, pioneered the major mode of travel of two decades later—the family car. In the exuberance of release from the Depression, and with a car in every garage, Americans joyously flooded the highways of the South.

With war boom babies in the back seat, they traveled to the beach in summer and the mountains in the fall. Quiet seaside villages like Myrtle Beach, S.C., and mountain towns like Gatlinburg, Tenn., grew into garish neon playgrounds. The family spent nights in tourist courts, stopped at roadside souvenir stands, visited alligator farms, toured Mammoth Cave, walked Civil War battlefields, and yes, saw Rock City. Later, such "attractions" as theme parks offered rides and Broadway-type entertainment in a milk-and-cookies family atmosphere.

Quickly, tourism became an industry with a manufacturing mentality to mass-produce. Kemmons Wilson of Memphis, founder of Holiday Inns, and other entrepreneurs stamped one motel after another from the same mold. Fast food franchises arched their signs above highways. Many of those motels and packaged food restaurants rise at exits of interstates that tie doorsteps to destinations, bypass towns, and hold the countryside at arm's length. Now, in driving 800 interstate miles, travelers may sleep in the same room every night, eat the same hamburger for every meal, and never see a town.

Why and to where do tourists today go on vacation? One large segment of the population indicates that three main factors, excluding cost, determine vacation destinations. Readers of *Southern Living* magazine, certainly the epitome of the middle-class southerner, say they travel primarily for scenery. And to most, scenery means mountains and seashore. Second, they go where they will find good restaurants and lodging: to resort condominiums on barrier islands and to quiet country inns in the mountains. And third, they choose routes and destinations to see historical sites. Even on pleasure trips to fish, swim, play golf and tennis, shop, hike, and canoe, southerners will stop a time or two to pay homage to the past.

Tourists who walk the narrow streets of Charleston pour some $460 million annually into the local economy. About 1 million visitors each year walk the battlefield at Vicksburg, Miss., and stroll through the re-created city of Colonial Williamsburg in Virginia. Through travel, southerners continue to learn of life of a century or two ago. In the 1930s garden club ladies in Natchez introduced a new genre of travel when it opened a few antebellum homes each spring to visitors. The name of such tours—pilgrimage—is appropriate for southerners' reverence of the past.

Many historic homes are open for lodging as well as tours, so guests may dream they dwelt in marble halls. At preserved villages like Old Salem in Winston-Salem, N.C., visitors watch costumed docents work at the crafts and cookery of two centuries ago. The Mississippi Museum of Agriculture and Forestry in Jackson moved an entire 100-year-old farm to its premises, where southerners hear words that have almost vanished from the daily vocabulary: singletree, laying-by time, bust the middles. Workers at the farm even plant a tiny patch of cotton and let the visitor try his or her hand at picking.

Historically, tourism for African Americans was a complex process. Uncomfortable and unhealthy Jim Crow railroad cars hardly encouraged travel over long distances. Automobiles gave more privacy and security, but difficulties in finding places to eat and sleep complicated touring. Blacks nonetheless developed particular travel locations, such as black-only beaches. With desegregation of the South's public facilities in the 1960s and a growing commercialization of black history, tourism among blacks visiting southern tourist destinations increased. *Alabama's Black Heritage* (1983) was a pioneering effort to promote African American heritage in the South, and other states and cities have targeted black tourists to heritage tourism sites.

GARY D. FORD
Southern Living

W. Fitzhugh Brundage, *The Southern Past: A Clash of Race and Memory* (2006); Ruth Camblos and Virginia Winger, *Shopping Round the Mountains* (1973); Charleston Trident Chamber of Commerce, *Tourism Profile, 1982–83*; John A. Jakle, *The Tourist: Travel in Twentieth-Century North America* (1985); Jeffrey Limerick, Nancy Ferguson, and Richard Oliver, *America's Grand Resort Hotels* (1979); Edward A. Mueller, *Steamboating on the St. John's, 1830–1885* (1980); Anthony J. Stanonis, ed., *Dixie Emporium: Tourism, Foodways, and Consumer Culture in the American South* (2008); Richard Starnes, ed., *Southern Journeys: Tourism, History, and Culture in the Modern South* (2003); *Southern Living* (December 1983, April 1984); *Travel Survey of Southern Living Subscribers* (1984).

Tourism, Automobile

The automobile represents many ideals of American culture such as individual freedom, technological dominance, and the pursuit of happiness, and the American South has long been a popular destination for many on the road and on the move. The temperate climate of the region, in addition to the lure of sandy white beaches and the beauty of the Appalachian Mountains, made automobile tourism in the South a popular recreational activity. Tourism is one of the top three economic forces in every state that constituted the Confederate States of America from 1861 to 1865. During the modern era, the South has experienced many changes brought about by the increased mobility and cultural exchange facilitated by automobile tourism. The influx of travelers and retirees to the region has caused a demographic and cultural shift.

Before the 20th century, the wealthy were the only ones able to engage in recreational travel. Many northern industrialists enjoyed the mild climate and healing waters—both oceans and hot springs—of the South. Many visited the region to vacation, build homes, and, perhaps late in life, migrate south for retirement. Northern capitalists J. P. Morgan, William Rockefeller, and Marshal Field all built elaborate homes and a country club on the once exclusive Jekyll Island in Georgia. The bucolic landscape and temperate climate of the South made the region especially alluring. Southern land was also inexpensive and largely undeveloped in the 19th century. As time went on, vacationing became a more accessible and common activity for all Americans.

When Henry Ford began to mass-produce the Model T in 1908, the first affordable automobiles began to open tourism to the average American. Yet the South left much to be desired in developed roads and infrastructure. The accessibility of the automobile combined with the Good Roads Movement to further democratize southern tourism. With the construction of the National Highway, connecting New York City to Atlanta, in 1909 and the Capital Highway, stretching from D.C. to Atlanta, in 1910 the North-South tourist trade was burgeoning. A few years later, in 1914, Carl Fisher was instrumental in developing the Dixie Highway, which connected Michigan to Fischer's developing resorts in Miami Beach, Fla. The Dixie Highway was developed with an eastern and a western route to maximize the tourist sites and towns along the way.

The trajectory of roads could make or break small communities that depended on tourist dollars. Following the development of the 1926 National Highway System, many new roads led to roadside attractions such as autocamps, filling stations, and a plethora of roadside stands selling various wares. Southern attractions have long played up the region's rich history, especially the Revolution and the Civil War. The biggest monument to the Confederacy began in 1915 when the United Daughters of the Confederacy started planning a bas-relief carving of Jefferson Davis, Robert E. Lee, and "Stonewall" Jackson on Stone Mountain in Georgia. The mountain is also infamous for being the site of the revival of the Ku Klux Klan in 1915. In the 1920s, Gutzon Borglum began the carving only to leave after disagreements with managers. The next artist destroyed Borglum's beginnings, and the project was not completed until the early 1970s. Today, Stone Mountain State Park draws many tourists. Stone Mountain is a tourist attraction that possesses both a complicated history and the allure of natural beauty and recreation.

One of the major reasons to pack the kids in the car was to see the country and experience different places. With all of the families on the road with more money and increased leisure time in the postwar era, there was a need for various roadside attractions. One of the most recognizable sites along the southern roadways is the yellow and red sign advertising Stuckey's pecan shop and roadside stand. Williamson Sylvester Stuckey went into the pecan business just as the southern roadside trade was booming. Stuckey is representative of many people who went into one business and ended up diversifying to take advantage of all those cars on the road needing gas and the tourists craving food and cheap souvenirs.

In addition to natural attractions such as beaches and mountains, the early era of automobile tourism also added destination tourism attractions such as Kentucky's Wigwam Village, South Carolina's South of the Border, Florida's Cypress Gardens, the resort of Gatlinburg, Tenn., and Arkansas's Dogpatch USA, just to name a few. Walt Disney World, located in Orlando, Fla., opened in 1971 and today is the nation's largest and most popular example of destination tourism. The South has always offered cultural and heritage tourism spanning from Colonial Williamsburg, to Revolutionary and Civil War battlefields, to the federal funding of a Gullah-Geechee Heritage Corridor to preserve the distinctive African American culture along the southeastern coast.

Early in the 20th century, auto camping took the form of "gypsying" and engaged the American values of independence and self-reliance. Later, as a growing consumer society evolved and the democratization of travel and leisure ensued, the roadside became a largely tame, commercialized, and homogenized landscape. There was a lull in the development of automobile tourism during the Great Depression and both world wars. Following World War II, a booming postwar economy and consumer culture led to an extensive expansion of tourism. In 1956 Eisenhower's push to develop a transportation system and the passage of the National System of Interstate and Defense Highways helped both to defend the country against foreign threats and to provide better transportation for its citizens. The development of good roads often led to sunny seaside resorts and campy roadside attractions as well as national defense. The dominance of high-speed superhighways in the 1970s served to destroy local color as well as decimate old neighborhoods and businesses. The places and people left behind were often poor and black, such as in Overtown, an African American community in Miami that was displaced by the building of Interstate 395. The interstate led to a more homogenized roadside culture with chain motels, gas stations, and restaurants. However, the South had developed a reputation for its distinctive regional flair and southern hospitality even in the face of a mundane commercial roadside.

Southerners are known for the emphasis they place on hospitality and recreation. The mythologized "southern hospitality" of the region's inhabitants is complicated by its hostility toward outsiders and history of racism. The influx of automobile tourism, which drew snowbirds and a more geographically diverse citizenry, has served to change a region that has often been hostile toward change. Tourism can lead to a more complex and open South; however, it also can lead to overdevelopment of the region's natural resources and the dominance of developers and large corporations that care little for regional flavor and local color. Tourism has often been seen as a double-edged sword because of the complexity of the positive and negative repercussions. Appealing to outsiders has often led to the proliferation of misconceptions and stereotypes about the South, such as the ignorant Hillbilly or the myth of the Lost Cause and idyllic antebellum South.

From the autocamps of the 1930s to the chain hotels of today, the South has sold itself as a land of southern hospitality, old-time charm, and beautiful landscapes. Local images and historical memory have often conformed to the expectations of tourists. The hospitality industry in the South was primarily segregated until the Civil Rights Act of 1964 desegregated public accommodations. Southern leisure culture still struggles with its legacy of segregation and racism. The automobile leveled class differences in America, and it also potentially offered more freedom to African Americans to travel undisturbed by Jim Crow segregation. However, automobile travel could be a dangerous gamble for African Americans traveling through the South. From the 1930s until the end of the 1950s travel guidebooks, such as *The Negro Motorist Greenbook* and *Travelguide*, provided African Americans with suggestions for "vacation and recreation without humiliation." However, "driving while black" could be a major problem in the South. For example, in 1948 Robert Mallard was attacked and killed by a Georgia mob for simply being a prosperous black man with a nice car. In the face of southern racism, guidebooks and word of mouth led to the development of strong black communities and businesses based in recreation. Beaches for African Americans, such as Florida's American Beach and South Carolina's Atlantic Beach, survive today. Many key moments in the civil rights movement of the 1950s and 1960s centered on the mobility of African Americans, such as Rosa Parks's protest against sitting in the back of a bus and the "Freedom Rides" that civil rights organizations undertook during the period. Southern automobile tourism serves as one battlefield for the meaning of modern citizenship, mobility, and freedom.

Automobile travel in the South deals with the serious nature of race relations and the frivolous aspects of campy roadside attractions. The act of driving to or through the South has certainly changed in the 21st century. While regions of the United States are much more connected today, there are still signs of a distinctive southern culture to be found while touring the American South.

NICOLE KING
University of Maryland at Baltimore County

Warren James Belasco, *Americans on the Road: From Autocamp to Motel, 1910–1945* (1979); Tim Hollis, *Dixie before Disney: 100 Years of Roadside Fun* (1999); David L. Lewis and Laurence Goldstein, eds., *The Automobile and American Culture* (1980); C. Brenden Martin, *Tourism in the Mountain South: A Double-Edged Sword* (2007); Cotton Seiler, *American Quarterly* (December 2006); Claudette Stager and Martha Carver, eds., *Looking beyond the Highway: Dixie Roads and Culture* (2006); Richard Starnes, ed., *Southern Journeys: Tourism, History, and Culture in the Modern South* (2003).

Tourism, Culinary

In 1936 Kentuckian Duncan Hines published the country's first restaurant guide, *Adventures in Good Eating*. In the introduction to the book, Hines explained that his "interest in wayside inns is not the expression of a gourmand's greedy appetite for fine foods but the result of a recreational impulse to do something 'different.'" With that declaration, one could argue, culinary tourism was born.

Culinary tourism is the search for vernacular eating and drinking experiences that are specific to place. Folklorist Lucy Long describes culinary tourism as the "intentional, exploratory participation in the foodways of an other— participation including the consumption, preparation, and presentation of a food item, cuisine, meal system, or eating style not one's own." Culturally, the concept has its roots in the development of automobile travel and the expansion of personal eating experiences outside the home. Once the Model-T began bouncing down the dirt roads of the South, drive-ins and roadside cafés sprang up to greet them, showcasing local and regional foods and growing in popularity as travelers were exposed to new recipes and ingredients.

Following the South's evolution of restaurants, and the later notion that individual cities such as New Orleans, Charleston, Memphis, and San Antonio (to name just a few) were culinary destinations, came the development of localized food festivals. Initially established to recognize a seasonal harvest or event, food festivals have grown into grand celebrations of a wide variety of southern foods and culinary traditions. One of the South's oldest food festivals is the Alabama Peanut Festival in Dothan, which began in 1938. Today, it is the nation's largest peanut festival, bringing more than 150,000 people annually to this small Alabama town for the 10-day event. The community of Breaux Bridge, La., started its Crawfish Festival in 1960, one year after the Louisiana Legislature named Breaux Bridge the Crawfish Capital of the World. These festivals, which began as simple community gatherings, have now grown into destination events, bringing people from all over the country to experience localized food traditions, putting iconic southern foods on the national stage.

New Orleans might be considered the epicenter of culinary tourism in the South. Celebrated for its multicultural heritage, the city is a mélange of cultural traditions—jazz, Mardi Gras, and St. Joseph's Day, to name a few—as well as culinary traditions unique to the area, and New Orleans has long been a specific destination for unique food experiences. There is hardly a tourist who has not visited the Crescent City without having a beignet or a bowl of gumbo, making New Orleans the perfect illustration of the relationship that culinary tourism has to cultural tourism. The two are inextricably combined.

In 1984 writer John Egerton traveled through 11 states to explore the idea that food is one of the most significant elements of southern culture. Three years later he compiled his findings in the seminal work *Southern Food: At Home, on the Road, in History*. Egerton's book was an early affirmation that "the traditional food and drink of people in the South—and the rituals surrounding their consumption of it—constitute the most defining, uniting, and enduring manifestation of the region's culture." *Southern Food* helped catalyze the food-ways scholarship movement, which started gaining both popularity and validation in the 1990s.

In 1999 the Southern Foodways Alliance (SFA), based at the University of Mississippi, produced the Mississippi Delta Hot Tamale Trail, a multifaceted online project that includes oral history interviews with tamale makers, essays that put hot tamales in a greater cultural context, and an interactive map. The SFA followed the Tamale Trail with three more culinary trails: Boudin, Gumbo, and Barbecue. The success or impact of these documentary projects cannot be measured, but their existence is certainly evidence that there is a need—and an audience—for resources that identify, illuminate, and support culinary tourism in the region.

The rise of travel- and food-related television shows has also spurred an interest in culinary tourism. The Food Network, founded in 1993, has capitalized on travel-themed programs that introduce viewers to people, places, and foods that they might not otherwise encounter. Alton Brown's Food Network series "Feasting on Asphalt," which premiered in 2006, follows Brown across the country as he seeks out small, family-owned establishments serving honest, local food. Cooking shows that feature southern chefs also offer inspiration for culinary tourism, because restaurants are also connected to many of the personalities who host such programs, such as Emeril Lagasse of New Orleans and Paula Deen of Savannah. Fans of their shows seek out a deeper connection with them and their food through the experience of eating at their establishments. The Food Network also features the series "All American Festivals," which celebrates regionalism through food, taking viewers across the country to get a taste of events such as the Grit Festival in Warwick, Ga., and the Cornbread Festival in Pittsburg, Tenn. And while one cannot be a culinary tourist from his or her couch, these kinds of shows can certainly inspire culinary travel.

Road guides written in the same vein as what Duncan Hines pioneered in the 1930s have experienced a resurgence in the past few decades, thus inspiring a new breed of culinary tourist. Calvin Trillin's *American Fried* (1974) and the first edition of Jane and Michael Stern's *Roadfood* (1977), two books that celebrate vernacular food across America, were contemporary precursors to the more specialized regional food guides that were to follow. In 2000 food writer and director of the Southern Foodways Alliance, John T. Edge, focused on the Deep South, publishing *Southern Belly: The Ultimate Food Lover's Companion to the South*, a compendium of information on restaurants and roadside cafés throughout the region. Much more than a collection of entries on where to find the best fried chicken or crispiest catfish, *Southern Belly* profiles the history of establishments from Arkansas to Virginia and the people who run them. This elevation of food as seen through a historical and cultural context is explored on a more subregional level in Fred Sauceman's three-volume work, *The Place Setting: Timeless Tastes of the Mountain South, from Bright Hope to Frog Level*. Focusing on the foodways of southern Appalachia, Sauceman offers colorful stories about the traditional foods of the area and the people behind the recipes.

It is not just restaurants and festivals that inspire people to hit the road. The greater awareness of and appreciation for artisanal producers has influenced culinary tourism in the region as well. Small, craft-oriented businesses such as Sweet Grass Dairy, producer of artisanal cow and goat cheeses in Thomasville, Ga., make items that highlight local foods and ingredients, celebrate generations-old production techniques, and are usually quick to open their doors for visitors.

In 2007 the Travel Industry Association published a report that 27 million travelers, or 17 percent of American leisure travelers, have engaged in culinary tourism since 2004. This statistic is an illustration of the growth of culinary tourism within the industry, as well as an effort to try to capitalize on its popularity. Many communities now showcase local food products, festivals, and culinary histories to entice visitors, with great results.

AMY EVANS STREETER
University of Mississippi

Rodger Lyle Brown, *Ghost Dancing on the Cracker Circuit: The Culture of Festivals in the American South* (1997); John T. Edge, *Southern Belly: The Ultimate Food Lover's Companion to the South* (2007); John Egerton, *Southern Food: At Home, on* the Road, in History (1993); Louis Hatchett, *Duncan Hines: The Man behind the Cake Mix* (2001); Duncan Hines, *Adventures in Good Eating* (1936); Lucy Long, *Culinary Tourism* (2003); Fred Sauceman, *The Place Setting: Timeless Tastes of the Mountain South, from Bright Hope to Frog Level* (2006); Jane Stern and Michael Stern, *Roadfood* (1977); Calvin Trillin, *American Fried* (1974).

Tourism, Cultural

Cultural tourism makes use of the South's history and cultural activities to attract visitors. Although tourists visit the region's natural attractions, commercial amusement and theme parks, and shopping venues, they also come to experience preserved aspects of the South's dramatic past and to enjoy its cultural expressions. State and local tourism boards increasingly target cultural, or heritage, tourism in attracting visitors, preparing special brochures, maps, timelines, Web sites, and other features to highlight cultural attractions. Although southern cultural tourism before the 1970s stressed white heritage and presented black culture in only stereotypical ways, contemporary tourist agencies are making special efforts to attract African American tourists, and in the process they contribute to reimagining southern culture as a black-white biracial culture.

Southern tourism increased dramatically in the 1920s, thanks to better roads south, a relatively prosperous national economy, and a self-conscious appreciation of heritage among middle- and upper-class white southerners who wanted to preserve architectural and other material features with historical significance. These efforts often drew from existing romantic imagery of the South. Despite the Great Depression of the 1930s, tourism efforts produced notable defining activities in the region. The Natchez Garden Club, for example, began the Spring Pilgrimage in 1932, attracting 1,500 visitors from 37 states for tours of 22 of the city's historic homes. The Pilgrimage also had a barbecue, a cotillion at the Natchez Hotel, a parade with an Azalea Queen and a Japonia King, and a "historical pageant." Renamed the Confederate Pageant, the latter became a key event of the Pilgrimage, presenting a vision of a refined white society and blacks singing plantation songs.

Charleston's Azalea Festival began two years after the Natchez Pilgrimage, in 1934, promoted by Mayor Burnett Rhett Maybank and utilizing the city's cultural resources and civic leadership. Costumed historical pageants had been added by the late 1930s, such as an Old South medieval-styled lancing tournament and the reenactment of a pirate's hanging. The Preservation Society gave house and plantation tours, while black singers performed spirituals in

"Plantation Echoes" and "negro street criers" competed. The Charleston Museum offered a rice-husking demonstration by black field hands who sang old work songs. The scale of the Azalea Festival's use of cultural, as well as environmental, features was an innovation, and its success inspired other communities across the region to utilize local resources and tie them to overarching southern mythology to attract tourists. Elite white Charlestonians succeeded in creating a marketable past, one that involved blacks in stereotypical ways. Brochures, advertisements, and souvenirs were marketed, highlighting Charleston's connections to the Lowcountry. Local boosterism and public spectacle connected this tourism effort to economic development and modern mass culture's consumerism, important models for the future.

White elites profited the most from these tourism efforts in Natchez, Charleston, and other cities in the early and mid-20th century. They gained new sources of wealth and prestige, buttressing the all-important role of respectability and gentility in the southern social system. These events were community activities that brought tourists and made jobs. Black street vendors, taxi drivers, café waitresses, hotel clerks, antique dealers, and other working-class people also benefited from these tourism efforts.

In the decades since these early tourism efforts, many southern locales, sites, institutions, and cultural experiences have been used to attract tourists. The Cherokee Reservation in western North Carolina presents Indians as hawkers for commercial goods on the street, dressed in Plains Indian garb not native to the Southeast; yet one can also learn from educational exhibits and firsthand experience about Cherokee heritage. The French Quarter in New Orleans is highly commercialized yet one can hear jazz and eat Creole and Cajun food while sitting in a carefully maintained historical district. Museums, music festivals, arts and crafts fairs, and countless other cultural experiences can be marketed as tourist attractions.

The Civil War is a key cultural tourism site in the South, given that most of the war's fighting took place in the region, leaving a landscape legacy of battlefields and related sites. The Civil War Trust's book *Civil War Sites: Official Guide to Battlefields, Monuments, and More* offers information on more than 600 sites in 32 states, with sites selected for historical significance and educational opportunities afforded by them. Many states organize Civil War tours in the forms of "trails" that provide linked information making it easier for tourists to visit many battle locations. The Tennessee Historical Commission sponsors one of the largest such efforts, the Tennessee Civil War Heritage Trail, with a brochure called *A Path Divided*, which gives information on 62 sites divided into the categories of Invasion by River, Fight for West Tennessee, Contest for Middle

Tennessee, East Tennessee Mountain War, and Hood's Tennessee Campaign. As the commission's Web site notes, the state's Civil War heritage is in "grave danger," as many sites are "fragile and vulnerable to damage." The goal of the brochure is "to help visitors to discover Tennessee's rich Civil War past and to understand better the convictions of the men and women who fought in it."

African American heritage has also become a major part of southern tourism efforts. Alabama led the way with its 1983 brochure promoting black heritage sites in the state. Governor George C. Wallace saw the attention to black sites as a sign of the state's aspirations toward racial reconciliation and a new image of Alabama. Civil rights museums and locales have been especially effective in attracting tourists. The King National Historic Site in Atlanta's Sweet Auburn District attracts more than a million visitors a years, and civil rights museums are now found in at least a dozen southern cities, including Savannah, Selma, Memphis, and Birmingham. The Birmingham Civil Rights Institute took 13 years to build and cost $12 million. It is part of a civil rights district in Birmingham that includes the Kelly Ingram Park and the 16th Street Baptist Church, bombed in 1963. Critics see the civil rights museums as sometimes presenting a heroic view of the movement that stresses leaders such as Martin Luther King Jr. at the expense of stories of more mundane grass-roots activism, but the Birmingham Institute presents its story to 100,000 visitors a year and offers exhibitions and educational activities that engage local activists like Fred Shuttlesworth as well as King.

Natchez, meanwhile, is also promoting black tourism in its Pilgrimage activities, with its *Southern Road to Freedom* staged in the First Presbyterian Church. It celebrates the story of Ibrahima, a slave brought to Natchez in the late 18th century who eventually gained his freedom and went back to Africa. The drama also highlights 1861 as a key year, as the Confederate Pageant does, but in this case the story of black Natchez emphasizes the beginning of the Civil War as a dividing line between oppression and the coming of freedom. The black and white pageants present a segregated history, though, with audiences often segregated as well. Natchez Pilgrimage lasts four weeks, attracts 100,000 tourists a year, and generates 1.5 million dollars a year.

Finally, in discussing examples of cultural tourism, one should mention the state of Mississippi's embrace of blues music. The Mississippi legislature created the Mississippi Blues Commission in 2004 to oversee efforts to promote and preserve the blues. It has 18 appointed commissioners, representing major organizations and geographic/political regions in the state that support blues initiatives. Its major activity has been support for a Mississippi Blues Trail consisting of sites that honor people, places, organizations, and events that have been important in blues history. "Welcome to the Mississippi Blues Trail," says the Web site devoted to it, "your unforgettable journey into the land that spawned the single most important root source of modern popular music." The site assures readers that sites "run the gamut from city streets to cotton fields, train depots to cemeteries, and clubs to shrines." Trail markers are scattered across the state, but the majority of them are in the Delta. Area promotions link the Blues Trail to such other tourist attractions as golf courses, hotels, and restaurants with "down-home southern cooking." The B. B. King Museum and Delta Interpretive Center opened in September 2008, a state-of-the-art museum with exhibitions and educational programming that aim to "build bridges between the community and the world while preserving the rich cultural and musical heritage of the Mississippi Delta."

CHARLES REAGAN WILSON
University of Mississippi

W. Fitzhugh Brundage, *The Southern Past: A Clash of Race and Memory* (2005); Steven Hoelscher, in *Southern Heritage on Display: Public Ritual and Ethnic Diversity within Southern Regionalism*, ed. Celeste Ray (2003); Renee C. Romano and Leigh Raiford, eds., *The Civil Rights Movement in American Memory* (2006); Anthony J. Stanonis, ed., *Dixie Emporium: Tourism, Foodways, and Consumer Culture in the American South* (2008); Richard Starnes, ed., *Southern Journeys: Tourism, History, and Culture in the Modern South* (2003); Tennessee Historical Commission, www .tn.gov/environment/history/path.divided/home.shtml; Stephanie Yuhl, *A Golden Haze of Memory: The Making of Historic Charleston* (2005).

Traveling Shows

A visit from a traveling show was a major event in the life of the southern small town in the late 19th and early 20th centuries. Colorfully decorated wagons and, later, trucks drove slowly through towns, with jugglers and acrobats drawing children and their parents out of their homes and into a happy procession of people anticipating fun at the show grounds. The coming of traveling shows signaled an unusual period of gaiety, when normal moral restrictions might be loosened and humdrum daily life enlivened. Most of these shows flourished from the end of the Civil War to World War I. After World War I grass-roots show business in the South continued to be dynamic, providing the training and experiences for many performers and businessmen in entertainment industries such as country music, jazz, the blues, and gospel. In addition to the circuses, carnivals, Wild West shows, and minstrels that had earlier become staples, there were tent shows, burlesque houses, magicians, freak shows, vaudeville bills, aerial daredevils, water circuses, and medicine shows.

The American circus, with its animal and clown shows, had antecedents in antiquity, but the real beginnings of the modern circus were in England in the mid-1700s. Animal trainers, acrobats, jugglers, and itinerant actors traveled through the American colonies, but the first recorded appearance of the circus in America was in 1791. Early circuses were city shows, and the predominantly rural South had less exposure than the North to circuses in the antebellum era, although circuses did appear along the lower Mississippi River in the 1820s. The basic pattern of the circus was established by the 1850s—circus parades to draw crowds, exhibitions under canvas walls or tents, trained animals, clowns, acrobats and aerialists, jugglers, ventriloquists, and freak shows. Multiple rings were introduced in the 1870s. The golden age of the circus was from 1870 to 1914. Phineas T. Barnum, George F. Bailey, W. C. Coup, and the Ringling brothers were leading circus entrepreneurs. In 1918 a merger brought the appearance of the Ringling Brothers and Barnum and Bailey Combined Shows. As circus audiences became larger in the early 20th century, the circus shows became more elaborate. The Wild West show became part of the event, and stages and rings were added, more dangerous animal acts were encouraged, and money was poured into acts, costumes, and pageants.

Circus owners adapted to the South by advertising their shows as classical and biblical, because they featured chariot races and religious depictions. The most popular circuses touring the South were John Robinson's Circus and Menagerie, W. C. Coup's Monster Shows, and the Grand New Orleans Menagerie and Circus (which had a Mademoiselle Eugene marching ahead of lions and tigers down southern streets to stir interest). In the 1890s almost 40 groups annually toured the region, from April to December, some of them touring only the South. Southerners turned out in large numbers for the circus, with rural people coming into town ahead of the circus in order to camp in or under wagons, watch the circus set up, and view the circus parade and opening ceremonies. Excursion trains brought thousands of people to the cities where the largest circuses were held. The appeal of the circus was universal, but the poor and children were its most fervent enthusiasts. Blacks and whites sat on opposite sides of the same tent. Gamblers and pickpockets frequently accompanied the circus, taking advantage of the rural folk coming out for the show, and the circus always seemed to bring out drinking and fighting. Community and religious leaders objected to them.

Only a dozen or so circuses continue to tour the nation today, but attendance at these is still large. Florida has served as the winter quarters for the Ringling Brothers circus, and Florida State University has become a prominent circus center because of the amateur productions on campus.

The carnival was another traveling show, closely related to the circus. "Pleasure gardens," modeled on London's Vauxhall and Ranelagh, were forerunners of carnivals, appearing in North America near the time of the American Revolution, offering the chance for visitors to stroll, eat, and drink. By the turn of the 20th century, trolley parks had emerged in eastern cities offering more exciting amusements. The beginnings of the American carnival are usually dated from the 1893 World's Columbian Exposition in Chicago, which included outdoor rides, fun houses, and games of chance. Coney Island opened the same year, but even before this, in the 1880s, the traditional state fairs had begun to set aside special areas for outdoor amusements.

Carnivals traveled the South, with their heyday between the world wars. Elaborate shows came to bigger cities, but smaller affairs hit the region's more typical small towns. They included set features: machine rides such as the Ferris wheel, roller coaster, and tunnel of love; the midway featuring food (such as popcorn, cotton candy, corn dogs, and caramel candy), shooting arcades, gypsy fortune tellers; the freak shows (featuring the Fat Lady, Tattooed Man, or midgets); and the girlie shows with risqué strippers. Gamblers, hustlers, and pickpockets of all sorts frequently accompanied the traveling carnival, as well as the circus. Harry Crews's article "Carny," which appeared in *Blood and Grits* (1979), portrays life on the road for carnival workers in the South; he discusses the distinctive vocabulary of "carny talk" and the social hierarchy among the carnival workers. Those who set up shows rank at the bottom of this society; the hustlers who run the working games rank higher; the "patch man," who exists to patch over conflicts that emerge within the carnival community and between it and the outside world, ranks still higher. Crews stresses that the farther south the carnival went, the rougher the shows were; a strip show that was relatively tame in Pennsylvania could be gross in Georgia.

The medicine show was a popular aspect of southern entertainment after the Civil War. During the fall, especially, when southern farmers had whatever money they would have during the year to spend, traveling salesmen of cheap patent medicines would appear. Few of these were of much value, as they were typically filled with alcohol or were strong purgatives that usually caused more illness than they cured. To attract attention, medicine salesmen would employ singers, such as the bluesman Sonny Terry or country singer Jimmie Rodgers (who sometimes worked in blackface), to put on a "medicine show" that would draw people together, creating an audience for the salesman to

hawk his goods. In normally quiet southern towns and rural areas, this entertainment, no matter how poor in quality, was worth listening to, and people
willingly came out to hear it. Performers would pass out Congo oil, liniments,
or similar remedies designed to cure whatever ailed anyone with money in
hand. Colorful pitchmen with names such as Joe "Fine Arts" Hanks, the Canadian Kid, Doc Zip Hibler, Mad Cody Fleming, Widow Rollins, and Population
Charlie were hustlers who went back and forth between medicine shows, carnivals, tent shows, and other forms of grass-roots show business.

The road company theater was another example of the traveling show in the
South. Before the Civil War, permanent theaters had existed in southern cities
such as Charleston, New Orleans, and Richmond, many of them presenting
road show spectaculars featuring exciting stage activities, musical performances, Shakespeare and other dramatic fare, and melodrama. After the war,
this continued, with new auditoriums and opera houses appearing. In Atlanta,
the 400-seat Davis Hall was built in 1865 as an essential part of the rebuilding of
the city. Dallas erected its first opera house in 1872. The new theaters and opera
houses were elaborately decorated with balustraded verandas, crimson velvet
wall hangings, glass chandeliers, and several tiers of seats for those of different
social classes. Blacks and prostitutes were generally restricted to the highest
galleries.

In 1869–70 the Wilmington, N.C., theater presented 50 evenings of entertainment, including Shakespearean plays, magicians, and Italian opera. Established theaters in cities presented the best American and European performers
and plays, but in smaller places the offerings were less ambitious. The average
theatergoer seemed to prefer the extravagant and sentimental, but originality
was valued little until after World War I. Italian touring companies performed
Rigoletto, Il Trovatore, and *Mignon*, among others; Shakespeare continued to be
a favorite; and less uplifting shows, especially melodramas with such titles as
Ten Nights in a Bar Room and *The Drunkard*, and spectacles with mechanical
thrills, as in the chariot race in *Ben Hur* and the railroad crossing the stage in
Under the Gas Lights, were also popular. Stock companies presenting these programs typically were in a town for a week or so, offering different shows daily.
By the 1880s a new star system emerged, leading to shows centered on a celebrity performer giving a single show. Broadway shows from New York—which
was the source for many of these performances throughout the period—also
went on the road in the early 20th century.

A special aspect of the touring theater was the tent show. The first theater
company to tour under canvas was an Illinois group in 1855, and the tent show
continued to be mainly a midwestern and southern phenomenon even after

permanent theaters proliferated in towns. Rural and small-town audiences seemed especially fond of these shows and continued to support them well into the 20th century. The average tent could hold almost 1,500 people. The tent show presented family-oriented dramatic performances, with three-act plays and specialty entertainers. They were clean shows, avoiding the kind of suggestive material in carnivals and vaudeville. After the movies became popular, the tent shows boasted of offering "a decent alternative to epics, orgies, sex, and horror." Traveling "rep" groups, with such names as Harley Sadler's Own, the Ted North Players, and Swain's Dramatic Show, played a town for three days to a week, offering their repertoire of the six to nine plays a season they had prepared. Usually presenting comedies, they also tried to include at least one serious play, sometimes an adaptation of a popular novel such as *The Virginian*, *The Trail of the Lonesome Pines*, or *The Shepherd of the Hills*.

The tent shows brought vaudeville to the South. It was not urban entertainment, as in the North, but rather performances designed to appeal to small-town folk. They offered popular singers such as Jimmie Rodgers, who served his apprenticeship in the 1920s in the traveling shows. Black blues singers also performed in this context, as did novelty bands such as Happy Cook's Kentucky Buddies. Impresarios such as W. T. Swain, known as Colonel Swain or "Old Double Eyes" to some who had done business with him, worked the South. Described by Nolan Porterfield as "sort of a cross between P. T. Barnum, William Randolph Hearst, and a snake-oil salesman," Swain typically wore a black suit, set off by a white bow tie and his silver gray hair. For four decades he was a major figure in the traveling theater of the mid-South and Southwest. Colonel Tom Parker, who eventually struck pay dirt as manager of Elvis Presley, was another typical tent show manager.

Almost 400 tent-show companies traveled the nation in 1925, mostly in the Midwest and South, visiting 16,000 communities and entertaining 76.8 million people. The Great Depression hit the shows hard, and eventually the competition from radio and television led to their decline. In the 1950s, 30 companies still toured under canvas, but by 1968 only 3 remained.

The tent road show contributed a popular character to show business lore and to regional imagery—Toby. He was the country bumpkin, a humorous figure who appeared in these shows around 1910. One manager, Fred Wilson, built the character into his shows and others copied him, until rural and small-town audiences knew him and looked forward to the character's appearance. A rustic, seemingly backward man, Toby would outwit and confuse the city slickers who tried to take advantage of him. Awkward, bumptious, but shrewd and full of common sense, Toby embodied the southern rural self-imagery of the Arkansas traveler. The character was adapted to different regions—in the Midwest, he was simply a rural hayseed; in the South, a hillbilly from the mountains; in Texas, he was a cowboy. By 1916 some 200 actors specializing in Toby, and always appearing the same—red-haired, freckled, with blacked-out tooth and farm clothes—traveled the circuit.

CHARLES REAGAN WILSON
University of Mississippi

George L. Chindahl, *History of the Circus in America* (1959); Joseph Csida and June Bundy Csida, *American Entertainment: A Unique History of Popular Show Business* (1978); John E. DiMeglio, *Vaudeville U.S.A.* (1973); Neil Harris, *Humbug: The Art of P. T. Barnum* (1973); Joe McKennon, *A Pictorial History of the American Carnival* (1972); Brooks McNamara, *Step Right Up: An Illustrated History of the American Medicine Show* (1976); Russel Nye, *The Unembarrassed Muse: The Popular Arts in America* (1970); Nolan Porterfield, *Jimmie Rodgers: The Life and Times of America's Blue Yodeler* (1979); Gregory J. Renoff, *The Big Tent: The Traveling Circus in Georgia, 1820–1930* (2008); William L. Slout, *Theatre in a Tent: The Development of Provincial Entertainment* (1972); Marcello Truzzi, *Journal of Popular Culture* (Winter 1972); Don B. Wilmeth, *American and English Popular Entertainment: A Guide to Information Sources* (1980), in *Concise Histories of American Popular Culture*, ed. M. Thomas Inge (1982).

Two Stepping

Two stepping is the basic form of partner dancing done within country fan culture. The dance, often called the Texas Two Step, has been part of southern (and especially southwestern) culture for many decades and is an integral part of honky-tonk rituals for fans both young and old. In 1978 *New York Times* writer William K. Stevens described it as a "controlled, old-fashioned country dance of considerable grace and elegance"; today, however, it is more often viewed as a marker of downhome or redneck identity, although the version of it performed in country dance competitions is a flashy, polished, and fast-moving display of technical prowess, always with boots and cowboy hat present.

The two step derives from a popular 19th-century "polite" social dance of the same name, although that one used a different basic pattern. That 19th-century two step was replaced in the 1910s by a new, trendier social dance called the foxtrot, named for its originator, vaudevillian Harry Fox. Dance teachers distilled Fox's jaunty performance into a set of standardized steps, the most basic of which alternated two glide steps with two quick, trotting steps in a pattern of "slow-slow-quick-quick." By the 1930s and 1940s, especially in the West,

Southwest, and Acadian regions—where partner dancing was an integral part of each community's social fabric—the foxtrot was so widely adopted that even where it was not referred to by name, its rhythms became the default social dance. As one lifelong country fan and dancer recently recalled, "Back then, it was just dancing. I guess it's what we call a two step today, but we just called it 'dancing.'" When the term "two step" resurfaced in country music and culture, it was applied to the most common style of dancing at the time—a simplified foxtrot—thereby creating the new definition of the two step as it is now done.

Between World War II and 1980, country fans in different regions maintained different dance traditions. Leon McAuliffe, longtime steel guitar player for the legendary western swing band Bob Wills's Texas Playboys, explained: "[West of the Mississippi] we played for dancing. East of the Mississippi they played a show . . . just for people to sit and listen." Although there was some two stepping in the Southeast during those years, the widespread adoption of the practice across the region did not occur until 1980, when the movie *Urban Cowboy* brought the dance and its native dance hall environs to rural and urban communities all across the country. The film's featured two-step sequences launched a fad that brought waves of instructional books and videos to a newfound market of country nightclub goers. Since that film, the term "two step" and the dance have become a synecdoche for country music and honky-tonks in general.

The basic form of the dance is done by partners in closed dance position, moving counterclockwise around the dance floor. In most country nightclubs, two-step songs make up approximately a third of the music played during a typical evening, while the rest is a combination of waltzes, polkas, line dances, and regional favorites such as the Cotton-Eyed Joe and Schottische. Two-step songs, which are usually in duple meter (2/4 or 2/2 time), are found in both traditional honky-tonk styles and pop-crossover styles of country music, as well as in Cajun music. The tempo of the dance has varied historically, but the current officially sanctioned tempo, according to the United Country and Western Dance Council, is 176 to 200 beats per minute, where each beat is implicitly defined as one quarter of a musical measure. Each "slow" step within the basic pattern occupies two beats, and each "quick" step occupies one beat, so the basic pattern of the dance ("slow-slow-quick-quick") requires one and a half measures of music. This phrase overlap—where the length of the dance pattern and the musical measures do not match—creates interesting rhythmic interactions between the music and the dancers' movements.

There are an increasing number of two-step variants danced in different communities. Many dancers who enter two-step competitions prefer to begin the dance with the "quick-quick" steps. In the thriving gay country dance scene, dancers sometimes modify the dance so that both leader and follower face the same direction, standing front to back, in what is called the shadow. In some regions, the basic rhythm of the two step is adjusted to a syncopated pattern. In others, such as Oklahoma, two step is replaced by a local variant known as shuffle (sometimes called triple-two), which substitutes a step-together-step pattern (a triple step) for each of the slow steps.

One of the earliest references to the dance in country song lyrics appears in Bob Wills's "New Spanish Two Step," an extremely popular country hit in 1946. In subsequent decades, country singers have frequently mentioned the dance as a way of affirming their authentic connection to country music traditions. George Strait sang "It's dance time in Texas where the wine and music flows / we'll do that Texas two step and that old Cotton-Eyed Joe" ("Dance Time in Texas") in 1985, while Mary Chapin Carpenter sang "Find a two-step partner and a Cajun beat" ("Down at the Twist and Shout") five years later in her recipe for the perfect evening out. Country artists have also used the dance's name as part of poetic wordplay in their songs, such as when Tracy Byrd sang, "The first step is the two step, then we'll talk" ("The First Step") in 1994. The dance has also been appropriated as a convenient verbal metaphor for smoothly circumventing political issues or other controversies.

Today, country fans throughout the South learn to two step at independent dance studios, at large country nightclubs, and from friends and family. Given the pervasive presence of the dance within the fan community, it is no surprise that parents frequently teach their children and grandchildren the basic two step, a practice that moves the dance squarely into the vernacular folk traditions of southern culture.

JOCELYN R. NEAL
University of North Carolina at Chapel Hill

James Bridges, director, *Urban Cowboy* (film, 1980); Tony Leisner, *The Official Guide to Country Dance Steps* (1980); Shirley Rushing and Patrick McMillan, *Kicker Dancin' Texas Style* (1984); Jerry C. Duke, "Country-Western Dance," *International Encyclopedia of Dance* (1998); United Country and Western Dance Council Official Rules (2007).

Visiting

Human beings have probably "visited" ever since they developed enough language and leisure to communicate about something other than access to food, safety, and a mate, but southern Americans have tended to make visiting especially central to their lives. Joe Grey Taylor (1982) quotes an Alabaman who, in the 1920s, described visiting as a "happy recreation," which was, nevertheless, taken "very seriously." Southern newspapers still include reports about people visiting from out of town, whether in a society column focused on the local elite or in reports from small town church congregations. Certain common expressions of hospitality have long reflected the belief that southerners should always give the appearance of being willing to set aside whatever they are doing to visit with someone: "Y'all come to see us sometime"; "Come again real soon"; and "Come set a spell." Southerners who announce that they have "had a good visit" with someone usually mean their conversation made them feel closer and that they are looking forward to seeing each other again.

The primary purposes of any visit have usually been to have fun and escape daily worries, to help each other solve problems, or to establish and reinforce personal ties. There has not been enough research to determine what visiting traditions, if any, have been exclusively southern, but many practices have been affected by their cultural and historical contexts. Until the 20th century, most southerners lived in relatively isolated rural settings, making them especially appreciative of any opportunity to talk with anyone, whether neighbors or strangers. Until the spread of air-conditioning, people wishing to escape both the summer heat and the isolation of their houses would sit on front porches where they could invite passersby to join them for a chat. The Sunday highlight for many churchgoers has been the chance to visit after the service either outside or in a "fellowship hall." At weddings, funerals, revivals, and other special gatherings, southerners have talked around tables "groaning" with massive platters of food (or, before football games, by the "tailgates" of each other's cars and trucks). Small sets of people wishing to be alone, particularly courting couples, have, throughout southern history, "gone for a ride," whether on horseback, in a carriage, or in an automobile.

The enduring social hierarchies in the South inspired complex regulations about who can see whom under what circumstances and how each individual should behave. Men have staked out special contexts for stag visits, including fishing, hunting, militia musters, political meetings, business luncheons, private clubs, locker rooms, bars, brothels, gambling, and various sports venues. Small town men have gathered to chat and play cards or checkers in front of courthouses, in barbershops and country stores (sometimes open late to serve as a male community center), and, in recent decades, at a common table in "meat and three" restaurants. Melton McLaurin (1987) noticed that men in his grandfather's store kept rehashing the same subjects rather than approaching topics that might stimulate tensions, but many male conversations have ended in fights, especially when they were fueled by alcohol.

Women have been most apt to visit in each other's kitchens or parlors, in beauty shops (significantly called "beauty parlors" by many southern women), or while shopping together. Urban ladies of the 18th century followed the English pattern of holding "tea-tables" at which they discussed fashions and people who were not present. Gossip has often been the special purview of females, allowing them to share opinions on who needed to be helped, reined in, or shunned. The primary "work" for the wives and daughters of wealthy planters, besides making sure that their servants did as bid, was to nurture relationships with other elites through frequent visits. One young antebellum wife complained about having to give up her quiet days at home "to pay morning calls" but acknowledged that it was "a duty we all owe society, and the sacrifice must be made occasionally."

Heterosexual visits have occurred most often at parties, whether casual and spur of the moment or formal and planned. Each generation of southerners in each class has set standards for what kind of visiting was suitable for young men and women with romance on their minds. Until they were ready to court seriously one special female, 19th century young males tended to gather in small groups and then visit a series of young women. Young people of the New South spent entire evenings riding a streetcar, much as their great grandchildren would "hang out" at a mall. For most of the 20th century, however, couples went on formal "dates," during which the young women were expected to feign interest in whatever fascinated their male companions.

Although visiting has never been an exclusive class privilege, access to particular gatherings has often been restricted. The wealthy have always had more leisure time as well as more money to spend on food, drink, servants, and congenial private and public spaces in which to entertain, but this may have made opportunities to visit more precious to people who had to spend most of the day working. Zora Neale Hurston, in *Their Eyes Were Watching God* (1937), describes members of an all-black community who "had been tongueless, earless, eyeless conveniences all day long" enjoying "the time for sitting on porches" when they might "hear things and talk." Members of the lower classes have faced restrictions on their ability to unify through visiting since the earliest slave traders prevented Africans with the same language from being chained next to each other. Mills and other workplaces have been decorated with "no talking" signs. In spite of this, workers have met clandestinely in the woods and swamps of plantations, during stolen moments when overseers were out of sight of workers, in workplace and school bathrooms, and during coffee and smoking breaks. Such visits have often included making jokes about the authorities being crossed.

The most significant visiting taboo in southern history has been that against people of different "races" interacting as if they were peers. White men could have sex with both willing and unwilling black women, but they were never to be caught eating at the same table with African Americans. White women and their enslaved or free black servants might gossip together and help each other in childbirth, but they were never to let their "friendships" develop to a point that might challenge their social differences. Byron Bunch, in Faulkner's *Light in August* (1932), criticized Lena Grove, the daughter of humanitarian carpetbaggers, for visiting sick black people "like they was white."

In the 20th century, historical developments such as the civil rights movement and the migration of northerners to the South eroded some of the restrictions concerning who can interact with whom. Visiting practices among 21st-century southerners are probably less distinctive than in earlier times, but visiting, for whatever reasons and in whatever form, remains a favorite pastime across the South.

CITA COOK
State University of West Georgia

John W. Blassingame, *The Slave Community* (1979); Joyce Donlon, *Swinging in Place: Porch Life in Southern Culture* (2001); Elizabeth Fox-Genovese, *Within the Plantation Household* (1988); Jacquelyn Dowd Hall et al., *Like a Family* (1987); Crandall A. Shifflett, *Coal Towns* (1991); Joe Gray Taylor, *Eating, Drinking, and Visiting in the South* (1982).

Water Skiing

With mild winters, hot summers, and many rivers and lakes, water sports are a significant recreation enjoyed by southerners. Aquaplaning behind outboard motor boats or sleek mahogany inboard runabouts was popular in the South in the 1920s. But the American Water Ski Association credits the beginning of water skiing to Ralph Samuelson of Minnesota, who on 22 June 1922, mastered the skill of riding behind a boat, holding onto a window-cord rope with two barrel staves for skis strapped on his feet.

Northern water skiers had the advantage of being snow skiers, but on northern lakes, never warm even in summers and often frozen in the winter, the water skiing season was short.

Down south, water skiing developed rapidly, and Cypress Gardens, which opened in 1936 in Winter Haven, Fla., became the water ski capital of the world. The genius behind Cypress Gardens was Dick Pope Sr., a flamboyant promoter for whom the saying "he can sell ice to the Eskimos" fit perfectly. But the real idea person, gardener, and plant collector was his wife, "Miss Julie," a native of Pike County, Ala., and a true southern lady not averse to hard work. The Gardens featured beautiful girls wearing antebellum gowns, a perfect Old South illusion following the 1939 movie *Gone with the Wind*.

While Pope was in the military in World War II, Miss Julie initiated the first water ski show. When a few soldiers showed up at the Gardens to see the show, Miss Julie quickly gathered her children, their friends, and employees who could ski or drive the boat, and sent them out to perform. It must have been good, because the story relates that 700 soldiers came to see the show the next day, and show skiing was born. The South, the nation, and the world learned from pictures how to do it. Belles in ballet skirts over bathing suits performed routines, clowns delighted audiences, and handsome lads flew off wooden ramps. The acts of the ski show were set. Although many sites offered water ski shows after the mid-1950s, it was the Cypress Gardens Water Ski Show that set the benchmark, spread the idea of water skiing, and provided outstanding tournament water skiers.

Competitive water skiing had its origins in Long Island, N.Y., and Holland, Mich., where Chuck Sligh nursed along the American Water Ski Association. Tournaments featured three events—jumping, tricks, and slalom. Tournament skiing quickly moved into Florida. In 1947 Cypress Gardens initiated the Dixie Tournament during spring break. Dick Pope Jr. was the first person to "ski" barefoot, a skill that many later learned.

The first world championship was held in France in 1949, but the next year it was hosted by Cypress Gardens, an event covered by the media, which made water skiing popular across the South. Henry Suydam began a water ski program at Rollins College in Winter Park, and other Florida and southern colleges followed.

Ida Cason Callaway Gardens in Pine Mountain, Ga., added water ski shows and ski instruction in 1955 and competition the following year. Callaway hosted the Southern Regionals in 1957 and the U.S. Nationals in 1958, but since 1959, the annual Masters Tournament built Callaway's skiing reputation.

The vast majority of southern water skiers, however, are not interested in competition. They are motivated by some inner drive and the desire to beat a relative or friend in mastering new skills. These weekend skiers enjoy the sport, skiing behind boats that are designed with special elevated tow hooks and that produce either flat or high wakes for different types of water skiing or any boat with enough power to pull a skier up.

The first wooden skis were replaced by laminated plastic, and Manila hemp ropes by plastic ropes. Short and wide trick skis were designed to facilitate turning from front to back and turns in the air, off wakes and ramps, and with the foot holding the rope. Skis pointed at both ends entered North America when European skiers brought "banana peel skis" to the 1957 World Tournament in Toronto. Tapered trick and slalom skis became a staple of southern skiers, but not before southern designs made the skis more stable. Florida has many water ski schools where skiers from all over the world come to be coached by former champions.

Several developments changed the leisure southern water ski world—the introduction of individual water craft in 1968 allowed young and old to race across the water with the same thrill of water skiing but without the learning curve or the strength, balance, and physical pain that came with water skiing. The wake board surpassed water skiing in popularity for weekend skiers, and skiing for disabled skiers became popular. Hydrofoil water skiing is the latest way to enjoy water skiing.

In 2010 water skiing is regulated by USA Water Ski in Polk City, Fla., where the offices of the American Water Ski Educational Foundation and Water Ski Hall of Fame are also located.

LEAH MARIE RAWLS ATKINS
Auburn University

Jack Andresen, *Skiing on Water* (1950); Dick Pope Sr., *Water Skiing* (1958); Mary M. Flekke, Sarah E. MacDonald, with Randall M. MacDonald, *Cypress Gardens* (2006).

Whittling

Whittling refers to woodcarving with a knife, usually a pocket knife. It is a pastime often associated with—but not confined to—the Appalachian South and has served many functions for southerners. In earlier days, whittlers often made practical products such as handles for hammers and axes, walking sticks, and various other everyday items. Some writers have emphasized the role of self-reliance in the popularity of whittling in southern Appalachia, relating the decline of whittling to the increased availability of consumer goods.

Despite the emphasis on making practical items, whittling also serves as an outlet for creativity. One of the most famous examples is the snake walking cane, once a popular whittling product in Appalachia. This type of cane con-

Dave Penland, a Confederate war veteran and mountaineer, whittling by the fireplace, Beech, N.C., c. 1920 (William A. Barnhill, photographer, Library of Congress [LC-USZ62-118644], Washington, D.C.)

sists of a standard-looking shaft but also features a snake of raised bark coiled around its length, usually whittled in detail down to the forked tongue.

According to most whittlers, visualization is essential to good whittling. Once a block of wood is sawed down to usable size, a good whittler will see the end product before carving out the broad contours. Finer details come next, followed by sanding. Whittling is commonly a time-consuming pursuit, and some items require weeks of work. While some whittlers sell their products, most whittle for personal use and enjoyment. At times, schools such as the John C. Campbell Folk School of Brasstown, N.C., have encouraged Appalachian southerners to capitalize on this folk tradition as a means of income.

Some whittled objects are wholly recreational in usage. A popular example is the whistle. Other whittled objects are purely aesthetic. These include whirligigs (windmills) and representational art—usually miniature depictions of animals. Whittlers apply artistic variations to these forms. Whittling also serves as a pastime, and it serves no other purpose for the significant percentage of whittlers who simply whittle sticks down to nothing instead of carving anything out of them. Some writers have indicated that this was a useful way for southern men to sit down for extended periods of time without projecting idleness.

"Arkansas," as sung by the Osborne Brothers, treats whittling as a marker of impoverished elderly southern men. The song asks,

Arkansas, are your rivers still flowing?
Is your cotton growing, white as snow?
Do the young men still piddle with the thought of growing rich
And slowly turn to old folks sittin', whittling on a stick?

Searcy, a small town in Arkansas's Ozark region, has been known as the nation's whittling capital since 1955, though the title is unofficial and its origins are unclear.

MILES LASETER
University of Mississippi

Wrestling

William Faulkner wrote that Thomas Sutpen, the Old South planter who is the central character of *Absalom, Absalom!*, would watch an evening of slave wrestling. At the end of "the spectacle," he would enter the ring, "perhaps as a matter of sheer deadly forethought toward the retention of supremacy, domination." He and a slave would soon be "naked to the waist and gouging at one another's eyes."

Physical grappling is an old tradition for southern men. In the colonial era well-off gentry planters presided over and sometimes joined in sports such as wrestling, which served as a communal bonding experience between social classes. One of the rituals in frontier areas of the antebellum South, which spawned real-life Thomas Sutpens, was the gouging match. It was a brutal sport where each man tried to pry his opponent's eyes out of their sockets using a thumb for leverage. Brutal though they were, wrestling and eye gouging were not surprising pastimes for men in a society where violence was common. Indians, animals, outlaws, and nature were threats to life; physical labor was long and grueling. Gouging matches tested a man's strength, dexterity, and ferocity. In *Life on the Mississippi* Mark Twain told of an appropriate product of this world, a self-styled Arkansas wrestling champion called "Sudden Death and General Desolation."

Itinerant wrestlers toured the South in the late 19th century, often with minstrel shows and fairs. By the beginning of the 20th century, though, wrestling was best known in American culture for its ethnic wrestlers, appealing to immigrants in northern cities. Just the names of Irish Dan Mahoney, Stan Zbyszko, Turkish-born Ali Baba, Killer Kowalski, or Bruno Sammantino could get ethnic pride juiced up, for or against these colorful figures. They created modern wrestling with its theatrical competitions, outlandish characters, and stylized violence. Professional wrestling became well anchored in the South in the 1950s. Television helped extend wrestling's appeal in the region, as smaller stations appreciated the low cost of producing live wrestling shows that had family appeal. The decade's popular wrestlers included masked men, including the Hooded Phantom and Zuma, the Man from Mars; patriots such as Mr. America; and the pretty boy, "Gorgeous George" Wagner. The wrestler narrative has to have villains as well as heroes, and the sight of German and Japanese wrestlers provoked post–World War II southern audiences. Gulf Coast Championship Wrestling promoted the sport in Alabama and Florida, and the National Wrestling Alliance sponsored matches in Virginia and the Carolinas. Other centers of the sport were in Memphis and Texas.

Professional wrestling thrived in the South after the war, just as it declined in popularity elsewhere, as other parts of the nation embraced professional football and baseball franchises, of which the South had few until recently. Professional wrestling did return to national prominence in the 1980s, with super celebrity Hulk Hogan (Terry Bollea) from Florida transcending the ring to become a star on television and in film. The National Broadcasting Company showed *Saturday Night's Main Event* beginning in 1985, the first national wrestling show since the 1950s. The emergence of an extensive network of cable television stations in the 1980s gave more opportunity for broadcast of wrestling events across the nation.

Although college football packs southern stadiums, stock car racing has historic roots and popular appeal in the South, and baseball remains popular, professional wrestling has long drawn southerners to small-town arenas. The wrestling season, of course, is 52 weeks long, and matches are promoted in countless towns and cities so small other sports would never give them a second thought. An estimated 60 percent of the national attendance is in the South. In 1984 a still-record 43,000 fans turned out at Texas Stadium in Dallas for a match.

The small town arenas are often drab, barnlike buildings with dirt floors and concrete seats, but their center typically contains a red, white, and blue wrestling ring brilliantly lighted by rows of television lights. The Friday or Saturday night entertainment is part athletic competition and part soap opera. Until recently, professional wrestling was the only sport many of these fans knew, and they have been intensely loyal and enthusiastic. In the wrestling ring, good and evil are distinct, and the fans pour into the arena to cheer the good guys and to jeer and curse the bad ones. Professional wrestling is the morality play of modern sports. If the good guy wins his match, that is simple justice, and if he loses, that is life. French theorist Roland Barthes indeed sees wrestling enacting "a purely moral concept: that of justice."

Wrestling promoters say their patrons are predominantly working class, with the average wrestling crowd made up of the kind of people whose pickups in the parking lot wear bumper stickers with messages such as "I Fight Poverty, I Work." Professional wrestling targets males 18 to 54, but about 20 percent of its audience is under 18. Seventy-five percent of television viewership of professional wrestling has a high school education or less, and about 70 percent has a household income under $40,000. Women represent a sizable proportion of the sport's audience, with one survey suggesting 36 percent of the television audience for wrestling is female.

Whether sport or entertainment in local arenas, professional wrestling is big business. By the 1990s southerners represented professional wrestling's core constituency, and its two leading entrepreneurs in that decade had southern origins. Atlanta-based Ted Turner's World Championship Wrestling (wcw) and North Carolina–born Vince McMahon's World Wrestling Federation (wwf) have dominated the sport since then. In 1995 the wwf grossed $55.8 million and the wcw earned $48.1 million from cable television pay-per-view showings alone. The wwf retail sales were more than $400 million in 1999. By the 1990s the South was the leader in producing American professional wrestlers, another factor giving a strong southern base to the sport. A 1995 survey revealed that 49 percent of American-born wrestlers were from the South, with Texas, Tennessee, and Florida among the top five states in birthing wrestlers.

The most frequently asked question by outsiders is whether professional wrestling is only entertainment. Are these guys athletes or entertainers? A fair answer is that they are both, that most of them have the skills, stamina, and strength for legitimate wrestling. But the wrestlers say that the fans, especially in the South, want to see "catch as catch can" competition, replete with exaggerated falls, wild punches, and frenzied action. Keeping the fans excited week after week, however, takes effort. This responsibility belongs partly to the promoter and partly to a "matchmaker," who is employed by the individual or group sponsoring matches in a region. The matchmaker's job is to decide which pairings of wrestlers, because of reputation or chemistry, are likely to please and excite the crowd.

Because the same dozen or so wrestlers compete against each other week after week around local circuits, the pairings have to be adjusted to maintain interest. Once the matchmaker gives the assignment to the wrestlers, they must build up as much interest as possible before the match and then make the match itself as exciting as possible. The prematch buildup is boosted with television shows taped and shown in each of the cities on the circuit a couple of days in advance of the live wrestling. The promoters pay for the television time, and the show includes some wrestling and a generous amount of interview time in which the wrestlers describe what they are going to do to their next opponents. The matchmaker will also bring in big-name outside wrestlers to increase attendance. The local wrestling world is often a family business. At one time promoters were related by blood or marriage, with promoters and wrestlers now often the second or third generation in the business.

Southern wrestlers have long adapted popular culture images of the region for what Louis M. Kyriakoudes and Peter A. Coclanis term their "stylized wrestling personas." The southern social types portrayed in the ring have reflected the South's changing role in American culture. Southern wrestling characters first appeared in significant numbers in the 1960s, which saw stereotypes of both the raw, degenerate, *Deliverance*-like mountain man and the more positive simple hillbilly, uncorrupted by modern civilization. Haystacks Calhoun, from Morgan's Creek, Ark., weighed in at 601 pounds and wrestled in knee-length overalls, while Crusher Blackwell tipped the scales at 400 pounds. The 1970s saw a rise in positive regional images among southern wrestlers. Dusty Rhodes, aka Virgil Runnels Jr., embraced working-class roots as the son of a Texas plumber. He proclaimed he was an "all around good guy, fighting for the American way of life." Kyriakoudes and Coclanis see him as a new type of southern wrestler, urban and blue collar, yet still a variant of the regionally specific good old boy. Patriotism was a popular theme for southern wrestlers in the 1970s as well, epitomized by Sergeant Slaughter, at first a villainously brutal drill instructor but then transformed during the Iranian hostage crisis into a heroic symbol of the United States. By the 1980s black wrestlers were increasingly popular, and one of them, Tony Atlas, Mr. USA, an African American body builder from Virginia, embraced patriotism, too, in grudge matches with a Russian wrestler. Ranger Ross, a black wrestler from Ft. Bragg, N.C., wore army boots and a camouflage jacket, while waving a large American flag as he entered the ring. Wrestlers effectively parodied southern icons, as in Honky Tonk Man's Elvis persona and Brother Love's representation of a hypocritical preacher suspiciously suggesting the disgraced preacher Jimmy Swaggart.

Wrestling remains a popular spectator sport in the South, but the embrace by sports fans of southern professional football, basketball, baseball, and hockey franchises, not to mention the stepped-up promotion of the always-popular stock car racing in the past decade, may be drawing diehard wrestling loyalists away from a sport with deep regional connections.

RANDALL WILLIAMS
New South Books
Montgomery, Alabama

Michael R. Ball, *Professional Wrestling as Ritual Drama in American Popular Culture* (1990); Roland Barthes, *Mythologies* (1957); Elliott Gorn, *American Historical Review* (February 1985), "The Manly Art: Bare-Knuckle Prize Fighting and the Rise of American Sports" (Ph.D. dissertation, Yale University, 1983); John Gutowski, *Keystone Folklore* (1972); Louis M. Kyriakoudes and Peter A. Coclanis, in *The Sporting World of the Modern South*, ed. Patrick B. Miller (2002); Gerald W. Morton and George M. O'Brien, *Wrestling to Rasslin': Ancient Sport to American Ritual* (1986); *Newsweek* (11 March 1985); Randall Williams, *Southern Exposure* (Fall 1979); Mark F. Workman, *Folklore Forum* (1977).

Aaron, Hank

(b. 1934) BASEBALL PLAYER.
Mobile, Ala., has produced several
great baseball players, including Willie
McCovey, Amos Otis, and Satchel
Paige. Perhaps the greatest of them all
is Henry Louis "Hank" Aaron. Born
5 February 1934 in Toulminville, a black
community in Mobile, he began playing
amateur baseball while in high school
at the Josephine Allen Institute. Playing
first with the Pritchett Athletics, Aaron
later played on weekends with a local
semiprofessional team, the Mobile Black
Bears. An exhibition game between the
Bears and the Indianapolis Clowns of
the Negro American League proved to
be Aaron's breakthrough into professional baseball.

The Clowns were impressed with
the young player's performance and
offered him $200 a month to join the
team. Aaron accepted, playing with
the Clowns in 1952 and compiling a
.467 batting average with his cross-
handed swing. Team owner Syd Pol-
lock attracted attention from the Boston
Braves when he ended a letter with the
postscript, "We've got an eighteen-year-
old shortstop batting cleanup for us."
On 12 June 1952 the Braves purchased
Aaron from the Clowns for $10,000 and
sent him to play in the Class C Northern
League at Eau Claire, Wis. After being
named rookie of the year there, he
was sent to Jacksonville, Fla., where
he played second base for the Braves'
Class A South Atlantic team. During the
off-season he trained in Puerto Rico to
play in the outfield and in 1954 won a
starting job with the Braves (which had
moved to Milwaukee) when outfielder

Bobby Thompson was injured during
spring training.

No longer a cross-handed hitter,
Aaron became best known for his hitting ability and power. In 1956 he won
the National League batting championship with a .328 average. Bypassing
such stars as Stan Musial and Red
Schoendienst, the league gave its most-
valuable-player award to Aaron the following year, the same year he clinched
the league pennant for the Braves with
an 11th-inning home run against the
St. Louis Cardinals. A Milwaukee real
estate firm supposedly accepted that
home run ball from Aaron as a $1,000
down payment on a home.

When the Braves moved to Atlanta
in 1966, Aaron hit 44 home runs and
signed a $100,000-a-year contract with
the team. In 1972 he signed a contract
for $200,000 a year, the largest player
salary in baseball history at the time.

During his major league career
Aaron steadily approached the record
number of home runs set by Babe Ruth,
who hit 714. In Cincinnati on 4 April
1974 Aaron hit his 714th home run.
Braves officials wanted him to hit his
record-breaking home run in Atlanta,
so they decided that he would not play
in the remaining games in Cincinnati. When Baseball Commissioner
Bowie Kuhn objected and threatened to
penalize the team, Aaron was put back
in the lineup, but he returned to Atlanta
without another hit.

The game in Atlanta on 8 April 1974
between the Braves and the Los Angeles
Dodgers was sold out and nationally
televised. A *New York Times* writer said
that "to many Atlantans, it was like

the city's festive premier of *Gone with the Wind* during the 1930s when Babe Ruth was still the hero of the New York Yankees and the titan of professional sports." That evening, Aaron hit his 715th home run, this one on a fastball thrown by pitcher Al Downing.

With a total of 755 home runs and numerous other major league records, "Hammerin' Hank" or the "Hammer," as Aaron was called, retired in 1976, after playing his final years with the Milwaukee Brewers. He was elected to the Baseball Hall of Fame in 1982. Since then, Aaron has worked for the Atlanta Braves as senior vice president and assistant to the president and for Turner Broadcasting as a corporate vice president of community relations and a member of TBS's board of directors. In 1990 Aaron published his best-selling autobiography *I Had a Hammer*, and in 2002 President George W. Bush awarded him the Presidential Medal of Freedom.

More than 30 years after it had been set, Aaron's home run record fell to San Francisco Giants slugger, Barry Bonds, on 7 August 2007, although Bonds's record-breaking feat was shrouded in controversy as he was under investigation for steroid use. Nevertheless, the always-gracious Hank Aaron pre-recorded a congratulatory video that was broadcast over the JumboTron at AT&T Park in San Francisco the night Bonds broke Aaron's long-standing record.

JESSICA FOY

Cooperstown Graduate Programs
Cooperstown, New York

Marjorie Dent Candee, ed., *Current Biography* (1958); *New York Times* (9 April 1974); Edna Rust and Art Rust Jr., *Art Rust's Illustrated History of the Black Athlete* (1985); Tom Stanton, *Hank Aaron and the Home Run That Changed America* (2004); Charles Van Doren, ed., *Webster's American Biographies* (1979).

Ali, Muhammad

(b. 1942) BOXING CHAMPION AND SOCIAL ACTIVIST.

"Float like a butterfly, sting like a bee" are the words most often attributed to Muhammad Ali, the Olympic gold medalist and world heavyweight champion boxer. Graceful yet powerful, as his catchphrase implied, Ali became just as famous for his stance against racial intolerance and his outspokenness against American society—in which he felt black men and women were treated as less than equal to whites—as he did for his incredible success in the ring. Named Cassius Marcellus Clay Jr. when he was born—Ali's father was named after the ardent 19th-century, Madison County, Ky., abolitionist Cassius Marcellus Clay—Ali's destiny as social critic seemed fated from birth. Ironically, however, Ali changed his name to Muhammad Ali after embracing the Nation of Islam, insisting that Cassius Clay was his "slave name."

Ali began his boxing career as a 12-year-old boy in his hometown of Louisville, Ky. When his new bicycle was stolen, he reported the theft to the first police officer he found, crying and claiming that he would beat up whoever had stolen the bike. As it happened, that officer was Joe Martin, a boxing coach at the Columbia Gym in Louisville. Martin told the distraught boy, "Well, you'd better come back here and learn how to fight," thus beginning his and Ali's trainer-boxer relationship.

"I was Cassius Clay then," Ali said years later in a *Sports Illustrated* story. "I was a Negro. I ate pork. I had no confidence. I thought white people were superior. I was a Christian Baptist named Cassius Clay." But by the time Ali was a high school senior he had begun exploring Islam, writing a senior paper on Black Muslims that nearly kept him from passing the class. He boxed as an amateur for six years, winning the light heavyweight gold medal in the 1960 Olympics in Rome. (Ali claims to have thrown his Olympic gold medal into the Ohio River after returning from Rome to Louisville and being refused service in a whites-only restaurant.) Ali turned professional that same year and won his first heavyweight boxing champion title in 1964 against Sonny Liston. Shortly thereafter he changed his name to Muhammad Ali, symbolizing his new identity as a member of the Nation of Islam.

The shift in Ali's religious faith came at a volatile time in American civil rights history. Ali became famous after winning the gold medal in Rome, and after winning his first boxing championship and announcing his conversion to Islam, he became an outspoken critic of American racial injustice, a message in line with his new Muslim faith. Ali's obvious prowess in the ring made him a highly visible symbol of black masculinity, and his comments outside the ring became a source of black pride,

propelling him into the role of a strong, straight-talking black leader.

In 1967 Ali refused to fight in the Vietnam War, claiming conscientious objector status on the basis of his religious beliefs. He later said to a *Sports Illustrated* reporter, "Why should they ask me to put on a uniform and go ten thousand miles from home and drop bombs and bullets on brown people in Vietnam while so-called Negro people in Louisville are treated like dogs?" As a result of his refusal to serve, Ali lost his boxing license and was stripped of his heavyweight boxing champion title.

In 1970 Ali regained his boxing license, and although he made millions in the ring, he was ostensibly opposed to the sport: "We're just like two slaves in that ring. The masters get two of us big old black slaves and let us fight it out while they bet: 'My slave can whup your slave.' That's what I see when I see two black people fighting." Nevertheless, Ali went on to fight in some of the most famous and highly promoted boxing matches in history, such as "The Fight of the Century," fought in Madison Square Garden against Joe Frazier; "The Rumble in the Jungle," fought in Zaire, Africa, against George Foreman; and "The Thrilla in Manila," fought in the Philippines, again against Joe Frazier. Ali lost the first bout by unanimous decision but won the latter two, further cementing his reputation as the epitome of black masculinity.

In time, as public support waned for the war in Vietnam and as the pace of violence against blacks in America slowed, Ali's antiwhite rhetoric diminished, but his passion for racial justice prevailed. In recognition of his contributions to the world of sports and to racial equality, during the 1996 Summer Olympics in Atlanta Ali served as the final bearer of the Olympic touch and received a replacement for the gold metal he won in 1960.

In all, Ali won nine heavyweight championship titles, and in 2001 he was the subject of the feature film *Ali*. Will Smith portrayed the champion, a role for which he was nominated for Best Actor in a Leading Role.

JAMES G. THOMAS JR.
University of Mississippi

Gerald Early, ed., *The Muhammad Ali Reader* (1998); Thomas Hauser, *Muhammad Ali: His Life and Times* (1991); Hunt Helm, *Louisville (Ky.) Courier-Journal* (14 September 1997); David Remnick, *King of the World: Muhammad Ali and the Rise of an American Hero* (1998).

Annual Interstate Mullet Toss

Opinions differ on how it got started. The confusion is compounded by the fact that the person credited with the idea—Jimmy Louis, one of the first musicians hired by the Flora-Bama Lounge and Package—tells two different stories. For some time, he and others vowed that Louis saw a cow-patty-pitching contest at a rodeo out west, and when the Flora-Bama's owners were looking for an excuse to throw a party (and make a little money) Louis suggested tossing a mullet. Maybe so. But in a 2006 documentary, *The Last Roadhouse*, Louis told the camera, "You want the truth about the Mullet Toss? It just come out of a fit of narcosis. I

got stoned one night and thought it up." Some say both stories are true. Either way, what began on the last full weekend in April 1984 as an excuse to sell and drink beer, and attracted only about 250 people at the start, today brings more folks to the Redneck Riviera than any other event, including the 4th of July.

Why a mullet? Why not? The mullet is considered by many to be a trash fish, a bottom feeder, whose persona is not unlike that (by reputation at least) of many who frequent the Flora-Bama and whose shape—minus the fins—is not unlike a particular part of the male anatomy. Although the Flora-Bama is said to be a place where you can find "a millionaire sitting next to a biker," one also finds that in that atmosphere identification with, and perhaps sympathy for, the lowly mullet makes perfect sense.

So what is it all about? Throwing a mullet. The rules are simple. Select your mullet from an ice bucket full of mullets. Stand inside a circle on the sand with your mullet in your hand and throw it—without leaving the circle. Then go and get your mullet, check your distance, put the mullet back in the ice. The circle is in Florida. The throw flies into Alabama—hence the "interstate" in the name.

Although records are kept, they are not kept well, so even though in 2004 one man threw his fish nearly 190 feet, *how* nearly is a matter of some debate. There are also categories for women, seniors, children, and others.

Like records for distance, crowd size is also difficult to pin down, but num-

In the air. Flora-Bama Interstate Mullet Toss, 2009 (Photograph courtesy of Harvey H. Jackson III)

bers in excess of 5,000 are considered conservative. Perhaps the best measure of the success of the event is the quantity of beer sold in the period between Friday, when it starts, and Monday, when it shuts down. Estimates are that in 2004 the Flora-Bama reportedly sold about 4,000 cases in three days. That is about 96,000, 12-ounce beers.

All for a mullet.

HARVEY H. JACKSON III
Jacksonville State University

Alan West Brockman and Joe Gilchrist, producers, *The Last American Roadhouse: The Documentary of the Flora-Bama* (film, 2006); Ryan Dezember, *Mobile Press-Register* (27 April 2008); Harris Mendheim, director, *Mullet Men: Second Place Is the First Loser* (film, 2000); Michael Swindle, *Mulletheads: The Legends, Lore, Magic, and Mania Surrounding the Humble but Celebrated Mullet* (1998), *Village Voice* (13 May 1997).

Appalachian Trail

The Appalachian Trail, a 2,178-mile footpath traversing the mountains from Maine to Georgia, is considered one of the most culturally valued and successful wilderness projects of the 20th century. Often referred to as the longest and skinniest National Park, the Appalachian Trail (A.T.) crosses 14 states and more than 60 federal, state, and local parks and forests. Marking the official route of this congressionally recognized National Scenic Trail, white paint blazes two-inch by six-inch vertical rectangles, found in both directions on everything from signs, bridges, rocks, trees, posts, or other objects approximately one-tenth of a mile apart.

Harvard graduate Benton MacKaye first proposed the idea for the A.T. in 1921. MacKaye's vision of the Appalachian Trail project was not the long-distance hiking trail known today but rather a pragmatic vision for wilderness conservation in the Appalachian region. The trail was completed almost 16 years after MacKaye's initial proposal of the Appalachian Trail project. However, during World War II, much of the trail route was lost as maintainers were unable to work. By 1951 the trail was officially declared complete once again. Since 1958, Georgia's Springer Mountain has been the southern terminus of the A.T., as indicated by a bronze plaque mounted on the summit. Approximately 4 million people set foot on the A.T. each year.

Of the "Triple Crown" of long-distance hiking trails (the Appalachian Trail, the Pacific Crest Trail, and the Continental Divide Trail), the A.T. is arguably the most internationally famous and most populated long-distance hiking trail in the United States. The A.T. attracts the largest number of thru-hikers (those attempting to hike the entire trail in one continuous journey each year). Since 1936, slightly more than 10,000 completed hikes made by thru-hikers and section hikers (those completing the trail in large sections over a period of time) have been recorded by the Appalachian Trail Conservancy. Of this number, approximately 200 have hiked the entire trail on more than one occasion. For the thousands of individuals who attempt to thru-hike the A.T. annually, only about one in four accomplish this goal, with thru-hikers taking anywhere from four to seven months to complete the trail. The majority of long-distance hikers on the Appalachian Trail are northbounders (i.e., NOBOS), meaning they begin in Georgia at Springer Mountain, located

in Amicalola Falls State Park, and hike north. While April Fool's Day is a traditional starting day for a northbound thru-hike, some long-distance hikers begin as early as February.

The Southern Appalachians include three states: Georgia, North Carolina, and Tennessee. The southern portion of the A.T. is dotted with many points of interest, including the summit of Georgia's Blood Mountain, which has spectacular views. The highest point on the A.T., Clingman's Dome, is located in Tennessee's Great Smoky Mountains National Park, and the trail enters the park at Fontana Dam, the highest dam east of the Mississippi River. North Carolina and Tennessee are both noted for their open grassy "balds," namely Tennessee's Max Patch, and Siler Bald and Wesser Bald, both located in North Carolina. Special hiking events also take place along the trail. Current and former hikers come together in Hot Springs, N.C., for Trailfest, while others celebrate the A.T. on White Blaze Day in Gatlinburg, Tenn. However, the largest gathering of long-distance hikers transpires every May in Damascus, Va., during the annual Trail Days Festival.

KRISTI M. FONDREN
University of Southern Mississippi

American Long-Distance Hiking Association-West, *ALDA-West: Triple Crown* (2009); Appalachian Trail Conservancy, *2,000-Milers: Facts and Statistics* (2008); Appalachian Trail Conservancy, *Step by Step: An Introduction to Walking the Appalachian Trail* (2008); Appalachian Trail Conservancy, *About the ATC: History* (2008); Karen Berger, *America's Triple Crown: Hiking the Appalachian, Pacific*

Crest, and Continental Divide Trails (2009), *Appalachian Trail: Something Unique* (2009); Dan "Wingfoot" Bruce, *The Thru-Hiker's Handbook, 16th Edition* (2006); Kristi M. Fondren, *Walking on the Wild Side: An Examination of a Long-Distance Hiking Subculture* (2009); Ronald Foresta, *Transformation of the Appalachian Trail* (1987); Benton MacKaye, *An Appalachian Trail: A Project in Regional Planning* (1921); Ben A. Minteer, *Wilderness and the Wise Province: Benton MacKaye's Pragmatic Vision* (2001); Roland Mueser, *Long-Distance Hiking: Lessons from the Appalachian Trail* (1998).

Ashe, Arthur

(1943–1993) TENNIS PLAYER.
Arthur Ashe grew up under racial segregation in Richmond, Va., and became a singular figure in American tennis, a notable humanitarian and social reformer, and a symbol of the South. The son of a policeman, he played on segregated playground tennis courts, but the U.S. Open championships are now played at the Arthur Ashe Stadium at Flushing, N.Y.

Lynchburg, Va., physician Walter Johnson took Ashe under his wing, as he did other promising African American tennis players, and Ashe soon moved to St. Louis to play tennis in an integrated environment and became the first African American to win the National Interscholastic League tennis championship. He attended the University of California at Los Angeles on a tennis scholarship in 1963 and became the first black member of the U.S. Davis Cup team the same year. He won the NCAA singles championship in 1965 and captured the U.S. Clay Court championship title in 1967. The following year he won both the U.S. Amateur and the U.S. Open tournaments and was on the winning Davis Cup team, all the while serving as a second lieutenant in the U.S. Army. For the next 12 years he was in the top-10 ranking of world tennis players. He won three Grand Slam major tournament championships, including the Australian Open (1970) and Wimbledon (1975), in addition to the 1968 U.S. Open. In his career, he won 33 singles titles.

Ashe retired in 1980, after having heart surgery the year before. He had been denied a visa to play in the South African Open, and after retirement he intensified his involvement in efforts to bring an end to apartheid there, calling for the nation to be expelled from the world tennis circuit. He was arrested in South Africa in 1985 for protesting apartheid and in Washington, D.C., in 1992 for demonstrating against treatment of Haitian refugees. He worked as a commentator for the American Broadcasting Company and HBO, and he authored *A Hard Road to Glory* (1988), a three-volume history of black athletes in the United States. He had a second heart surgery in 1983 and discovered in 1988 that he had contracted HIV from a blood transfusion during his second operation. He founded the Arthur Ashe Foundation for the Defeat of AIDS and used his misfortune to promote efforts to prevent and treat the disease. In 1992 he established the Arthur Ashe Institute for Urban Health to work to improve medical care for underserved populations. Ashe died 6 February 1993.

Ashe's father, a widower, intentionally raised his son to have the manners and discipline traditionally associated with a gentlemanly ideal. "I wanted him to be a gentleman that everybody could recognize," the senior Ashe said. Writer Digby Balzell, reflecting on Ashe's life, wrote, "The moral life of Arthur Ashe has constantly renewed my faith in the staying power of the gentlemanly ideal." Ashe's personal qualities helped him in negotiating the stresses and complexities of transcending the color line in high-pressure sporting contexts. His own qualities and their representation by others positioned him as a specifically southern gentleman. Despite controversy at the time, Richmond erected in 1995 an Arthur Ashe monument on Monument Avenue, previously marked only by statues to white heroes of the American Revolution and the Confederacy.

CHARLES REAGAN WILSON
University of Mississippi

Arthur Ashe, with Frank DeFord, *Arthur Ashe: Portrait in Motion* (1975), with Arnold Rampersad, *Days of Grace: A Memoir* (1993); Matthew Mace Barbee, in *Southern Masculinity: Perspectives on Manhood in the South since Reconstruction*, ed. Craig Thompson Friend (2009); E. Digby Balzell, *Sporting Gentlemen: Men's Tennis from the Age of Honor to the Cult of the Superstar* (1995); Robin Finn, *New York Times* (8 February 1993).

Atkins, Leah Marie Rawls

(b. 1935) WATER SKIER.
Alabama's first world water skiing champion, Leah Marie Rawls Atkins, reigned supreme in the sport from 1951 to 1958. In her first year of competition, at the age of 16, she won first place overall at the Ontario championships in South Hampton, Canada. Following this early success, she continued to establish records and win championships in both national and international arenas. Her impressive tally of accomplishments includes winning the United States women's overall national championship and the women's overall world championship in 1953. She also became the first woman senior judge and first woman board member of the American Water Ski Association, in 1976, and was the first woman inducted into the Alabama Sports Hall of Fame. In 2004, Atkins received the American Water Ski Educational Foundation award for extraordinary contributions to the sport.

Atkins was born in Birmingham, Ala., 24 April 1935, and grew up spending time at her parents' cabin on the Warrior River, where she learned to swim and ride the surfboard at the age of four. Later she learned to water ski, and when she saw photographs of people doing tricks on water skis at Cypress Gardens, she began trying to do them herself. Success did not come easily, but Atkins was tenacious; although she finished last in every event at the 1950 Lake Guntersville ski competition advertised as Alabama's first state championships, she still considered the trip worthwhile because that competition is where she learned to jump. Because of Atkins's determination to compete, her father hired men's champion Henry Suydam as her coach. The following year, she won her first event in junior girl's tricks. Suydam's coaching turned her career around and she domi-

Leah Marie Rawls Atkins, Alabama's first world water skiing champion
(Photograph courtesy of Stacye Hathorn)

nated women's water skiing for the next seven years. When she moved up to the women's division, she won the U.S. nationals in California, then the world championship in Toronto.

Incredibly, Atkins married and began her family in the middle of her water skiing career. When they married in 1954, she and her husband, George, lived on Lake Martin where they practiced three times a day for competition. Atkins taught skiing lessons and performed Sunday ski shows. While in residence on Lake Martin, Atkins once unwittingly performed a service for her state by rescuing Governor Gordon Persons when she spotted him in his stalled boat waving a white towel.

She took a brief hiatus from her water skiing career for the birth of her first child in 1955 but was back in the thick of the competition by 1957. In 1958, Atkins taught skiing in Italy, and it was there that year that she skied in her last tournament. Her second child was born in 1959, and she subsequently turned her focus entirely towards academic pursuits. Although often referred to in the press as a "pretty blonde," Atkins proved to have her fair share of brains. She earned a Ph.D. degree in history from Auburn University and taught at three Alabama universities. She was the founding director of the Samford London Study Centre and also the founding director of the Auburn University Center for the Arts and Humanities (now the Caroline Marshall Draughon Center) where she remained for the last 10 years until her retirement. Dr. Atkins has created quite a legacy having published many articles and books on Alabama history. Moreover, she and her husband have a family of 4 children and 13 grandchildren.

STACYE HATHORN
Alabama Historical Commission

Alabama Sports Hall of Fame, www.ashof .org; Jimmy Smothers, *Alabama Gadsden Times* (26 August 2007, 28 August 2007).

Atlantic Beach, South Carolina

Atlantic Beach, S.C., is one of the last surviving beachfront communities on the East Coast with a history of African American ownership and self-governance. A small parcel of land at just under 100 acres, Atlantic Beach offered one of the few recreational beaches open to blacks during Jim Crow segregation. Despite the racism of the early 20th-century South, Atlantic Beach, also known as the Black Pearl, became a vibrant spot for African American leisure culture.

Black-owned since the early 1930s, when businessman George Tyson purchased the land, Atlantic Beach was designed to be a "haven for blacks" on the Grand Strand. When Tyson ran into financial problems, the Atlantic Beach Company, a group of local black professionals, took over his failing mortgage in 1943. Dr. Leroy W. Upperman, the last surviving member of the company until his death in 1996, pointed out that it was "not out of altruism, but as a business venture" that the company sought to develop a beach for African Americans.

During its "golden era," from the 1940s through the 1960s, Atlantic Beach hosted entertainers such as James Brown, Ray Charles, Martha and the Vandellas, Count Basie, Billie Holiday, and the Drifters, who performed in but could not stay at the whites-only hotels of neighboring oceanfront communities. Atlantic Beach was designed for all African Americans and welcomed domestics and schoolteachers as well as famous entertainers. The small community persevered through hardships, such as harassment by the Ku Klux Klan in 1950 and the devastation of Hurricane Hazel in 1954.

Following the Civil Rights Act of 1964, which desegregated public accommodations, new opportunities and freedoms were opened for African Americans in the South, and Atlantic Beach, like many other black businesses and communities, struggled to maintain its economy and sense of place. In 1966 Atlantic Beach incorporated as a municipality of Horry County. Just two years later in 1968, when the surrounding towns consolidated into North Myrtle Beach, Atlantic Beach opted to maintain its autonomy as a black beach with black control. The small independent town still struggles with economic and social issues.

In 1980 the Carolina Knight Riders, a local African American motorcycle club, and Atlantic Beach politicians joined forces to start the Atlantic Beach Bikefest. The festival began to grow exponentially in the 1990s by drawing younger motorcycle enthusiasts from around the country. The Atlantic Beach Bikefest began to cause controversy in the late 1990s when it grew beyond the borders of the small black beach into the larger and predominantly white tourist town of Myrtle Beach. Tourists' claims of discrimination drew national media attention and an investigation into civil rights violations. In 2003 the NAACP helped plaintiffs claim suit against the city of Myrtle Beach and local business for discriminatory practices. These tensions pushed the Grand Strand, essentially the entire northern coast of South Carolina, to grapple with its sense of "southern hospitality." While all of the suits were settled in 2006 for the plaintiffs, the black motorcycle festival controversy is still unresolved, and the region still struggles over tourist dollars and political boundaries.

The town of Atlantic Beach has weathered many problems related to corrupt politics and sour development deals as well as internal crime and external racism. The hopes for a successful redevelopment—one that considers the important identity and history of the town—are still alive. The Black Pearl remains a symbol of the strength of African Americans in the South to persevere and build physical and psychological communities during the era of legal segregation and the resulting challenges of maintaining that sense of place and community as desegregation offered wider access and mobility for African Americans in the region.

NICOLE KING
University of Maryland at Baltimore County

Jeffrey Collins, "Once-Segregated South Carolina Beach Town Fights to Survive," Associated Press (30 January 2009); Catherine H. Lewis, *Horry County, South Carolina, 1730–1993* (1998); Barbara F. Stokes, *Myrtle Beach: A History, 1900–1980* (2007); Will Moredock, *Banana Republic: A Year in the Heart of Myrtle Beach* (2003).

Big Bend National Park

According to Indian legend, when the Great Spirit had finished making the Earth he dumped all of the leftover rocks in what is now Big Bend country. Sometime later, yet still over a hundred years ago, a Mexican cowboy described Big Bend country as a place "where the rainbows wait for the rain, and the big river is kept in a stone box, and water runs uphill and mountains float in the air, except at night when they go away to play with other mountains."

What is now Big Bend National Park sits on the U.S.-Mexican border along the Rio Grande and covers 801,000 isolated acres of southwestern Texas wilderness. The Rio Grande, the Chihuahuan Desert, and the Chisos Mountains constitute the three distinct geological divisions within the park—Big Bend often considered to be "three parks in one"—and because of these diverse areas the park's climate is one of extremes. Altitudes range from 1,800 at the river to over 7,800 feet in the Chisos Mountains (highest point is Emory Peak at 7,832 feet, which is accessible by hiking trail). During the summer months, ground temperatures in the Chihuahuan Desert can reach a sweltering 180 degrees, but winters are normally mild, with temperatures hovering around a balmy 80 degrees. Because of the harsh summer climate, most hiking and camping in Big Bend is done between the months of November and April.

Average rainfall in the Chisos Mountains reaches 20 inches, creating a vast diversity between plant and animal life in the mountains and on the desert floor. Because of the range's relative isolation, several species of plants and animals can be found only in the Chisos Mountains, making the park a nature lover's paradise. Cacti and wildflowers carpet the desert, and the flora changes to grasslands as one approaches the mountains. As the elevation continues to increase, taller plant life such as the evergreen sumac, mountain mahogany, and the Texas marone replace leafy shrubs and bushes. In all, Big Bend is home to more than 1,200 species of plants (including pink and blue bluebonnets, yucca flowers, lechuguillas, and 60 species of cacti), 3,600 species of insects, 450 species of birds, 75 species of mammals, and 67 species of amphibians and reptiles. Animals include panthers, Mexican black bears, kangaroo rats, jackrabbits, roadrunners, rattlesnakes, tarantulas, and coyotes. Summer tanagers, painted buntings, vermillion flycatchers, sandpipers, killdeers, golden eagles, and cliff swallows attract birdwatchers from across the globe.

The Rio Grande forms 118 miles of border between the United States and Mexico through the Chihuahuan Desert. The name of the park is derived from the U-turn the river takes on its border, redirecting the river's southeasterly flow northeastward, and the flow of the river varies between a languid current perfect for floating downstream and intense white-water rapids. (Those who chose to navigate the Lower Canyon of the Rio Grande are required by the National Park Service to sign an Assumption of Risks and Agreements of Release and Indemnity form.)

Popular scenic canyons made by the river long ago include the Santa Elena Canyon, Mariscal Canyon, and Boquillas Canyon, and garfish and turtles that live in the river illustrate the evolutionary record that extends back 50,000 years when the area was a lush, swamplike savannah.

Big Bend, because of it remoteness, is one of the least-visited national parks in the United States, attracting only 300,000 to 350,000 visitors annually. The entrance to the park at Persimmon Gap lies 70 miles from the nearest town. It is, however, one of the largest parks in the National Park System. It is popular with adventurous hikers and backpackers and offers more than 150 miles of trails for day hikes and backpacking. Some of the most popular trails include the Chimneys Trail, Marufo Veg Trail, Outer Mountain Loop, and Dodson Trail. Other attractions include the Santa Elena Canyon and Mule Ears Peaks, two impressive rock towers seemingly thrust upward from the middle of the desert floor.

JAMES G. THOMAS JR.
University of Mississippi

Arthur R. Gómez, *A Most Singular Country: A History of Occupation in the Big Bend* (1990); John Jameson, *The Story of Big Bend National Park* (1996); J. O. Langford with Fred Gipson, *Big Bend: A Homesteader's Story* (1952); Ross A. Maxwell, *The Big Bend of the Rio Grande: A Guide to the Rocks, Landscape, Geologic History, and Settlers of the Area of Big Bend National Park* (1968).

Blue Ridge Parkway

The most popular unit within the U.S. National Park Service system, the Blue Ridge Parkway annually records more than 16 million visitors. The focal point of this linear park is a 469-mile stretch of two-lane, landscaped road that traverses the crests of the Blue Ridge Mountains and adjoining ranges. The parkway was constructed to accommodate tourist driving and to encourage recreational enjoyment of southern Appalachia. While used for local transportation, the parkway attracts millions of visitors who travel considerable distances for a range of recreational opportunities. In addition to showcasing the region's natural beauty via scenic vistas and overlooks, the parkway provides access to hiking trails, picnic areas, campgrounds (for recreational vehicles as well as tent camping), and bodies of water—streams, rivers, ponds, and man-made lakes—for fishing and boating. Although no admission fees are charged for its use, the parkway is closed to commercial vehicles. All cars are required to observe a strictly enforced speed limit (generally 45-miles-per-hour, though slower speeds are posted in some sections).

The parkway was not the first tourist road planned for the Blue Ridge. In 1909 Colonel Joseph Hyde Pratt, attempting to capitalize on the growing popularity of automobiles in the United States, proposed a ridge-top toll road in a section of North Carolina's and Georgia's Blue Ridge. When World War I forced cancellation of the project, only one short segment of that road had been constructed (near Pineola, N.C.).

In the 1920s, growing out of the national trend toward constructing scenic parkways, a federally constructed tourist

road, Skyline Drive, was built in the recently designated Shenandoah National
Park, located in the northern Virginia
Blue Ridge. By the mid-1930s, another
tourist road—originally called the
Appalachian Scenic Highway but soon
renamed the Blue Ridge Parkway—was
designated to connect Skyline Drive/
Shenandoah National Park with another
newly established Appalachian park to
the south: Great Smoky Mountains National Park. When completed, the Blue
Ridge Parkway would enable tourists to
travel between the two national parks
through rural and at times undeveloped
mountain landscapes without the visual
interference of billboards and other
manifestations of modern, commercial
civilization. Another justification for the
parkway was that it would provide economic relief to Depression-era residents
of the Blue Ridge region.

Given its length and the difficulties
of land acquisition and road construction, the parkway, begun on 11 September 1935, took 52 years to complete.
The upper part of the road coursed
through Virginia, while North Carolina won the bid over Tennessee for
the parkway's lower route. Necessary
rights-of-way were obtained by the government through the voluntary sale of
properties by landowners or through
the exercising of eminent domain laws.
Three Depression-era federal programs—the Civilian Conservation
Corps, the Works Progress Administration, and the Emergency Relief Administration—channeled funds for the
employment of laborers to work on the
parkway's roadbed, landscaping, and
recreational facilities.

The parkway begins at the southern
terminus of Skyline Drive near Waynes-
boro, Va., and courses 355 miles southward along the crest of the Blue Ridge
range, at which point the road veers
southwestward for more than 100 miles
across such other mountain ranges
as the Blacks, the Great Craggies, the
Pisgah Ledge, the Great Balsams, and
the Plott Balsams. The parkway ends
near Cherokee, N.C., at the eastern
entrance to the Great Smoky Mountains
National Park.

Internationally renowned as a
masterpiece of engineering and design, the parkway incorporates banked
curves, extensive landscaping intended
to create a "natural" appearance, and
intricate stone masonry in many of the
parkway's tunnels, bridges, and viaducts. In the last-completed section
of the parkway—a short stretch over
Grandfather Mountain—is the Linn
Cove Viaduct, a state-of-the-art suspen-
sion bridge that has become the parkway's most photographed feature.

The parkway encompasses or borders a number of popular tourist destinations. In Virginia are the exhibition of
historical Appalachian farm buildings
at Humpback Rocks, the James River/
Kanawha Canal, the Peaks of Otter,
Mabry Mill (an often photographed
waterwheel gristmill), and the Blue
Ridge Music Center (a museum and
concert venue for interpreting and promoting regional music). Sites of interest
along the parkway's North Carolina section include Doughton Park,
Moses H. Cone Memorial Park, Julian
Price Park, Linville Falls, the Museum
of North Carolina Minerals, Craggy

Gardens, the Folk Art Center (an outlet for the exhibition and sale of regional crafts), Mount Pisgah (formerly part of the adjacent Biltmore Estate), and the Shining Rock Wilderness Area (a popular area for backpacking).

While the majority of campers, hikers, anglers, and bicyclists enjoy the Blue Ridge Parkway between May and late October, the road remains in use during colder months, though particular sections may be closed to vehicles in the wake of storm-related damage.

TED OLSON
East Tennessee State University

Leonard M. Adkins, *Walking the Blue Ridge: A Guide to the Trails of the Blue Ridge Parkway* (2006); Ted Olson, *Blue Ridge Folklife* (1998); Tim Pegram, *The Blue Ridge Parkway by Foot: A Park Ranger's Memoir* (2007); Anne Mitchell Whisnant, *Super-Scenic Motorway: A Blue Ridge Parkway History* (2006).

Bowden, Bobby

(b. 1929) COLLEGE FOOTBALL COACH.

The legendary football coach of the Florida State University Seminoles, Bobby Bowden ranks at or near, along with Joe Paterno, the top of the list of all-time winningest coaches in Division I collegiate football history.

Robert Cleckleer "Bobby" Bowden was born on 8 November 1929 in Birmingham, Ala. At 13, Bowden was bedridden for six months with rheumatic fever. Listening to radio broadcasts made him a fan of Crimson Tide football. He recovered and excelled at football, earning All State honors in

1948 at Woodlawn High School. With a scholarship to the University of Alabama he hoped to play quarterback, but he eloped in 1949 to marry his high school sweetheart, Ann Estock. In 1952, he transferred to Howard College and earned All-America honors. He was a member of Pi Kappa Alpha fraternity and graduated in 1953.

Bowden remained with the Bulldogs as an assistant coach at Howard College, 1954–55, and moved to South Georgia Junior College, 1956–58, before landing the head coach job at Howard College (now Samford University). From 1959 to 1962, Bowden posted a 31–6 record as coach of his alma mater. Bowden next went to Florida State University as the wide receivers coach under Bill Peterson, and then he went to West Virginia in 1965. Bowden served as offensive coordinator for four seasons before taking over the head coaching responsibilities in 1970. In six seasons, from 1970 to 1975, he coached the West Virginia Mountaineers to a 42–26 mark.

At 46 years old, Bowden accepted the head coach position at Florida State University in 1976. Within four years, a team that had won only four games over the previous three seasons was propelled to an 11–1 record in 1979. That team fell short of the national championship with a loss at the Orange Bowl.

From 1987–2000 Bowden's Seminoles finished the season ranked in the top five. During those 14 seasons Florida State was 152–18–1 and earned the national championship titles in 1993 and 1999. Bowden's teams also played in the championship game at three other bowl games over that stretch.

Since joining the Atlantic Coast Conference in 1992, Bowden won the conference title 12 times. Bowden was named conference coach of the year in 1993 and 1997. The field at Doak Campbell Stadium in Tallahassee was named for him in 2004.

Coach Bowden enjoyed recruiting, and his personal magnetism attracted talented players to FSU. Two Heisman trophy winners played under Bowden: quarterbacks Charlie Ward in 1993 and Chris Weinke in 1999. Twenty-four Seminoles were been named consensus All-Americans. Moreover, during his tenure 28 players were selected in the first round of the NFL draft. Since 1993, more than 100 Seminoles have been drafted into the pros.

Bowden is an iconic figure of college football. As a coach he enjoyed the limelight and the prestige he earned. He easily fielded the questions of the press, charmed football fans at speaking engagements, and enjoyed attention at public functions.

With a 33–21 win over West Virginia in the 2010 Gator Bowl, Bobby Bowden coached his final game as FSU head coach. His record as a head coach ended at 389 wins, 129 loses, and 4 ties.

LLEWELLYN D. COOK
Jacksonville State University

Mike Bynum, *Bound for Glory: The Horatio Alger Story of FSU's Bobby Bowden* (1980); Mike Freeman, *Bowden: How Bobby Bowden Forged a Football Dynasty* (2009).

Bryant, Paul "Bear"

(1913–1983) FOOTBALL COACH.
Born 11 September 1913 to a sharecropping family in Moro Bottom, Ark., Paul "Bear" Bryant became the most successful college football coach in history. The youngest of 11 children of Wilson Monroe and Ida Kilgore Bryant, Paul Bryant was born on a farm and sold farm goods to help his invalid father and his mother. At age 12 he earned his nickname by fighting a bear at the Lyric Theater in Fordyce, Ark. He played football for the Fordyce High School Red Bugs and received a football scholarship to the University of Alabama, where he played end.

Bryant was an assistant coach at the University of Alabama and at Vanderbilt University, then served two years in the U.S. Navy during World War II. He was head coach at Maryland, Kentucky, Texas A&M, and Alabama. After coaching his last game in the Liberty Bowl in Memphis, Tenn., in December of 1982, Bryant had a record 323 victories. He died in January 1983, and his funeral was one of the largest in southern history, with an estimated 500,000 people turning out to see the funeral procession from Tuscaloosa to the Birmingham burial site.

Bryant was one of the modern South's preeminent mythic figures. A product of the rural poverty so typical of the South in his youth, Bryant rose to national success. The Bear Bryant story is a rags-to-riches American tale, told in the southern vernacular. In his origins, Bryant symbolized the poor sharecropping South, but he became a middle-class hero to well-off southerners who made football a part of their lifestyles.

During Bryant's early years at Alabama, he was the center of controversy. In 1963 *Saturday Evening Post* accused

Paul "Bear" Bryant, University of Alabama football coach, 1970s (Courtesy of the Paul W. Bryant Museum/University of Alabama)

Bryant of involvement in a scheme to throw a game. A jury trial exonerated him, but the national press followed this episode with charges Bryant encouraged unnecessary violence on the field. His coaching success and sheer longevity led to fundamental changes in his reputation by the 1970s. Sportswriters created a legend about Bryant with their stories of his toughness, generosity, compassion, shrewdness, and democratic egalitarianism. "Generations from now they will speak in hushed tones about the backwoodsy man from Fordyce whom the city slickers couldn't beat," wrote Memphis sportswriter Al Dunning when Bryant died. The *New Yorker* magazine referred to him as an "actual genius." Observers compared him with Douglas MacArthur, John Wayne, and, most frequently, George Patton.

Although he was a national figure,

southerners felt a special claim on Bryant. He was most admired in the South because he was a winning leader. For a people whose heroes sometimes symbolized lost causes, Bryant was a change. The Bryant legend was not just one of power and victory. Observers stressed his character and class, his concern for making athletes decent people. In his early career there were recruiting scandals and stories of his meanness, but these were forgotten when sportswriters began his apotheosis in the 1970s. The Bryant legend embodied aspects of earlier regional mythology — the New South hope of education transforming the region; the fighting South, with football as Celtic sublimation; and the Jeffersonian agrarian dream with Bryant as wise rural rustic. The Bryant legend is part of the Sports South myth, which views sports as central to the modern southern identity. Bryant was slow to recruit black athletes in the 1960s, and some observers saw him as the sports equivalent of another Alabamian of the era, George Wallace. But he later became one of the first Deep South coaches to recruit black athletes, seeing his need for their talents to remain competitive. He ironically came to embody the hope for a biracial South, in which southern blacks and whites, working together, will achieve great things off the football field as well as on it.

CHARLES REAGAN WILSON
University of Mississippi

Birmingham News Staff, *Remembering Bear* (1983); Andy Doyle, in *The Sporting World of the Modern South*, ed. Patrick B. Miller (2002); Keith Dunnavant, *Coach: The Life of Paul "Bear" Bryant* (1996); James Peterson and Bill Cromartie, *Bear Bryant: Count-down to Glory* (1984); Charles Reagan Wilson, *South Atlantic Quarterly* (Summer 1987).

Busch Gardens

Busch Gardens Tampa, one of several Florida theme parks, is Tampa's most popular tourist attraction and a leading example of urban-based amusement venues in the South. When Busch Gardens opened in 1959, it encompassed 15 acres of vegetation, birds, and limited amusements adjacent to a brewery that tourists and local residents could visit for no charge. The original gardens evolved into an elaborate African themed park that attracted more than four million visitors annually at the height of its popularity.

August A. Busch Jr., the chairman of the board and president of Anheuser Busch, sought a southeastern location for a brewery. Busch was familiar with the Tampa area because the St. Louis Cardinals, the major league baseball team that he owned, held its spring training in St. Petersburg. Busch initially purchased 152 acres and then expanded its holdings to 265 acres in late 1965, and eventually to its present size of 335 acres. During its first several years, Busch Gardens attracted about 1.5 million visitors annually, more than any other attraction in Florida. It included a hospitality house overseeing a lagoon where visitors could enjoy complementary glasses of Budweiser.

Busch Gardens opened a monorail in 1966 to carry passengers above its newly created Wild Animal Kingdom, recreating the African Veldt. The area included several animal species found in Africa, such as chimps, lions, rhinos, cheetahs, and elephants. In 1970, when Disney was about to open its Orlando facility, Busch decided to compete. He announced to expand Busch Gardens and charge admission for the first time.

Busch Gardens added several different sections including Nairobi, Serengeti, Stanleyville, Congo, and Timbuktu. The park also included a large amphitheater and a movie theater. In late 1975, advertising for Busch Gardens emphasized the African theme and branded the park as "The Dark Continent." Advertisements included such headlines as "The Best Part of a Florida Vacation Is Spending a Day in Africa" and "Instead of a Zoo, We Created a Continent." According to the general manager, the "Dark Continent" offered visitors "a place where the entire family can step back in time and relive the misery, intrigue and adventure associated with big game, native folklore and classic feature films made on location in Africa." Eventually, "The Dark Continent" was dropped and the name Busch Gardens Tampa Bay was adopted. Starting in 2006, visitors entered Busch Gardens Africa, a brand introduced to correspond with the Anheuser-Busch park in Williamsburg, Va., whose name was changed to Busch Gardens Europe.

In addition to its several types of rides, animals, elaborate vegetation, and a variety of shows, Busch Gardens offers roller coasters. Its first roller coaster, the Python, opened in 1976. The Scorpion followed in the Timbuktu area in 1980. Kumba opened in 1993, claiming to be the largest steel roller coaster in the

Southeast. Montu, an Egyptian-themed coaster, opened in 1996. Gwazi, the "Southeast's largest and fastest double wooden coaster," was completed in 1999. SheiKra was introduced in 2005, billed as North America's first dive coaster.

Busch Gardens has been positively recognized by theme park analysts and aficionados. *Forbes* magazine recognized it in 2005 as among the world's top-10 amusement parks. In 2000 *Forbes* reported that frequent riders of steel roller coasters voted Montu as their second favorite, and the Golden Ticket Awards presented by *Amusement Today* have several times recognized Montu as one of the country's top-10 steel roller coasters. Busch Gardens has also won several awards from the International Association of Amusement Parks and Attractions, including prizes for the quality of its entertainment and its landscaping.

Busch Gardens has played a significant role in Tampa's economy, consistently rated as the most important draw for tourists and a major employment generator. During the 1980s it ranked in the top-10 private-sector employers in Hillsborough County. The Busch brewery in Tampa closed in 1995. In mid-2008, Belgian brewer InBev NV acquired Anheuser-Busch, and the acquisition included the 10 Anheuser-Busch theme parks. In 2009 InBev sold all Busch properties to the Blackstone Group, which removed the last remaining traces of Anheuser-Busch ownership other than the name.

ROBERT KERSTEIN
University of Tampa

Dana Anderson, *Journal of Popular Culture* (Fall 1999); Ken Breslauer, *Roadside Paradise: The Golden Age of Florida's Tourist Attractions, 1929–1971* (2000); Mark Gottdiener, *The Theming of America: Dreams, Media Fantasies, and Themed Environments* (2001); Karen Haymon Long, *Tampa Tribune* (27 January 2002); Gary Mormino, *Land of Sunshine, State of Dreams: A Social History of Modern Florida* (2005).

Case, Everett

(1900–1966) COLLEGE BASKETBALL COACH.

Indiana native Everett N. Case helped bring basketball insanity to North Carolina. Hired by North Carolina State in 1946, he successfully transplanted Indiana's high school basketball mania to North Carolina at the college level through a combination of aggressive on-the-court play, successful teams, and tremendous promotional abilities. His legacy includes his name on the ACC tournament MVP trophy, the popularity of that conference tournament, and the tradition of cutting down nets after great wins.

When N.C. State hired him on the recommendation of renowned coach Chuck Taylor, Case already held a record of 726–75, including four Indiana state championships. After a trip to Raleigh, Case sensed that the university and the area were ripe for basketball madness. His 1946–47 team, nearly all from Indiana and, like Case, fresh out of the service, was an instant success. The 1946–47 running and pressing "Hoosier Hotshots" won the Southern Conference tournament and received a bid to the NIT. State lost in the regional semifinal to Kentucky—coached by Adolph Rupp. It was the only meeting of these titans of college basketball.

In the fall of 1949, the new 12,000-seat William Neal Reynolds Coliseum opened, the largest arena on the East Coast at the time. Case took immediate advantage of the coliseum, inaugurating the Dixie Classic tournament during Christmas week that same year. Matching the Big Four schools of UNC, Duke, Wake Forest, and host State against four of the nation's top programs, the tournament instantly became a success.

Case's teams went on to win 45 games in a row in Southern Conference play and remained undefeated in six tournaments. State continued its dominance in the new Atlantic Coast Conference, winning the first three ACC titles. Case's success motivated other schools to upgrade their programs. UNC brought in Frank McGuire after his St. John's Redmen beat Case twice in one year. Wake Forest hired Bones McKinney, and Duke hired one of Case's boys, Vic Bubbas. These fine coaches, as well as problems in Case's locker room, made the 1955–56 team the last truly dominant State team for nearly two decades.

Recruiting violations, a national cheating scandal, and his own health hounded Case's second decade at State. Case recognized the importance of recruiting early on, running afoul of Indiana high school officials. At State, the program suffered a one-year, then a four-year probation—at that time the longest ever handed out by the NCAA—primarily for the then-common prac-

tices of holding tryouts and paying travel expenses of recruits.

If Case continually tested the NCAA recruiting rules, he was proactive in fighting gambling corruption. Revelations that gamblers were bribing college players, especially in the area around New York City, rocked the nation in 1951. Case brought in agents of the FBI and the N.C. State Bureau of Identification to warn players about being involved with gamblers. In 1961 the scandal broke anew, again in New York City. The web of money and point shaving soon entangled players at both State and Carolina. Three State players admitted taking money from gamblers. The penalty for both universities was a deemphasis of college basketball in order to lessen its allure for gamblers. Games were limited to 18, geographic restricts were placed on scholarships, and the Dixie Classic was ended.

Two years later Case's declining health took a turn for the worse. Over the course of the 1962–63 season, he suffered from shingles and gout and finally had gall bladder surgery. Confident that the next year's squad would be one of his best, he attempted to coach one more year, but after the second game of the year, a close loss at Wake Forest, his declining health forced him to retire. Pete Maravich took over the team, which won the ACC tournament, defeating the heavily favored Duke.

Everett Case died in his home in Raleigh on 30 April 1966 of heart disease related to myeloma. Of the 57 young men he coached, 23 returned to Raleigh for the funeral. His will divided his estate among all the boys who had played for him.

Case left a legacy of success. He was 397–135 at State, with six straight conference championships and 10 in all. Case was an innovative coach who brought new techniques to the game—charting, game films, and scouting. His up-tempo offense and aggressive defense changed the game of college basketball and attracted fans. State led the nation in on-campus attendance seven years in a row. The legacy of all the Big Four coaches of this era, particularly Case, is the premier college basketball conference in the country.

PAUL R. BEEZLEY
Jacksonville State University

Casinos, Mississippi

During the late 20th century, casino gambling, previously restricted to Las Vegas, Nev., and Atlantic City, N.J., spread rapidly across the nation. In the states of the old Confederacy, Indian bands developed casinos in North Carolina, Mississippi, Florida, and Alabama. Louisiana and Arkansas have "racinos" that operate at dog and horse tracks. Mississippi and Louisiana adopted the "riverboat" approach.

Of all the places taking advantage of this new wave of gambling in the South, by far the most successful are two spots in Mississippi—the Gulf Coast and Tunica County, just south of Memphis. Politicians from these regions collaborated to secure casino legislation in 1990. Both parts of the state were in dire need of economic revitalization in the 1980s. The Delta had long been one of the poorest parts of the nation, and the resort communities on the Gulf Coast had entered a period of relative decline.

The initiative to legalize casinos in Mississippi began in the late 1980s. Supporters chose a low-key strategy. Rather than styling their bill as a statewide revenue measure that would require a 60 percent vote, they crafted it as local legislation for specific counties. Thus, as local legislation requiring only a simple majority vote, the casino bill slipped through and was signed by Governor Ray Mabus in spring 1990. Fortunately for the casino advocates, the attention of antigambling forces was focused on defeating a statewide lottery bill pending in the same session.

Casino opponents launched lawsuits to overturn the new law, but they were unsuccessful. Soon, several coastal counties and Delta counties authorized gambling. On 1 August 1992, Isle of Capri in Biloxi was the first to open. Within two years more than two dozen casinos had commenced operation although some soon moved or closed.

Tunica County's position near Memphis ensured that it would be the principal locus of Delta casinos. Though even closer to Memphis, the voters of DeSoto County spurned casinos. There was an early shakeout period during which small dockside operations folded while well-financed big barges with adjacent hotels came to dominate the market. In 1992 there were only 16 hotel rooms in all of Tunica County. By 2000 there were 6,000 rooms with more on the way, and Tunica had become the nation's third largest gaming center. In 2004 the county boasted some 14,000 slot machines and more than 400 tables in more than a half million square feet of gaming space. By that time nine casinos were well established with Sam's Town, Hollywood, Horseshoe, and the Grand (now Harrah's) dominant.

A similar pattern of early small operators followed by bigger establishments emerged along the Gulf Coast. On the eve of Hurricane Katrina, the dominant coastal properties with large hotels and big-name entertainment were Grand-Biloxi, Grand-Gulfport (now Island View), Imperial Palace (now IP), and, most notably, the luxurious 1,740-room Beau Rivage.

On 29 August 2005 the storm surge from Hurricane Katrina devastated the casinos along the coastal beaches and seriously damaged the back bay properties as well. Katrina proved that floating barges were too vulnerable on the hurricane-prone coast, so the legislature, anxious to restore jobs and preserve tax revenue, amended casino law to allow casinos to relocate up to 800 feet from shore. Three casinos did not rebuild, but the other properties, including Isle, IP, Grand, and Beau Rivage, soon remodeled and resumed operation. The Hard Rock, which had been under construction when the storm hit, finally opened over a year later.

Although much smaller in scale than those near Tunica and on the Gulf Coast, several casinos operate in the southern river region at Vicksburg, Greenville, Lulu, and Natchez.

Two important decisions were key to the success of Mississippi's casinos. First, the bill drafters opted for Las Vegas–style gambling with strong regulations to guarantee the integrity of the games but with relatively low taxes, no limit on the number of casinos, and very few operational restrictions. This gave Mississippi operators a distinct competitive advantage over casino boats in Iowa, Missouri, Illinois, and Louisiana, which were beset with higher taxes and stiffer regulations such as required cruising and loss limits.

The second important provision in the law allowed flexibility in the type and placement of the floating casinos. The image of "riverboat" casinos is one of tourists gambling on modern replicas of 19th-century sternwheelers, but the Mississippi legislation set no such requirements on casino appearance. Most Mississippi casinos developed the technique of surrounding huge barges with land-based lobbies, shops, and hotels to create the effect of one large building even though the actual gaming floor was technically floating. Tunica County developers dug ditches as "tributaries" of the Mississippi so that their barges could float in shallow manmade lagoons well back from the edge of the river.

From an economic standpoint, Mississippi casinos were successful even beyond the vision of the legislators who authorized gambling in 1990. Ten years later, only Nevada and New Jersey derived more tax revenue from gaming. Tunica County and the coastal gaming counties built new schools, roads, and other public facilities. In 2004 the state's 29 nontribal casinos employed nearly 30,000 with a payroll of $885 million and served 8–12 million customers, more than three-quarters of whom were from out of state. The incredible growth that Mississippi casinos experienced in the 1990s has slowed because of increased competition from surrounding states. But thanks to a good head start and a continued favorable regulatory and tax environment, the Mississippi casino industry continues to exhibit steady, if slowed, growth.

BRADLEY R. RICE
Clayton State University

Denise von Herrmann, ed., *Resorting to Casinos: The Mississippi Gambling Industry* (2006), *The Big Gamble: The Politics of Lottery and Casino Expansion* (2002); Steve Bourie, *American Casino Guide 2009* (2008).

Christmas

The first celebration of Christmas in North America was likely by the Spanish in the 1500s, and it certainly took place in the South, although whether in Florida or the Southwest is unknown. The first recorded commemoration of Christmas in the British colonies on the mainland was in Jamestown, Va., in 1607. About 40 of the original 100 colonists, unsure of their survival, gathered in a primitive wooden chapel for a somber day. Until well into the 19th century, the Protestants of New England looked with suspicion upon Christmas as a "popish" day, but southerners generally encouraged a joyous celebration.

Gentleman farmers, in particular, regarded the day more as a time of relaxation and social activity than as a religious holiday. They preserved such European customs as caroling, burning the Yule log, and decorating with greenery. But the environment worked to make a distinctive festival.

Native seafood and turkey replaced the traditional European dishes of beef and goose. White southerners added regional touches such as eating fried oysters, drinking eggnog with rum, and going on a Christmas morning hunt for foxes or other small game. Pines replaced European firs and cedars for the Christmas tree, and Spanish moss was used as a primitive "angel hair" for decorating in the Deep South. The poinsettia became a custom in 1825 when a Charleston man with that name brought a red flower back from Mexico as a gift, and others were soon decorating with poinsettias.

The French in Louisiana introduced the tradition of Christmas fireworks, setting off firecrackers and firing rifles. Until the World War I era, southerners rarely used fireworks on the Fourth of July but did punctuate the Christmas holiday with them. A long-standing Cajun custom is the Christmas Eve bonfires, known as *feux de joie* (fires of joy), burning all night along the Mississippi River from Baton Rouge to New Orleans.

Three southern states were the first in the nation to make Christmas a legal holiday—Louisiana and Arkansas in 1831 and Alabama in 1836. The plantation was the center for the most elaborate and distinctive antebellum southern celebration of Christmas. In backcountry rural areas, plantation houses became the scene of sometimes-extravagant Christmas partying, eating, and playing, including the morning hunt. For slaves, Christmas had special meaning. December was a slow work month on the typical plantation, and it became the social season for them. The slaves' holiday lasted from Christmas to New Year's Day. The setting off of fireworks became a noted custom among the slaves as well as the whites. The end of Christmas at the New Year saw a more somber mood often settle among slaves as slave hiring and contracts often turned over, sometimes resulting in slave auctions and family separations.

Christmas as currently celebrated, in broad outline, was an invention of the 19th-century Victorians, who sentimentalized the day and made it the focus for new traditions. By the 1930s the celebration of Christmas had become even more secular than before, with the exchange of gifts for adults and Santa Claus for children. The religious aspects of Christmas were played down by the Victorians, but by the mid-20th century this dimension had become stronger. Some Protestant churches even imitate, in modified manner, the Catholic midnight Eucharist. In Jewish communities the festival of Hanukkah has expanded and absorbed many of the characteristics of Christmas.

Christmas has become the holiday par excellence in the South as elsewhere in the United States. Merchants begin to prepare for it and to advertise their offerings long before Halloween. The Santa Claus parades come early in December, if not sooner, and parties are given throughout the month. Fireworks, the antebellum custom, are still seen. Christmas trees adorn the streets, and one southern state, North Carolina, is a national leader in the number of trees harvested and first in terms of dollars made per tree. Christmas pro-

grams and music are the fare on television and radio. Cards and presents flood the post offices. Charities set up stalls on street corners and with ringing of bells summon passersby to make contributions. Churches, of course, have special services. A few southern families make some effort to celebrate the 12 days culminating on 6 January, a day sometimes called "Old Christmas" (which is perhaps a faint recollection of when Britain adopted the Gregorian calendar in 1752, changing the celebration of Christmas from the 6 January date on the Julian calendar). In New Orleans the season of Carnival officially begins with Twelfth Night parties on the eve of Old Christmas. Many communities now sponsor candlelight tours of historic places at Christmas, reinforcing the holiday's ties to the idea of tradition itself.

ALLEN CABANISS
University of Mississippi

William M. Auld, *Christmas Traditions* (1968); John E. Baur, *Christmas on the American Frontier* (1961); Emyl Jenkins, *Southern Christmas* (1995); Harnett T. Kane, *The Southern Christmas Book: The Full Story from the Earliest Times to the Present: People, Customs, Conviviality, Carols, Cooking* (1958); Joanne B. Young, *Christmas in Williamsburg* (1970).

Cobb, Ty

(1886–1961) BASEBALL PLAYER.
Tyrus Raymond "Ty" Cobb, arguably the greatest of all professional baseball players and the first nationally known southern player, was born on 19 December 1886 in Banks County, Ga. His father was William Herschel

Cobb, an itinerant schoolmaster who, after moving his family to Royston in Franklin County, Ga., served as state senator, county school superintendent, and editor of the local newspaper. His mother, Amanda Chitwood Cobb, was the daughter of a prominent Banks County landowner.

Tyrus Cobb showed early signs of being an intelligent, hard-driving youngster, impatient with his own and others' shortcomings. Skinny but fast and well coordinated, he starred on the town baseball team and acquired a burning ambition to pursue the game professionally. That ambition clashed with the wishes of his equally strong-willed father, who intended his elder son to be a lawyer, physician, or career military man. Finally, Tyrus won W. H. Cobb's permission to try out with the Augusta team in the South Atlantic League. Although he was a failure at Augusta in 1904, Cobb came back the next year to lead the league in hitting and thus gained the attention of major league scouts. The 18-year-old Cobb was about to join the Detroit Tigers in the American League when he learned that his father had been shot to death by his mother, who claimed she had mistaken him for a prowler.

Arriving in Detroit late in August 1905, "Ty" Cobb (as sportswriters soon dubbed him) finished that season with the Tigers. The next spring, while his mother was tried and acquitted on a charge of voluntary manslaughter, young Cobb struggled to gain a regular place on the Detroit ball club. It was, he said long afterward, "the most miserable and humiliating experience I've

ever been through." Cobb was subjected to the customary harassments and petty cruelties that rookies usually had to endure in that day. But as a sensitive, troubled young man, a proud southerner among ballplayers who were mainly Irish-American northerners, Cobb reacted strongly against such treatment and ended up a friendless loner on the Detroit team. The death of his father and his painful early experiences with his teammates largely account for why he became, as he later described himself, "a snarling wildcat," driven to prove himself to everybody, including himself, season after season and game after game.

Prove himself he did. In 1907 Cobb won the American League batting title, in the course of leading the Tigers to the first of three straight league championships. For 11 of the next 12 years he outhit everyone in the American League and frequently led as well in runs scored and bases stolen. Unquestionably the top star of baseball's "dead-ball" era, Cobb remained an outstanding player after the advent of the "lively ball" in 1920 and the emergence of the power-oriented style of baseball heralded by Babe Ruth's home run exploits. From 1921 through 1926 Cobb managed the Detroit team and continued to play the outfield; his final two years as a baseball player were with Connie Mack's Philadelphia Athletics. He retired with an astonishing lifetime batting average of .367 and some 42 other records.

Already a millionaire by the time he hung up his uniform, Cobb ultimately built his personal fortune to $10 million. A man who had quarreled and brawled with teammates, umpires, opposing players, spectators, and many people off the field, Cobb continued to be a hard man to get along with in his long years of retirement. In 1947 his marriage of 39 years to Charlie Marion Lombard Cobb, an Augusta native, ended in divorce, and nine years later a second marriage, to Frances Fairburn Cass Cobb of Buffalo, N.Y., came to a similar end. Moreover, he became estranged from his surviving three children. By the time of his own death from cancer on 17 July 1961, in Atlanta, few people remained whom Cobb could call his friends. His renown in baseball, however, remains undiminished.

CHARLES C. ALEXANDER
Ohio University

Charles C. Alexander, *Ty Cobb: Baseball's Fierce Immortal* (1984); Ty Cobb, with Al Stump, *My Life in Baseball: The True Record* (1993); John D. McCallum, *The Tiger Wore Spikes: An Informal Biography of Ty Cobb* (1956); Don Rhodes, *Ty Cobb: Safe at Home* (2008); Lawrence S. Ritter, *The Glory of Their Times: The Story of the Early Days of Baseball Told by Men Who Played It* (1974); Al Stump, *Cobb: A Biography* (1996).

Colonial Williamsburg

Something more ubiquitously American than uniquely southern permeates the air about Colonial Williamsburg. What appears to epitomize southern genteel traditions is more a slice of general Americana—a replica of history as all Americans might wish it had been—than a monument to the Tidewater aristocracy that bred generations of influential southerners.

The real Williamsburg, founded in 1699, appeared less tidy and behaved less decorously than today's bewigged guides would have the tourists believe. About 2,000 people lived permanently in what served Virginia more as a political and cultural mecca than as a trading center. At least half those residents were black, slaves who served the wishes of the other half. The pace of life shuffled along leisurely except during the "Publick Times"—generally held once each season during the 1700s, but daily fare for the interpretive 1900s—when either the provincial courts or legislatures held sessions. Williamsburg surged and ebbed to its own social tides through the colonial period, until 1781 when the capital was moved upriver to Richmond. Then, except for the frenzy of the Peninsula campaign in 1862, it declined into dormant insignificance.

Revival came at the hands of the local rector, W. A. R. Goodman, who convinced John D. Rockefeller Jr. to bequeath part of the family fortune to fund a restoration project. Work began in 1926, and by the 1930s buildings were being opened to the public. Rockefeller spent over $80 million in 40 years as 600 postcolonial structures were demolished, more than 80 existing period buildings restored, and replicas reconstructed over excavated foundations. His success spawned other restoration projects across the South, notably those in Salem and Savannah. Yet Williamsburg has persisted as the most popular "preserved" area. By the 1960s more than 15 million visitors had crowded the 130-acre site, and a second phase of restoration and reinterpretation was instituted to meet demand. Popularity peaked during the American Revolution Bicentennial.

A cultural commitment is explicit in the purpose behind Colonial Williamsburg—to interpret American history in light of acknowledged national values. John D. Rockefeller III, son of the restorer, said: "Colonial Williamsburg must help make history—not simply serve as a reminder of history." As such, there is more to the pristine atmosphere than a mere commercialization of a past regional graciousness. The guided tours stress less the lifestyles of the gentry than the values of liberty they came to hold. Journalist Bill Moyers has argued that in a place where "people lived routinely and seldom easily," more modern Americans, from all regions, find cultural significance from a presentation "too tidy to be real," but too encompassing to be missed. In 1994 Bill Moyers's comment proved all too true when a mock slave auction provoked the ire of black religious and civil rights groups, including the Virginia chapter of the Southern Christian Leadership Conference and the Virginia branch of the NAACP. Before the production, a small group of demonstrators gathered, accusing Colonial Williamsburg of sanitizing history, but the show went on nonetheless. After a moving dramatization of the horrors of slavery, at least one of the protest organizers retracted his objections to the production, claiming, "Pain had a face. Indignity had a body. Suffering had tears."

Colonial Williamsburg found itself in a fiscal decline during the late 1980s, throughout the 1990s, and into the 2000s, dropping in attendance from

1.1 million in 1985 to 707,000 in 2008. By 2006 the historic district was operating at a $36 million deficit. Because of waning of tourism dollars, the 2000s saw development encroach upon Colonial Williamsburg. In February 2007 developers announced that they were building more than 300 new homes on the historic Carr's Hill tract, and in December 2007 Colonial Williamsburg made the decision to sell Carter's Grove, a 750-acre plantation on the north shore of the James River, as well as a number of other landholdings.

GARY FREEZE
University of North Carolina at Chapel Hill

Richard Handler and Eric Gable, *The New History in an Old Museum: Creating the Past at Colonial Williamsburg* (1997); Rhys Isaac, *The Transformation of Virginia, 1740–1790* (1999); Robert P. Maccubbin, *Williamsburg, Virginia: A City before the State, 1699–1999* (2000); Marcus Whiffen, *The Public Buildings of Williamsburg, Colonial Capital of Virginia: An Architectural History* (1958); George Humphrey Yetter, *Williamsburg Before and After: The Rebirth of Virginia's Colonial Capital* (1988).

Daytona 500

The Daytona 500 is a 500-mile automobile race run annually in Daytona Beach, Fla., as the opening event in the NASCAR Sprint Cup Series (NSCS) championship season. Daytona sports one of the few beaches in the United States where the sand is packed hard enough to drive on, and auto racing on Daytona Beach itself dates back to the turn of the 20th century. But the modern history of the Daytona

500 dates to 22 February 1959, when the first 500-mile race was held at the newly opened Daytona International Speedway, the venue for the February season opener ever since.

Lee Petty, the father of Richard Petty, won the 1959 Daytona 500, and the track's history and that of the Petty clan have been closely aligned ever since. Son Richard won NASCAR's most prestigious race seven times. (Petty's record-setting 200th career win was also at Daytona but in the July race, not the 500.) Sociologist John Shelton Reed once pointed out that Petty is one of only three men known throughout the South as "The King," the others being Jesus and Elvis.

For more than a half century, the Daytona 500 has been NASCAR's biggest, richest, most prestigious event. The total purse for the 2008 race was $18,700,000, with $1,506,040 going to winner Ryan Newman of Indiana. Annual attendance at the event is not reported but is reliably estimated to be on the order of a quarter million fans.

The 1979 Daytona 500 was the first NASCAR championship race to be covered by live television. CBS viewers of the event witnessed one of the most spectacular finishes in the race's storied history. The two race leaders, Cale Yarborough and Donnie Allison, crashed in Turn Three of the final lap, allowing Richard Petty to shoot past for his sixth Daytona 500 victory. The excitement at the finish line was as nothing compared to the Yarborough-Allison fistfight that broke out in Turn Three.

Daytona 500 winners comprise a who's who of NASCAR. In addition to the Pettys, event winners have included such storied names in American racing as Junior Johnson, Fireball Roberts, Mario Andretti, Cale and LeeRoy Yarborough, A. J. Foyt, Bennie Parsons, Bobby Allison, Darrell Waltrip, Dale Earnhardt, and Jeff Gordon. Bobby Allison was 50 years old when he won the race in 1988, the oldest winner ever. Jeff Gordon was the youngest (age 25 years, 6 months) when he won his first Daytona 500 (of three) in 1997.

NASCAR has had a long if thin history of female competitors beginning with Sara Christian, who competed in NASCAR's inaugural season in 1949. But the only woman ever to compete in the Daytona 500 was Janet Guthrie in 1977. Guthrie was also the first woman to drive in the Indianapolis 500.

Twenty-four race car drivers have been killed at the Daytona track, but only one died in the Daytona 500 itself. Dale Earnhardt ("The Intimidator") was killed in a wreck on the last turn of the final lap of the 2001 event. (Eight other drivers have died in Daytona 500 practice runs or qualifying attempts.) Earnhardt's death was truly the end of a NASCAR era and stimulated widespread discussion about driver safety and NASCAR's role in assuring it. The only like event in recent memory that has had an equivalent impact on the popular culture was the death of Princess Diana (who, it seems appropriate to add, also perished in a high-speed automobile crash).

As part of its Bicentennial Celebration, in May 2001 the Library of Congress recognized the Daytona 500 as a "Local Legacy" of enduring historical and cultural significance. In the recognition ceremony, Florida congressman John Mica, remarked, "The Daytona 500 has become known as the Great American Race, and is a source of entertainment for countless Americans. . . . [Its] designation as a Local Legacy will help ensure that our future generations continue to appreciate [its] significance."

JIM WRIGHT
University of Central Florida

Ed Hinton, *Daytona: From the Birth of Speed to the Death of the Man in Black* (2002); Daytona 500 Web site: www.daytona 500.com; J. J. O'Malley, *The Daytona 500: 50 Years, the Great American Race* (2007); Bob Zeller, *Daytona 500: An Official History* (2002).

Dizzy Dean, Arkansas-born baseball player and sportscaster, 1930s (National Baseball Library, Cooperstown, N.Y.)

Dean, "Dizzy"

(1911–1974) BASEBALL PLAYER.

Jay Hanna "Dizzy" Dean, who was born in Lucas, Ark., in 1911, toiled in cotton fields all over the South as the son of a poor migratory farmer. Dean never advanced past the second grade. Enlistment in the army during the Great Depression gave him comparative stability and a nickname that lasted, "Dizzy."

Dean's return to civilian life brought him a contract in the far-reaching St. Louis Cardinal farm system and a quick advancement to the parent club. It was his first step en route to an eventual place in baseball's Hall of Fame. Dean's fastball became a feared weapon for the Cardinals. Many hitters knew what it was to be knocked down by a loud and proud Dean. A high-and-tight Dean fastball was described very accurately by the opposition as "high neck in."

The boldness of the flame-throwing Dean gained just as much attention as his pitching. His first employer, Branch Rickey, quickly learned this when he confronted Dean, telling the young pitcher he was quite a braggart. Dean's reply, quoted in dialect, was an unblinking "'Tain't braggin' if you kin really do it!" The combination of excellent pitching and colorful personality made Dean one of the sport's greatest gate attractions and, in turn, one of its wealthiest ballplayers. Yet, his eccentricities drove many crazy. In one game, troubled by an umpire's call and what he believed to be poor backing by his own team, he decided to lob the ball to opposing hitters.

One of many high points in Dean's career was the 1934 World Series. After winning the first game, he was put on a shortwave hookup to Antarctica to talk with famed explorer Admiral Richard E. Byrd. "Howdy, Dick Byrd," shouted Dean. In the fourth game of the Series, in a pinch-running role, he was flattened by an infielder's throw and carried off on a stretcher. He reported later, "They X-rayed my head and found nothing." The statement was used to full advantage by the press. Then, in the seventh and final game, he shut out the Detroit Tigers.

A broken toe, the result of a line drive during an all-star game, reduced Dean's efficiency considerably and led to an earlier retirement than desired. Dean had learned well, however, how to take advantage of his uniqueness and was soon entertaining people from the radio booth, doing play-by-play broadcasts. The hillbilly image was played to the hilt—and very profitably. A Dizzy Dean broadcast introduced such terms as slud, swang, press-peration, airs (errors), and spart (spirit), as well as players called Scorn (Skowron), Bearer (Berra), Mannul (Mantle), and Richison (Richardson), always intermingled with a very liberal sprinkling of "ain't." When his cornpone English brought protests from teachers, among others, Dean candidly assessed, "A lot of people who ain't saying ain't, ain't eating." If he had a favorite word, though, it was "I."

Wealthy and retired, Dean moved "down home" to the Ozarks to live out his life. He is buried in Wiggins, Miss., and the Dizzy Dean Museum, which is a part of the Mississippi Sports Hall of Fame, displays his memorabilia in Jackson, Miss.

JOHN E. DIMEGLIO
Mankato State University

Robert Gregory, *Diz: The Story of Dizzy Dean and Baseball during the Great Depression* (1993); John Heidenry, *The Gashouse Gang: How Dizzy Dean, Leo Durocher, Branch Rickey, Pepper Martin, and Their Colorful, Come-from-Behind Ball Club Won the World Series—and America's Heart—during the Great Depression* (2008); Curt Smith, *America's Dizzy Dean* (1978); Vince Staten, *Ol' Diz: A Biography of Dizzy Dean* (1992).

Disney World

Walt Disney World, near Orlando, Fla., is a vacation resort complex that ranks as one of the South's most popular holiday spots and draws nonsoutherners to the region as well. It includes three amusement parks (the Magic Kingdom, MGM Studios, and the Animal Kingdom), numerous hotels and resorts, campgrounds, golf courses, shopping centers, and the EPCOT Center (Experimental Prototype Community of Tomorrow). This complex, which opened in 1971, is on 25,000 acres of land (40 square miles, or twice the size of Manhattan Island) and, like a municipality, provides many of its own services. It represents the fruition of Walt Disney's ideas, which were first expressed in the opening of Disneyland, near Anaheim, Calif., in 1955.

Disneyland pioneered as the prototype theme park, but later parks, such as Six Flags over Georgia (Atlanta), Six Flags over Texas (Dallas), Opryland (Nashville), and even Dollywood (Pigeon Forge, Tenn.), which all borrowed heavily from Disney, focused on aspects of the past or present southern experience. Both Disneyland in California and Disney World in Florida originated ideas that relate to city planning and architecture, such as the extensive use of mass transit and the design of spaces to entertain people.

The Magic Kingdom, Disney World's first amusement park, covers 100 acres with activities — ranging from exhibits and rides to services such as restaurants — oriented around particular conceptual or historic themes. These themes come from Disney's perceptions of popular ideas about the American experience — and include small-town Midwest America about 1900 in Main Street USA, American history in Frontierland, the importance of technology in Tomorrowland, and literary and mythic figures and themes in Fantasyland. Despite their location in the South, few of these popularizations embodied in Disney World relate directly to the region, although in 2008 Disney World brought 17 million people to central Florida, making the park the most visited theme park in the world.

In 1982 Disney World opened its second theme park adjacent to the Magic Kingdom: EPCOT Center. The inspiration for EPCOT Center was the Experimental Prototype Community of Tomorrow, Walt Disney's idea of a utopian city of the future, a place where technology and machines improved quality of life, cars would travel underground, and alternate forms of transportation, such as the monorail, would operate efficiently above ground. The theme park took the ideals of a futuristic city and incorporated them into informative and educational rides. In addition to the world of the future, internationally themed rides, shops,

and restaurants, which highlight the individual cultures and traditions of 11 countries around the world, form a ring around a "lagoon" in the center of the park in anachronistic juxtaposition with the futuristic essence of the rest of the park. Eventually, as the future became the present, the future that Disney and the park's creators imagined has begun to seem dated, resembling science fiction more than the actual future. Today, the park is simply known as Epcot.

In 1989 Disney opened Disney-MGM Studios, a park modeled on the theme of a Hollywood motion-picture studio. Rides and live entertainment are based on famous films and Disney-produced pictures and television shows, such as *Toy Story*, *Playhouse Disney*, *Raiders of the Lost Ark* ("Indiana Jones Epic Stunt Spectacular!," a live-action production that includes a plot, several stunts, and a great deal of fire), and *Sunset Boulevard*. In 2007 Disney officials announced that the park's name would be rebranded as Disney's Hollywood Studios.

In 1998 Disney opened its fourth and largest single park: Animal Kingdom, a 500-acre, wildlife-themed park that contains a number of real-animal habitats, fictional African and Asian villages, international restaurants (such as the Restaurantosaurus and the Yak & Yeti), elaborate parades with Disney characters dressed in safari garb, thrill rides, and live stage productions of well-known Disney films, such as *Festival of the Lion King* and *Finding Nemo: The Musical*.

Most of the rides, shows, and performances throughout the parks are given by extremely sophisticated, computer controlled ("audio-animatronics") robots, appropriate perhaps to the high-technology of South Florida. These robots ensure identical presentations for each audience. Numerous forms of mass transit, ranging from a monorail to buses to horse-drawn wagons, move visitors around the parks and allow easy access to other parts of the resort. The parks have many other architectural and city planning features that make the experience pleasant for visitors as well as serving as models for what humanized technology can do.

Disney's graphics, architecture, and technology blend to create a "magic" aura where visitors can suspend their disbelief and enjoy themselves. The rides, robots, and attractions allow them to return for a moment to their own childhood and to relive the mythic origins of the nation. The parks, with their own versions of American history, folklore, and technology, serve as a unifying experience for the millions of Americans who have visited them. The parks provide a shared cultural experience, a common interpretation of history (albeit somewhat fantasized), and a vision of the future that results in greater cultural sameness among southerners as well as among other groups of Americans.

DAVID M. JOHNSON
North Carolina Agricultural and Technical State University

JAMES G. THOMAS JR.
University of Mississippi

Richard E. Foglesong, *Married to the Mouse: Walt Disney World and Orlando* (2003);

Carl Hiaasen, *Team Rodent: How Disney Devours the World* (1998); Margaret J. King, ed., *Journal of Popular Culture* (Summer 1981); David Koenig, *Realityland: True-Life Adventures at Walt Disney World* (2007); Jeff Kurtti, *Since the World Began: Walt Disney World, the First 25 Years* (1996); Charles Ridgway, *Spinning Disney's World: Memories of a Magic Kingdom Press Agent* (2007); Walt Disney Productions, *The Story of Walt Disney World* (1973).

Dogpatch USA

Dogpatch USA was an Arkansas theme park based on the popular and long-running Al Capp comic strip, *Li'l Abner*. Located in a remote and rugged area of the Ozarks, Dogpatch USA survived for about a quarter century, closing its gates for good in the early 1990s.

Inspired by the success of Branson's Silver Dollar City, which had opened in 1960, a group of businessmen in the small town of Harrison, Ark., about 40 miles south of Branson, formed Recreation Enterprises, Inc., for the purpose of founding their own tourist attraction. The Arkansas investors obtained permission from Capp to use his characters and allowed the Boston-based comic to invest in Recreation Enterprises, Inc. The result was Dogpatch USA, a theme park located on the site of an abandoned farming community known as Marble Falls, situated in a rural area 10 miles south of Harrison.

Capp flew in from Boston to attend the grand opening on 18 May 1968, and thousands of visitors got their first glimpses of the zany hillbilly denizens of Dogpatch—Li'l Abner and the Yokums, Daisy Mae and the Scraggses, Lone-

Arkansas governor Orval Faubus and his wife beneath the statue of Gen. Jubilation T. Cornpone near the entrance of Dogpatch USA (Photograph courtesy of Special Collections, University of Arkansas Libraries, Fayetteville)

some Polecat, Hairless Joe, and a massive statue of Gen. Jubilation T. Cornpone, the town's Civil War hero, at the entrance to the park. They also got to see the saggy-roofed log buildings that local workers had constructed to resemble the slovenly dwellings of Capp's imaginary mountain village. Taking a page from Silver Dollar City's successful theme park efforts, Dogpatch USA featured Ozark musicians and craftspeople, resulting in an awkward mix of blatant hillbilly stereotyping and cultural celebration. An economic impact study had predicted that the park would ultimately bring in more than a million visitors per year and contribute $5 million annually to the local economy, but the investors did not seem convinced. At the close of the first season, they sold Dogpatch USA to a Little Rock businessman, the first of many times the park would change hands.

The new owner, Jess Odom, an-

nounced plans to spend millions of dollars to make Dogpatch USA the equal of such amusement parks as Six Flags and Disneyland. At the very least, Odom knew how to attract publicity, for in early 1969 he generated national headlines by hiring former Arkansas governor Orval Faubus as general manager of the park. Although Faubus's tenure at Dogpatch USA would prove a brief one, Odom upgraded the park's attractions by building a railroad, a roller coaster, and other rides and by hiring a creative director to supervise the actors portraying Li'l Abner, Daisy Mae, and the other characters. In the early 1970s, Odom constructed Marble Falls Estates, a ski resort and convention center, adjacent to Dogpatch USA.

In spite of the millions that Odom and his successors spent on the park, Dogpatch USA never achieved anything close to the success of Silver Dollar City, or any other solvent theme park for that matter. The park's remote location limited attendance, and after Capp retired in 1977 the characters of fictional Dogpatch became increasingly peripheral to the mainstream of American popular culture. In addition, Odom's Marble Falls Estates hemorrhaged money, leaving his whole enterprise in danger of folding. Odom eventually abandoned his dreams of a winter wonderland in the Ozarks, and Dogpatch USA, which had managed at least marginal profits during its first decade, struggled to entice visitors to the Ozark backcountry. The park occasionally turned a profit in the 1980s, but the debts accrued by Odom's other properties continued to pile up until they choked Dogpatch

USA out for good. After a series of desperate moves—a season of free admittance, abandonment of Capp's characters, and more emphasis on native crafts and folk traditions—Dogpatch USA closed its gates in 1993.

In the years since Dogpatch's demise, the abandoned theme park has become a favorite haunt of "underground" explorers and local teenagers; the many varieties of souvenirs peddled for 25 years at Dogpatch USA have become collector's items. Local residents perhaps wrote the last chapter in the Dogpatch saga in 1997 when they successfully petitioned the U.S. Postal Service to change the community's name back to Marble Falls. The exaggerated hillbilly stereotypes are gone, but so are the valuable dollars that helped sustain a rural region that remains among the poorest in Arkansas.

BROOKS BLEVINS
Missouri State University

Brooks Blevins, *Hill Folks: A History of Arkansas Ozarkers and Their Image* (2002), *Arkansas, Arkansaw: A State and Its Image* (2009); Rodger Brown, *Southern Changes* 15:3 (1993); Donald Harington, *Let Us Build Us a City: Eleven Lost Towns* (1986).

Dollywood

Located near the Great Smoky Mountains National Park in Pigeon Forge, Tenn., Dollywood is an iconic southern amusement park that is both important to the economy of the Appalachian region and a powerful example of the commodification of southern culture.

Dollywood is the most recent and most successful of several amusement parks to share the same site in Pigeon

Forge. The first—Rebel Railroad, built in 1961 by North Carolinians Grover and Harry Robbins—offered visitors a trip back to the Civil War with rides and attractions that echoed both staunch regionalism and the Lost Cause. The pro-Confederate theme included a train ride that culminated with a Yankee attack thwarted by southern soldiers and their tourist allies. After some commercial success, the Robbins brothers, who also owned the Tweetsie Railroad Park in North Carolina, sold Rebel Railroad to Art Modell and the Cleveland Browns in 1970. The Browns rechristened the park Goldrush Junction and adopted the imagery of the Old West, but soon realized that depictions of mountain culture were more profitable. The 1970s saw a resurgence of hillbilly imagery in American popular culture, and the Browns believed that a return to Appalachian roots would enhance the park's tourist appeal, but such hopes were never fully realized.

The strange marriage of the Appalachian theme park and one of the National Football League's worst franchises ended with the sale of Goldrush Junction to Branson, Mo., entrepreneurs Jack and Pete Hershand. The Hershands helped to establish Branson as a tourist destination in the 1960s and 1970s in part through their Ozark-themed park Silver Dollar City. They soon turned the Pigeon Forge park into an Appalachian Silver Dollar City, complete with mountain musical shows, craft demonstrations, Appalachian-themed rides, and daily recreations of the Hatfield-McCoy feud.

In 1985 country music superstar and

Sevier County native Dolly Parton became the Hershands's partner, bringing her image, her money, and her marketable name to enhance the park's appeal. The renamed Dollywood used Parton's star power and her unabashed love for her native mountains to breathe new life into the park and Pigeon Forge.

The new partners set about enhancing the park's Appalachian themes. Attractions such as the Mountain Sidewinder and Daredevil Falls water rides emphasized the region's landscape, while the White Lightning rollercoaster simulated a chase between moonshiners and the law. After enjoying these rides, visitors could find a meal at Aunt Granny's Dixie Fixins or visit a museum dedicated to Parton's life. Although many of Dollywood's early attractions offered a healthy dose of campy, clichéd, and stereotypical depictions of mountain people, such images evolved over time. Parton and her partners realized that the park's stereotypical portrayal of mountain culture did not reflect societal realities, but they also knew that tourists wanted to experience something of mountain culture—real or imagined— during their visits. Although unflattering and negative Appalachian stereotypes can still be found in Dollywood's imagery and attractions, the partners realized that more positive portrayals of mountain culture could also draw visitors. This duality reflects Parton's own willingness to make light of her mountain roots while simultaneously taking great pride in the region's people, heritage, and culture. More recently, the park employed artisans who demonstrate mountain crafts such as candle making, blacksmithing, and woodcarving and offer their wares for sale at craft shows on the park grounds. Dollywood even blended southern agriculture and religion to draw tourists, hosting a Gospel & Harvest Celebration to showcase the region's religious musical heritage and foodways. While critics of the park and its portrayal of mountain people exist and have at times been quite vocal, the park draws more than 2 million visitors annually and has generated tremendous growth in Sevier County.

Dollywood's history demonstrates the ways that southern tourism entrepreneurs have used image, culture, and stereotypes to carve out a niche in the region's tourist economy. The park stands as an important example of how the South is packaged and sold to tourists, as well as the tensions that accompany a tourism economy.

RICHARD D. STARNES
Western Carolina University

Scot Haller, *People Magazine* (5 May 1986); C. Brenden Martin, *Tourism in the Mountain South: A Double-Edged Sword* (2007); J. W. Williamson, *Hillbillyland: What the Movies Did to the Mountains and What the Mountains Did to the Movies* (1995).

Drive-in Theaters

The drive-in movie theater—synonymous with the Fabulous Fifties, poodle skirts, rock and roll, and the golden age of American car culture—was the creation of a New Jersey inventor and automotive soap salesman named Richard Hollingshead Jr. In 1933 Hollingshead opened the first drive-in theater in Camden, N.J. Three years later he sold the business and turned his attention to collecting royalties from the patent. This proved useless, as a patent court ruled that Hollingshead's invention—essentially an amphitheater for cars—was unpatentable. The result was a financial setback for Hollingshead, but it ultimately led to the widespread appearance of drive-ins across the United States, particularly in the South, where they proliferated in greater numbers than in any other region of the country.

The earliest drive-in to be built in the South was the Drive-in Short Reel Theater in Galveston, Tex. It opened in July 1934 and operated for less than one month before it was destroyed in a storm. (It was not rebuilt.) Florida saw its first drive-in open in 1938, and other southern states followed soon after. Nevertheless, drive-ins were not as popular with the movie-going public when they first appeared as they would be later on. It would be almost two decades before every state in the nation had one, let alone every sizable town.

The earliest drive-ins were generally regarded as novelties, met with amusement but low expectations. Outdoor theaters were nothing new, certainly not in the South. In the days before air-conditioning, when many indoor theaters closed down during the stifling summer months, film exhibitors experimented with temporary outdoor screens in parks, on beaches, and even in the middle of towns. The addition of automobiles to the seating arrangement was certainly novel, but it did not necessarily improve the experience. Technical difficulties (particularly with sound equipment) plagued drive-ins

from the start, and economic conditions in the 1930s made their initial prospects for success unfavorable. This situation, combined with a nationwide moratorium on new theater construction during World War II, meant that drive-ins had to wait until after the war was over to attract significant audiences and investors.

The prosperous postwar era created the perfect set of circumstances that allowed the drive-in to flourish. Employment was up, the rush to the suburbs was on, and American families had disposable income to spend. The statistics on drive-in theater construction are revealing. As of 1946, there were just over 100 drive-ins scattered throughout the United States. Two years later, census data shows that figure leaping to 820; six years after that, 3,775. The upward trend was especially noticeable in the South. In Georgia, the number of drive-ins climbed from 13 in 1948 to 128 in 1954. In the same six-year period, Florida saw a rise from 22 to 158 drive-ins; North Carolina, from 66 to 209; and Texas, from 88 to 388, surpassing every other state. By 1958 an all-time high of 4,063 drive-ins across the country accounted for more than 20 percent of all ticket sales in the American motion picture industry.

The drive-in theater embodied something of the spirit of America in the 1950s—it represented expansion, indulgence, consumption, and an intense love of the automobile. In the comfort of their success, drive-in owners began to exhibit a kind of gaudy showmanship, not only in their flashy neon marquees but in their creative appeals to local or regional identity. The Cedar Valley Drive-In in Rome, Ga., disguised itself as a southern plantation, with the screen tower concealed behind a neoclassical facade, complete with Greek columns. Other drive-ins adopted names and marketing schemes designed around hometown sports teams, industries, and allegiances. There were the Razorback in Little Rock, Ark.; the Varsity in Tuscaloosa, Ala.; the Bourbon in Paris, Ky.; the Battlefield in Vicksburg, Miss.; as well as numerous Rebels, Magnolias, Azaleas, and Dixies.

Of course, not all southern audiences experienced a night at the drive-in equally. Just as most indoor movie houses were segregated, many southern drive-ins had separate entrances, restrooms, concession facilities, and parking areas for African Americans. Some drive-ins, such as the Lariat in Fort Worth, Tex., catered to blacks only, while others excluded them altogether.

During the late 1950s and early 1960s, attendance at drive-ins began to trail off, as television rapidly changed the way Americans thought of an evening's entertainment. The quality of the moviegoing experience also worsened, as drive-ins were often stuck screening low-rent films on their second or third run, while indoor theaters (many owned and operated by Hollywood production companies) showed newer and better fare.

In a last-ditch effort to stay open, many drive-ins resorted to screening pornographic "skin flicks," a practice that actually did more to hurt their chances of survival. In 1969 Alabama governor Albert Brewer made national headlines by ordering state troopers to shut down six different drive-ins for violating the state's antiobscenity law. Other states around the country pursued a similar course, forcing scores of drive-ins out of business.

By the 1970s, indoor film houses were adding screens and turning into multiplexes capable of housing six, seven, and eight screens in a building and running films throughout the day and night. Drive-ins, open only at night, could hardly compete. Moreover, as cities expanded toward the suburbs and land values rose, many drive-in owners sold out. All of these factors and more signaled the beginning of the end for the drive-in. By the 1990s, the number of drive-ins in the United States had dwindled to a few hundred.

Recently, however, the decline has actually started to reverse, if only gradually in a few pockets around the country. The trend is most noticeable in sparsely populated rural areas in the South, where land is cheap and the nearest multiplex is a considerable distance down the road. With few exceptions, these new drive-ins are more toned-down affairs than their predecessors. Gone are the colonial mansions, elaborate marquees, and ostentatious displays of yesterday. Construction tends to be simple and functional, while sound and projection technology has vastly improved. Film quality has also improved, as distributors hustle to get new releases on every available screen before the DVD release. As a result, drive-ins no longer have to run second-rate fare. Now they screen the same blockbusters playing at multiplexes with stadium seating. Although they will probably never reach their former numbers again, drive-ins have found a niche in the modern South by adapting to suit modern tastes.

AARON WELBORN
Washington University in St. Louis

Elizabeth McKeon and Linda Everett, *Cinema under the Stars: America's Love Affair with the Drive-in Movie Theater* (1998); Don Sanders and Susan Sanders, *The American Drive-in Movie Theatre* (1997); Kerry Segrave, *Drive-in Theaters: A History from Their Inception in 1933* (1992).

Earnhardt, Dale

(1951–2001) NASCAR DRIVER.
A seven-time Winston Cup champion, Dale Earnhardt was one of the most successful, popular, and unpopular drivers in NASCAR history. For many people Dale Earnhardt epitomized the rough-edged Piedmont working-class roots of the sport with his hard-charging, win-at-all costs style of driving. At the same time, however, he transcended those roots to become one of the wealthiest and most influential athletes in the history of American sport.

Earnhardt was born in the Piedmont mill town of Kannapolis, N.C. His father, Ralph Earnhardt, was a stock car racing legend on small dirt tracks and asphalt "bullrings" in the Carolinas and won the 1956 NASCAR sportsman championship. Dale served as a virtual apprentice with his father as he traveled with him learning the art and craft of both racing and stock car mechanics. He dropped out of school at 16 and went to work in a local cotton mill, was mar-ried at 17, a father at 18, and divorced at 19.

Earnhardt began his racing career in 1970 in a pink 1956 Ford Club Sedan owned by his brother-in-law. He soon became a fixture on local Piedmont tracks and quickly moved up through the ranks, occasionally securing a chance to drive underfunded cars at Winston Cup races. Racing, however, put him deeply in debt, brought him little fame outside a narrow circle, and even helped cause a second divorce.

His luck changed in 1979 when, on the verge of bankruptcy, he impressed car owner Rod Osterlund enough to secure a full-season ride in a well-financed car. He won his first race in NASCAR's top division that year and rookie-of-the-year honors. The next year brought five wins, his first Winston Cup championship, and $671,990 in winnings. In little over a year and a half, Earnhardt had gone from being virtually destitute to standing at the top of the racing world. However, long-term success did not come easily for him. Osterlund sold the team in the middle of the 1981 season and Earnhardt was again consigned to inferior equipment.

Earnhardt's career took off once again in 1984 when he returned to drive for one of his earlier car owners, Richard Childress. The pairing with Childress proved magical as over the next 17 years Earnhardt won 67 Winston Cup races and six championships in the number 3 Chevrolet. Along the way his stubbornness and his penchant for rough and aggressive driving—"I didn't mean to wreck him, I just meant to rattle his cage"—earned him the nicknames of "Ironhead," "The Intimidator," and, after adopting a black paint scheme, "The Man in Black." Earnhardt's style and his success on the track made him both the most beloved driver on the NASCAR circuit—particularly to working-class fans—and the most hated, and he seemed to revel in both roles.

Earnhardt became almost as important to the sport as a pioneer in the marketing of his image. His business savvy, and that of third wife, Teresa, helped make him one of the wealthiest celebrities in the United States through souvenir sales, endorsement contracts, and solid investments. The once shy, uncouth, ninth-grade dropout even became a smooth celebrity spokesperson and helped to solidify the place of NASCAR in the national consciousness as an up-and-coming national pastime and not just a redneck sport for southern "good old boys."

Earnhardt defied the odds late in his career and continued to be a consistent winner even in his late 40s. Indeed, his rivalry with the polar opposite, California-born Jeff Gordon gave NASCAR one of its most compelling story lines in the 1990s and helped to further boost the sport's popularity. His career and life ended, however, on 18 February 2001 when he was killed in a last-lap wreck at the Daytona 500. While the outpouring of grief was most intense around his Piedmont North Carolina home, the cover photos and major tribute pieces in every major news and entertainment venue in the nation dramatically testified to Dale Earnhardt's, and NASCAR's, national

popularity and influence. There was a silver lining to Earnhardt's death in a renewed emphasis on safety in NASCAR. In the aftermath of his accident, NASCAR mandated a number of safety features—ironically, some resisted by Earnhardt during his life—that have made the sport notably less dangerous.

Dale Earnhardt's death ended an important era of NASCAR history. He would prove to be the last of the southern Piedmont-born, high-school-dropout, tough-as-nails, working-class NASCAR heroes that had been so important to the sport's origins and growth. At the same time, Earnhardt had helped transform the sport through his extraordinary talent and business savvy into an increasingly popular national pastime.

DANIEL S. PIERCE
University of North Carolina at Asheville

Charlotte Observer Editors, *Dale Earnhardt: Rear View Mirror* (2001); Kevin Mayne, *3: The Dale Earnhardt Story* (2004); Leigh Montville, *At the Altar of Speed: The Fast Life and Tragic Death of Dale Earnhardt* (2001).

Easter

Easter is a Christian religious holiday celebrating Christ's victory over death, an occasion that has especially resonated in the South with its large evangelical Protestant population that highlights the centrality of rebirth. Christian groups of all varieties make it a joyous day, the Sunday when more people typically attend church than any other. It is also a spring ritual that marks a seasonal turn toward earthly renewal.

Southerners enjoy the traditional symbols of Easter. The Bermuda lily (or simply, Easter lily) is widely displayed in churches, homes, and businesses. Families decorate colored Easter eggs; Easter morning finds Easter baskets filled with candy and fruit; and public parks and home yards are sites for Easter egg hunts—all highlighting the importance of children to the day. Easter bunnies are associated with the holiday, a symbol of fertility like the egg. Some families give baby chicks as a seasonal gift at Easter. Chocolate eggs, bunnies, and chicks represent only one example of commercial use of the season's symbols. Southerners have long bought or made new clothes, "Easter finery." Other Americans might wait until Memorial Day to wear white shoes or clothes, but southerners knew that Easter was the correct time for that display. Ham is the typical food that anchors Easter dinners, but the growing popularity of lamb is seen in food writer Damon Lee Fowler's Savannah Easter Dinner menu that includes roast lamb with bourbon and mint. Since the 1950s, television has structured many families experience of the holiday, as they gather on Easter night to watch religious-themed films like *The Ten Commandments* or *The Robe.*

Americans in general mark Easter with parades, and southerners are no exception. The parade in St. Augustine, Fla., makes much of that city's historic role as the oldest permanent settlement in the nation. Its Parada de los Caballos y Coches is a picturesque event that includes horse-driven Spanish carriages, decorated floats, beauty queens, military drill units, men on horseback, and women marching in antique costumes. The parade is part of the city's Easter week festival that began in 1958.

Religious activities are central, though, to Easter. Some faiths have clergy wearing white vestments, with most having special music for the day, whether "Christ the Lord Is Ris'n Today, Alleluia!" in liturgical churches, or "Up from the Grave He Arose" in evangelical tradition. Late morning Sunday congregational services are preceded by early "sunrise services" at dawn. These services are often interdenominational and began in outdoor locales of special beauty or significance—on mountaintops or hillsides, in parks, in cemeteries, on ocean beaches or riversides, or at historical landmarks. Probably the first Easter sunrise service was held by the Moravians in 1771 at Salem, N.C. The preliminary activities began as early as 1:30 A.M. with a Moravian band awakening townspeople. The service formally began at dawn on Salem Square in front of Old Salem's Home Moravian Church. Other older sunrise services took place at scenic Natural Bridge, Va., Arlington National Cemetery in Virginia, the Stephen Foster Memorial on the Suwannee River at White Springs, Fla., and Cypress Gardens' Lake Eloise. Today, many southern cities host nonsectarian sunrise services.

Easter Rock is an Easter vigil ritual that has been documented in rural Louisiana African American churches since before the Civil War. It ceremonially goes through Jesus's time in the tomb and his resurrection. Participants gather at ten o'clock on Saturday

night and hear singing. The culmination is a procession of people dressed in
white entering the church, led by a man
carrying a "banner" representing Christ
symbolism. Twelve women, known as
"sancts," follow the leader, carrying
kerosene lamps as they move. Devo-
tionals and homilies are given, and a
table is set up filled with cakes, punch,
and lamps. The "rock" ceremony is the
syncopated marching around the table,
accompanied by the congregation's call-
and-response acapella singing and the
sound of the steps of the rockers. One
participant in the ceremony in the early
20th century said the name "Easter
rocks" came from the fact that "everything rocks."

Perhaps the most famous literary
portrayal of Easter reflects the spirit
of Easter Rock. William Faulkner, in
The Sound and the Fury (1929), writes
of the black woman Dilsey, servant of
the decaying Compson family, who
attends an Easter morning worship conducted by the Reverend Shegog. Dilsey
takes the idiot child Benjy to the black
church, despite complaints from blacks
and whites about this violation of segregation. Shegog preaches of the Egyp-
tian bondage and the children of God.
He preaches of the Crucifixion of Jesus
and the Resurrection. The congregation sways to the emotional rhythms of
the sermon, Benjy sits "rapt in his sweet
blue gaze," and Dilsey "sat bolt upright
beside, crying rigidly and quietly in the
annealment and the blood of the remembered Lamb."

CHARLES REAGAN WILSON
University of Mississippi

Hennig Cohen and Tristram Potter Coffin,
eds., *The Folklore of American Holidays* (3rd
ed., 1999); Jane M. Hatch, ed., *The American
Book of Days* (3rd ed., 1978).

Everglades National Park

Dedicated in 1947, Everglades National
Park was the first park within the national system founded to protect an
area's biological endowments. In the
view of policy makers and wilderness
advocates, the tabletop flat terrain of
the Everglades lacked an awe-inspiring
natural monument—a cascading waterfall, a looming mountaintop, an incredible geyser—that had been a pre-
requisite for other national parks. Yet
the Everglades had considerable recreational possibilities, another important standard required for national park
status.

The men and women who spent
nearly 20 years campaigning for the
establishment of an Everglades national
park recognized they were trying to
sell to the public a place most Americans regarded as a swamp and waste-
land. Although the park proponents
worked hard to convince others to see
unique beauty in the region, they leaned
heavily on the recreational benefits the
great expanse offered. For several decades before the founding of the park,
the Everglades were popular for hiking,
camping, boating, fishing, and hunting
(an activity later prohibited in the park)
opportunities. In the late 19th and early
20th centuries, some of the country's
best-known ornithologists, including
Harold H. Bailey, found great leisure
in bird watching in the Everglades. It
was by way of this activity that Mar-

jory Stoneman Douglas, a park founder who in the late 20th century emerged as a central figure in the campaign to restore the beleaguered Everglades ecosystem, first became intimate with the Everglades. Ernest Coe, a semiretired landscape architect who in the 1920s launched the campaign to establish a national park, spent countless sublime hours hiking and camping in the Everglades. When parks in the North closed during cold months, Coe argued, the subtropic park in South Florida would serve as a prime recreational spot during the winter season.

Boosters in the state who supported the park believed Everglades would attract one million tourists a year (a number not reached until decades later). Governor Spessard Holland, who was instrumental in the final push for the park's creation, envisioned motor tourists driving down through the long state and stopping to spend their money at filling stations, restaurants, motels, and roadside attractions before reaching Everglades National Park at the tip of the peninsula.

In the 21st century, the recreational attractions in the approximately 1.4-million-acre Everglades National Park remain largely unchanged. Most of the park's roughly one million visitors are daytime sightseers, although a significant number of tourists overnight in the park's lodge or campground at Flamingo or boat out to and rough it on a remote chickee (a thatched-roof platform on stilts) in the mangrove forests. For birders, the area's 300 avian species, from pink flamingoes to the endangered Cape Sable seaside sparrow, are one of the park's most striking features, with numbers reaching into the tens, sometimes hundreds, of thousands during the winter–early spring nesting season. This also is the most popular season, with mosquitoes at a minimum, for tourists, who are eager to catch a glimpse of alligators and American crocodiles, the latter of which are unique to Everglades National Park. Everglades has 156 miles of canoe and hiking trails and a 15-mile biking trail leading to an observation tower on the Shark Valley tram road. Visitors tour the waters primarily in canoes, kayaks, and captained pontoon motorboats. Sport fishing ranges from salt to fresh to brackish water and concentrates among the thousands of acres of shallow-water flats, mangrove islands, and channels. During open state season, recreational crabbing is allowed, offering stone crabs and blue crabs. Hiking trails wend through the park's diverse landscape, including sawgrass marshlands, wet prairies, pine flatlands, palmetto scrubland, and hardwood hammocks, where tourists can see wild orchids, bromeliads, the smooth-barked gumbo limbo tree, and the large golden silk orb-weavers (the largest nontarantula spiders in North America). Popular recreations in the larger Everglades, airboating and swamp-buggy rides are prohibited activities in the park.

JACK E. DAVIS
University of Florida

Ernest F. Coe, *Landscape Architecture* (October 1936); Jack E. Davis, *An Everglades Providence: Marjory Stoneman Douglas and the American Environmental Century* (2009); Everglades National Park, www.nps

.gov/ever; Everglades National Park Information Page, www.everglades.national-park.com/info.htm.

Evert, Chris

(b. 1954) TENNIS PLAYER.

Chris Evert is the most successful woman tennis player to come from the South, and during a two-decade career she established herself as one of the greatest women athletes of the 20th century. In 1985 the Women's Sports Foundation honored her as the Greatest Woman Athlete of the previous quarter century. When she retired from professional competition in 1989, she had 157 singles titles and 8 doubles titles.

Born 21 December 1954 in Fort Lauderdale, Fla., Christine Marie Evert was the daughter of James Evert, a professional tennis teacher at Holiday Park Tennis Center in Fort Lauderdale. She began hitting tennis balls against the walls at age six, and her father was soon giving her intense lessons as part of a middle-class family where tennis was an everyday affair. Evert and her sister became professional tennis players, and her brother played intercollegiate college tennis at Auburn. Chris Evert won her first competitive play at age 10, and at age 15, at the Carolinas Tournament in 1970, she upset Margaret Court, then the top-ranked women's tennis player. Within a year she had won the Virginia Slims Master's Tournament, become the youngest woman selected for the U.S. Wightman Cup team, and competed in her first U.S. Open tournament. After graduating from St. Thomas Aquinas High School in Fort Lauderdale in 1972, she declared her professional status as

she turned 18. By 1974 she had claimed the top ranking in women's tennis.

Evert had more than 1,300 match wins. Her career doubles record was 117–39. Evert won her first Grand Slam singles title in 1974 and won 55 consecutive matches that year. In her career, she won 18 Grand Slam singles championships. She captured the French Open seven times (1974, 1975, 1979, 1980, 1983, 1985, 1986), the U.S. Open six times (1975, 1976, 1977, 1978, 1980, 1982), Wimbledon three times (1974, 1976, 1981), and the Australian Open twice (1982, 1984). She was the world's top ranked player from 1974 to 1979. With her great success, she gained the nickname "Ice Maiden of Tennis" for her domination of the sport and her calm, focused manner while playing. The Associated Press named Evert female athlete of the year four times and *Sports Illustrated* honored her as sportswoman of the year in 1976. She served as president of the Women's Tennis Association from 1975 to 1976 and from 1983 to 1991.

Evert's success paralleled the rise of women's tennis in the late 20th century. Television regularly broadcast woman's tennis, making her a well-known celebrity and popularizing her baseline game and two-handed backhand for the next generation of women players.

CHARLES REAGAN WILSON
University of Mississippi

Johnette Howard, *The Rivals: Chris Evert vs. Martina Navratilova: Their Epic Duels and Extraordinary Friendship* (2006); Chris Evert Lloyd, with Neil Amdur, *Chrissy: My Own Story* (1982); Betty Lou Phillips, *Chris Evert: First Lady of Tennis* (1977).

Favre, Brett

(b. 1969) FOOTBALL PLAYER.
Brett was widely thought to be the most
accomplished quarterback in professional football in the 1990s and first decade of the 21st century. While playing
for the University of Southern Mississippi in 1990 Brett Favre was involved in
a terrible auto crash after which a large
section of his intestine had to be removed. Five weeks later he returned to
the lineup to defeat heavily favored Alabama. Crimson Tide Coach Gene Stallings declared, "You can call it a miracle
or a legend or whatever you want to, I
just know that on that day, Brett Favre
was larger than life." It would not be the
last time that would be said.

Brett was born in 1969 to a family in
Kiln, Miss., with a Cajun and Choctaw
background. Coached in high school
by his father, he played quarterback in
a run-dominated offense that saw him
passing very little. This probably contributed to the fact that he was offered
only one scholarship to a Division I
school, the University of Southern Mississippi—and that was to play de-
fensive back. Though he was deep in
the quarterback depth chart, he was
brought in during a 1987 game against
Tulane. He threw two touchdown passes
and led the team to a win, all the while
nursing a massive hangover.

Favre partied extremely hard in
college and had a child with his then-
girlfriend Deanna (whom he met
in Catholic Sunday school when he
was seven and later married). He did
manage to earn a degree in special education, and his aptitude in that field
later demonstrated itself in his chari-

table foundations and in the time he
takes with children.

He was not highly sought after in
the NFL draft, even given his college
success. Eventually the Atlanta Falcons
picked him up, but they had no real use
for a hard-drinking Cajun with a laser
gun for an arm. They traded him in 1992
to Green Bay, where general manager
Ron Wolf and coach Mike Holmgren
saw something, although they were not
quite sure what.

During his first several seasons,
Favre infuriated fans and coaches with
his passes that regularly broke fingers—often those of the opposing team.
Gradually Holmgren calmed Favre
down and built a team around him
that was able to win Super Bowl XXXI
(1997), while his quarterback garnered
three consecutive MVP awards. During
this time Favre went into voluntary
rehabilitation for an addiction to pre-
scription painkillers. This was highly
successful and the addiction never returned. In 1996 he married his college
girlfriend, Deanna, and the couple has
two daughters.

Mike Holmgren departed in 1998,
and, though the Packers were never able
to duplicate their success under him,
Favre went on to have a career as one
of the best quarterbacks in NFL history
and the holder of nearly every major
record that a quarterback can possess.
Most notable among these are more
than 460 touchdowns, 64,000 yards
passing, 5,600 pass completions, and,
in true Favre style, more than 300 inter-
ceptions. Most astonishing, however, is
his record of more than 287 consecutive games started, a statistic that com-

pares to Cal Ripken's streak in baseball, especially at one of the most demanding positions in sports.

Perhaps his most special game came in Oakland in 2003. One day after his father was killed in an auto crash, and with his family's encouragement, he decided that he could not let his team down and that his father would have wanted him to play. Before a nation-wide audience on Monday Night Football, Favre threw for 4 touchdowns and 399 yards, winning 41–7. There was not a dry eye in the country after that game, and even the Raider Nation gave him a standing ovation.

Though Green Bay is in the heart of the Northwoods, Brett Favre never lost his southern manners and appeal. Green Bay and Wisconsin took him in as a favorite son. In a place where the average temperature high is below freezing for several months at a time, Brett from Kiln, Miss., was known for winning the cold-weather games. He said he did not like the cold much, but his play always seemed to give lie to the statement. In the off-season he would return to his farm in Mississippi with his family and every season be right back in Green Bay. That is, until 2008. After 16 seasons in, Favre retired and, like many high-level athletes today, subsequently unretired. Management, it seemed, was unimpressed. What happened next was unthinkable to many Packers fans. Brett Favre was traded to the New York Jets.

Now, if Brett Favre in Green Bay seemed strange (though it appeared the most natural thing in the world after a few years), the Kiln native under the scrutiny of the New York fans and press seemed more than incongruous. Nevertheless, he succeeded there as well, taking a team that was 4–12 in 2007 to the brink of the playoffs, while the Packers, whom he took to the NFC championship game that year, finished below .500 in 2008. Favre retired again after the 2008 season, but then came out of retirement in 2009 to lead the Minnesota Vikings to the NFC championship game, where they lost to the New Orleans Saints 31–28 in overtime.

Favre has exported his southern bonhomie on a national scale, though on a quieter level than Terry Bradshaw, and with less commercial savvy than Peyton Manning. He comes across to people as genuine, and his work ethic and endurance under trying conditions are things that can be embraced all over the country, from southern Mississippi to the frozen tundra of Green Bay, from the media center of New York City to, perhaps finally, Minnesota's Twin Cities.

DONALD S. PRUDLO
Jacksonville State University

Deanna Favre, *Don't Bet Against Me* (2007); Sam Lucero, *Catholic News Service* (25 October 2007); Bonita Favre and Brett Favre, *Favre* (2004); Gary D'Amato, *Milwaukee Journal-Sentinel* (17 October 2005); Jimmy Traina, *Sports Illustrated* (5 October 2002).

Flora-Bama Lounge and Package

It is not often that a bar becomes a cultural attraction beyond the distance one of its patrons can (or should) safely drive after closing time, but the Flora-Bama Lounge and Package is one bar that has become just that. Billed as "The

Last American Roadhouse," it has been featured on local and national television, written up in a variety of publications, and immortalized in the music of Jimmy Buffet. It is dear to the hearts of the many who have enjoyed its hospitality and an imagined destination in the minds of those who leave their recliners only for trips to the refrigerator.

To have a roadhouse one needs a road, so there was no Flora-Bama until the highway between Orange Beach, Ala., and Perdido Key, Fla., was completed in 1962. Two years later the bar and package store was built, just on the Florida side of the border, to take advantage of the Sunshine State's more liberal liquor laws. But because the establishment butted right up against Alabama, the motto "Let's do it on the line" was a natural.

The early days were rough. A suspicious fire burned down the first Flora-Bama, but it was rebuilt and, being almost the only place to get a beer on that lonely stretch, it became a popular watering hole for locals and visitors.

In 1978 two events coincided to make the Flora-Bama what it is today. Joe Gilchrist and Pat McClellan bought the place and made music an essential part of the "Bama" entertainment. That same year an article in the *New York Times* ("Todd and Stabler Offseason Game: Living It Up on 'Redneck Riviera'") highlighted the Flora-Bama as the home of the "midnight rambler and honky-tonk rounder." The rest, as they say, is history.

With Gilchrist tending bar and musicians making their music, the Flora-Bama evolved into a go-to place and the epicenter of the Redneck Riviera. Even-

tually it grew into a sprawling complex of bars and stages where bands played to packed audiences that consisted of bankers, bikers, and all the variety in between. It is a place where, according to one observer, "you can holler 'Bubba' and 15 people will respond." University of Alabama football hero and All-Pro quarterback Kenny Stabler called it "the best watering hole in the country," and so far no one has challenged him or argued otherwise.

As beach communities grew up around it, the Flora-Bama became a major tourist attraction, though one where attractions were typically Flora-Bama. The year kicks off in January with the Polar Bear Dip, where alcohol-insulated patrons take to the frigid Gulf. Spring is brought in with the Annual Interstate Mullet Toss, and in the fall there is the Frank Brown International Songwriter's Festival, which honors a legendary bouncer and celebrates the Bama's reputation as a place where entertainers can play their own compositions and not be forced to cover "popular" hits.

In September 2004 the Flora-Bama was almost lost when Hurricane Ivan roared ashore, destroying or damaging most of the building and sweeping away scores of bras that hung from the ceiling and classic inscriptions that decorated the restroom walls. For nearly a year, fans waited patiently while temporary structures, many of them trailers, were brought in and set up in a fashion reminiscent of the warrenlike arrangement of the original complex. When all was in place (and, in some cases, even before), the Flora-Bama was open for business.

And what a business it is. Events like the Mullet Toss yearly break attendance records, beer sales continue to climb, while legends and lies about what was done on the line are passed about as the gospel truth.

Meanwhile, after a lot of legal wrangling, the Escambia (Fla.) County Board of Adjustments agreed to a variance that would allow the Flora-Bama to be rebuilt in a way that the owners promised would be true to "the style, structure and mystique of the pre-Ivan Flora-Bama for generations to come." The management warned friends that "it will be tricky to rebuild, because you have been keeping us as busy as ever," but no one complained. That's what is to be expected if you are "the Last American Roadhouse."

HARVEY H. JACKSON III
Jacksonville State University

Alan West Brockman and Joe Gilchrist, *The Last American Roadhouse: The Documentary of the Flora-Bama* (film, 2006); Ryan Dezember, *Mobile Press-Register* (27 April 2008); Robert F. Jones, *Sports Illustrated* (19 September 1979); Harris Mendheim, director, *Mullet Men: Second Place Is the First Loser* (film, 2000); Howell Raines, *New York Times* (21 June 1978); Ken Stabler and Berry Stainback, *Snake: The Candid Autobiography of Football's Most Outrageous Renegade* (1986); Michael Swindle, *Mulletheads: The Legends, Lore, Magic, and Mania Surrounding the Humble but Celebrated Mullet* (1998), *Village Voice* (13 May 1997).

Fourth of July

The Fourth of July celebrates the independence of the United States and has been an important holiday in the South since the American Revolution. Typical activities have included parades, picnics, patriotic speeches, baseball games, ceremonies honoring veterans, the reading of the Declaration of Independence, and assorted community events. As elsewhere in the nation, fireworks have long been a part of the celebration, both in community-sponsored large fireworks shows and privately, among individuals. City ordinances control fireworks in most cities, but the familiar roadside fireworks stands pop up on edges of cities in early summer. Williamsburg, Va., with its pronounced colonial history focus, sponsors its Prelude to Independence beginning in May, with 18th-century cannons fired and bells rung at the College of William and Mary and at historic Bruton Parish Church. In addition to these historic spots, independence activities take place at special sporting events, such as stock races, including Daytona's Firecracker 400 in Florida.

The history of the Fourth of July in the South reveals it to have long been a contested holiday, focusing on issues of sectionalism and race relations. In the early 19th century, the Fourth of July was a vital commemoration that promoted national feeling in the young republic. A Raleigh, N.C., orator in 1851 praised the Union on the holiday and its "importance to the maintenance of our liberties, and the safety, peace and prosperity of the whole country." This nationalist spirit was expressed, though, in local and regional contexts. For antebellum white southerners, the Declaration of Independence and the Fourth of July did not relate to issues of slavery but of compromise and union. With the beginning of the Civil War, few southern communities marked the day, but the Confederacy continued to lay claim to the heritage and heroes of the American Revolution and saw the South as the champion of the legacy associated with the Fourth. After the war, southern states rejoined the Union, but white southerners until the turn of the 20th century refused to commemorate the Independence Day. A Wilmington, N.C., newspaper said the Fourth "should be passed by our people in dignified silence."

Black southerners, however, embraced the Fourth of July and its key document of the Declaration of Independence as symbols of their new freedom. Historian W. Fitzhugh Brundage notes that southern blacks "virtually laid claim to Independence Day." African American memoirist Mamie Garvin Fields recalled of her Charleston childhood in the 1890s that "the oldtime Southerners," meaning whites, saw the Fourth as a "Yankee holiday and ignored it." For her and other blacks, though, she said, "Oh, my, but the Fourth was a big day." During Reconstruction, blacks occupied the South's public spaces for their joyous celebrations of American nationalism. Parades, military bands, and African Americans in militia uniforms proclaimed the new power and position of African Americans in the postwar South. But these rituals stirred white anxieties and sometimes led to white violence against blacks. As late as the 1890s, though, blacks in Richmond, Va., celebrated the holiday with parades and military musters at the state Capitol and even staged events at the Robert E. Lee statue on Monument Avenue.

The centennial celebration of American Independence in 1876 was a notable event in North-South reconciliation that would lead to diminished African American participation in civic celebrations of the holiday. Northern celebrations often omitted a role for blacks—thus denying a fundamental meaning of the Civil War and the extension of the ideals of the Declaration of Independence—but highlighting the white South's historic role in founding the nation. White southerners fought in the Spanish American War, reviving a sense of American patriotism in the region and leading to their increased honoring of the Fourth. Patriotic organizations like the Daughters of the American Revolution were active in the South from the Progressive Era onward, promoting the rise of a new patriotism that emphasized the common Revolutionary heritage of North and South. Whites now held whites-only civic ceremonies, with black commemorations moved to separate locations in black neighborhoods. Historian Fletcher M. Green could still observe, though, that as late as the 1950s, "little attention is paid to July Fourth by the people of North Carolina," although he referred only to whites in that conclusion.

The bicentennial celebration of American independence in 1976 led to a new embrace of the Fourth of July by southern communities. The desegregation of southern public facilities in the 1960s promoted the most integrated and enthusiastic celebration in the region's history. Bicentennial events, programs, and projects included restoration of historic districts and downtown areas, the commissioning of musical events with patriotic themes, construction or expansion of civic buildings and museums, and the staging of festivals and exhibits around historical themes. The American Revolution Bicentennial Administration provided public funding and general coordination, with state commissions active throughout the South.

CHARLES REAGAN WILSON
University of Mississippi

W. Fitzhugh Brundage, *The Southern Past: A Clash of Race and Memory* (2005); Hennig Cohen and Tristram Potter Coffin, eds., *The Folklore of American Holidays* (3rd ed., 1997); Matthew Dennis, *Red, White, and Blue Letter Days: An American Calendar* (2002); Jane M. Hatch, *The American Book of Days* (3rd ed., 1978).

Gibson, Althea

(1927–2003) TENNIS PLAYER.
Althea Gibson was the first African American to win a Grand Slam major tennis tournament, becoming known as "the Jackie Robinson of tennis" for her achievement. Born to sharecropping parents in Silver, S.C., Gibson grew up in Harlem, beset by poverty and behavioral difficulties but excelling in athletics. Walter Johnson, a Virginia physician who had long worked to develop young black tennis players, became her mentor. After further training in Wilmington, N.C., she won the first of her 10 national championships in American Tennis Association all-black tournaments. In the segregated world of tennis then, she was kept out of tournament

Althea Gibson, "the Jackie Robinson of tennis," 1956 (Fred Palumbo, photographer, Library of Congress [LC-USZ62-114745], Washington, D.C.)

competition with whites until breaking the color barrier in 1950, playing in the U.S. championship at Forest Hills, N.Y. In the same year, she graduated from Florida A&M University, having played basketball as well as tennis.

Gibson won the Italian championship (1955), the French championship in singles and doubles (1956), and the Wimbledon championship in doubles (1956) and singles (1957). The latter prestigious win earned her a ticker-tape parade in New York City, and in her breakout year of 1957 she was ranked No. 1 in world tennis and the Associated Press named her female athlete of the year. She won the Wimbledon singles and doubles titles in 1958 and defended her singles title at the U.S. championship the same year. Women's tennis was entirely amateur in Gibson's era, and she retired in 1958, playing in exhibition tours thereafter, including working with the Harlem Globetrotters. Gibson recorded an album, *Althea Gibson Sings* (1958), and published an autobiography, *I Always Wanted to Be Somebody* (1958).

The International Tennis Hall of Fame inducted Althea Gibson in 1971. Four years later she became the New Jersey Commissioner of Athletics. She worked in other government positions as well but suffered a stroke in 1992. She died in 2003 in East Orange, N.J. She had long remembered receiving the Wimbledon trophy and shaking hands with Queen Elizabeth II, thinking that experience "was a long way from being forced to sit down in the colored section of the bus going into downtown Wilmington, N.C."

CHARLES REAGAN WILSON
University of Mississippi

Althea Gibson, with Richard Curtis, *So Much to Live For* (1968); Billie Jean King, with Cynthia Starr, *We Have Come a Long Way: The Story of Women's Tennis* (1988); George Vecsey, *New York Times* (29 September 2003).

Gilley's

Gilley's, in Pasadena, Tex., was founded by Sherwood Cryer as "Shelly's." Its success, like its present name, dates from 1971, when Cryer went into partnership with Mickey Gilley, a country music singer and piano player once probably best known as Jerry Lee Lewis's cousin. Billed at one time as "the World's Largest Saloon" (it could accommodate 4,500 customers), it eventually offered, besides the traditional drinking and dancing, such challenging entertainments as a punching-bag machine and "El Toro," a mechanical bull for customers to ride. Dancing at the club was to music supplied by Gilley, by the house band (the Bayou City Beats), or by visiting country music entertainers, and it included group dances such as the Cotton-Eyed Joe (punctuated with rhythmic chants of "Bullshit!") and the schottische.

Despite these attractions, Gilley's was little known outside the Houston area, except in country music circles, before 1978, when *Esquire* published an article by Aaron Latham on the club and some of its patrons. Latham's article was accompanied by a photographic feature on designer Ralph Lauren's new line, "embracing the rugged natural look of the American cowboy." When the movie *Urban Cowboy*, starring John Travolta, was actually filmed in Gilley's, scores of more or less frankly imitative establishments sprang up across the country. These "cowboy" bars sometimes replaced discos that had been inspired by Travolta's performance in *Saturday Night Fever* and catered to much the same clientele, even more urban and less plausibly cowboy than the young oil workers Latham had chronicled. The most bravura of these new establishments was also in Texas, a Fort Worth club called "Billy Bob's" that offered live bull riding in place of Gilley's machine-simulated version. (Rumors that a patron had been stomped and gored did not hurt at all.) Billy Bob's was even larger than Gilley's, and on one occasion Merle Haggard treated all 5,095 customers to drinks.

The era of "Texas chic" soon faded,

but not before Gilley's had become a major tourist attraction with its own magazine, its own brand of beer, and complete line of souvenirs. Mickey Gilley himself had become a major country music singer with a number of hits to his credit, including "Don't the Girls All Get Prettier at Closing Time"— a traditional number at the club.

Southerners themselves have often collaborated in—and occasionally profited from—the marketing of the South. But the story of Gilley's reflected a new development in the nation's old, on-again/off-again love affair with the South. Gilley's represented, and *Esquire* and Hollywood marketed, a blue-collar South newly popular in the 1970s, populated by the same good old boys (and girls) whom the mass media had generally portrayed a decade earlier (in such movies as *Easy Rider* and *Deliverance*, for instance) as vicious rednecks. The increasing national respectability of their music, the popularity of Burt Reynolds and the *Dukes of Hazzard*, and, not least, the "Urban Cowboy" phenomenon—all attest to a metamorphosis that was one of the stranger aspects of a strange decade. This attention presaged a rising popular culture interest since then in rednecks and other varieties of white working-class southern culture. The original Gilley's, meanwhile, was demolished in 2006, but a new Gilley's—with 91,000 square feet of entertainment and meeting space—opened in 2003, complete with "El Toro."

JOHN SHELTON REED
University of North Carolina at Chapel Hill

Bob Claypool, *Saturday Night at Gilley's* (1980); Robert Crowe and Gregory Curtis, *Texas Monthly* (November 1998); Aaron Latham, *Esquire* (September 1978).

Graceland

Graceland, formerly the estate of an aristocratic Memphis family, became the home of the rock and country icon Elvis Presley from 1957 until his death in 1977. Graceland has since ceased to be a private residence and now enshrines the memory and meaning of Elvis. Located off Highway 51, about eight miles from downtown Memphis, Tenn., Elvis's former home is a favored destination for thousands of fans every year. The largest single gathering takes place on August 18, the anniversary of Elvis's death. Thousands of the curious, the contemptuous, and the utterly worshipful make a pilgrimage that involves tours of the home, candlelight vigils, and a slow procession by the grave of the King of Rock and Roll.

Elvis purchased the estate for himself and his parents, Vernon and Gladys Presley. Frequent renovations completely transformed the colonial-style estate. Elvis had wanted, first, an enlarged bedroom and living area for his mother and, secondly, requested that a soda fountain, "a real soda fountain with cokes and an ice cream thing," be installed in the kitchen.

Ironically, Elvis purchased Graceland to find relief from the constant attention of his persistent fans. The mansion sat on a little over 13 acres with a lush, forested park stretching from the front door down to the iron gates and stone wall that surrounded the property. Graceland, however, became so closely identified with its owner in large part because fans, and Elvis himself, worked to prevent the home from becoming a truly "private" residence. The large stone wall offered devoted fans the opportunity to mark, stencil, and chalk their love to Graceland's owner. Presley himself seemed to invite such attention, at one point stringing bright blue Christmas lights from Highway 51 all the way up to the mansion's front steps. Presley also made it a practice to dramatically leap the walls and sign autographs at least once a day. During his frequent absences, the gates opened between 8:00 A.M. and 5:00 P.M. and fans were allowed to walk the grounds and even look in the windows.

Elvis, and his heirs, emphasized the rural past of Graceland, hoping to play on both Presley's southern roots and the "cowboy" imagery he dearly loved. Elvis himself attempted to build on this mythic image in 1967 when he purchased more than 160 acres south of Memphis off of Highway 51. Purchasing innumerable pickup trucks, horses, and cattle, as well a trailer for himself and Priscilla, he named the spread "The Flying G Ranch" (the "G" maintaining the connection to Graceland).

Following Elvis's death, Graceland underwent extensive renovations in 1980–81 under the guidance of Priscilla Presley. A restaurant and hotel complex now sits across the highway from the mansion, boasting an enormous gift shop containing Elvis memorabilia of every description. Today, a bus carries visitors from the hotel-restaurant complex, through the front gates and up to the very steps of the mansion, much as lucky fans who crowded outside the gates in the 1950s and 1960s would occasionally be taken in a large hot pink jeep to the house to have dinner with Elvis, his family, and friends.

W. SCOTT POOLE
College of Charleston

Peter Guralnick, *Last Train to Memphis: The Rise of Elvis Presley* (1994), *Careless Love: The Unmaking of Elvis Presley* (1998); Karal Anne Marling, *Graceland: Going Home with Elvis* (1996).

Great Smoky Mountains National Park

Federally mandated in 1934 to be one of three major units of the National Park Service in southern Appalachia, the Great Smoky Mountains National Park incorporates 814 square miles and encompasses most of the Great Smoky Mountains on the North Carolina–Tennessee border. The park incorporates the high-elevation ridgeline as well as the side ridges and valleys of the Smokies, a spur range of the Blue Ridge (the latter courses in a southwestward direction from south-central Pennsylvania to northern Georgia). Great Smoky Mountains National Park was linked with Shenandoah National Park, located in a section of the Blue Ridge in northern Virginia, by means of the Blue Ridge Parkway, a 469-mile federal scenic road that traverses southward along the crest of the Blue Ridge and various spur ranges before ending in the Smokies. These three units of the National Park Service were initially promoted in the 1920s by the automobile and tourism industries, and all three would receive extensive federal support during the presidency of Franklin D. Roosevelt. While the various properties acquired for the establishment of Great Smoky Mountains National Park were purchased with financial donations from the citizens of North Carolina and Tennessee and by philanthropist John D. Rockefeller Jr., infrastructural projects within the park were primarily funded by the New Deal programs of the Roosevelt administration.

The park offers numerous recreational activities. Most popular is auto touring, owing in part to the fact that the park has never charged an entrance fee. Each year millions of visitors drive on the Newfound Gap Road (U.S. Highway 441), which bisects the park, and on the Little River Road and the Cades Cove Loop Road to experience panoramic vistas of mountains and forests and to access high elevation sites (such as Clingman's Dome, at 6,643 feet above sea level). Additionally, the park offers numerous opportunities for nature observation—of wildflowers, wildlife (especially black bear, white-tailed deer, and elk—the last-named species having recently been reintroduced into the Smokies), and other natural entities (such as the phenomenon of the synchronous fireflies at Elkmont). Other recreational activities within the park are bicycling (particularly in Cades Cove), fishing (in approximately 700 miles of streams, for native brook trout as well as for introduced brown and rainbow trout), hiking (on more than 800 miles of trails, including a 70-mile stretch of the Appalachian Trail), horseback riding (on more than 500 miles of

trails allowable for horses), picnicking (at 11 maintained picnic areas), and camping (at more than 100 backcountry campsites or shelters accessed via hiking or horseback as well as at 10 developed campgrounds established for tents and recreational vehicles). Some people opt to make the steep trek up Mount LeConte to stay overnight at LeConte Lodge, originally built in the 1920s.

The park operates several historical exhibitions, most notably the Mountain Farm Museum (behind the Oconaluftee Visitor Center) in North Carolina, and, in Tennessee, the collection of 19th-century buildings in Cades Cove (including log and frame houses, two churches, and a mill). Structures that predate the park are also preserved, on the North Carolina side of the park, in Cataloochee Valley (which features, among other buildings, a church, a log cabin, and a frame house), and, in Tennessee, along the Old Settlers Trail (which is routed past numerous old home sites). The park maintains a total of 80 historical buildings in all.

Information or assistance from park rangers and other park staff may be obtained at campgrounds, at certain historical exhibits, as well as at three visitor centers (Sugarlands and Cades Cove Visitor Centers in Tennessee and Oconaluftee Visitor Center in North Carolina).

For the unparalleled ecological diversity it harbors within its boundaries, Great Smoky Mountains National Park was designated an International Biosphere Reserve in 1976, a UNESCO World Heritage Site in 1983, and a Southern Appalachian Biosphere Reserve in 1988. The Great Smoky Mountains Association, a nonprofit educational organization, cosponsors the Great Smoky Mountains Institute at Tremont, which is operated inside the park to foster wider public appreciation for the park's natural and cultural history.

TED OLSON
East Tennessee State University

Michael Frome, *Strangers in High Places: The Story of the Great Smoky Mountains* (1994); Great Smoky Mountains Association, *Hiking Trails of the Smokies* (2003); Daniel S. Pierce, *The Great Smokies: From Natural Habitat to National Park* (2000); Michael Ann Williams, *Great Smoky Mountains Folklife* (1995).

Hamm, Mia

(b. 1972) SOCCER PLAYER.
Mariel Margaret "Mia" Hamm was a crystallizing figure in the growth of women's soccer in the United States. Born 17 March 1972 in Selma, Ala., Hamm was the daughter of an Air Force officer and played soccer while growing up on military bases in Texas, Virginia, and Italy. She played for the University of North Carolina at Chapel Hill, and the Tar Heels won four National Collegiate Athletic Association women's soccer championship titles in five years while she played there, earning Atlantic Coast Conference (ACC) female-athlete-of-the-year honors in 1993 and 1994. When she graduated, she held ACC records in goals (103), assists (72), and total points (278).

Hamm began playing on the United States women's national soccer team at age 15, and at age 19 she was the youngest American woman to win a World Cup championship. She competed for the women's national team for 17 years, and the team won the gold medal at the 1996 and 2004 Summer Olympics. The Federation Internationale de Football Association named her world player of the year in 2001 and 2002. Soccer USA named her female athlete of the year five times (1994–98). Hamm retired from soccer competition after the 2004 Olympics, having scored 158 goals in international competition, a record for the sport of soccer. In 2007 she was voted into the National Soccer Hall of Fame.

Hamm grew up in the aftermath of Title IX's mandate for gender equality in sports, and she made use of new resources that enabled her to train and play competitively in route to becoming a world-class athlete. She then embodied the possibilities of athletic achievement for young women and spurred interest in soccer throughout the nation.

CHARLES REAGAN WILSON
University of Mississippi

Mia Hamm, *Go for the Goal: A Champion's Guide to Winning in Soccer and Life* (2007); Charles Maher, in *Women and Sports in the United States: A Documentary Reader*, ed. Jean O'Reilly and Susan K. Cahn (2007), *USA Today* (18 January 2008).

Hilton Head Island, South Carolina

As forested refuge for nomadic Indian tribes, as the site for 17th-century Spanish and French fortifications, and as the location of antebellum Sea Island cotton plantations, Hilton Head Island has lured people through its climate and its geographic diversity.

Now one of the South's most famous resort areas, Hilton Head had historic significance in the 19th century. On 7 November 1861, 17 Union warships blocked South Carolina's Port Royal Sound, capturing the Confederate stronghold of Fort Walker on the island. The Port Royal anchorage remained the principal base of federal naval operations for the duration of the war, and Hilton Head's Port Royal Plantation, quartering some 30,000 troops, was transformed into a boomtown, complete with hotels and a theater. Along with other southern sea islands, Hilton Head became the focus for a social and agrarian experiment, in which large plantations and town property were claimed by the federal Treasury Department and redistributed to freedmen.

Called a "dress rehearsal for Reconstruction," the Port Royal experiment influenced the formation of federal policy concerning the status of emancipated slaves. Its schools, military training, and wage labor programs acted as a proving ground for freedmen and provided experience for postwar Reconstruction leaders such as General O. O. Howard, head of the Freedman's Bureau, and Congressman Robert Smalls. Many of the freed slaves who remained on Hilton Head Island were of Gullah descent and maintained their existence on the island with subsistence farming.

Soon, however, prosperous northern investors were attracted to the Sound.

Huge tracts of land, and sometimes whole islands, were purchased for use as hunting preserves and winter havens. The largest of South Carolina's barrier islands—12 miles long and covering about 42 square miles—Hilton Head escaped sole proprietorship and became instead a popular combination of resort and residential development.

Gulf breezes keep temperatures on the island at a semitropical 60° to 80° range throughout the year. Many visitors to the island are attracted by its pristine beaches and ocean activities, such as waterskiing, parasailing, surfing, sailing, scuba diving, fishing and crabbing, and dolphin cruises. But Hilton Head's attractions are not just along the shoreline; nature lovers go to enjoy the island's numerous nature preserves. The ocean and networks of freshwater lagoons, meadows, forest area, and marshland support some 260 varieties of birds, as well as bream, bass, and blue marlin. Sea oats and palmetto share the landscape with magnolia, pine, and live oak. These nature preserves offer visitors and residents opportunities for fishing, canoeing, kayaking, hiking, biking, bird watching, and horseback riding.

Cultural activities and events also abound at Hilton Head; historic tours and Gullah heritage tours are popular, and numerous art galleries and cultural exhibits attract museum-goers. The island also has its own orchestra, which performs regularly. Avid shoppers enjoy frequenting plentiful boutiques and art galleries (more than 200) and both indoor and outlet malls.

Hilton Head offers its more than

2.5 million annual visitors an abundance of recreational diversity. There are 8 marinas, 23 golf courses, and more than 300 tennis courts on the island. Seafood restaurants are popular among visitors and residents alike. Accommodations range from hotel rooms to oceanfront villas with names like Bayberry Dune and Xanadu. Abounding in secluded white sand beaches and quiet nature trails but only hours from the urbane charm of Charleston, Hilton Head represents a fusion of society and serenity that has a characteristically southern flavor.

ELIZABETH M. MAKOWSKI
MARY AMELIA TAYLOR
University of Mississippi

Michael Danielson and Patricia Danielson, *Profits and Politics in Paradise: The Development of Hilton Head Island* (1995); Guion Griffis Johnson, *A Social History of the Sea Islands* (1930); Hilton Head Island Chamber of Commerce, www.hiltonhead island.org; Willie Lee Rose, *Rehearsal for Reconstruction: The Port Royal Experiment* (1964); *Southern Living* (April 1982); David D. Wallace, *South Carolina: A Short History, 1520–1948* (1961).

Hooters

Ask most males why they eat at a Hooters restaurant and they will likely tell you that the chicken wings are delicious. Although that certainly may be true, others would contend that the siren call that attracts large numbers of men to Hooters is not related to the food. Established in 1983 in Clearwater, Fla., Hooters of America, Inc. has grown from a single establishment in the Sunshine State to a chain of some 450 locations throughout the world, including international branches in Greece, Singapore, Korea, England, and Australia, to name a few. According to Hooters' corporate history, more than 68 percent of Hooters patrons are male and between the ages of 25 and 54. While the restaurant does not cater to families, it admits that some 10 percent of its patrons are children.

The original Hooters Restaurant in Clearwater was the brainchild of Alisa Lamellae, who found cheap land on which to build—a former dumpster-washing facility. The original concept for Hooters was more of a bar than a full-service restaurant. The scantily clad servers were always part of the equation, though. In 1984 Robert H. Brooks and a group of Atlanta investors bought franchise rights outside of the six-county Tampa area. Brooks and his investors often clashed over leadership of the chain until they bought out the original owners with $60 million and limited franchising rights in exchange for the Hooters trademark.

Under Brooks's leadership, Hooters grew exponentially (corporately speaking), establishing a presence in every state and in 20 countries. He explained Hooters' success as "Good food, cold beer, and pretty girls never go out of style." Brooks did, however, assert that he never realized what the owl symbolized in the Hooters logo. In 2004 Hooters Airline tried to offer air travelers the same wholesome goodness that Brooks asserted one could find in the restaurants. Flight attendants wore the now familiar short orange shorts and snug fitting white tank tops. But the airline ceased operations in 2006, citing the high cost of jet fuel.

In 1991 the U.S. Equal Employment Opportunity Commission (EEOC) accused Hooters of sexual discrimination against men because all of the company's servers were women. Hooters had made no claim to the contrary, but the company addressed the accusations by organizing a "100 Hooter girl march" on Washington, D.C., while encouraging Hooters patrons to conduct a postcard campaign in support of the chain to Congress. The EEOC never brought suit on the matter. Six years later, in 1997, men in Chicago and Maryland filed class action lawsuits against Hooters, claiming that the restaurant chain discriminated against men in hiring servers. The matter was settled out of court. Hooters vigorously defends the use of the female form in restaurants, asserting without a hint of irony on its corporate Web site that "the Hooters girl is as socially acceptable as a Dallas Cowboy cheerleader, *Sports Illustrated* swimsuit model, or a Radio City Rockette."

Hooters maintains, however, a strong presence in the male-oriented, sports bar, chicken wings restaurant scene and has increased that role by sponsoring NASCAR racing teams and hosting the Annual Hooters International Swimsuit Pageant, which chooses Miss Hooters International from among the chain's Hooters Girl employee population.

For all its assertions of a wholesome, All-American, atmosphere, Hooters remains a point of contention between those who support the chain and its image and those who feel that it is an exploitation of the female form.

GORDON E. HARVEY
Jacksonville State University

Dean Foust, *Business Week* (13 June 2005); Hooters Corporate History, www.hooters.com/about; Douglas Martin, *New York Times* (18 July 2006).

Hot Springs National Park

Forty-seven hot springs flowing from the slope of Hot Springs Mountain in the foothills of Arkansas's Ouachita Mountains gained much attention in the early 19th century as a treatment for rheumatism and other ailments. Today, these naturally occurring springs serve as the centerpiece of Hot Springs National Park, one of the state's most popular tourist destinations.

Archaeological and other historical evidence suggests that Native Americans bathed in Hot Springs Creek prior to the arrival of Europeans. Before the Louisiana Purchase, the area surrounding the springs remained a virtually uninhabited wilderness; after that time, the thermal waters gained a widespread reputation for their healing, therapeutic qualities.

Early on, visitors flocked to the area in search of a cure. For example, in the 1820s the *Arkansas Gazette* reported 61 people representing seven different states at the springs "for health and pleasure." Belief in the thermal waters' efficacy in treating rheumatism and paralytic afflictions caused the valley's popularity to grow with each passing year.

In 1820 the Arkansas Territorial Assembly requested that Congress grant the site to the newly established Arkansas Territory, but Congress refused. Instead, on 20 April 1832, Congress created the Hot Springs Reservation by setting aside "four Sections of land including said Springs" for future use of the United States, making it the oldest area in the National Park System. This act intended to deny private landownership within a mile of the springs, but the government failed to enforce the measure so the town continued to grow within the federally reserved area.

The uncertainty surrounding landownership in the area hindered progress. Hot Springs' population increased little from the time of Arkansas statehood until the Civil War, reaching only 201 by 1860, but its fame as a health resort grew steadily. While the land dispute discouraged large investments or improvements for residents or visitors, a number of structures sprang up in the narrow valley alongside Hot Springs Creek. Bathing procedures remained primitive and visitors utilized crude facilities throughout the antebellum period.

Following the Civil War, the place took on an entirely different character. Numbers of tourists increased dramatically as patrons from all parts of the country poured in to spend their money. After 1869 the number of visitors grew by about 50 percent each year, and by the early 1870s Hot Springs enjoyed widespread popularity across the nation as a health resort. When Garland County was established in 1873, the city of Hot Springs became the county seat. The town included 24 commercial

Vintage postcard of Hot Springs National Park (Charles Reagan Wilson Collection, Center for the Study of Southern Culture, University of Mississippi)

hotels and boardinghouses, with capacity of 1,500 to 2,000 visitors per day. After the U.S. Supreme Court finally vested title to the springs in the federal government in 1877 and allowed private ownership in the surrounding area, bathing facilities and services enjoyed even further expansion. The once sleepy little village rapidly acquired characteristics of a wide-open boomtown.

The government took an active interest in its Hot Springs Reservation in the late 19th century. Federal improvements helped transform the frontier town to a cosmopolitan spa: construction of a grand entrance to the Reservation, mountain drives, elaborate fountains, and an arch covering Hot

Springs Creek along Central Avenue, all contributed to a more pleasing appearance. And government officials regulated activity involving the springs by establishing standards for bathing prices and related services.

For decades to follow, growth and development within the bathing industry paralleled growth and development of the city itself. Bathing reached a peak by the end of World War II, when over one million baths per year were provided to patrons. As the industry reached its zenith during the first half of the 20th century, luxury accommodations dominated the town's landscape, and the city bristled with activity. The town gained a reputation as an entertainment-rich destination, complete with illegal gambling, thoroughbred racing, and an assortment of amusement parks. Everyone—movie stars, politicians, rich, poor, and even gangsters—frequented "The American Spa." The town's slogan, "We Bathe the World," rang true.

In 1916 Congress established the National Park Service, and the Park Service assumed control of the Hot Springs Reservation. The reservation officially became Hot Springs National Park on 4 March 1921. A combination of factors resulted in the sharp decline of Central Avenue and its bathing industry by the 1960s: improved medical techniques, a general trend away from downtown shopping, and the elimination of gambling, all contributed to the downturn.

Hot Springs' Bath House Row was listed in the National Register of Historic Places on 13 November 1974. The most ornate of the Central Avenue structures, the Fordyce Bath House, became the National Park's visitor center, and only one of the of eight existing bathhouses continues to offer baths today. The remaining six facilities sit vacant. Now, as the reservation approaches its 175th anniversary, park officials plan to offer leases of the other structures to the private sector for renovation and development in an attempt to revitalize Hot Springs National Park's world famous Bath House Row.

WENDY RICHTER
Ouachita Baptist University

Orval Allbritton, *Leo & Verne: The Spa's Heyday* (2003); Dee Brown, *The American Spa: Hot Springs, Arkansas* (1982); Francis J. Scully, *Hot Springs, Arkansas and Hot Springs National Park: The Story of a City and the Nation's Health Resort* (1966).

Johnson, Junior

(b. 1931) SPORTS CAR DRIVER AND MOONSHINER.

Robert Glenn "Junior" Johnson is the most famous resident of Ingle Hollow in Wilkes County, N.C. Neighbors used to admire him for his adeptness at outwitting and outmaneuvering tax agents on moonshine runs. Now they and fans throughout the South and the nation revere him for his accomplishments as a stock car driver.

Johnson's father operated a still in Wilkes County, one of the most productive moonshine regions in the country. The size of his profit often depended on whether Junior could deliver the product to customers in nearby cities and towns without getting caught; so

Junior learned to drive fast and skillfully, often evading would-be captors by implementing his "bootleg turn," a technique that evolved into the "power slide" he later used as a stock car driver to maintain and accelerate speed coming out of turns on the racetrack. In 1955 agents caught him, not on a delivery, but standing in front of the still. He served just over 10 months in a Chillicothe, Ohio, prison.

At the time of his arrest, Johnson was already well on his way to becoming a successful stock car driver. He had won championships in the Sportsman and Modified classifications and, in 1955, captured the first of his seven Grand National victories. Ten years later he retired as a driver, having won the Daytona 500 and 49 other races. He was one of the sport's most popular figures.

Beginning in 1965, Johnson hired drivers for his cars and, with employees like Bobby Allison, Cale Yarborough, and Darrell Waltrip, his success continued, with his drivers winning 139 races. Recognized as a master mechanic, Johnson worked as a consultant to General Motors while still operating from his home in Ingle Hollow, where he and his staff built parts, made repairs, and worked to keep the team's cars among the fastest on the track. In 2007 Johnson teamed up with Piedmont Distillers in Madison, N.C., to begin making Midnight Moon, a small-batch moonshine made in the Johnson-family tradition.

Success has not separated Johnson from his heritage in the rural South. He is a prototypical good old boy who likes coon hunting and chicken farming.

He even helped found the Holly Farms Chicken company in North Wilkesboro, N.C. Writer Tom Wolfe called him the "Last American Hero," and Johnson's neighbors would probably agree. His bootlegging days may be well past— even if his moonshining days are not.

JESSICA FOY
Cooperstown Graduate Programs
Cooperstown, New York

Pete Daniel, *Lost Revolutions: The South in the 1950s* (2000); Larry Griffin, *Car and Driver* (April 1982); Charles Leerhsen, *Newsweek* (16 November 1981); Neal Thompson, *Driving with the Devil: Southern Moonshine, Detroit Wheels, and the Birth of NASCAR* (2006); Tom Wolfe, *Esquire* (March 1965).

Jones, Bobby

(1902–1971) GOLFER.
Born on 17 March 1902 in Atlanta, Ga., Robert Tyre "Bobby" Jones Jr. was a child prodigy at golf, studying under Stewart Maiden, a Scottish pro who worked at Atlanta's East Lake course. Jones played in the 1916 U.S. Amateur Tournament when he was only 14 years old. He went on to win 13 major championships, culminating in 1930 with his sweep in a single season of the "Grand Slam of Golf," which was then the championships of the British Amateur, the British Open, the U.S. Open, and the U.S. Amateur. New York City treated him to an enormous ticker tape parade that year, appropriate to one who had become a national hero. Later, he received a similar outpouring of affection from his hometown in Atlanta. At the height of his fame, at age 28, Jones announced his retirement. He returned

to his law practice and business endeavors in Atlanta, starting a long involvement with the A. G. Spalding Company, making a series of instructional film shorts for Warner Brothers studios, and conceiving and assisting in the design of the Augusta National Golf Course in Augusta, Ga., home of the Masters Tournament.

Jones's career reflected the rise of spectator sports in the South and the nation during the 1920s. Although golf was not as popular in the South as in the Northeast and on the West Coast, Jones nonetheless consciously worked to increase its popularity in his home region. He conceived the idea of the Augusta course, because "my native Southland, especially my own neighborhood, had very few, if any, golf courses of championship quality." He regarded it "as an opportunity to make a contribution to golf in my own section of the country."

Jones was frequently referred to as the embodiment of the southern gentleman. Journalist and commentator Alistair Cooke wrote that Jones was "a gentleman, a combination of goodness and grace, an unwavering courtesy, self-deprecation, and consideration for other people." Graceful in his athletic performance, poised at all times, modest in his success, and self-consciously "southern" in his attitudes, Jones symbolized a transitional figure—the traditional regional image of the gentleman in a new 20th-century mass culture context. Through the press and radio in the 1920s, the exploits of "The Emperor Jones" were publicized, and he thereby helped popularize golf with southerners and others who had once dismissed it as an effete game for the wealthy.

CHARLES REAGAN WILSON
University of Mississippi

Mark Frost, *The Grand Slam: Bobby Jones, America, and the Story of Golf* (2004); Stephen Lowe, *Georgia Historical Quarterly* (Winter 1999); Robert Tyre Jones Jr., *Golf Is My Game* (1959).

Jordan, Michael

(b. 1963) BASKETBALL PLAYER.

It would surprise most basketball fans—who associate Michael Jordan so closely with the Tar Heel State—that he was born in Brooklyn, N.Y. But his family moved to Wilmington, N.C., when he was a child, and it was there that his basketball prowess first became obvious. But he became nationally famous in 1982 when, as a freshman at the University of North Carolina, he hit a 17-foot jump shot to give his team the NCAA championship. Jordan remained in Chapel Hill two years after that, receiving All-American and national player-of-the-year honors, and then, in 1984, joined the professional Chicago Bulls. During his National Basketball Association career, he led his team to six NBA titles and was named NBA player of the year five times. A tremendous competitor, a great shooter, a tenacious defender, and—most famously—a spectacular leaper, he soon became known by the name "Air Jordan." Often called the greatest basketball player of all time, he was also named by ESPN in 1999 the greatest North American athlete of the 20th century. By the end of his career—partly because of his superiority on the court, partly because of his visibility as a pitchman for numerous products—he may also have become the most recognizable athlete in the world.

FRED HOBSON
University of North Carolina at Chapel Hill

David Halberstam, *Playing for Keeps: Michael Jordan and the World He Made* (2000); Michael Jordan, Mark Vancil, and Sandro Miller, *I Can't Accept Not Trying: Michael Jordan on the Pursuit of Excellence* (1994); David L. Porter, *Michael Jordan: A Biography* (2007).

Jubilees

The word "jubilee" means a season or occasion of joyful celebration. The term comes from the Hebrew *yobel* which was a ram's horn used as a trumpet. Along the eastern shore of Mobile Bay, in Baldwin County, Ala., the cry of "Jubilee!" has, for over a century, trumpeted one of nature's strangest natural occurrences. During a jubilee, large numbers (in various combinations) of flounder, crabs, shrimp, eels, catfish, stingrays, needlefish, and other bay creatures come into shallow water seemingly offering themselves to anyone alert enough to witness the event. During a large jubilee, scores of people can be seen gathering, netting, or gigging hundreds of pounds of seafood in a short period of time. A "jubilee network"—in which friends have contact lists that they have pledged to alert in the event of a jubilee—can assume an almost cultlike secrecy and organization.

Although jubilees have been reported in other parts of the world, none occur with the frequency as those found in Mobile Bay. Although unpredictable, the bay jubilees usually occur between June and September and can last from about 20 minutes to several hours—almost always between midnight and sunrise. Some summers will see no jubilees while others have experienced up to 15. In 1959 there were eight reported jubilees in the month of July. The prime area of the Jubilee is on the eastern shore of the bay along 15 miles of shoreline stretching from Daphne ("Jubilee City") south to Mullet Point. In rare cases, jubilees have occurred as far south as the northern tip of the Fort Morgan Peninsula. Even more rare is a jubilee on the western side of Mobile Bay, but these have been documented near Deer River and Dog River. Although the term jubilee was not used until the early 20th century (the earliest known written use of the term was in 1912), reports of jubilee-like events go back to just after the Civil War. On 17 July 1867 the *Mobile Daily Register* reported "EXCITEMENT AMONG THE FISH—Yesterday all the fish in the Bay seemed to be making for the Eastern Shore. Large numbers of crabs, flounders, and other fish were found at the water's edge and taken in out of the wet. They were counted by the bushel."

Decades ago, jubilees were attributed to everything from phosphorescent sparks in the water, to springs or gas vents in the bay, to minerals washed from the inland river systems. Many newspaper accounts in the late 1800s credited the odd marine happenings to excessive levels of salt water coming into the Bay from the adjacent Gulf of Mexico. More recent scientific study has determined that jubilees are actually caused by decaying organic matter that is washed south into the bay from the Mobile Delta. As this matter decomposes, there is a large increase in oxygen-consuming microorganisms. Pockets of oxygen-depleted water move to the shore producing a "corralling" effect on bottom-dwelling bay inhabitants. Starved of oxygen, the creatures lose their normal muscular abilities— appearing reluctant to swim or even to escape their human predators. The typical jubilee will last no more than a few hours. When water conditions improve, the fish will recover and ease back into deeper waters, none worse for the wear—except for the many that will soon appear on south Alabama tables.

Predicting jubilees has become a cottage industry on the eastern shore. In late summer, jubilee enthusiasts look for an easterly wind coinciding with an incoming tide. The wind blows surface water out into the middle of the bay while the tide directs the stagnant water to the shore. Some observe that on the day before a jubilee the weather will be cloudy or overcast and the bay will be calm or slick. These conditions help prevent the replenishing of oxygen in the water. Veteran jubilee watchers will say that, just before a jubilee, the water "looks funny" with perhaps a brownish or yellowish brown tint. If these conditions appear, a designated person might assume a night watch—checking along the shore every hour for signs that a jubilee has commenced. The social net-

work is then activated and the normally tranquil shoreline suddenly takes on a partylike atmosphere as the aroused human scavengers harvest the bounty.

LONNIE A. BURNETT
University of Mobile

Auburn University Marine Extension and Research Center, *The Jubilee Phenomenon* (2003); Jack C. Gallalee, *Jubilees* (1973); Edwin B. May, *Limnology and Oceanography* (May 1973); David Rainer, *Outdoor Alabama* (2008).

Juneteenth

Juneteenth is the popular name among black people in Texas for their emancipation day, which they celebrate on 19 June. On that day in 1865 Major General Gordon Granger officially announced the freedom of slaves when he arrived at Galveston to command the District of Texas following the Civil War.

Three black folktales provide other explanations of the date. In one version, Texas landowners refused to announce emancipation until the 1865 harvest had been gathered by the slaves. According to a second story, a black man journeyed by mule from Washington to Texas and arrived in June 1865 with word of the abolition of slavery. The other legend has the end of slavery declared as late as June because an earlier messenger was killed on the way to Texas.

The celebration of 19 June as emancipation day spread to the neighboring states of Louisiana, Arkansas, and Oklahoma, and later to California as black Texans migrated west. It has appeared occasionally in Alabama and Florida, also as a result of migration.

Large celebrations began in 1866 and continued to be held regularly into the early 20th century, although blacks in some Texas towns honored emancipation on 1 January or 4 July—days favored in some other states. Observations of Juneteenth declined in the 1940s during World War II but revived with 70,000 black people on the Texas State Fair grounds at Dallas during 1950. As school desegregation and the civil rights movement focused attention on the expansion of freedom in the late 1950s and early 1960s, Juneteenth celebrations declined again, although small towns still observed Texas's emancipation day. In the 1970s Juneteenth was revived in some communities, especially after two black members convinced the Texas Legislature to declare Juneteenth an unofficial "holiday of significance . . . particularly to the blacks of Texas."

Typical celebrations over the years included parades, picnics, baseball games or other competitive contests, speeches on freedom and future goals, and dances. Leaders in the black community normally organized the events, although occasionally in the 20th century a business or a black fraternal group assumed that role.

ALWYN BARR
Texas Tech University

Randolph B. Campbell, *Southwestern Historical Quarterly* (July 1984); *Ebony* (June 1951); Doris Hollis Pemberton, *Juneteenth at Comanche Crossing* (1983); Wendy Watriss, *Southern Exposure* (no. 1, 1977); William H. Wiggins Jr., *O Freedom! Afro-American Emancipation Celebrations* (1987).

Kentucky Derby

The Kentucky Derby, America's premier race classic for three-year-old thoroughbreds, showcases some of the South's most established traditions: honorable sporting competition, high fashion, and the love of pageantry. This mile-and-a-quarter test has been run at Churchill Downs in Louisville, Ky., since May 1875. The race originally was proposed as a match between Kentucky's and Tennessee's best three-year-old horses. However, its founder, Colonel M. Lewis Clark of Louisville, after visiting the racecourses of Europe, changed the inaugural to a derby patterned after England's one-and-a-half-mile Epsom Derby.

The names and traditions associated with the Kentucky Derby are a tapestry of American racing history. There was Matt Winn (1861–1949), the colorful track president who had seen every Derby and whose flair for showmanship transformed the race into a national and world event. There was Isaac Murphy (1871–96), the legendary black jockey with three winning rides. And Colonel E. R. "Bet-a-Million" Bradley, whose four winners—Behave Yourself (1921), Bubbling Over (1926), Burgoo King (1932), and Brokers Tip (1933)—like all his horses, began their names with the letter *B*. The year 1919 produced Sir Barton, the first Triple Crown winner, and 1941, Whirlaway, the chestnut speedster with the flying tail. Then, too, there were "R-r-r-racing fans, this is Clem McCarthy" calling the race on national radio (1928–50); Citation (1948), one of eight horses to carry the devil's red silks of Calumet Stables to victory;

Churchill Downs, Louisville, Ky. (Kentucky Department of Travel)

and Penny Tweedy's wonder horse, Secretariat, the race record holder (1.59²⁄₅, 1973). And, of course, there were Donerail (1913) and Mine That Bird (2009), the shocking come-from-behind winners that provided the biggest upsets in the Derby's history.

The Derby is not just about the horses, jockeys, and placing bets, however; it is steeped in traditions that reinforce southern ideals of community entertainment, social interaction, and fashion. During the two weeks before Derby Day, the Louisville community celebrates the Kentucky Derby Festival, which offers events such as fireworks, steamboat and hot-air balloon races, parades, concerts, and even a marathon. Since 1972, the governor of Kentucky has been hosting a Derby Day breakfast at the capitol for all Kentuckians and their Derby guests. At the Derby, numerous traditions emerge to make

the race unique. The mint julep, closely associated with southern cuisine, has long been considered the traditional beverage of the Kentucky Derby; the combination of sugar, ice, mint, and bourbon is served at the Derby in traditional silver julep cups and commemorative glasses. One Kentucky distiller said that drinking mint juleps is like wearing the Derby's fashionable hats: both traditions are usually symbolically observed only at the Derby.

Hats are indeed one of the most iconic traditions of the Derby. The large, elaborate, stylish hats complement the fashionable outfits worn by people who dress the part of traditional Derbygoers, who take their appreciation of high fashion from the Royal Ascot race in England and from the antebellum South. The most elaborate outfits are often found in Millionaire Row, the expensive box seats in the stands around the track. Many celebrities are often in attendance—even royal figures; Queen Elizabeth II and Prince Phillip of England attended the Derby in 2007. The Infield is crowded with less auspicious crowds, many of whom make their own "wacky" hats and bring picnic coolers and beer, ready to enjoy the infield's light-hearted revelry. Even people who do not attend the race have an opportunity to experience the Derby's traditions. Many watch the race and practice southern hospitality at elegant house parties as they entertain guests with typical southern cuisine and, of course, mint juleps.

Run on the first Saturday in May, the Derby is an American tradition, an unofficial holiday that focuses on the spectacle of finely conditioned animals competing in the ultimate two-minute test. For the winner, there is racing immortality, the traditional blanket of roses, a purse in excess of $100,000, and the chance to win America's racing Triple Crown. For the audience, there is an opportunity to enjoy the traditions and to savor a flavoring of timeless culture. When the familiar strains of "My Old Kentucky Home" are sung as the horses are led onto the track, everyone becomes both a Kentuckian and a southerner. In this sense, the Kentucky Derby is more than a race; it is, instead, an expression of national heritage.

JAMES C. CLAYPOOL
Northern Kentucky University

MARY AMELIA TAYLOR
University of Mississippi

James Barron, *New York Times* (5 May 1990); Peter Chew, *The Kentucky Derby: The First 100 Years* (1974); Joe Drape, *New York Times* (2 May 2009); Annie Harrison, *The Kentucky Derby: Its Traditions and Triumphs* (1980); Laura Hillenbrand, *American Heritage* (January 1999); Chuck Martin, *Cincinnati Enquirer* (30 April 2003).

Lambert's Café

Lambert's Café opened during the Second World War in a small town in the heart of southeast Missouri. Claiming to be the only home of "Throw'd Rolls," the establishment takes its slogan from its peculiarly raucous system of serving hot, dinner rolls. This family-owned operation began with one restaurant in Sikeston, Mo., located between St. Louis and Memphis, Tenn., but has since opened Lambert's II in Ozark, Mo., in 1994 and Lambert's III in Foley, Ala., in 1996.

Earl and Agnes Lambert entered the restaurant business on 13 March 1942 after borrowing $1,500 dollars from a friend. The café soon became popular with local residents, but hungry travelers have increasingly provided Lambert's with a steady stream of customers from outside the southeast Missouri region since the opening of Interstate 55.

After Earl's death in 1976, his son, Norman Lambert, and wife, Patti, became part owners alongside Earl's widow, Agnes. That same year, Lambert's Café assumed its famous moniker as the "Home of Throw'd Rolls." Norman, who had heretofore passed out rolls to customers from a pushcart, was unable to navigate through the thick lunch-hour crowd. When a customer became irritated with the slow pace, he yelled at Norman to "throw the [expletive] thing." Norman Lambert obliged, and Lambert's servers have been throwing fresh, hot rolls to customers ever since.

Lambert's Café serves traditional southern dishes such as fried chicken, catfish, chicken-fried steak, and country ham. Servers—wearing the bow ties and suspenders made famous by Norman—offer customers unlimited servings of side items (known as pass-arounds) with their meal. According to Lambert's, they serve 48,960 pounds of white beans, 8,496 gallons of red pepper relish, over 73,000 pounds of fried Arkansas okra as well as 23,760 large cans of sorghum molasses to go along with 2,246,000 "throw'd rolls" each year.

In addition to creating the restaurant's claim to fame, Norman Lambert lent his distinctive personality to the restaurant's décor during his 20-year stint as owner. Walls covered with various antiques and portraits of Missouri mules surround patrons who sit at unadorned tables and drink from plastic mugs and fruit jars while tunes stream loudly from a player piano. As Norman Lambert, who passed away in 1996, once told the Associated Press, "It's a 'hey bud,' 'hey dude' place. Bottom line, there's a lot more Chevy's out there than is Cadillacs."

Ben Lambert has operated Lambert's Café alongside his mother, Patti, since Norman's death. The family continues to display Norman's "13 Golden Rules" with prominence. The first of these is "Do unto others as you would have them do unto you," and the last is to do "simple things, but in exceptional ways." These rules add to the bucolic charm

that draws customers by the tour bus-load to Lambert's Café.

Highly rated food and service, along with the novelty of flying dinner rolls, also drew many famous patrons, including Clint Eastwood, Stan Musial, Elvis Presley, Conway Twitty, and Tammy Wynette. Another famous face pitched the restaurant in an early 1990s commercial sponsored by the Missouri Department of Tourism. Actor and St. Louis native John Goodman encouraged tourists to visit Lambert's for an unpretentious eating experience. The café's massive portions and endless pass-arounds led the *Travel Channel* to name Lambert's the best place to "pig out" in the United States, and *Southern Living* magazine named the family eatery the "Best Small Town Restaurant" in 1996.

ASHTON ELLETT
University of Georgia

Harry Cline, *Western Farm Press* (1 December 2007); Jerry Shriver, *USA Today* (25 May 2007); Michael Stern and Jane Stern, *St. Petersburg Times* (8 October 1987).

Louisiana State Lottery Company

The Louisiana State Lottery Company had its genesis in 1866 when the legislature, controlled by Confederate veterans, passed an act permitting lottery vending in the state. Two years later a Republican-dominated legislature assisted by Charles T. Howard, a skilled lobbyist, pushed through a bill chartering the Louisiana State Lottery Company. The 25-year charter gave the company a monopoly on the sale of lottery tickets and exempted the organization from state taxes, except for an annual license fee of $40,000. Its capital stock was set at $1 million with 10,000 shares valued at $100 each. Operations began on 31 December 1868.

By the time the Republican government fell in 1877 the company was a lucrative and politically powerful enterprise. Anxious to maintain its privileges and to foil opposition from Louisiana's Redeemers, lotterymen in 1879 allied themselves with the reactionary Bourbon faction of the Democratic Party, wrote a new state constitution that ousted unfriendly state officials, installed lottery supporters in key government positions, and gave legal sanction to lotteries until 1 January 1895.

With opposition temporarily stayed, lotterymen improved the image of the organization by undertaking philanthropic endeavors and enshrining their enterprise in the sacrosanct shroud of the Lost Cause. Two ex-Confederate generals, P. G. T. Beauregard and Jubal Early, presided over drawings, thereby ensuring honesty. Yet, with 47 percent of its gross receipts retained as profit, there was little need for chicanery. Conservative estimates of profits accrued in the 1880s range from $8 million to $14 million annually, and by 1890 the company reportedly took in from $20 million to $30 million.

At the peak of its economic and political power, opposition to the company increased locally and nationally. From 1890 to 1892, debates over the renewal of the company's charter raged throughout the state, split both major parties, divided the Populists, and submerged all other issues. The antilottery

forces won the battle in Louisiana, but the U.S. Congress, taking direct aim at the Louisiana Lottery, delivered the fatal blow by passing a bill denying the use of the mails to lotteries. Because 90 percent of the Louisiana Lottery's proceeds came from states other than Louisiana, this legislation dried up profits and closed down operations in the state in December 1893. In January diehard lotterymen transferred the company to Honduras, and for some years they sponsored illegal activities in the United States. Federal law enforcement authorities checked these operations, and the company collapsed in 1907.

CAROLYN DELATTE
McNeese State University

Berthold C. Alwes, *Louisiana Historical Quarterly* (October 1944); Henry C. Dethloff, *Louisiana History* (Spring 1965); William I. Hair, *Bourbonism and Agrarian Protest: Louisiana Politics, 1877–1900* (1969).

Mammoth Cave National Park

Located in south-central Kentucky, Mammoth Cave National Park is the longest recorded cave system in the world, officially identified as the Mammoth Cave System. The national park was established in 1941, now encompassing 52,830 acres above ground and 360 miles of mapped tunnels and passageways below, with newly found tunnels adding to that number yearly.

The history of the Mammoth Cave region extends across several millennia—perhaps as far back as the Paleo-Indians, who roamed the Mississippi Valley more than 11,000 years ago—but it is uncertain when modern man began exploring the cave. Legend

Mammoth Cave National Park, Kentucky (Kentucky Department of Travel)

has it that John Houchins first "discovered" the cave in 1797 when giving chase to a wounded bear while hunting, yet other accounts place its discovery before then. The first person to map the cave system and give name to many of its features was Stephen Bishop. By the War of 1812, Mammoth Cave was mined for bat guano, which contains calcium nitrate, an ingredient used to make gunpowder. In the decades following the war, after the price of gunpowder had significantly fallen, the cave became one of America's first and most popular tourist attractions, and ownership of the cave changed hands a number of times, eventually being purchased by Franklin Gorin in 1838. Gorin, a slave owner, used his slaves as guides for tourists who wanted to explore the increasingly famous cave. Stephen Bishop, one of Gorin's slaves, was sold in October 1839, along with Mammoth Cave, to Dr. John Croghan. Through the 1840s and into the 1850s, Bishop explored, mapped out, and guided visitors through Mammoth Cave. Today, many features of the cave still bear the names that Bishop gave them, such as Pensacola Avenue, the Snowball Room, Bunyan's Way, Winding Way, Bottomless Pit, Great Relief Hall, and the River Styx.

In 1849 Dr. Croghan died, but not before attempting to turn portions of the cave into a sanitarium for tuberculosis patients, believing the vapors within the cave contained healing powers. Some of his patients died shortly after relocating to the cave; all the rest grew progressively worse. Within a year he had abandoned his sanitarium experiment. Croghan died, incidentally, of the disease he was attempting to cure, and Bishop, one year after his manumission in 1856, also died of tuberculosis at the age of 36.

By 1926 advocacy for the preservation of Mammoth Cave had grown among wealthy Kentuckians. Private citizens donated funds to purchase much of the land within the proposed park, and the right of eminent domain secured the remaining tracts. On 1 July 1941 Mammoth Cave National Park was officially dedicated, and the cave system below the park continues to grow. As recently as 2005 a connection linking the Mammoth system to another cave system, Roppel Cave, was discovered east of the park. It is generally accepted that explorers will continue to discover unexplored pathways in the coming years and that thousands of yet-to-be-discovered animal species exist in the cave system.

Today the wondrous subterranean world of Mammoth Cave is visited by nearly 2 million visitors annually. Tourists travel from all over the world to explore Mammoth Cave's labyrinthine passageways. Features of particular interest within these caverns are the 192-foot-high Mammoth Dome, the 105-foot-deep Bottomless Pit, walls sprinkled with sparkling white gypsum crystals, conical stalagmites and stalactites, giant vertical shafts, the underground Echo and Styx rivers, and rare and endangered animal species such as the southeastern bat, the eyeless crayfish, and the Mammoth Cave shrimp. But while most visitors are attracted to the park to venture below ground, above ground the 52,830-acre park contains lakes and rivers, a 300-acre old-growth forest, rolling hills, miles of hiking trails, and a complex and diverse ecosystem.

JAMES G. THOMAS JR.
University of Mississippi

James D. Borden and Roger W. Brucker, *Beyond Mammoth Cave: A Tale of Obsession in the World's Longest Cave* (2000); Roger W. Brucker and Richard A. Watson, *The Longest Cave* (1976); Horace Carter Hovey, *One Hundred Miles in Mammoth Cave in 1880: An Early Exploration of America's Most Famous Cavern* (1982); Johnny Molloy, *A Falcon Guide to Mammoth Cave National Park* (2006); Robert K. Murray and Roger W. Brucker, *Trapped!: The Story of Floyd Collins* (1979); Bob Thompson and

Judi Thompson, *Mammoth Cave and the Kentucky Cave Region* (2003); William B. White and Elizabeth L. White, eds., *Karst Hydrology: Concepts from the Mammoth Cave Area* (1989).

Manning Family

ARCHIE MANNING (b. 1949), PEYTON MANNING (b. 1976), AND ELI MANNING (b. 1981) FOOTBALL PLAYERS.

Archie Manning, patriarch of the first family of southern football, arrived at the University of Mississippi in 1967. The red-haired, gangly, and relatively unheralded recruit from Drew, Miss., took over at quarterback as a sophomore under legendary coach John Vaught. Manning soon gained regional and national renown as a superb passer as well as a talented runner. He led the Rebels to three bowl games, including a Sugar Bowl victory over Arkansas. Archie's stature grew to heroic proportions in the South during the 1969 Sugar Bowl campaign, in which he was the Rebels' leading rusher. He produced two unforgettable games during that eight-win season. The first came in a losing effort against Alabama in the first nationally televised college football night game. He amassed an SEC record 540 yards of total offense against the victorious Crimson Tide.

Later in the season, he led the Rebels to a 38–0 upset of first-ranked Tennessee, a game known as the Jackson Massacre. Some Volunteer fans had worn "Archie Who?" buttons to the game, and afterward, an exultant Ole Miss fan recorded "The Ballad of Archie Who," which sold 35,000 copies and

featured the line, "That's All-American Archie / You know Archie Who." Today, Archie Manning's number 18 is both the speed limit on campus and one of the football program's two retired jersey numbers.

Shortly after Archie married his college sweetheart, Ole Miss Homecoming Queen Olivia Williams, the New Orleans Saints drafted Archie. He was the second overall pick in the 1971 NFL draft. He played there for 12 seasons. He completed his 14-year career with season-long stints with the Houston Oilers and the Minnesota Vikings. Despite never having a winning season in the pros, he went to two Pro Bowls and was the NFC's MVP in 1979. He is a member of the college football and New Orleans Saints halls of fame.

The Mannings remained in New Orleans after Archie's retirement, and all three of his sons lettered in multiple sports at Isidore Newman High, a private school near the Garden District. The oldest, Cooper, signed with Ole Miss as a wide receiver, but a spinal cord disorder ended his career. Peyton, the most intense and serious brother, bucked the family trend and offended many Rebel fans when he decided to sign with the University of Tennessee. He later said he would have signed with Ole Miss if Cooper had still been playing. Peyton started eight games as a freshman and every game of the next three seasons. He led the Vols to four bowl appearances, three top-10 finishes, and an SEC title. He was the MVP of Tennessee's victory over Auburn in the 1997 SEC championship game. He fared well against Alabama, beating the

Vols' traditional rival three consecutive years. He led the "Pride of the Southland" band in "Rocky Top" to celebrate the 1997 victory, one of the most memorable moments of his collegiate career.

The Indianapolis Colts drafted Peyton with the first overall pick in 1998, and he started every game of his rookie season. He became known as league's most devoted student of the game and quickly became one of the league's elite quarterbacks. Despite stellar play throughout his career, he drew criticism for his perceived inability to win the big one. After all, Tennessee never beat Florida with Peyton at the helm, and the Colts always seemed to come up short to the New England Patriots in the playoffs. But he finally got past the Patriots in the 2006 AFC championship game, and the Colts went on to win the Super Bowl. Peyton engineered an 80-yard drive in the final minutes of Super Bowl XLI that produced the go-ahead touchdown and earned him the game's MVP award. Peyton has also won the league MVP award a record-tying three times and has made nine Pro Bowl appearances.

Following his prep career at Isidore Newman, Eli signed with Ole Miss, where Peyton's former offensive coordinator and mentor, David Cutcliffe, was head coach. In spite of the intense pressure of living up to the Manning name at his father's alma mater, the soft-spoken and undemonstrative youngest Manning kept a characteristically even keel at Ole Miss. The Rebels enjoyed winning seasons in each of the three years Eli started at quarterback, and his senior campaign netted 10 wins, an SEC West co-championship, and a 31–28 Cotton Bowl victory over Oklahoma State. Eli set or matched 47 Ole Miss records, including career completions (829) and career passing yards (10,119).

The San Diego Chargers selected Eli Manning with the first overall pick of the 2004 NFL draft, but he threatened to sit out if not traded to another team. The New York Giants landed the youngest Manning. Eli took over the starting job late in his rookie season, and he led the Giants to the playoffs in 2005 and 2006. But critics—including some of his teammates—questioned his leadership ability. In 2007 he overcame these criticisms by leading the Giants to a 10–6 season that culminated in a Super Bowl victory. To beat the undefeated Patriots in Super Bowl XLII, he made one of the most dramatic plays in the game's history late in the fourth quarter. On a critical third down, he twisted out of the grasp of a defender, bailed out of a collapsed pocket, and completed a 32-yard pass into traffic. With less than a minute remaining, Eli completed the drive with a 13-yard touchdown pass. Just a year after Peyton was the Super Bowl's MVP, Eli earned the same honor, and both played in that year's Pro Bowl.

The first family of southern football gets a great deal of exposure off the field as well. The quarterbacking Mannings are featured on dozens of national commercials, and an ESPN commercial featured the whole family. Peyton has hosted *Saturday Night Live*, and Eli has been on the cover of *Men's Vogue* magazine. The Mannings are also known for tremendous charitable contributions. In

1999 Peyton created the Peyback Foundation to help disadvantaged children in Louisiana, Tennessee, and Indiana, and in 2007, as a result of Peyton's charitable contributions to the hospital, St. Vincent's Hospital in Indianapolis renamed its children's hospital Peyton Manning Children's Hospital at St. Vincent's. In December 2008 Eli helped raise funds to open the Eli Manning Children's Clinics at the Blair E. Batson Hospital for Children in Jackson, Miss.

MILES LASETER
University of Mississippi

Archie Manning and Peyton Manning with John Underwood, *Manning* (2000); Ralph Vacchiano, *Eli Manning: The Making of a Quarterback* (2008).

Maravich, Pete

(1947–1988) BASKETBALL PLAYER. Peter Press Maravich was born on 22 June 1947 in Aliquippa, Pa., near Pittsburgh. He learned the fundamentals of basketball from his father, "Press," and spent hours each day developing his shooting, dribbling, and passing artistry. When his father became head coach at Clemson University in 1956, Pete played at high schools in South Carolina and North Carolina, where he earned the nickname "The Pistol" because he shot accurately from his hip.

Pete took a scholarship to LSU when his father became head coach there in 1966. In three years with the varsity (1967–70), "Pistol Pete" scored 3,667 points, averaging 44.2 points per game. In 83 games for the Tigers, he scored 50 points or more 28 times. He set every scoring record at LSU, as well as 34 SEC

records, and 11 NCAA marks. In 1970 he led LSU to a 20–8 record and was named All-American and U.S. Basketball Writers Association player of the year and won the Naismith Award. Although he raised the quality of basketball at LSU, Pete never played in the NCAA tournament.

In 1970 the 6'5" Maravich was the third pick in the NBA draft and signed a five-year, $1.9 million contract with the Atlanta Hawks, making him the highest paid athlete in the United States. After four seasons with the Hawks, including two selections to the NBA All-Star team, Maravich was traded to the New Orleans Jazz in 1974. He prospered with the Jazz, making the All-Star team in 1977, 1978, and 1979, and leading the NBA in scoring with 31.1 points per game during the 76–77 season.

In 1979 Maravich moved with the Jazz to Utah, but he was waived in January 1980 and was acquired by the Boston Celtics as a free agent. He spent the rest of the season as a bench player supporting a rising star, Larry Bird. As the next season approached, Maravich announced his early retirement.

Maravich suffered from nagging knee injuries since 1978. In the NBA, the five-time All-Star had scored 15,948 points in 658 games (24.2 points per game). He became a recluse for two years, struggling with depression and alcoholism. He reemerged in 1982 as a born-again Christian, determined to use his celebrity to promote his new faith around the country. He and his family moved to Covington, La.

In 1986 "Pistol Pete" was inducted into the NBA Hall of Fame. Eight years after his retirement, while working with James Dobson's ministry in Pasadena, Calif., the 40-year-old Maravich collapsed during a pickup basketball game. The heart attack that claimed his life on 5 January 1988 was determined to have resulted from a congenital heart defect. He was buried at Resthaven Garden of Memory in Baton Rouge, La.

Louisiana governor Buddy Roemer named the LSU home court the Pete Maravich Assembly Center in 1988. LSU retired his number 23 in 2007. "Pistol" Pete Maravich left a legacy to basketball that is found in every lanky, bushy-haired youngster with droopy socks who devotes countless hours, after practice ends, to honing his skills.

LLEWELLYN D. COOK
Jacksonville State University

Mark Kriegel, *Pistol: The Life of Pete Maravich* (2007); Tom Saladino, *Pistol Pete Maravich: The Louisiana Purchase* (1974).

Mid-South Wrestling

Former professional wrestling star "Cowboy" Bill Watts bought out his former employer, Tri-State Wrestling, in 1979 and redubbed it the Mid-South Wrestling Association, which covered territory in Louisiana, Mississippi, Oklahoma, and eventually Arkansas and parts of eastern Texas. At the time, Watts was seen as a very savvy promoter in the professional wrestling world, backing shows that garnered high ratings and that sported a large fan base. Mid-South Wrestling focused on high-energy matches featuring a more physical style and episodic format than some of his competition.

Watts's Mid-South brand gained in popularity during the early 1980s, in large part because of his dynamic and exotic cast of (primarily southern) wrestlers, which included the Junkyard Dog, the One Man Gang, Kamala the Ugandan Giant, King Kong Bundy, the Fabulous Freebirds, Dusty Rhodes, the Great Kabuki, and "Hacksaw" Jim Duggan. Mid-South Wrestling's success led Ted Turner to ask Watts to air the matches on the TBS cable channel in 1985 as an alternative to the World Wrestling Federation (WWF) show that aired on Saturday nights. With increased popularity, Watts positioned himself to take over the two-hour Saturday night block occupied by the WWF, but his luck ran out when National Wrestling Alliance (NWA) promoter Jim Crockett Jr. bought the slot from the WWF's Vince McMahon and became the exclusive wrestling promotion for TBS. The deal forced the removal of the *Mid-South Wrestling* program from the TBS schedule.

In March 1986 Mid-South Wrestling went national and was renamed again as the Universal Wrestling Federation (UWF). Many newcomers, including Steve Williams, D. J. Peterson, and Scott Hall, joined Universal. But despite the federation's success, it could not compete against Jim Crockett Promotions and the WWF. Watts sold the UWF to Jim Crockett in the spring of 1987, and many of the federation's top names went on to either the NWA, WWF, or World Class Championship Wrestling (WCCW). Crockett's circuit was sold to Ted Turner and eventually became World Championship Wrestling (WCW).

In the early 1990s, Watts found himself back in the spotlight as WCW president.

MARK COLTRAIN
Central Piedmont Community College

Scott Beekman, *Ringside: A History of Professional Wrestling in America* (2006); Carolyn Kolb, *New Orleans Magazine* (November 2004); Kristian Pope and Ray Whebbe, *The Encyclopedia of Professional Wrestling: 100 Years of History, Headlines, and Hitmakers* (2003).

Myrtle Beach, South Carolina

Myrtle Beach is a popular tourist destination in South Carolina known for its beaches, entertainment venues, seafood restaurants, golf courses, and shopping. The city, which draws 10 million tourists per year, is the main attraction along the Grand Strand.

Myrtle Beach, currently the largest city in Horry County, was not developed until the early 20th century. The sparsely populated area was isolated by rivers and swamps and had generally poor soil for farming. The local economy was based primarily on aspects of the timber industry, fishing, and subsistence farming.

Franklin G. Burroughs, a prominent businessman who settled in the area in the mid-19th century, saw the coast as a potential resort. Burroughs and Benjamin Grier Collins formed the Burroughs & Collins Company in 1895. The company built the first railroad line from Conway, the county seat, to the coast; opened the first motel, the Seaside Inn; and built a simple pavilion and boardwalk in the first years of the 20th century. Burroughs & Collins began to sell small beachfront lots to individuals from Conway for vacation cottages. In 1912 the land-rich Burroughs & Collins Company was in need of capital and partnered with Simeon B. Chapin, a northern businessman. They formed the Myrtle Beach Farms Company to develop a resort along the coast. The Great Depression was devastating for America, but Myrtle Beach grew and prospered.

In 1926 John T. Woodside bought 65,000 acres from Myrtle Beach Farms and contributed greatly to the infrastructure, planning, and development of Myrtle Beach. Woodside built the first golf course—today there are more than 100—and the Ocean Forrest Hotel, a lavish structure referred to as the "million dollar hotel." The hotel's grand opening was a few months after the stock market crash of 1929. Woodside ended up defaulting, and the land reverted back to Myrtle Beach Farms with many improvements. In the late 1930s, the city of Myrtle Beach received its charter; however, World War II soon disrupted the developing tourism industry. The war effort bought a strong military presence to the area. The Myrtle Beach Air Force Base became a social and economic force from 1940 until it closed in 1993.

With increased leisure time, the development of better roads, and a strong economy, tourism flourished in postwar America. In 1950 Burroughs & Collins opened the Myrtle Beach Pavilion Amusement Park, which became a local institution and center of socialization. Mom-and-pop tourist courts, motels, restaurants, and amusements flourished alongside the white, sandy beaches. As a

southern resort, Myrtle Beach's amusements were for whites only until the
late 1960s. Blacks were instrumental to
Myrtle Beach's development, including
building and working in the tourism
industry. Strong, tight-knit African
American communities existed in the
resort town.

The devastation of Hurricane Hazel
in 1954 and the subsequent rebuilding
efforts contributed to Myrtle Beach's
transition from quaint seaside resort
to the national tourist destination it is
today. Low-cost flood insurance became available in 1968 and facilitated
bigger developments along the shore.
The 1970s brought the first high-rise
hotel, the Yachtsman, and by the end of
the decade overdevelopment had become a problem. In 1990 Myrtle Beach
Farms Company joined with Burroughs
& Collins Company to form Burroughs
& Chapin Company, Inc. In the late
20th century, Myrtle Beach suffered
from poor planning, lack of ecological
conservation, and complaints about the
dominance of Burroughs & Chapin.

Burroughs & Chapin closed the
Pavilion Amusement Park in 2006. The
resulting hole left in the center of the
city was representative of the changes
and challenges facing Myrtle Beach in
the 21st century. Burroughs & Chapin
plan to build condos to replace the
amusement park. Many of the park's
historic artifacts have moved to the
Pavilion Nostalgia Park at Broadway
at the Beach, a 350-acre Burroughs &
Chapin entertainment compound with
chain stores, restaurants, bars, theaters,
and a miniature golf course.

Today, Myrtle Beach still has the

beautiful beaches that originally drew
people to its shores. The buildings
alongside the coast are much taller, the
natural environment is less pure, and
the development is under a corporate
rather than a family model. Yet one of
the South's most popular and democratic tourist destinations continues to
grow and change with the tides.

NICOLE KING
University of Maryland at
Baltimore County

Catherine H. Lewis, *Horry County, South*
Carolina, 1730–1993 (1998); Barbara F.
Stokes, *Myrtle Beach: A History, 1900–1980*
(2007); Will Moredock, *Banana Republic:*
A Year in the Heart of Myrtle Beach (2003).

NASCAR

Daytona Beach, Florida–based NASCAR
(National Association for Stock Car
Auto Racing) is the largest and most
important sanctioning body for auto
racing in the United States. It is best
known for its premier stock car series,
currently known as Nextel Cup. Like
Coca-Cola and Wal-Mart, NASCAR is a
southern born-and-bred brand that has
grown to have national and even international significance and influence. At
the same time, its management style
and many of its major features retain a
uniquely southern character.

Stories of the origins of NASCAR
generally revolve around two key components: "good old boy" illegal liquor
haulers and Daytona Beach mechanic/
auto racer/promoter William Henry
Getty "Big Bill" France. To be sure,
illegal liquor haulers, primarily from the
Piedmont South, had a significant impact on the origins of NASCAR as the

majority of the early stars of southern stock car racing had their first high-speed driving experiences behind the wheels of late 1930s Ford V-8s loaded down with white liquor.

The move from high-speed evasion of law enforcement on the back roads of the Piedmont and its foothills to racing on red-clay fairgrounds tracks was a natural one for the liquor haulers. In the early years of southern stock car racing, these wild individuals generally dominated the regional racing scene as they possessed more disposable income than the average southerner, superior equipment, mechanical know-how, and extensive high-speed driving experience. The outlaw image of many of the drivers helped to attract working-class fans to the tracks to cheer on these individuals who defied both law and convention.

Bill France became friends with many of these liquor-hauling racers as he both competed against them in stock car races in the late 1930s and early 1940s and promoted some of the largest and most important pre–World War II races on Daytona Beach. After World War II, France focused his energies on building a stock car racing empire. In addition to the drivers, France used the financial capital provided by other southerners who were deeply involved in the illegal liquor business. Most of the key early car owners, mechanics, and track owners in the Piedmont had deep ties to moonshining and bootlegging. Indeed, the very financial foundation of Bill France's empire was built on the proceeds of the manufacture, transport, and sale of hundreds of thousands,

if not millions, of cases of white liquor and bonded "red" liquor.

In 1947 France sought to expand what was essentially a regional enterprise and brought together promoters from the Northeast and Midwest to found NASCAR. From the start, its organization was unique to any other professional sport's sanctioning body as it was almost solely owned and controlled by France, who possessed dictatorial powers. At the same time, however, France had a paternalistic side and gained the trust of most important stock car drivers, car owners, and promoters.

In the 1950s the sport experienced tremendous growth as France and his associates expanded NASCAR's reach across the nation, sanctioning races in its top division in 28 different states in every major region of the country, and even beyond, in Ontario, Canada. In the same period drivers from 38 states and 3 Canadian provinces competed in these races. While NASCAR's reach did expand, the Piedmont South was still the home of most of its star drivers and its most significant races. Perhaps NASCAR's most important innovation during the period was the creation of lower divisions of weekly racing on the burgeoning number of Piedmont short tracks. This expansion enabled working-class individuals to start racing for little cost and move up through the ranks. Indeed, most of the second generation of NASCAR stars got their start in this manner, rather than at the wheel of a liquor car.

NASCAR's increasing connections to the American auto industry also helped to facilitate this growth. In the early 1950s, car dealers began to note the rise in sales when a particular make of automobile was successful in stock car racing. Bill France and others in NASCAR successfully promoted the notion of "win on Sunday, sell on Monday," and Detroit began to provide significant technical and financial support to top car owners and drivers.

NASCAR entered a new era of expansion in the late 1950s and 1960s, as new, paved superspeedways were built, older dirt tracks were paved, and new stars came on the scene. Bill France led the way by constructing NASCAR's most important showcase in 1959, the Daytona International Speedway. The construction of Daytona put France in the enviable position of owning not only the sanctioning body but also its most important venue. Other high-speed paved tracks followed at Charlotte and Rockingham, N.C., Atlanta, Ga., Bristol, Tenn., the Irish Hills near Detroit, and Talladega, Ala.

During the early 1960s, Detroit played an even greater role in NASCAR, pouring millions of dollars into the sport. Competition between the automakers became intense, and Bill France had to walk a fine line to appease the automakers while preventing one make from winning all of the races. France alternately banned the Chrysler Hemi engine in 1965 and then the Ford overhead-cam engine in 1966. In each year, the factory teams boycotted, leaving France with dominance by a single make and without the attraction of some of his top drivers, including

Richard Petty, who joined the Chrysler boycott in 1965.

France also encountered problems from his drivers in the 1960s. The more powerful automobiles and the high-speed tracks combined to produce a dangerous mix for drivers, especially when tire technology failed to keep pace. A number of NASCAR's top stars lost their lives during the period, including two-time champion Joe Weatherly and the most popular driver in NASCAR, Glen "Fireball" Roberts. Drivers also noted that while their expenses and NASCAR's revenues were increasing, prize money remained static. In 1961, and again in 1969, drivers attempted to unionize. Although both efforts were led by some of the most successful and popular drivers in NASCAR, Bill France adeptly crushed both movements. Indeed, one of the most southern aspects of NASCAR is the way France defeated the union movements using every tried and true tactic employed by Piedmont mill owners to defeat the United Textile Workers of America.

Having successfully handled these controversies, France turned the reins of power over to his son William Clifton France—generally known as Bill Jr.—in 1972. Before he left, however, he helped NASCAR take its most significant step into the modern era when he secured sponsorship for his flagship Grand National series from the R. J. Reynolds Tobacco Co. Flush with dollars it could no longer spend on television advertising because of a new federal ban, R. J. Reynolds poured millions into the series—now named the Winston Cup—transforming it from a sport of small dirt track and paved bullrings to large superspeedways. In the same year, Richard Petty wooed STP to sponsor his race car and the sport entered a new era of corporate sponsorship.

Television also began to have a greater and greater impact on the sport and helped Bill France Jr. promote its growing popularity. Incredibly exciting finishes in nationally televised Daytona 500s in both 1976 and 1979 brought greater exposure to the sport and created hordes of new fans. Increasing numbers of live broadcasts soon followed, especially when the fledgling cable network ESPN began making NASCAR broadcasts one of its staples in 1981.

In the 1980s and 1990s, NASCAR experienced explosive growth owing to its greater television exposure and a bevy of talented and attractive new stars. Growth in the sport was heightened even more by the rivalry in the 1990s of the polar opposites Dale Earnhardt and Jeff Gordon. Earnhardt was the epitome of the NASCAR "good old boy," a native of a Piedmont mill town who dropped out of high school at 16, worked in a cotton mill, and moved up through the ranks of local drivers at area short tracks. In contrast, native Californian Gordon was the face of the new NASCAR, seemed to be the All-American boy, became a go-kart champion before he entered elementary school, and was as talented as a spokesperson for his sponsors as he was as a driver. Their rivalry could not

have been better scripted in Hollywood and brought millions of new fans to the sport.

As the sport grew in popularity its image changed dramatically. Increasingly, new tracks were built outside the Piedmont South and the majority of new fans and drivers came from outside the region. Tracks began to pop up near Dallas, San Francisco, Los Angeles, Las Vegas, Kansas City, Chicago, even in New Hampshire. *Fortune* 500 companies noticed the sport's national appeal and the loyalty of its fans to products endorsed by their favorite driver. Companies including DuPont, Proctor and Gamble, Anheuser-Busch, Coors, McDonalds, Kodak, and Kellogg's joined the auto-related companies such as Texaco, Valvoline, GM Goodwrench, and Ford Quality Care to pour millions into the sport in sponsorship dollars. It soon became as important for drivers to be effective celebrity spokespersons for their myriad sponsors as it was for them to have the courage and skill to handle a 3,400-pound stock car in a battle with 42 other drivers.

While the sport did change dramatically in the 1990s and early years of the 21st century, it still retains significant evidences of its roots in the Piedmont South. The center of the NASCAR universe is the area around Charlotte, N.C., where the vast majority of its drivers live and most of the race shops are located. NASCAR is also the most overtly evangelical Christian sport on the American scene and not only holds regular chapel services for its drivers but opens every race with a public prayer, generally one ending with "in Jesus's name." Pre-race festivities are also very patriotic and often include tributes to American troops and flyovers of military aircraft. In a reflection of its connections to the Piedmont, where African Americans were not allowed to work in cotton mills until the late 1960s, NASCAR is also the whitest professional sport in the United States. Indeed, in its almost 60 years of existence, NASCAR has had only one African American driver—Wendell Scott in the 1960s and early 1970s—compete in its top series on a consistent basis. NASCAR has recently instituted an aggressive diversity program to bring both minority and female drivers into the sport.

Perhaps the most strikingly southern aspect of NASCAR is the unprecedented control over the sport still exercised by the France family. Indeed, its hegemony over the sport is nothing if not reminiscent of the control exercised by Piedmont cotton mill owners through their ownership of both factory and mill town. NASCAR drivers are still the only major professional athletes without union representation. Not only does the France family own NASCAR itself, but it also owns 12 of the 22 tracks that host races in its top division through the publicly traded, but France-family con-trolled, International Speedway Corpo-ration. This control has made the France family incredibly wealthy. Forbes Maga-zine estimated in 2006 the wealth of Bill France's two sons—Bill Jr. and Jim—at $1.5 billion each.

Today, races in NASCAR's top divi-sion regularly attract 150,000 or more fans to tracks featuring luxury corporate skyboxes and valet parking. Millions more watch the live broadcasts on net-work television. Indeed, NASCAR racing consistently draws a larger television audience than any other sport with the exception of the NFL. While the sport has come a long way from its roots as a blue-collar spectacle acted out on the dirt tracks of the Piedmont South by a bunch of "good old boy" liquor haulers, it is still the most characteristically southern sport in the nation.

DANIEL S. PIERCE
University of North Carolina at Asheville

Pete Daniel, *Lost Revolutions: The South in the 1950s* (2000); Greg Fielden, *Forty Years of Stock Car Racing*, 5 vols. (1988); Peter Golenbock, *American Zoom* (1993); Paul Hemphill, *Wheels: A Season on NASCAR's Winston Cup Circuit* (1997); Tom Higgins and Steve Waid, *Brave in Life: Junior Johnson* (1999); Ed Hinton, *Daytona: From the Birth of Speed to the Death of the Man in Black* (2001); Mark Howell, *From Moon-shine to Madison Avenue: A Cultural His-tory of NASCAR's Winston Cup Series* (1997); Daniel S. Pierce, *Atlanta History* (no. 2, 2004), *Real NASCAR: White Lightning, Red Clay, and Big Bill France* (2010), *Southern Cultures* (Summer 2001); Sylvia Wilkinson, *Dirt Tracks to Glory: The Early Years of Stock Car Racing as Told by Its Participants* (1983).

Negro Baseball Leagues

Under segregation, by custom and sometimes by law, interracial sports en-counters were prohibited in the South. As a direct result, black southerners developed their own sports world, and baseball was by far the most popular sport of the period.

Each town or rural area had a black baseball team that competed against other local black teams in games that had great cultural importance and entertainment value in those communities. The larger towns had better teams, and the very best players became professionals. The top of the black baseball hierarchy was the Negro League—sometimes called the Negro Major Leagues.

Though headquartered in the North for economic reasons, the Negro League had a distinctly southern accent. The league's founder, Rube Foster, was an expatriate Texan; and the majority of players, always southerners, were recruited from southern teams during spring training or during regular Negro League barnstorming forays into the South. In addition, the Negro League contained a smattering of southern teams at various times including the Birmingham Black Barons, Memphis Red Sox, Atlanta Black Crackers, Jacksonville Red Caps, and Nashville Elite Giants. A Southern Negro League functioned as the strongest Negro minor league. Supplementing the professional and semiprofessional teams of the South were church teams and teams organized around the workplace.

The movement of black athletic talent from South to North mirrored the migration of blacks in general from the South during segregation. Yet the visibility of the black baseball stars and their association with the communities from whence they came provided a unifying influence for all black Americans. Southern blacks were able to follow their baseball heroes through the na-tional black newspapers that circulated throughout the South, and northern black teams appealed to the still strong southern loyalties of the black fans through promotions such as "Texas Day," "Alabama Day," or "North Carolina Day."

The life of the traveling black ballplayer was difficult. Players were on the road constantly seeking a ball game and a payday, and they augmented the league schedule with exhibitions whenever possible. Sometimes they played three or four games in a single day. At the same time, in an age before television and air-conditioning, the ballplayers provided eagerly sought entertainment and were treated as bona fide celebrities in the black community. When the black players competed against and frequently defeated white major league players during postseason exhibitions in the North and West, they became genuine heroes in black America.

After Jackie Robinson became the first black to enter the major leagues in the 1947 season, black baseball rapidly declined as the black fans deserted their teams to watch integrated baseball. Southern-born Negro Leaguers who achieved prominence in the major leagues after integration include Willie Mays, Hank Aaron, Jackie Robinson, Ernie Banks, and Satchel Paige; but as recounted in the rich folklore that sprang up about Negro baseball, many of the greatest black players never played in the major leagues.

DONN ROGOSIN
Beckley, West Virginia

John Holway, *Voices from the Great Black Baseball Leagues* (1975); Neil Lanctot, *Negro League Baseball: The Rise and Ruin of a Black Institution* (2004); Robert Peterson, *Only the Ball Was White: A History of Legendary Black Players and All-Black Professional Teams* (1992); Donn Rogosin, *Invisible Men: Life in Baseball's Negro Leagues* (1983); Jules Tygiel, *Baseball's Great Experiment: Jackie Robinson and His Legacy* (1983; 2nd ed., 2008).

Paige, Satchel

(1906–1982) BASEBALL PLAYER.
LeRoy "Satchel" Paige was born in Mobile, Ala., on 7 July 1906. As a youngster he was a porter at the railroad station, where he was given the nickname "Satchel" because he built a device that enabled him to carry many more bags than normal. He was in trouble early in life and spent over five years at the Industrial School for Negro Children at Mount Meig, Ala.

As a teenager he attracted attention for his baseball pitching, and he began playing professionally in 1924 for the Mobile Tigers, a black semipro club. By 1928 he had risen to the highest level of black baseball, playing with the Birmingham Black Barons of the Negro National League. He achieved his greatest fame in the Negro Leagues pitching for the Pittsburg Crawfords during the 1930s and the Kansas City Monarchs during the 1940s, but he pitched for as many as 250 independent ball clubs, usually on a one-game exhibition basis.

His fastball was virtually impossible to hit, and his reputation spread well beyond the world of black baseball, aided by his enormous showmanship and inexhaustible energy. In exhibition games he was frequently advertised as "guaranteed to strike out the first six men," and he was known to call in the outfield or instruct his infielders to sit down.

His reputation was enhanced by a series of historic encounters with white major league players that followed the major league World Series. These games, during the era of segregation, enabled black and white ballplayers to assess each other's skills. Dizzy Dean called Paige the greatest pitcher of his era, and major league testimony to Paige's ability is abundant. Paige's many victories over white major leaguers gave him a symbolic importance to blacks during segregation, and black baseball fans everywhere followed Paige's exploits through the highly developed sports pages of the national black newspapers.

Shortly after the integration of baseball by Jackie Robinson, Paige became the first black pitcher in the American League with the Cleveland Indians in 1948. He pitched for Cleveland in 1948 and 1949, with the St. Louis Browns in 1951–53, and briefly with the Kansas City Athletics in 1965, all of which helped qualify him for a major league pension.

Paige was the ultimate barnstorming baseball player, pitching virtually every day. His talent was extraordinary, and his success was coupled with a flamboyant, comic style that augmented his reputation. Paige's career illustrated the typical Negro League history of southern roots and northern achievement. In 1971 Paige was elected to the Baseball Hall of Fame, the first Negro Leaguer admitted under a new admissions policy. Paige died in 1982 in Kansas City, Mo.

DONN ROGOSIN
Beckley, West Virginia

William Price Fox, *Satchel Paige's America* (2005); Donn Rogosin, *Invisible Men: Life in Baseball's Negro Leagues* (1983); Edna Rust and Art Rust Jr., *Art Rust's Illustrated History of the Black Athlete* (1985).

Petty, Richard

(b. 1937) SPORTS CAR DRIVER.
Among modern southern sports legends, few have had as sustained and dedicated a following as Richard Petty, often dubbed "King of the Road" in stock car racing. Petty's dominance of the asphalt ovals in the South has created a following that adores him as much for his traditional lifestyle as for his driving exploits.

His racing record has been impressive. In his first 25 seasons (1958–83), Petty won 198 races, far more than any of his competitors. His earnings exceeded $4.5 million. Although slow to gain prominence—he went winless his first two seasons—Petty dominated the tracks from the early 1960s to the mid-1970s. His peak performances came from 1967 through 1971, when the familiar Petty blue Plymouth was driven into victory lane in 40 percent of the 233 races he entered. Over the course of his career, Petty accumulated 200 career wins, including winning the prestigious Daytona 500 seven times, receiving seven Winston Cups for the best seasonal performance among drivers, and finishing among the first 10 drivers in 70 percent of the 900 races he entered.

Yet more than simple performance explains the hold of the Petty legend on so many southerners. Intensely personal and familial traits exist in stock car racing. Fans become attached to a particular driver and espouse his cause as if he were kin. Petty's career style has been both an extension of and a reaction to such traits. He frequently spends hours after races signing autographs. He has been known, when eliminated early in competition, to use public restrooms to change his clothes. When a movie was made about his life, Petty himself played the lead role. Such closeness to his fans has bred deep loyalties. Through the years those who become Petty fans remain Petty fans.

The depth of such attachments can be best explained by the common origins Petty shares with most of his fans. His background, like theirs, is deeply rooted in the rural South. Petty grew up in the Uwharrie hills of Randolph County, N.C. He remained there until late in his career. Racing has been a hereditary trait among the Pettys. Richard succeeded his father, Lee, and Richard's own son, Kyle, became a professional NASCAR driver himself. Kyle's son, Adam, the fourth in a long line of race-car-driving Pettys, was an up-and-coming driver until 2000, when he died in a crash while practicing for an upcoming event. Much like traditional rural skills such as weaving and smithing, racing is passed along through generations.

Petty fans remained loyal because the racer remained just like them, even though he achieved uncommon financial success. The Pettys have lived "like folks," even though they are co-owners

Held each year in October, the Angola Rodeo, which began in 1965, is the longest-running prison rodeo in the nation. (Photograph courtesy of the State Library of Louisiana)

of the NASCAR racing team Richard Petty Motorsports. They reinforce the ambitions of their fans, who through stock car racing have striven to hold on to the identities of their impoverished, rural past as they seek the urbane riches of the Sunbelt.

GARY FREEZE
University of North Carolina at Chapel Hill

Ed Hinton, ed., *Daytona: From the Birth of Speed to the Death of the Man in Black* (2001); Bill Libby with Richard Petty, *"King Richard": The Richard Petty Story* (1977).

Prison Rodeos

Convicts riding bulls and broncos is quite a sight, and spectators can watch the phenomenon in only two places—McAlester, Okla., and Angola, La. The rodeo at the penitentiary in Huntsville, Tex., ended in 1986 after a 55-year run.

Angola Prison is a huge 18,000-acre complex where inmates raise much of the food they consume. The prison rodeo started in 1965 as a diversion for convicts and employees, but it was not opened to the public until two years later. It grew steadily in popularity so that now the public flocks to Angola twice a year to see inmates compete in seven rodeo events. The rodeo became so large that a new 7,500-seat arena was constructed in 2000. Organizations consisting of trusted prisoners are allowed to set up booths to sell handmade crafts and food such as peanuts, sausages, and fried onions to the spectators.

Shopping the booths is a key part of the festival-like atmosphere that visitors enjoy.

The rodeo at the Oklahoma State Penitentiary started in the 1940s—some say in imitation of the already famous Texas Prison Rodeo. It features convict cowboys not just from the "big house" in McAlester in the eastern part of the state but also from other institutions in the Oklahoma correctional system. Unlike Louisiana's, Oklahoma's "Outlaw Rodeo" also includes events open to nonconvicts and sanctioned by the International Professional Rodeo Association (IPRA). Staged in August in a usually full arena with 14,000 seats, it is billed as the only rodeo "behind prison walls."

BRADLEY R. RICE
Clayton State University

Angola Prison Rodeo, www.angolarodeo.com; Texas Prison Rodeo History, www.txprisonmuseum.org.

Redneck Riviera

Although the name has been used to identify everything from a failed real estate venture in central Florida to a cluster of upscale houseboats on Kentucky's Lake Cumberland, "Redneck Riviera" is most often used to describe a stretch of south Alabama beach running from the mouth of Mobile Bay east to just past the Alabama-Florida line. (Some include the Florida Panhandle, but purists don't.)

The 'Bama beach was what Howell Raines wrote about in the *New York Times* back in 1978, when he may have been the first to use the term in print. Raines was describing the place where former University of Alabama, then pro-football quarterbacks Kenny Stabler and Richard Todd played during the off-season. From Gulf Shores to past Orange Beach was as fine a collection of bars and roadhouses as there was anywhere on the Gulf Coast—the Pink Pony, the L.A. ("Lower Alabama") Pub & Grub, the Bear Point Marina, and the Seagull, all capped off by the Flora-Bama Lounge and Package. The Flora-Bama, located mostly in Florida to take advantage of more liberal liquor laws, was where "Let's Do It on the Line" was said to be more than a slogan.

When asked about the life he led down there, Stabler reportedly replied, "I live the way I want to live and don't give a damn if anybody likes it or not. I run hard as hell and don't sleep. I'm just here for the beer." So were a lot of other people.

Although the term "redneck" often conjures images of white-trash racists, race was not much of an issue for folks down on the "Riviera" because there were so few African Americans—in 1990, Orange Beach had two black residents. Gulf Shores had only one. As a result, without race in the equation, visitors and residents could and did concentrate on those other aspects of redneck culture that Stabler so eloquently described.

The people who did this, the creators of the Redneck Riviera, were, for the most part, members of the rising post–World War II Lower South middle-class, who came to the coast to fish a little, swim a little, drink a little, eat seafood, and generally do what they could not do back home—at least publicly. Many of the visitors came with their families, helping to calm more excessive urges.

Then in the 1960s and 1970s, a younger, more raucous crowd appeared on the scene, and as these newcomers mingled with the older residents, Robert F. Jones, writing for *Sports Illustrated*, noticed two categories emerging: the "upper-crust, matronly, Rotarian with cash register eyeballs," and those like "the Stabler gang, raffish, sunburnt, hard of hand and piratical of glance." But the two were not as different as one might think. Indeed, given the opportunity they were ready to merge into what historian Emory Thomas described as "a new generation of raffish Rotarians, pirates with cash register eyeballs, and hard handed matrons."

That opportunity came with Hurricane Frederic. On 12 September 1979 the storm hit the Alabama coast with 120-mile-per-hour winds and a record storm surge. Vacation cottages and "mom and pop" businesses were washed away, and in the recovery the "raffish Rotarians" discovered that there were baby boomers with money to invest. So they bought up and built up, and the Redneck Riviera became a condo row.

Today, much of that stretch of coast is lined with high-rise, upscale condominiums, most absentee owned, that rent to college kids at spring break, "snowbirds" in the winter, and anyone who has the money in the summer. But still tucked in among this new construction, not yet squeezed out by trendy restaurants and sports bars, are a few of the roadhouses and the seafood joints that gave the Riviera its "redneck" character. The Pink Pony is still there. So is the

Flora-Bama, where the Annual Interstate Mullet Toss recaptures some of the "redneckery" for which the strip was once famous—though more controlled and calculated than when local roadhouses were described as "beer-and-a-black-eye places." And there were the Gulf and bayous to fish in and the beach to lie out on, though access to both continues to cause controversy.

But more than anything, there is the legacy of a more freewheeling time and a reputation for antisocial behavior that continues to inspire visitors to cut loose and be a redneck, if only for a little while. So long as the folks back home don't find out.

HARVEY H. JACKSON III
Jacksonville State University

Robert F. Jones, *Sports Illustrated* (19 September 1979); Alan West Brockman and Joe Gilchrist, producers, *The Last American Roadhouse: The Documentary of the Flora-Bama* (film, 2006); Harris Mendheim, director, *Mullet Men: Second Place Is the First Loser* (film, 2000); Howell Raines, *New York Times* (21 June 1978); Ken Stabler and Barry Stainback, *Snake: The Candid Autobiography of Football's Most Outrageous Renegade* (1986); Michael Swindle, *Mulletheads: The Legends, Lore, Magic, and Mania Surrounding the Humble but Celebrated Mullet* (1998); Emory M. Thomas, *Travels to Hallowed Ground: A Historian's Journey to the American Civil War* (1987).

Robert Trent Jones Golf Trail

The Retirement Systems of Alabama (RSA), a $32 billion pension fund for state employees and teachers in Alabama, financed the largest golf course construction project at one time in history. The $255 million project was conceived, according to Dr. David G. Bronner, CEO of RSA, to stimulate economic development in Alabama by attracting industrial development, tourists, and retirees. It is called the Robert Trent Jones Golf Trail, otherwise known as simply "the Trail," and consists of 468 holes on 26 courses at 11 distinct sites.

These sites run from the mountains in north Alabama to the coast in south Alabama and are located no more than 15 minutes from a major interstate and are less than two hours apart. There are five 54-hole complexes, five 36-hole complexes, and one 18-hole resort course. Each course has distinctive geographical features, which, as a group, highlight the natural beauty of Alabama's diverse landscape. The RSA has also developed upscale hotels adjacent to the golf complexes on the trail.

Huntsville's complex is built in a natural bowl with a river, creeks, and ponds against a panoramic mountain backdrop. Birmingham's complex is nestled around Red Mountain and Shades Mountain with hills and has many downhill shots between mountains, creeks, and lakes. Auburn/Opelika's complex is located on a 600-acre lake with gently rolling terrain and majestic woodlands. Mobile's complex carves through wetlands with a jungle environment and surprising elevations for a course on the Gulf Coast. Dothan's complex accents rolling hills with creeks, ponds, and large moss-covered oaks. Greenville's complex is located on the highest point for miles around with a beautiful lake, hills, and valleys wooded with forests of pine and hard-

wood. Anniston/Gadsden's complex is on a series of spring-fed lakes in rolling topography with pretty forests surrounded by gorgeous mountains. Prattville's complex has courses that play along the Alabama River and Cooter's Pond, which offer more than 1,500 acres of natural beauty and spectacular views overlooking Montgomery. The Shoals complex offers a spectacular view from a bluff overlooking Lake Wilson and the Tennessee River. Point Clear's complex on the eastern shore of Mobile Bay has some of the most beautiful live oak trees on the Gulf Coast. The Ross Bridge complex is carved into the rolling terrain of Shannon Valley and meanders through indigenous landscape along the banks of two significant lakes connected by a spectacular waterfall dropping 80 feet.

The hotels in historic Mobile and Montgomery have sparked downtown revitalization efforts, including new businesses, entertainment, and restaurants. These golf complexes were designed to accommodate large corporate golf outings, as well as charity fund-raising events. They have excellent meeting facilities, and the adjacent hotels have spas and complete state-of-the-art conference facilities. The quality of these golf courses is exceptional. The golf courses, hotels, and housing and the associated advertising and publicity have helped to enhance the image of the state of Alabama. There have been more than 5,000 positive articles written in the media about this project. There have been many hours of worldwide television coverage of professional golf tournaments at the golf complexes. Ross

Bridge hosts the PGA Champions Tour, and Mobile and Prattville host the LPGA Tour for weekly tournaments. Other collegiate and professional tours have been hosted on the Trail sites.

The courses, hotels, and adjacent housing developed in phases. Phase one of this development was the construction of the golf courses. Phase two was the construction of the hotels and phase three (just beginning) is the construction of resort/retirement housing adjacent to three of the complexes (Ross Bridge, Grand Hotel, and Grand National).

People from all over the world have visited Alabama to play golf on the Trail. The Trail has helped to increase tourism revenue in Alabama from $1.8 billion in 1992 to more than $9 billion in 2008, significantly changing the recreational culture and economy in Alabama.

MARK FAGAN
Jacksonville State University

David Anderson, *New York Times* (17 June 2000); Michael O'Neal, *New York Times* (13 September 2002).

Robinson, Eddie

(1919–2007) FOOTBALL COACH.
Eddie Robinson was born 12 February 1919 in Jackson, La., to sharecropper parents. At age eight he moved with his parents to Baton Rouge, where, according to Robinson, he watched a high school football team practice and decided he wanted to be a coach. Robinson played football at McKinley High School in Baton Rouge and at Leland College. After graduating in

1940, he worked during the day at a Baton Rouge feed mill and at night on an ice truck. In 1941 Grambling hired Robinson as head football coach, and he began his legendary career.

Robinson's success in developing the football program at Grambling was phenomenal. When he first arrived on campus, Robinson assumed chores assigned to support staffs at larger schools, such as mowing the playing field, taping ankles, and even writing game stories for the newspapers. With the support of the Grambling administration, Robinson built the fledgling program into one of the most respected collegiate programs in the country. Robinson was always a popular figure in the world of black college football, but broader fame came in the late 1960s after sports commentator Howard Cosell did a television documentary on the success of Grambling football. More than 200 of Robinson's Grambling players went on to play on professional teams, a record that testified to Robinson's success as a coach. Robinson's coaching style changed little during his years at Grambling. His teams used the wing-T formation on offense and a pro-style 4–3 on defense.

During the fall 1985 season, Robinson won his 324th game, surpassing the record previously held by Paul (Bear) Bryant of Alabama. Although some observers charge that Robinson's record meant less than Bryant's because most of his victories came against Division I-AA-caliber teams, others point out that Robinson has had to overcome difficulties Bryant never faced at Alabama, such as low recruitment and operating budgets and racial discrimination. Robinson retired in 1997 with 408 wins, the most of any head coach in Division I-AA.

KAREN M. MCDEARMAN
University of Mississippi

Paul Hemphill, *Southern Magazine* (December 1986); Rick Reilly, *Sports Illustrated* (14 October 1985); William C. Rhoden, *New York Times* (16 September 1985); Eddie Robinson, *Never Before, Never Again: The Stirring Autobiography of Eddie Robinson, the Winningest Coach in the History of College Football* (1997).

Rupp, Adolph Frederick

(1901–1977) COLLEGE BASKETBALL COACH.

A generation after Adolph Rupp's death, he remains one of the most successful and best-remembered college basketball coaches. In a college career that spanned 41 years, all of them spent at the University of Kentucky, he compiled a record of 876 wins and a .822 winning percentage. Rupp's name joins his college coach, Forrest "Phog" Allen of Kansas University, as a titan in the history of the sport.

Rupp's businesslike seriousness about the game brought success immediately upon his arrival at Kentucky. He coached UK to near total supremacy in the Southeastern Conference (SEC), winning the regular season 27 times and taking the conference tournament 13 times. In six Final Four appearances, his teams won four championships, including a streak of three in a row between 1948 and 1951. Rupp, along with other coaches like Everett Case, brought real innovation to the college game. Pairing an up-tempo offense with a tight man-to-man defense quickened the game and changed the style of play permanently. This fast-paced and exciting style quickly won over legions of fans and helped to make college basketball one of the most popular sports in the country.

Several controversies arose over the course of Rupp's long and successful career. Despite Rupp's assurances that his players were above reproach, Kentucky was caught up in the national cheating scandal of 1951, leading to the cancellation of the 1951–52 season. Rival coaches felt Rupp exercised undue influence over the NCAA Tournament, particularly in the selection and seeding of teams. He never pretended to be a father figure to his players, and his demand for militaristic discipline left many players feeling alienated from the coach. He demanded perfection from his teams, and he got it. However, it was Rupp's failure to integrate the team that remains the most significant blemish to his reputation.

Rupp was well aware of the changing racial situation of the 1960s. Unlike many other southern colleges, Kentucky regularly played integrated teams. As one of the most prominent coaches in the country, many people believe he was in a position to recruit African Americans, and hasten the change. While he faced tremendous pressure to integrate his team, from both outsiders and the president of the university, he also felt the pressure from conservative alumni and boosters, plus the reality of playing throughout the South. Rupp's personal resistance to change, and his total confidence in his own righteousness, also hindered the move. Kentucky's first African American player joined the team in 1970, making it one of the last two schools in the SEC to integrate its basketball team.

Rupp died on 10 December 1977 at age 76. That night Kentucky played at his alma mater, Kansas, in a game dedicated to him.

PAUL R. BEEZLEY
Jacksonville State University

Dan Chandler and Vern Hatton, *Rupp: From Both Ends of the Bench* (1972); Russell Rich, *Adolph Rupp: Kentucky's Basketball Baron* (1994).

St. Cecilia Ball

A private, exclusive subscription ball, the St. Cecilia is an outgrowth of the oldest musical society in the United States. One of a variety of social, charitable, cultural, and educational organizations in antebellum Charleston, the St. Cecilia Society was founded in 1762. Gentlemen amateurs came together "to indulge a common taste and to pass an agreeable hour" and organized two concerts each month for members, featuring talented musicians both within the city and nationally.

By 1773, when visiting Bostonian Josiah Quincy decreed its first violinist "incomparably better" than any he had ever heard, the society had a membership of 120 and a professional orchestra comparable in size to European ensembles of the period. Though carefully managed by its officers—the peerage of

Charleston—difficulties in obtaining musicians and the increased popularity of dancing led to a gradual change in emphasis. After 1822 subscription balls entirely replaced the concerts.

There were three St. Cecilias during the winter "gay" season: one in January and two in February, the latter cautiously arranged to avoid interfering with Lent. The balls were held on Thursdays (St. Cecilia's day) in St. Andrew's Hall, Broad Street, and, after that hall was destroyed in the fire of 1861, in the Hibernian. Invitations were hand delivered to members, and new membership in the society was strictly limited, typically, to the sons or grandsons of current members. When a man was elected, the names of the ladies of his household were added to "the list." Their names were removed only upon death or departure from the city, "change of fortune affecting them not at all."

When invited as guests, visiting strangers were expected to follow the traditions of the ball, designed to ensure "the greatest decorum." Young ladies always arrived and returned home with chaperons who, during the course of the ball, sat on a slightly raised platform surrounding the dance floor. Men engaged girls for dances by signing a card. Before each dance, the orchestra signaled ladies to return to their chaperons to await the next partner.

At midnight the president of the society led the march to supper with the newest bride in the group on his arm. Replete with fine food and wine, silver and monogrammed Irish linen, the elegant suppers were capped by a "scramble of the men for a sugar figure placed on the top of a huge fancy structure of spun sugar," which each tried to secure as a souvenir for his partner.

Still held yearly, the St. Cecilia balls have changed little since the 1800s. In an effort to preserve social distinctions and traditions without, in the words of a former society president, "stirring up jealousies and animosities which seriously impair the goodwill normally existing between members and nonmembers," secrecy continues to surround both rules for admission and customs of the ball, leading outsiders to view the affairs with a mix of awe and incredulity. "It is remarkable," wrote one early 20th-century journalist, "that such exclusive and elective balls, bound by such rigid rules, and so opposed to new members, should exist so long in the whirling change of American life."

ELIZABETH M. MAKOWSKI
University of Mississippi

Ainslee's Magazine (October 1905); Frederick P. Bowes, *The Culture of Early Charleston* (1942); Nicolas Michael Butler, *Votaries of Apollo: The St. Cecilia Society and the Patronage of Concert Music in Charleston, South Carolina, 1766–1820* (2007); John J. Hindman, "Concert Life in Ante Bellum Charleston" (Ph.D. dissertation, University of North Carolina, Chapel Hill, 1971); James Hutchisson, *Charleston Magazine* (March 2006); Mrs. St. Julien Ravenel, *Charleston: The Place and the People* (1907).

Seaside, Florida

Although Seaside, Fla., has become an award-winning prototype for the much-hyped New Urbanism movement, that was not what Robert Davis,

its developer-founder, wanted it to be at the start. Davis's vision—shaped by 1950s beach nostalgia, 1960s communal romanticism, and 1970s neighborhood preservation experience—inspired him to take the 80 Gulf of Mexico–fronted acres between Panama City and Destin that he had inherited from his grandfather and create "an old-fashioned town." He envisioned that there neighbors of all classes, occupations, and circumstances would live in "cracker cottages" with wide front porches and picket fences all tightly packed and neatly arranged so that "a mother with a baby carriage can walk from one side of town to the other in 15 minutes."

What he created instead was what *Time* magazine called "the most astounding design achievement of its era," a collection of unique houses built along brick streets laid out to draw people to the convenient town center and make automobiles unnecessary. Even before it was finished it had become "the most celebrated new American town of the decade" and had garnered some of architecture's most prestigious awards. So complete was the scheme and so total was the package that it was easy to believe that it had all been planned that way from the start—but it had not.

Davis had hoped that his development would become a "real town," with growth governed by a code so simple that anyone "handy with tools" could design and build his own house. The town center would include a small grocery for necessities, a hardware store for the handyperson, and other small shops to meet the needs of residents. And it began that way, with a weekend market, a "Dog Days Festival," and the "Shrimp Shack," a bar and grill created out of a "sharecropper shack" brought in for the purpose. But while Davis liked what he called "the seedy, vigorous quality" of what he was creating, local folks complained of its "slung up" appearance and expressed a hope that the developer would built something "with a bit of distinction and class."

Distinction and class soon arrived. First a cover article in *Southern Living* called attention to the town, and baby boomers, with Reagan-era money, decided to spend it there. Snapping up lots, investors built architect-designed houses in colors so vivid that neighbors began to call it "pastel hell." And to help them make the mortgage payments, Davis opened a rental agency.

When the houses became rental units the whole nature of the town changed. Talk of making it a place where people lived ceased, and Seaside became a "holiday town," like the ones Davis had seen in Europe. The hardware store became a designer shop, the market became a place where recreational chefs could shop, and the other stores were transformed into upscale tourist attractions. All of it, according to the *New York Times*, was "as restlessly tasteful as any place on the planet."

But not everyone was happy. Looking at the increasingly trendy designs and the "populist prettify" of the town, one of Davis's early collaborators complained that they set out to "build Kansas" and ended up "building Oz." Indeed, this very unreal quality led producers of the 1998 movie *The Truman Show* to select it as the setting for the town that was nothing more than a TV set.

Yet Davis accepted each element in the evolution of Seaside and found a way to make it appear as if he had planned it that way from the start. And perhaps he had. For despite the fact that the town had become a tourist attraction and "a horizontal condominium," the design remained to attract attention of New Urbanists.

It is hard to say whether Seaside inspired the New Urban Movement or was inspired by it, but the fact remains that Davis's creation, with its compact, pedestrian friendly design fit neatly into the ideas advanced by those theorists. Hoping to break the pattern of suburban sprawl with its "numbing sameness" and wean modern man of his dependence on the automobile, New Urban planners advocated small communities, just like Seaside, and Davis's plan for educational facilities, a church, even a cemetery, to go with the market center and residences seemed to create the sort of living space the reformers wanted. What did it matter if only a few people lived there year round, Seaside could become the model for others to follow.

So, at the beginning of the 21st century, Seaside is part resort, part laboratory, and part prototype for development along the Florida Gulf Coast. It is also a reflection of the hopes and dreams, foibles and fantasias, of the southerners who visit and spend their money.

HARVEY H. JACKSON III
Jacksonville State University

Harvey H. Jackson III, in *Southern Journeys: Tourism, History, and Culture in the Modern South*, ed. Richard D. Starnes (2003), *Atlanta History* (Fall 1998); Stephen Brooke, *Seaside* (1995); Davis Mohney and Keller Easterling, eds., *Seaside: Making a Town in America* (1991).

"See Rock City"

The imperative "See Rock City" became an icon of roadside advertising beginning in the late 1930s. Hand-painted "See Rock City" signs, along with folksy and extravagant claims about Rock City Gardens, a small tourist park near Chattanooga, Tenn., graced some 900 structures, mostly barns, along rural roads and highways in 19 states. Many of the barn signs survive and have been repainted in recent years, but they are less visible to tourists who have migrated away to the interstate highway system.

The "See Rock City" ad campaign transcended the tourist attraction it was designed to support. A Chattanooga developer and promotional whiz, Garnet Carter, opened Rock City Gardens in 1932 on Lookout Mountain. The park features walkways through unusual and impressive limestone formations, plus a cliff-top viewing area where visitors are said to be able to see parts of seven states. Carter collaborated with Fred Maxwell, of the Southern Advertising Company of Chattanooga, on an idea to paint signs on barns and other structures with good exposure to motorists. The technique had been used before. Beginning in 1897, the Bloch Brothers Tobacco Company paid farmers for the right to paint Mail Pouch chewing tobacco ads on barn sides, and eventually thousands of them dotted the landscape from New York to Kentucky.

Clark Byers, a painter for the Southern Advertising Company, was the man most responsible for executing the "See Rock City" campaign. Between 1937 and 1968 Byers painted Rock City ads in big, white, blocky letters set against a black background on the plank sides and tin tops of barns. He and his helpers also painted ads on other structures with good roadside visibility: silos, country stores, garages, even post offices. To persuade farmers to turn their barns into billboards, Byers offered free paint jobs, nailed down loose tin, and handed out Rock City thermometers. Later, after imitators got into barn signs, many farmers received rent, usually $3 a year to start. Byers searched for suitable structures along the main routes of the day such as US 41, the old Michigan-to-Miami Dixie Highway. He made up ad slogans on the spot, fitting words to barn space using a yardstick, chalk, and some string. The ads touted Rock City Gardens as a wondrous place no tourist should miss. Among his slogans:

> "When you see Rock City, you see the best."
> "Bring your camera to Rock City, photographer's paradise."
> "See beautiful Rock City, world's 8th wonder."

The barn signs, while quaint today, were part of a trend some derided. Historian Thomas D. Clark, in his 1961 book *The Emerging South*, observed that "the Southern landscape has been sacrificed in many places to this mad campaign to snatch the tourist dollar. Scarcely a roadside post, tree, fence, or barn has escaped the signmaker." Ads beckoned tourists to Civil War battle-fields, Ruby Falls, Silver Springs, Dog-patch, various caverns, and other at-tractions. The Highway Beautification Act of 1965, championed by Lady Bird Johnson, changed the landscape by re-stricting the placement of outdoor ads, particularly billboards, along U.S. high-ways and interstates. Signs along these routes had to meet new zoning, spacing, lighting, and size requirements. Many Rock City barn signs had to be blacked out, but some were allowed as spe-cial "landmark" signs. Other Rock City barns persist along sleepy back roads.

Whether icon or eyesore, the Rock City barn has earned affection. Rock City Gardens annually sells tens of thousands of birdhouses modeled after the old barns. "We beautified the high-ways with these signs," Clark Byers said in a 1996 interview. He even painted "See Rock City" on the roof of his own house. Byers, who lived near Rising Fawn in northwest Georgia, died in February 2004 at age 89.

WESLEY LOY
Anchorage, Alaska

Thomas D. Clark, *The Emerging South* (1961); Wesley Loy, *Reckon* (Winter 1996); Associated Press, "Clark Byers, Painter of 'See Rock City'" (21 February 2004).

Showboats

Beginning in the 1830s and reaching a peak from 1870 to 1910, showboats steamed the waterways of the Atlantic Coast and the Mississippi River Valley,

bringing spectacular entertainment to people in communities along the way. Some showboats were little more than flatboats with primitive structures on top, but the most elaborate were floating palaces, which had fancy decor and comfortable quarters. Among the most famous showboats were Edwin Price's Water Queen, William Chapman's *Floating Theatre*, Norman Thom's *Princess*, Spaulding and Rogers's *Floating Circus Palace*, John McNair's *New Era*, and Augustus French's *New Sensation*. Loud calliopes and brightly colored flags announced the coming of the showboats, and a parade and free con-cert would be held if the community was big enough. The showboats pre-sented family fare, including musical performances, sentimental melodramas, minstrel routines, acrobatics, fiddlers' contests, humorous speeches, and magic shows. Thousands of people in isolated river towns and on plantations turned out enthusiastically, and uncritically, to see the shows.

In the 20th century, showboats de-clined because of competition from other forms of mass culture, especially the movies. In the early 1900s, though, even more elaborate showboats than before were built, such as the *Cotton Blossom*, the *Goldenrod*, and the *Sunny South*. They were large, sometimes seating almost 1,000 people, and they began specializing in dramatic perfor-mances and stage plays from the New York theater. This did not reverse the decline, though, as the number of show-boats on the Mississippi fell from 22 in 1910 to 4 in 1938.

Showboats have become so identi-

Moonlight on "the Old Man River," Mississippi River, Greenville, Miss., postcard, c. 1900 (Ann Rayburn Paper Americana Collection, Archives and Special Collections, University of Mississippi Library, Oxford)

fied with southern entertainment history that contemporary southerners have shown a renewed interest in them. In 1948 Vicksburg, Miss., for example, purchased the *Sprague*, a huge towboat built in 1901, and converted it into a showboat of sorts. Metro-Goldwyn-Mayer studios used it in 1950 for the musical film *Showboat*. It then housed a river museum in Vicksburg and served as the stage for a Gay Nineties melodrama, *Gold in the Hills*.

The *Delta Queen* became the most famous paddle-wheel steamer cruising the Mississippi in the 20th century. The 285-foot-long, 58-foot-wide steamer regularly made the trip from Cincinnati to New Orleans as well as numerous shorter trips. Its sister ship, the *Mississippi Queen*, was a larger, more modern vessel. Those on their cruises were entertained with presentations of shows such as *The Mississippi*

Gambler and Mark Twain's *Huckleberry Finn* and *Tom Sawyer*. The sound of the calliope playing "My Old Kentucky Home," "Are You from Dixie?," or "Way Down in New Orleans" summoned people to river towns to greet the boat as it steamed into port, seemingly recreating the 19th-century showboat experience. Amusement parks such as Nashville's Opryland used steamboats (the *Andrew Jackson*) as stages for musical entertainment, and museums such as Memphis's Mud Island have used riverboat replicas—all evoking memories of an earlier southern form of amusement. The *Delta Queen* docked in Chattanooga, Tenn., in February 2009 and became a boutique hotel there, complete with a lounge, live music, and theatrical performances that evoked an older river culture. Louisiana and Mississippi have old-style riverboats that offer gaming and entertainment in a setting that evokes the Old South show-boats.

CHARLES REAGAN WILSON
University of Mississippi

Philip Graham, *Georgia Review* (Summer 1958), *Showboats: The History of an American Institution* (1951); Jacquette White, *New Orleans Times-Picayune* (30 January 2009).

Silver Dollar City

Silver Dollar City is a modern theme park with roots in one of the Ozark region's earliest tourist attractions. Though today just one part of an entertainment megacorporation, Silver Dollar City remains one of the most popular theme parks in the Upper South and one of the primary catalysts for the transformation of the Branson, Mo., area into a leading American tourist destination.

Silver Dollar City was established in 1960, but its roots stretch back to the late 19th century when a Canadian entrepreneur opened Marble (later renamed Marvel) Cave to tours in rural Stone County, Mo., some five miles west of Branson. In the early 20th century with the almost simultaneous arrival of the railroad and publication of Harold Bell Wright's best-selling novel, *The Shepherd of the Hills*—set in the Branson vicinity—the cave became a popular summer tourist destination. Among the thousands who visited the cave were Chicago engineer Hugo Herschend and his family. In 1950 Herschend and his wife, Mary, began operating Marvel Cave and buying hundreds of acres surrounding it.

A decade later, after Hugo's death, Mary Herschend and her two sons, Jack and Peter, built Silver Dollar City at the entrance to Marvel Cave. Originally conceived as a sideline to the cave—a place for visitors to mill around while waiting for their tour—Silver Dollar City opened on 1 May 1960, with five late 19th-century, frontier-style buildings (general store, inn, ice cream parlor, and blacksmith and doll shops) and two reconstructed log buildings. The theme park combined elements of the Wild West mythology sweeping American popular culture at the time with popular imagery of the highland South. The original park was designed by the planner of Oklahoma City's Frontier City USA, and within a couple of years the western touch at Silver Dollar City included two stage coaches and a park railroad, the Frisco Silver Dollar Line. The earliest visitors were serenaded by the bluegrass-picking Mabe Brothers, local performers who would later open Branson's first music theater, and park employees performed a Hatfield-McCoy feud/shootout on the city's main street.

Through aggressive and novel marketing, such as the theme park's practice of giving customers change in silver dollars, by the mid-1960s Silver Dollar City was the leading tourist attraction in southwestern Missouri. An event at the end of the decade would give it national publicity. In 1969 Paul Henning, a Missouri native who had vacationed in the Branson area as a boy, agreed to film a few episodes of his hit television sitcom, *The Beverly Hillbillies*, at Silver Dollar City. Though the name "Silver Dollar City" was not used in the episodes, which featured the Clampetts' journey back to the Ozarks to find Elly May a husband, the media exposure generated record crowds in the growing frontier town, and the momentum continued into the following decade. By the mid-1970s Silver Dollar City employed 260 full-time and 1,200 seasonal workers and attracted 1.4 million visitors annually.

As Silver Dollar City's attractions multiplied—roller coasters, water-rafting rides, annual craft festivals, a permanent hillbilly vaudeville troupe—the Herschends looked to expand into other entertainment venues. In 1976 Silver Dollar City's founders purchased Gold Rush Junction Park in Pigeon Forge, Tenn., and renamed the renovated park Silver Dollar City (now Dollywood). The Herschends also partnered with Dolly Parton to create the Dixie Stampede dinner theater in Pigeon Forge in 1988, with subsequent openings in Myrtle Beach and Branson. Over the past three decades, the Silver Dollar City Corporation (now known as Herschend Family Entertainment [HFE] and headquartered in Atlanta) has developed or purchased water parks, music theaters, shopping malls, amphibious tours, and urban aquariums in widely scattered locales from Branson to Camden, N.J.

Tourists who visited the little cluster of faux-frontier buildings in 1960 would not recognize Silver Dollar City today. Thousands of visitors daily spend hours in the park without realizing there is a cave underneath it—and still open for tours. By the early 21st century, Silver Dollar City had expanded into a sprawling minicity with its own neigh-borhoods, dozens of rides, 100 craftspeople, four in-park music and performance theaters, and one of the world's largest Christmas light displays. Though Silver Dollar City has adopted many of the trappings of other modern, successful theme parks, its craftspeople, such traditions as the Hatfield and McCoy feud and the train robbery, and the active role of the Herschend brothers in HFE provide a link to its genesis in the rural Ozarks half a century ago.

BROOKS BLEVINS
Missouri State University

Aaron Ketchell, *Holy Hills of the Ozarks: Religion and Tourism in Branson, Missouri* (2007); Crystal Payton, *The Story of Silver Dollar City: A Pictorial History of Branson's Famous Ozark Mountain Theme Park* (1997).

Smith, Dean

(b. 1931) BASKETBALL COACH.
Dean Edwards Smith, named in 1997 by ESPN as one of the five greatest American college coaches of any sport, was born in Emporia, Kan., on 8 February 1931. The son of teachers (his father was also a coach), he excelled in all sports on the high school level and attended the University of Kansas as a serious math student and a solid though hardly spectacular basketball player who filled a reserve role on a Jayhawks' national championship team. After serving as an assistant coach at the Air Force Academy, in 1958 he became an assistant at the University of North Carolina to Frank McGuire, the dapper New Yorker who had led the Tar Heels to the 1957 NCAA basketball championship (against Smith's own Jayhawks, led

by Wilt Chamberlain). When McGuire, a lavish spender loath to abide by the Chapel Hill ethos of high thinking and plain living, resigned under some fire in 1961, Smith was elevated to head coach.

Not winning but cleaning up the Carolina program was his primary assignment in the beginning, a fortunate turn for him because his first four teams were only marginally over .500, and none challenged for supremacy in the Atlantic Coast Conference. But in the mid-1960s he broke through with a number of high-profile recruits, and in 1967, 1968, and 1969 he won the ACC tournament and went to the NCAA's Final Four. This was the beginning of a nearly unprecedented run in college basketball, one that resulted in 13 ACC regular season championships, 17 regular season championships, 11 Final Fours, and 2 national championships, in 1982 and 1993. In 1976 he coached the U.S. Olympic basketball team to a gold medal. Smith was named national coach of the year four times and ACC coach of the year nine times. He coached 26 All-Americans, among them Billy Cunningham, James Worthy, and Michael Jordan, all later included among the top 50 NBA players of all time. Jordan came to be considered the greatest basketball player ever. When Smith retired in 1997, he was the winningest major college coach in history, having posted 879 victories.

But Smith's significance went beyond victories and championships. A staunch advocate of civil rights in the segregated South of the early and mid-1960s, he brought black players into his basketball program and helped to integrate the town of Chapel Hill. He took a number of stands — unpopular in a conservative South — on other social and political issues. He demanded that his athletes be students first, and over his 36-year career they graduated at a 96 percent rate. In 1983 Smith was elected to the Basketball Hall of Fame, and in 2000 to the National Collegiate Basketball Hall of Fame.

FRED HOBSON
University of North Carolina at Chapel Hill

Art Chansky, *Blue Blood: Duke-Carolina: Inside the Most Storied Rivalry in College Hoops* (2006); Rick Reilly, *Sports Illustrated* (19 March 2003); Dean E. Smith, *A Coach's Life* (2002).

South by Southwest

Held each March in Austin, Tex., the South by Southwest Music and Media Conference (SXSW) was organized to bring together aspiring musicians and entertainment industry representatives from around the country. Founded by four music enthusiasts, the first conference was held in 1987, showcasing 200 primarily unsigned, regional bands to 700 conference registrants at 15 venues around the city. Now an industry mainstay, the 20th annual festival in 2006 featured more than 1,800 bands, attracted 12,000 registrants, and included 80 official performance venues. In 1994 SXSW expanded to include the South by Southwest Film Conference and Festival and South by Southwest Interactive, covering the technology industry. It is estimated that the combined conferences now generate as much as $110 million annually for the city of Austin.

The 10-day string of sxsw events hosts creators, industry personnel, and everyday aficionados. In addition to the presentation of new projects and products, a large portion of the festival consists of panel discussions, where professionals discuss developments, strategies, and other components of their respective fields. Though the three festivals do not occur simultaneously, sxsw promotes the intertwined nature of each platform, and many registrants attend multiple conferences.

Though Austin is widely noted as a robust film and tech location, the Music and Media Conference remains the centerpiece of South by Southwest. Deviating somewhat from its original mission to showcase the best unsigned bands in North America, the festival now hosts musicians and music-related enterprises from all over the world, both amateur and established. Though still branded an independent ("indie") event, success has attracted mainstream sponsors, such as PepsiCo, Levi's, and major tobacco and alcohol companies. Yet alongside showcases sponsored by major corporations or media entities, much of the festival remains devoted to bands in search of representation. In addition to official sxsw events, unaffiliated concerts take place throughout the city in spaces that range from traditional venues and converted small businesses to parking lots and backyards.

Austin's demographic history, a hodgepodge of Mexican, Slavic, German, and other indigenous and colonial peoples, contributes to the musical landscape of a city long billed the "Live Music Capital of the World."

In popular music history, Austin was the epicenter of country music's Outlaw or Cosmic Cowboy movement of the 1970s, attracting generations of musicians and fans to the city. Establishments such as the Armadillo World Headquarters (1970–81) gained a national reputation with performers from a spectrum of popular genres because of eclectic crowds and show billing. Though this era faded in the early 1980s, the associated aesthetic of promoting diverse music and culture continues to serve as model for the conferences.

ODIE LINDSEY
Austin, Texas

Austin Business Journal (27 February 2008); David Carr, *New York Times* (17 March 2009); Handbook of Texas Online Web site, www.tshaonline.org; South by Southwest Web site, www.sxsw.com.

South of the Border

The South of the Border roadside attraction stretches for over 300 acres along Interstate 95 right across the South Carolina border. The kitschy tourist stop with a faux-Mexican border town theme consists of a variety of accommodations for the weary traveler, including a miniature golf course, a truck stop, a campground, motel rooms, souvenir shops, various restaurants, amusement rides, and strange animal statues. The first sign of the bright neon complex, which lights up at night like a little Las Vegas of the South, is the looming Sombrero Tower. In addition to the "largest sombrero in the world," the complex uses hundreds of flashy billboards to advertise its various attractions. The famous billboards, and the complex itself, disrupt the monotony of driving the interstate highway. The tourist complex is conveniently located midway between New York City and Miami, Florida.

Behind the sombrero lurk layers of controversy and intrigue. Jewish southerner and notorious businessman-politician Alan Schafer opened South of the Border in 1949. Following the repeal of Prohibition in 1933, Schafer turned his family's Dillon County general store into a successful beer distribution business. When neighboring Robeson County, N.C., went dry, Schafer bought a small cinderblock establishment located on the North Carolina–South Carolina border to lure consumers across the state line to purchase legal alcohol. The original South of the Border "beer depot" also benefited from its placement along Highway 301, which was developing a brisk tourist trade at the time. Owing to the success of the business and the social stigma associated with the sale of alcohol, Schafer expanded the beer depot into a diner. In the 1950s, South of the Border added its first motel rooms, convenience stores, and various other services both to lure tourists passing through and to serve the locals of Dillon County.

Schafer presented himself as an independent and progressive figure in the dicey local political scene in rural Dillon County. He registered African American voters in 1948 when a Supreme Court ruling forced primaries, the important elections during the period of the solidly Democratic South, to be open to all races. Furthermore, Schafer claimed South of the Border

was open to all races from the start and that "we checked only the color of their money, not their skins." However, the openness of South of the Border was not advertised and certainly was only under specific conditions, considering the racial strictures and the climate of the small-town South during the 1950s and 1960s.

While turning South of the Border from a small bar and diner into a 300-acre wonderland of consumer kitsch, Schafer also chaired the local Democratic Party from 1963 to 1981 and gave generously to local charities. His political power was diminished in the early 1980s following a vote-buying scandal during the local sheriff election, which resulted in Schafer's serving time in federal prison. Schafer maintained he was fighting for the underdog and against the concentration of power in Dillon County. In 1998 he was also entangled in a contentious governor's race in South Carolina centered on the legality of video gambling, which was a featured amusement at South of the Border. During the 1990s, South of the Border also came under attack for stereotypical and insulting depictions of Mexican culture. Pedro, the sombrero-and-serape-wearing mascot who abounds throughout the complex and its billboards, was a point of contention for consumers concerned with offensive advertising.

Through all of the changes in southern culture throughout the 20th century, Schafer built one of the most lasting and recognizable tourist stops in the South. Following his death in 2001, his family has continued to run South of the Border. The roadside attraction has not changed much in the last decade. Schafer's innovative flair left a lasting and distinctive mark on the landscape of southern roadside culture and tourism.

NICOLE KING
University of Maryland at Baltimore County

Rudy Maxa, *Washington Post* (1979); Herbert Ravenel Sass, ed., *The Story of the South Carolina Low Country* (1956); Anthony J. Stanonis, ed., *Dixie Emporium: Tourism, Foodways, and Consumer Culture in the American South* (2008); Durward T. Stokes, *The History of Dillon County, South Carolina* (1978).

Spoleto Festival USA

Spoleto Festival USA is the American equivalent to Gian Carlo Menotti's Festival of Two Worlds, staged annually since 1957 in the Umbrian town of Spoleto, Italy.

With a long tradition of support for theater companies and music societies, such as the venerable St. Cecilia, and unique architectural beauty paralleling its Italian counterpart, Charleston, S.C., was selected in 1977 as the site for this interdisciplinary arts festival. For two-and-one-half weeks each spring, from the end of May to the first week in June, as many as a dozen events a day highlight both traditional and experimental forms in the visual arts, music, theater, and dance. Offerings range from Bellini's *La Sonnambula*, Rachmaninoff concerts, and medieval liturgical drama to performances by the Alvin Ailey American Dance Theater. Pianist Misha Dichter, Dizzy Gillespie (a native South Carolinian), Yo-Yo Ma, the Dance Theatre of Harlem, and members of such distinguished ensembles as the Saint Paul Chamber Orchestra and the Pittsburgh Symphony have appeared on Spoleto stages.

Piccola Spoleto (Little Spoleto) supplements these paid-admission events. Emphasizing local and regional talent and children's activities, Piccolo Spoleto holds performances in community centers, schools, and churches throughout Charleston.

Education is an important part of Spoleto. Each year hundreds of young musicians from conservatories and universities across the nation audition to join the Spoleto Festival USA Orchestra. In 2007 the orchestra consisted of 113 musicians. Opportunities to work with international talents extend to administrators and technicians as well, because in addition to performance, apprentice programs cover most aspects of arts management and production.

More than a showcase for the arts, Spoleto Festival USA links the established polished performer with the innovative, young artist and European cultural traditions with those of the South.

ELIZABETH M. MAKOWSKI
University of Mississippi

John Ardoin, *Opera News* (October 1983); Andrew Porter, *New Yorker* (15 July 1985); *Southern Living* (May 1980); Harold Rosenthal, *New Grove Dictionary of Music and Musicians*, vol. 18, ed. Stanley Sadie (1980); www.spoletousa.com.

Stabler, Ken "Kenny" Michael (aka "Snake")

(b. 1945) FOOTBALL PLAYER AND
"RENEGADE."

The South has produced its share
(maybe more than its share) of athletes whose accomplishments off the
field add as much to their reputations
as the records set when suited up. But
few have ever matched Kenny "Snake"
Stabler. If he is not, as the subtitle of his
autobiography proclaims, "Football's
Most Outrageous Renegade," it would
be hard to say who is.

Stabler came roaring out of Foley
(Ala.) High School, where a twisting
touchdown run got him the nickname
"Snake," and onto the campus of the
University of Alabama, where he became Paul "Bear" Bryant's star quarterback and the legendary coach's burden
to bear. In 1965, with fellow quarterback
Steve Sloan, he led the Tide to a national
championship. The next year, with
Stabler the sole signal caller, Alabama
finished off a perfect season beating
Nebraska 34–7 in the Sugar Bowl.
However, the team wound up third
in the polls, behind Notre Dame and
Michigan State—something that has
rankled Tide fans ever since. During his
senior year, Stabler was kicked off the
team for, in his own words, "skipping
practice, failing classes, and collecting
speeding tickets as if they were chances
in a raffle." Bryant later let him return,
but Alabama finished a disappointing
8–2–1. However, "Snake's" redemption
came with his famous "run in the mud,"
a 47-yard scamper on a rain-soaked
field to beat arch rival Auburn.

Drafted in the second round by the
Oakland Raiders, Stabler signed a four-
year contract—$16,000 the first year
with $2,000 raises each of the next three
seasons, plus a $50,000 signing bonus.
With the money in hand, he dropped
his classes and hung around campus
until time to report for training camp.
Though some thought a left-handed
quarterback would not make it in the
pros, once Stabler became a Raider he
set out on a career that took his team to
100 wins in his first 150 starts (a record
then) and to a Super Bowl victory in
1977. During his stay with the Raiders,
he was twice named AFC player of the
year and was the NFL's passing champion in 1976.

In 1980, after a contract dispute, he
was traded to the Houston Oilers, where
he played one season. Then he was
traded to the New Orleans Saints, where
he finished his career three years later.

Two of the three quarterbacks from
the NFL's All-1970s team have been
named to the Pro Football Hall of Fame.
Terry Bradshaw has. Roger Staubach
has. But despite all his accomplishments, Ken Stabler has not. In a recent
listing of the top 10 players not in the
Hall of Fame, Stabler was number six.
Some say it is because of how his career
ended, a journeyman quarterback with
a losing team. Some say it is part of an
NFL plot against the Oakland Raiders.
But most believe it has more to do with
what Stabler did off the field than on it.

As *Snake*, his "candid" autobiography reveals, Stabler was not far wrong
when he reportedly told the press "I live
the way I want to live and I don't give
a damn if anybody likes it or not. I run
hard as hell and don't sleep. I'm just

University of Alabama star quarterback Kenny Stabler (number 12) in a game against the University of Tennessee, 1966 (Courtesy of the Paul W. Bryant Museum/University of Alabama)

here for the beer." But though his off-field activities during the season may have soured the NFL brass to what he accomplished in the game, it was what he did when the season ended that has endeared him to many southerners and made him a legend along what is known as the "Redneck Riviera." In a 1978 article in the *New York Times* and in a 1979 piece in *Sports Illustrated*, writers Howell Raines and Robert F. Jones told of how Stabler and friends lived it up on the Alabama Coast and in the process turned themselves into the prototype of what the "Redneck Riviera" was all about. With "Wickedly Wonderful Wanda" on his arm, this quintessential good ol' boy lived as if tomorrow would never come.

Of course, tomorrow came. Once out

of football, he eventually got into broadcasting and landed a job as a "color commentator" with "Alabama radio network," which broadcasts Crimson Tide games. But personal problems continued to devil him. Messy divorces, the last of which also involved a dispute over a Gulf Coast house and back income taxes, made headlines. Then a DUI arrest (not his first) led to him voluntarily leave the broadcast booth for the 2008 season. But he was found not guilty of the drunken driving charge, and at last report, his divorce and tax problems seemed on the way to being settled. With those matters resolved, it was reported that "Snake" would be back on the radio, much to the delight of Alabama fans, most of whom overlook his indiscretions and remember instead the glory days.

HARVEY H. JACKSON III
Jacksonville State University

Robert F. Jones, *Sports Illustrated* (September 19, 1979); Howell Raines, *New York Times* (21 June 1978); Ken Stabler and Berry Stainback, *Snake: The Candid Autobiography of Football's Most Outrageous Renegade* (1986).

Summitt, Pat

(b. 1952) BASKETBALL COACH.
Pat Head Summitt has been coach of the University of Tennessee Lady Vols since 1974 and is the winningest college basketball coach in history. Born in Clarksville, Tenn., Summitt played high school basketball in nearby Henrietta, later becoming an All American at the University of Tennessee at Martin. She won a silver medal as a member of the United States women's national basketball team in the 1976 Summer Olympics. Summitt's success as the Lady Vols coach mirrored the rise of women's college basketball, as she won the first Southeastern Conference (SEC) Women's Tournament at the end of the 1970s and made it to the Final Four in the first National Collegiate Athletic Association (NCAA) Women's Tournament in 1982.

Summitt's team won its first national championship in 1987 and went on to win a total of eight national titles. Her 1997–98 team had an undefeated 39–0 record, and the Lady Vols went on from there to win three consecutive SEC titles and three SEC tournaments. During the 2004–5 NCAA tournament, Summitt reached 880 wins, breaking University of North Carolina coach Dean Smith's record of 879, setting a new record in NCAA basketball history. The University of Tennessee honored the coach, naming the court at the Thompson Boling Arena, where the team plays, as "The Summitt" to commemorate win number 1,000 in February 2009.

Pat Summitt is a seven-time SEC coach of the year, has been NCAA coach of the year seven times, and was named the Naismith coach of the century. The HBO documentary, *A Cinderella Season: The Lady Vols Fight Back* (1997), chronicles the 1996–97 season, which ended with a 23–10 record and a second straight national title.

CHARLES REAGAN WILSON
University of Mississippi

Christine Baker and Becky Hammond, *Why She Plays: The World of Women's Basketball* (2008); Karen Crouse, *New York Times* (24 January 2009); Sally Jenkins and Pat

Head Summitt, *Raising the Roof: The Inspiring Story of the Tennessee Lady Vols' Undefeated 1997–98 Season* (1998).

Talladega Superspeedway

Just off Interstate 20 between Birmingham and Atlanta sits Talladega Superspeedway, a 2.66 mile asphalt tri-oval that is NASCAR's longest racetrack. Opened in 1969, the track was built by NASCAR founder William "Big Bill" France and his International Speedway Corporation.

In the1960s the Talladega site was abandoned airport runways and soybean fields largely inaccessible from nearby cities. A major motorsports facility at the site would be feasible only if highway access could be arranged. Alabama governor George Corley Wallace agreed to get the necessary highways built, and in exchange France agreed to chair the Democrats for Wallace presidential campaign in Florida, France's home state.

The track opened to controversy. Concerned about the excessive speeds made possible by the track's length, width, and steep 33-degree banking, a drivers' union led by Richard Petty went on strike the night before the inaugural race. Petty's concerns were well founded. The qualifying speeds for that first race were near 200 miles per hour, and the available tires would hold up for only a few laps. In direct defiance of Petty's Professional Drivers Association, France announced, "There will be a race, but if you want to go home, go home." Petty and most of the other NASCAR regulars did so. The first 500-mile race at Talladega, run on 14 September 1969, was contested by a field of independents and won by the previously unknown and soon forgotten Richard Brickhouse (his only NASCAR victory). France's decision broke the back of Petty's union and left permanent ill feelings between the two NASCAR giants.

Because of the track geometry, NASCAR's cars can run wide open all the way around the track with no need to decelerate in the corners. As such, the fastest competition lap ever achieved in NASCAR, a qualifying lap of almost 213 miles per hour, was turned in at Talladega by Bill Elliott in 1987. (Rusty Wallace turned a practice lap of 216 mph in 2004.) In all, nine drivers qualified for that race at speeds over 210 mph.

Early in the 1987 race, driver Bobby Allison blew an engine and then a tire, went airborne, and tore out an entire section of catch fence along the track's front straightaway. Only dumb luck prevented 200-mph chunks of race car from killing dozens of spectators. Allison's wreck made it obvious that slower speeds were necessary for the safety of both drivers and fans and this led to the much-despised "restrictor plates," thin metal plates that sit between the carburetor and intake manifold, limit the flow of fuel and air, and dampen the horsepower down from about 750 to about 450. Since 1987, restrictor plates have been required at all Talladega and Daytona races.

Even with restrictor plates, today's Talladega stock cars run at speeds over 190 miles per hour and often in thick packs three or four cars wide, the entire field of 43 bunched up nose-to-tail, bumper-to-bumper. This virtually guarantees at least one high-speed multicar crash at every Talladega event, a mishap known as the Big One. The Talladega Big Ones often take 15 or 20 cars out of competition at once.

Dale Earnhardt notched the most victories at Talladega (10), the last in 2000, four months before his death. Since Earnhardt's death, his son, Dale Earnhardt Jr., has won five races at the famed track. Other multirace Talladega winners include Richard Petty, David Pearson, Buddy Baker, Darrell Waltrip, Bobby Allison, Bobby's son Davey Allison (killed in a helicopter crash at Talladega in 1993), Cale Yarborough, Ernie Irvan, and Jeff Gordon.

JIM WRIGHT
University of Central Florida

Thomas Gillespie, *Angel in Black: Remembering Dale Earnhardt* (2008); Peter Golenbock, *Miracle: Bobby Allison and the Saga of the Alabama Gang* (2007); Bob Latford, *Built for Speed: The Ultimate Guide to Stock Car Racetracks* (2002); Talladega Superspeedway, www.talladegasuperspeedway.com; Jim Wright, *Fixin' to Git: One Fan's Love Affair with NASCAR's Winston Cup* (2002).

Texas Western vs. Kentucky

1966 NCAA NATIONAL BASKETBALL CHAMPIONSHIP.
On 19 March 1966 Coach Don Haskins and his Texas Western College (now the University of Texas at El Paso) squad defeated the No. 1 ranked University of Kentucky and legendary coach Adolph Rupp, 72 to 65, for the NCAA national basketball championship. Despite the lack of future NBA superstars or a miracle finish, this game remains remarkable as the first and only time an all-black starting five faced an all-white team for an intercollegiate championship. The victory by the young men of Texas Western, all of African descent, coming as it did in the midst of the Freedom Struggle, held tremendous symbolic and practical importance.

Texas Western did not pioneer the integration of college basketball. African Americans played ball at smaller universities from the 1920s forward. Bill Garrett integrated big-time college basketball when he began playing at Indiana University in 1947. The next two decades saw integrated teams spread throughout the North and West and produced some of the true superstars of basketball history, including Bill Russell at San Francisco State, Oscar Robinson at Cincinnati, and Lou Alcindor at UCLA. However, even integrated programs maintained unwritten racial quotas that largely prevented more than three black players on the court at one time. Loyola of Chicago broke this rule when it won the 1963 NCAA championship, starting four African Americans against Cincinnati, which started three black players itself. While most southern teams remained strictly white, at the national level the integrated squads were well established.

In the immediate aftermath of Texas Western's victory over an all-white southern team considered one of the greatest basketball powerhouses in history, college basketball changed. Racial myths that believed an all-black team would descend into chaos without the steady guidance of at least one white player were shattered. That the victory came against Rupp, who was resisting the pressure to recruit black players, made it all the more significant. To remain competitive now required recruiting the best players regardless of race. The number of African Americans at major programs increased greatly over the next few years, and Vanderbilt integrated the SEC in 1967 when Perry Wallace joined the team. The players at Texas Western did not pioneer the integration of college basketball, but they did put the final nail in segregated basketball's coffin.

PAUL R. BEEZLEY
Jacksonville State University

Rebecca Craver and Charles H. Martin, eds., *Diamond Days: An Oral History of the University of Texas at El Paso* (1992); Frank Fitzpatrick, *And the Walls Came Tumbling Down: Kentucky, Texas Western, and the Game That Changed American Sports* (1999).

Toasts and Dozens

In Greenville, Atlanta, Memphis, or other towns and cities in the South, you might hear preadolescent, lower-class black boys playfully hurling rhymed insults at each other. The language is rough, and the themes are risqué, but the composition is creative. They are playing the "dozens," as they often call it. "I fucked your momma on the levee," a Greenville, Miss., youth told his playmate while others looked on. "She said, 'get up baby, your dick's getting too heavy.'" The onlookers roared with delight. After shouts of encouragement

to the butt of the insult, he replied "I fucked your momma in New Orleans, her pussy started poppin' like a sewing machine." The challenge was put to the first boy to top the retort. He came back strongly with "I fucked your momma on a fence, selling her pussy for 15 cents; a bee come along and stung her on the ass, started selling her pussy for a dollar and a half."

The dozens are social entertainment, a game to be played, but they have also sparked considerable sociopsychological comment. Folklorist Roger Abrahams observed, for example, that the dozens represent a striving for masculine identity by black boys. They try symbolically to cast off the woman's world— indeed, the black world they see as run by the mother of the family—in favor of the gang existence of the black man's world. In dozens playing, the black boy is honing the verbal and social skills he will need as an adult male. A form of dozens playing, usually called "ranking," has also been collected among white boys, but most collections have stressed the black dozens, also called "woofing," "sounding," and "joning."

Although Roger Abrahams did his classic study of black verbal contests and creativity in Philadelphia, his informants had deep roots in the South. Other southern connections to the dozens are found in a spate of southern blues songs popular from the 1920s on. "The Dirty Dozen" was first recorded by Georgia's Rufus Perryman, known as Speckled Red, in 1929. Other versions quickly followed by southern artists including Tampa Red, Little Hat Jones,

Ben Curry, Lonnie Johnson, and Kokomo Arnold. The content of the dozens was apparently in circulation even before these recordings; folksong collectors Howard W. Odum and Newman I. White found references in the field to the dozens before World War I. Alan Dundes and Donald C. Simmons have suggested an older existence of the dozens in Africa.

Also collected from lower-class blacks has been a form of narrative poetry called by their reciters "toasts." Toasts use many of the rhyming and rhythmic schemes and the rough imagery of the dozens but are performed by young men as extended poetic recitations rather than ritualized insult. Indeed, Abrahams called toasts the "greatest flowering of Negro verbal talent" (although similar recitations are also known among whites).

The performance of toasts is intended to be dramatic. The settings are placed in barrooms and jungles; the characters are badmen, pimps, and street people; and the props are often drugs, strong drink, and guns. Here is an excerpt, for example, from a common toast, "The Signifying Monkey."

> Down in the jungle near a dried-up
> creek,
> The signifying monkey hadn't slept
> for a week
> Remembering the ass-kicking he had
> got in the past
> He had to find somebody to kick the
> lion's ass.
> Said the signifying monkey to the
> lion that very same day,

> "There's a bad motherfucker heading
> your way.
> The way he talks about you it can't
> be right,
> And I know when you two meet
> there going to be a fight.
> He said he fucked your cousin, your
> brother, and your niece,
> And he had the nerve enough to ask
> your grandmom for a piece."
> The lion said, "Mr. Monkey, if what
> you say isn't true about me,
> Bitch, I'll run your ass up the highest
> tree."
> The monkey said, "Now look, if you
> don't believe what I say,
> Go ask the elephant. He's resting
> down the way."

Other popular toasts in oral tradition include "Stackolee," "The Titanic," "Joe the Grinder," and "The Freaks (or Junkers) Ball."

The origin of the term and the tradition of toasts is uncertain. Bruce Jackson suggested roots in prison and hobo life. Roger Abrahams looked to the influence of recitations common on the blackface minstrel stage and in subliterary comic forms. The name toasts may be derived from once-popular books of after-dinner speeches, jokes, and drinking toasts, or from underworld slang.

Several collections of toasts come from the South. In the North most texts come from the cities. Although some southern examples are reported in cities such as New Orleans and Austin, southern texts often come from the rural and small-town South. In Mississippi, David Evans, William Ferris, and Simon J. Bronner collected them in small towns. Bruce Jackson's book on toasts, *Get Your Ass in the Water and Swim Like Me* (1974), had texts primarily collected from prisons in Texas and Missouri. The connection to southern life is usually passed up by interpreters of toasts in favor of links to the life of the underworld and the urban ghetto. Relations exist, however, between the themes and heroes of the toasts and those of southern black folksongs including "Stackolee" and "The Titanic." The blues also are influenced by the erotic and violent verses of the toasts. Other connections are found between southern black animal folktales featuring the monkey and the toast "Signifying Monkey." Indeed, Richard Dorson reported prose versions of "Signifying Monkey" in his classic collection *American Negro Folktales* (1967) taken from southern-born blacks.

Dozens and toasts stand out because they are framed as play or performance, and they contain strong themes and sounds. Dozens and toasts creatively manipulate imagery and metaphor to bring drama to words. The boy telling dozens may eventually tackle the more sophisticated toasts. Mastering the techniques in these traditional performances gives the teller an important sense of prestige and power that is reserved for the man of words in black society. Their dozens and toasts entertain friends and pass the time; they communicate values and feelings. The tellers of dozens and toasts are narrators of imagined scenes and cultural critics for the audiences to which they perform. The tellers also draw attention because they are themselves characters in the social drama of communication through folklore.

SIMON J. BRONNER
Pennsylvania State University
Capitol Campus

Roger D. Abrahams, *Deep Down in the Jungle: Negro Narrative Folklore from the Streets of Philadelphia* (1970), *Positively Black* (1970); Simon J. Bronner, *Western Folklore* (April 1978); Richard M. Dorson, *American Negro Folktales* (1967); William Ferris, *Jazzforschung* (1974–75); Bruce Jackson, *Get Your Ass in the Water and Swim Like Me: Narrative Poetry from Black Oral Tradition* (1974); William Labov, Paul Cohen, Clarence Robins, and John Lewis, in *Mother Wit from the Laughing Barrel*, ed. Alan Dundes (1973); Lawrence Levine, *Black Culture and Black Consciousness: Afro-American Folk Thought from Slavery to Freedom* (1977); Paul Oliver, *Aspects of the Blues Tradition* (1970); Dennis Wepman, Ronald B. Newman, and Murray B. Binderman, *Journal of American Folklore* (July–September 1974).

Walker, Herschel

(b. 1962) FOOTBALL PLAYER.
In 1980 Herschel Walker began a three-year football career at the University of Georgia during which he established himself as the Deep South's first universally acclaimed black collegiate superstar. Having set numerous high school records in the tiny south Georgia town of Wrightsville, Walker led his team to one national and three Southeastern Conference championships, claiming for himself not only statistical records and the Heisman trophy, but a unique place in the hearts of his region's white football fanatics.

Despite the often-unpleasant experiences of his black predecessors in southern collegiate athletics, most white football fans refused to let several centuries of racial paranoia come between them and an athlete who could run like Herschel Walker. Walker received some racist hate mail, but even his controversial early departure from the University of Georgia for a lucrative contract with the New Jersey Generals of the United States Football League and his challenge of the white South's ultimate racial taboo—dating and marrying a white woman—did little to damage his overall popularity in Georgia and throughout the region. He joined the National Football League Dallas Cowboys in 1986 and went on to play for the Minnesota Vikings (1989–91), the Philadelphia Eagles, (1992–94), and the New York Giants (1995), only to return to the Cowboys for his final two seasons (1996–97).

Southern whites developed an affection for Walker because of both his physical prowess and the unassuming grace with which he wore their adulation. (Jack Armstrong, the "All-American boy," was a smart-mouthed street punk by comparison.) Walker's conservatism and reticence brought criticism from some black militants and white activists who felt that black athletic heroes should speak out on racial issues. Walker refused to become a social reformer, however, steering clear of civil rights demonstrations in his native Wrightsville and thwarting the efforts of the most determined interviewers to lead him into controversial areas.

Mature and intelligent, Walker realized it was in his best interest to watch what he said and did. He remained, despite his fame, a country boy, profoundly influenced by two determined, God-fearing parents. Walker's mother and father instilled in their children courtesy and humility familiar in the rural and small-town South. The key to Herschel Walker's identity and appeal was his down-to-earth southern upbringing. That upbringing, however, included no color-coded parental instructions to stay in his "place." No one, black or white, doubted that Walker knew what he could do, and his interracial courtship and marriage indicated that he had no qualms about violating southern social norms that he did not accept.

It is difficult to determine whether Herschel Walker parted the waters of racism in the South or simply walked expertly across them. His miracle was primarily a personal one. A decade after Georgia's "Redcoat" marching band had dropped "Dixie" from its title as well as its repertoire, many of the same fans who had lost their hearts to Herschel continued to demand that the band resume playing the song that black southerners saw as the anthem of slavery, segregation, and the Ku Klux Klan. Across the football-mad South, racial epithets still reached the ears of black players and fans, and many whites still objected to starting lineups that were predominantly black. Such evidence suggested that the level of acceptance that Walker achieved would remain an exception until another uniquely "All-American on-and-off-the-field" black superhero came along to again strike white fans colorblind.

JAMES C. COBB
University of Georgia

Sue Burchard, *Herschel Walker* (1984); Pat Conroy, *Southern Living* (September 1983); Terry Todd, *Sports Illustrated* (4 October 1982); Herschel Walker, *Breaking Free: My Life with Dissociative Identity Disorder* (2008).

Womanless Weddings

From time to time, grown men hook themselves into bras, struggle into dresses, and perform a womanless wedding in front of family and neighbors. Deeply rooted in the community, a womanless wedding is a mock wedding performed by an all-male cast. Although womanless weddings have taken place throughout the United States, these folk plays are believed to occur most frequently in the Southeast, where they are staged by both whites and African Americans.

Mainstream organizations—such as churches, schools, fire departments, chambers of commerce, and various civic and fraternal clubs—sponsor the plays, which are typically organized and directed by women. They are performed in venues such as church halls and school auditoriums before a cross section of the community. Most frequently, a womanless wedding's avowed purpose is to raise funds for a good cause; occasionally organizers include womanless weddings as entertainment at a social function, mainly to help create a sense of community. Casts feature prominent citizens: for example, mayors, ministers, coaches, bankers, doctors, lawyers, and police chiefs. Costumes range from reasonably realistic wedding attire to outlandish outfits such as hillbilly overalls or glaringly mismatched ensembles. The actors often play with male and female physical attributes by using huge balloons to represent breasts, for instance, or wearing off-the-shoulder frocks that reveal hairy chests.

Tracing the folk play's history is difficult, although it seems reasonable to assume it is distantly related to European festival customs. Oral histories describe early 20th-century womanless weddings as ad-libbed affairs, with little plot and no formal script. However, shortly after World War I, companies began producing scripts for use in community theatricals. During this period, commercially published womanless wedding scripts appeared, both as booklets and in anthologies. For a fee, some companies furnished personnel to help stage local productions. One such company, the Sympson Levie Company of Bardstown, Ky., and Jackson, Mich., has been credited with "inventing" the womanless wedding, its best-selling offering, although the company most probably drew on existing traditions.

Womanless weddings were a particularly active tradition in southern towns and rural areas during the 1920s and 1930s. With increased mobility and more numerous entertainment options, however, performances became sporadic by the turn of the 21st century. Still to this day, communities and groups revive the folk play now and again. Although directors sometimes write an original script for such productions, usually they hunt up a published version at the local library or, more often, inherit from another group a script several generations removed from its original published source. Regardless, organizers freely make changes both out of respect for the community's sensibilities and culture and because of practical circumstances, such as cast size.

Often hosted by a master of ceremonies, the play usually has two acts: the wedding processional and the ceremony. The attendees often include a weeping mother, a jilted sweetheart, and an out-of-control baby, sometimes accompanied in older versions by an actor in blackface playing a mammy. During the ceremony, the bride, played by the largest cast member, is joined in matrimony to the groom, the smallest available man. Their vows reflect a decidedly unromantic view of marriage as an institution that is frequently not in the groom's best interests. Coerced to the altar by the bride's father, sometimes armed with a shotgun, the groom contemplates escape routes. The bride is older, ugly, stupid, and desperate to marry, often because she is pregnant or has already had a child. Successful performances include a great deal of improvisation, with the interplay between the actors and the audience shaping the performance. Much of the humor springs from audience members' seeing men they know well, often authority figures, behaving in raucous, ludicrous ways that contrast with their everyday

roles. On occasion, a mock wedding reception follows, giving cast members and the audience a chance to mingle.

The main organizing principle, then, is inversion: men become women, adults become children, whites become blacks, the sacred turns into the profane. By breaking down customary boundaries and allowing normally taboo subjects out into the open, communities acknowledge and express their complicated, often ambivalent feelings about the social realities and forces that affect their everyday lives, especially marriage, gender roles, sex, religion, authority, social class, racial relations, and rural life.

Closely related variants include mock weddings where both males and females cross-dress; womanless beauty pageants and talent shows where all the contestants are men in drag; and Tom Thumb weddings, performed by children.

JANE HARRIS WOODSIDE
Johnson City, Tennessee

Arthur Depew, *The Cokesbury Party Book* (1932); Hubert Hayes, *A Womanless Wedding* (1936); Mrs. James W. Hunt, *The Womanless Wedding* (1918); Theodore Johnson, ed., *Baker's Stunt and Game Book* (1928); Walt Larrimore, *Bryson City Secrets* (2006); Laurence Senelick, *The Changing Room: Sex, Drag, and Theatre* (2000); Michael Taft, *North Dakota History* (Fall 1989); Brenda Veradi, *Voices: The Journal of New York Folklore* (Fall–Winter 2000); Jane Harris Woodside, "The Womanless Wedding: An American Folk Drama" (M.A. thesis, University of North Carolina at Chapel Hill, 1987).

Zaharias, Mildred "Babe" Didrikson

(1911–1956) GOLFER, BASKETBALL
PLAYER, TRACK AND FIELD ATHLETE.
In 1950 the Associated Press proclaimed Babe Didrikson Zaharias the
female athlete of the half century, and
her achievements in golf, basketball,
and track and field make her one of the
most accomplished athletes to come out
of the American South. Born 26 June
1911 in Port Arthur, Tex., and educated
in nearby Beaumont, Zaharias was a
product of Norwegian immigrant parents and the working-class culture of
east Texas that was a turbulent and dynamic place at time when the area experienced a southwestern oil boom. She
was athletic from childhood, a tomboy
often playing roughhouse games with
neighborhood boys. Her nickname
"Babe" came from the playgrounds of
Beaumont. She could throw a baseball
harder than any boys around and hit
home runs that seemed so towering as
to evoke their hero Babe Ruth, so that
when they started calling her Babe she
had her lifelong nickname.

After the 1920s the American Athletic Union (AAU) regulated women's
sports, and Zaharias's first major athletic accomplishments came when
playing basketball for the Dallas Golden
Cyclones, whom she led to a national
championship (1931) and two other
finals (1930, 1932). She worked as a
typist for Employers Casualty Company
in Dallas, whose owner encouraged
her to compete not only in basketball
but also in AAU track and field competitions. Between 1930 and 1932, she
entered meets in seven different events.

In the 1932 AAU nationals, she competed
in 8 of 10 events staged, winning five of
them (shot put, baseball toss, long jump,
80-meter hurdles, and javelin throw)
within three hours. At the 1932 Olympics in Los Angeles, she earned gold
medals in the 80-meter hurdles and
the javelin throw and a silver medal in
the high jump. In December 1932 she
became a professional athlete, playing
on the Babe Didrikson All-American
Basketball Team, and in 1934 she
pitched at Major League Baseball spring
training games.

Despite these achievements, and
the celebrity that came with them, Zaharias gained greatest renown as a
golfer. She played in her first golf tournament, the Fort Worth Women's Invitational, in 1934, and in 1935 she won
the Texas Women's Golf Association
amateur championship. The lack of professional opportunities for women in
golf led her to do an exhibition tour
with famed golfer Gene Sarazen, which
brought her new wealth and more acclaim in the sports world. She married
professional golfer George Zaharias in
1938. In the early 1940s she played in
professional golf matches, but later regained her amateur status, winning the
1945 Western Open, Texas Open, and
Broadmoor Invitational. The following
season she won 17 tournaments in a
row. She turned professional again after
that and became a founding member of
the Ladies Professional Golf Association (LPGA) in 1949. She won 31 LPGA
events in her career, capturing three
U.S. Women's Open Titles (1948, 1950,
1954) and three Women's Titleholders

tournaments (1947, 1950, 1952). Cancer cut short her career, as she died 27 September 1956.

Zaharias was significant as a major force in popularizing women's sports in American culture. When she began, many American sports leaders discouraged women's involvement in competitive sports as unfeminine and even unhealthy; the U.S. Olympic Committee into the 1930s sanctioned women's involvement in only a few sports. Commentators often tried to marginalize Zaharias as a "mannish" woman athlete, but she became friends with sports reporters who helped make her an admired sports hero for her genuine accomplishments. She was flamboyant, engaging, and reached a level of success in so many sports that she is recognized as one of the nation's best all-around athletes.

CHARLES REAGAN WILSON
University of Mississippi

Susan E. Cayleff, *Babe: The Life and Legend of Babe Didrikson Zaharias* (1996); R. R. Knudson, *Babe Didrikson: Athlete of the Century* (1985); Babe Didrikson Zaharias, *The Life I've Led* (1955).

INDEX OF CONTRIBUTORS

Page numbers in boldface refer to articles.

Early, Jubal, 316
Earnhardt, Dale, 16, 276, **286–87**, 327, 354
Earnhardt, Dale, Jr., 354
Earnhardt, Ralph, 286
Easter, 123, **287–89**
Easy Rider, 299
Eatonville, Fla., 158
Edge, John T., 226
Edisto, S.C., 38
Edmunds, Richard, 3
Edmundson, George, 109
Edwards, Edwin, 116
Egerton, John, 225
Eisenhower, Dwight, 222
Elder, Lee, 121
Elizabeth I (queen of England), 68
Elizabeth II (queen of England), 68
Elliott, Bill, 353
Ellis, Jimmy, 54
Emergency Relief Administration, 262
Emerging South, The (Clark), 341
Emory University, 199
England, 189
Equal Employment Opportunity Commission, 305
Esquire, 298, 299
Eunice, La., 169
Evans, David, 356
Everglades National Park, **289–90**
Evert, Chris, 216, **291**

Fairfax, Lord, 111
Fairs, **74–79**, 232
Falmouth, Ky., 79
Family reunions, 15, **80–81**
Farmer, Sydney, 214
Faubus, Orval, 281
Faulkner, William, 118–19, 136, 163, 240, 244, 289
Favre, Brett, **292–93**
Ferris, William, 356
Festivals, **81–84**; music, **84–88**
Fiddle contests, 85, 86, **88–90**, 168
Field, Marshall, 221
Field and Stream, 96

Fields, Mamie Garvin, 44, 296
Field trials, **90–92**
Finley, John T., 143
Fireballing, **92–94**
Fisher, Carl, 221
Fishing, 5, **94–98**
Flagler, Henry, 39, 181, 218
Flaming Lips, 87
Flatt, Carlton, 104, 105
Flora-Bama Lounge and Package, 15, 252–53, **293–95**, 333, 334
Florida, 252, 289–90, 312, 333, 340; parks, 22, 266, 278–80; beaches, 38, 41; beach resorts, 39, 181; growth, 41; fishing, 95; horses, 125; juke joints, 138; pets, 165; running, 195; tourism, 218, 222; water skiing, 241, 242; wrestling, 245, 246; gambling, 269; Christmas, 271; drive-ins, 284
Florida, University of, 35, 73, 102, 109–10
Florida Marlins, 30
Florida State University, 102, 110, 232, 263, 264
Florida Times Union, 39
Foley, Ala., 314
Folksong USA (Lomax and Lomax), 187
Fontaine Ferry Park, 21
Food Network, 225
Football, 11, 12, 263–65, 292–93, 319–21, 336–37, 350–52, 357–59; college, **99–102**; high school, **103–5**; professional, **105–8**; traditions, **109–10**
Forbes, 267, 328
Ford, Henry, 221
Foreman, George, 54–55, 251
Forest Hills, N.Y., 297
Forrest, Nathan Bedford, 127
Fort Lauderdale, Fla., 41
Fort Mill, S.C., 24
Fort Myers News-Press, 39
Fort Worth, Tex., 285, 298
Foster, Rube, 329
Fourth of July, 123, 124, 194, 195, **295–97**
Fowler, Damon Lee, 288
Fox, Harry, 235

Gulf of Mexico, 94, 96
Gulfport, Miss., 22
Gulf Shores, Ala., 41, 42
Gulfside Summer Assembly, 45
Gullah, 64, 303
Guthrie, Janet, 276
Gymnastics, 13–14, 59

Haggard, Merle, 298
Halifax Journal, 39
Hall, Joe, 36
Hall, Scott, 322
Hamm, Mia, **302**
Hammocks Beach, 40
Hammond, John, 2
Hampton, S.C., 82
Hanes Hosiery, 32
Haney, Carlton, 86
Hannah, Barry, 216
Hanover County, Va., 85
Hardaway, Benjamin H., 126
Hard Road to Glory, A (Ashe), 255
Harris, Joel Chandler, 215
Hartsfield, Zeke, 122
Haskins, Don, 35, 354
Hatteras Island, 97
Hawes, Bess Lomax, 64
Haynie, Sandra, 120
Health Resorts in the South, 181
Heisman, John, 99
Heisman trophy, 102
Helena, Ark., 79
Hendersonville, N.C., 218
Henning, Paul, 344
Heritage USA, 24–25
Herkimer, Lawrence "Herkie," 59
Herschend, Hugo, 344–45
Herschend, Mary, 344–45
Hershand, Jack and Pete, 282
Highland Beach, 43
Highway Beautification Act, 342
Hilton Head Island, S.C., 41, 120, 182, **302–4**
Hines, Duncan, 224, 226

Historically black colleges and universities, 101, 145–47, 203
Hobson, Fred, 37–38
Hogan, Ben, 119
Hogan, Hulk, 245
Hog-dogging (hog hunting), 47, 50, 51
Holidays, **122–25**. *See also individual holidays*
Holland, Spessard, 290
Hollingshead, Richard, Jr., 283–84
Holmes, Larry, 54
Holmgren, Mike, 292
Holyfield, Evander, 54
Honky-tonks, 138–39, 235, 236
Honor and Slavery (Greenberg), 193
Hooters, **304–5**
Hopkins, Linton, 186
Horry County, S.C., 40, 45
Horse racing, 112–13, 115, 125–26, 312–14
Horses, **125–29**, 164, 312–14
Hot Springs, Ark., 29, 115
Hot Springs, N.C., 254
Hot Springs, Va., 180
Hot Springs National Park, **305–7**
Hound Ears, N.C., 191
House parties, **129–32**
Houston, Tex., 26, 28, 30, 59, 122, 127, 192
Houston Astros, 30
Houston Oilers, 105, 106, 319, 350
Houston Rockets, 37
Houston Texans, 106
Howard, Charles T., 315
Howard, Frank, 100
Howard, O. O., 303
Howard College, 263
Howard University, 204, 206
Hughes, Solomon, 122
Humane Society of the United States, 50
Hunt, Lamar, 216
Hunt clubs, 135–36
Hunting, 5, 90–92, 127, **132–37**, 174–76
Huntington Beach, Calif., 44
Huntsville, Ala., 193, 335
Huntsville, Tex., 332

Segregation, 34, 43, 44, 139, 223, 259, 285

Selma, Ala., 229

Shape-note singing convention, 19

Sharp, Cecil, 201

Sharpe, William, 40

Sheehan, George, 194

Shelbyville, Tenn., 127

Shenandoah National Park, 262, 300

Shepherd of the Hills, The (Wright), 344

Sherrill, Jackie, 102

Shoal Creek, Ala., 58

Shopping, **195–98**

Showboat, 343

Showboats, **342–44**

Shula, Don, 105, 108

Shuttlesworth, Fred, 229

Sikeston, Mo., 314

Silver Dollar City, 15, 24, 280, **344–45**

Simmons, Donald C., 356

Six Flags New Orleans, 25

Six Flags over Georgia, 25, 278

Six Flags over Texas, 25, 278

Slave States of America, The (Buckingham), 184

Slavery, 7, 63, 65, 66, 205, 271–72, 311

Sligh, Chuck, 241

Sloan, Steve, 350

Smalls, Robert, 303

Smith, Carl "Buster," 171

Smith, Dean, 36, 37, **345–46**, 352

Smith, Ervin, 171

Smith, Captain John, 212

Smith, Tubby, 36

Smith, Will, 252

Snake (Stabler), 350

Snead, Sammy, 120

Soccer, **198–201**, 302

Sound and the Fury, The (Faulkner), 118, 289

South Africa, 255

South by Southwest, **346–47**

South Carolina, 347, 348; beaches, 38, 259; fairs, 76; festivals, 82; fishing, 94, 95, 98; football, 104; fox hunting, 112; gambling, 113; gardening, 118; golf, 119; ring shouts, 187; ring tournaments, 189; tourism, 218; tourism, 222; wrestling, 245

South Carolina, University of, 109, 110

Southeastern Climbers Coalition, 191–92

Southeastern Conference (SEC), 33, 34, 101, 337, 352, 357

Southern, Terry, 60

Southern Belly (Edge), 226

Southern Christian Leadership Conference, 375

Southern Exposition, 76

Southern Exposure, 32

Southern Food (Egerton), 225

Southern Foodways Alliance, 225, 226

Southern Golf Association, 119

Southern League, 30

Southern Living, 74, 219, 315, 340

Southern Mississippi, University of, 292

Southern Tennis Association, 216

Southern University, 35, 101, 203

South of the Border, 15, **347–49**

South Padre Island, 41

Southwest Conference, 100

Southwestern Athletic Conference, 34, 101

Spanish American War, 296

Sparrow's Beach, 45

Spaulding and Rogers, 342

Speaker, Tris, 29

Spinks, Leon, 54

Spoleto Festival, 82, **349**

Sporting News, 27

Sports Afield, 96

Sports Illustrated, 251, 291, 334, 351

Springville, Ala., 79

Spurrier, Steve, 102

Square dancing, 56, **201–2**

Stabler, Kenny, 16, 294, 333, **350–52**

Stallings, Gene, 292

Starkville, Miss., 34

State fairs, 232

Stearns, Marshall and Jean, 205

Steele, Ala., 191

Step It Down (Jones and Hawes), 64

Stepping, **203–7**

Stern, Jane and Michael, 226